THE TREATMENT OF MARKET POWER
Antitrust, Regulation, and Public Enterprise

THE TREATMENT OF MARKET POWER
Antitrust, Regulation, and Public Enterprise

William G. Shepherd

1975

COLUMBIA UNIVERSITY PRESS

New York and London

Library of Congress Cataloging in Publication Data
Shepherd, William G
 The treatment of market power.

 Includes bibliographical references and index.
 1. Competition—United States—Mathematical models.   2. United States—Economic policy—Mathematical models.   3. Big business—United States—Mathematical models.   I. Title.
 HD2795.S48   338.8′0873   75-19459
 ISBN 0-231-03773-2

Copyright © 1975 by Columbia University Press
Printed in the United States of America

For George

Preface

PERHAPS NO CLINICAL DIAGNOSIS or treatment of market power is possible, but I have tried to offer one in this book. The subject touches on sensitive social nerves of power and meaning, and so even the most scholarly dialogue about it often slips over into debate and then into rhetoric and passion.

Yet this hyperbole does reflect the importance of the subject, as I explore it in these pages. And such a root problem needs even more than the images and policies that have evolved in recent decades. The corporate economy is with us, for good or ill, or both. If our images of its nature and effects are distorted, then our social policies toward it are likely to be harmful (or perhaps merely hoaxes played upon ourselves), rather than wise and efficient.

My windows upon this topic are three: I have done research on several parts of the topic; I have had the mixed blessing of participating in policy choices in certain ways. And I have learned from others through their writings and much friendly discussion.

My research will be noted at various points in the text. My policy experience included service as Special Economic Assistant to the Assistant Attorney General for Antitrust, U. S. Department of Justice, during 1967–68. This experience gave me a firsthand look at the full range of antitrust activities, as well as some access to other policy agencies. It also showed me that intelligent policy requires a sound sense of priorities, or else it may block or even violate its own objectives.

As for discussions with my colleagues, I have benefited to the point of exploitation. Discussions and exchanges over many years cannot be sorted out neatly, and I have gained different things from different friends. Donald J. Dewey has enriched my understanding in many ways, and he provided penetrating advice on all parts of the book. James R. Nelson and John Perry Miller have tried for a number of years to reduce my naïveté. Charles H. Berry and W. H. Locke Anderson have tried to make my econometric work firmer; Richard E. Caves, Walter Adams and Harry M. Trebing have encouraged a deeper understanding of a wide range of topics; Daniel R. Fusfeld, James Pickett, Geoffrey Faux, and Gar Alperovitz have urged against narrow concepts of the problem; and Shorey Peterson has reminded me at many points that the critical issues, above all, can and should be treated with lucidity, poise, and good humor. Other colleagues in Ann Arbor who have given generously include Michael W. Klass, Lester Taylor, Richard B. Mancke, William J. Adams, F. M. Scherer, and Peter O. Steiner.

Among other colleagues in the United States, I wish particularly to thank William S. Comanor, Leland L. Johnson, John M. Blair, Lee E. Preston, Oliver E. Williamson, David D. Martin, Willard F. Mueller, and George J. Stigler. In Britain, I have learned much from Alexander Cairncross, Ralph Turvey, Alasdair I. MacBean, Peter E. Hart, Basil Yamey, Christopher D. Foster, Denys L. Munby, and E. F. Schumacher.

Donald F. Turner created the Special Economic Advisor's post at the Antitrust Division. He and the remarkable cascade of industrial and policy events during 1967–68 saw to it that my policy experience would be intensely instructive. I also learned much there from Donald I. Baker, Lionel Kestenbaum, Edwin M. Zimmerman, and Robert A. Hammond. I doubt that there will ever again be such a convergence of legal talent, and of intense and baffling industrial issues, as there was then at the Division.

For the publisher, Bernard Gronert has handled the book most sympathetically. Leslie Bialler edited the manuscript with unflagging care and patience.

Alice Y. Sano's typing of the manuscript has been equally remarkable. I have also benefited at various times from research support and facilities provided by The University of Michigan, the London School of Economics, Stanford University, and the Brookings Institution.

From such generous help, one might expect a better book than has come to be. For each of the faults, I accept and expect blame. But if my readers will be irritated instead to do further rethinking of their own, that will make the best of it.

W. G. S.
Ann Arbor

September 1975

Contents

Chapter One Introduction 1

PART ONE CONCEPTS FOR POLICY CHOICES

Chapter Two Defining Structure and Performance 23

Chapter Three Evaluating Industrial Policies 62

Chapter Four The Basic Policy Yields in Actual Markets 87

PART TWO POLICY ALTERNATIVES IN PRACTICE

Chapter Five Policy Instruments 139

Chapter Six The Financial Sector 169

Chapter Seven Conventional Markets: Restorative Treatments 183

Chapter Eight Conventional Markets: Preventive Treatment 216

Chapter Nine "Utility" Sectors 225

Chapter Ten The Supply of Weapons 259

Chapter Eleven Industrial Policies in an Equalitarian Society 270

Chapter Twelve A Summary 291

APPENDICES

A Methods and Data 297

B Changes in the Leading Dominant Firms 304

C Estimates of Yields from Certain Antitrust Actions 314

Index 321

THE TREATMENT OF MARKET POWER
Antitrust, Regulation, and Public Enterprise

CHAPTER ONE
Introduction

IN EACH GENERATION, the best minds try—and usually fail, until too late—to understand the society's basic problems and their cures. So it is with industrial policies, those "treatments" (antitrust, regulation, and public enterprise are now the conventional three) for the problem of "corporate power." Events outpace the treatments—which are themselves obscurely arranged and poorly understood.

These industrial policies first took form during 1900–1915, and the scientific study of industry dates back to the 1930s. Yet it is evident that today we still do not understand the structure and character of industry very well. Nor do industrial policies now seem to be efficient. The field of study now known as "industrial organization" is the lens through which we have been trying to observe industry. But it has grown rather narrow and technocratic, with certain orthodox concepts and a mandarin prose. And the conventional policies now seem to be costly and indirect, part of the problem itself as well as, possibly, a solution. Indeed, the professional language we use has itself come to contain biases against an adequate understanding.

We need to enlarge the analysis of industry, restoring certain important parts that have come to be excluded. We need also to understand better the methods for defining and choosing "optimal" policies. Then, comparing what we have with the realistic alternatives, we may be able to define an "adequate" or even "optimal" set of basic policies for the future.

This book tries to move in these directions. Much of the volume sums up existing and earlier strands of thought, though some of it is new (and therefore untested). Rather than replaying the familiar themes, it picks out changes and extensions. The core idea is simple enough: an "optimal" set of policies is defined by its costs and benefits. Cost-benefit thinking is already budding in some academic discussions of antitrust and regulation. Here I try to frame it more fully and skeptically, and then try to evaluate several types of policy choices in that context.

This chapter lays out the formulations for the analysis. The cardinal points are: (1) Analysis needs to extend outside the familiar focus on market structure, to include the *context* in which markets function, and the *content* of activity inside firms (these terms are defined below and in chapter 2); (2) Optimal sets of policies involve both the right *magnitudes* of effort and resources, and the correct inner *design,* and the *effects* of policies are the essential test of their fitness; (3) Policies arise within a political economy, so they need to be evaluated and designed accordingly.

We shall see that optimal policies may not be definable. Even if they are definable, they may be impossible to apply. Indeed, the subject is rich in irony and, for many, cynicism. Still we may at the least be able to state the language of policy choice so that it fits reality a little more closely. And certain clear policy errors may be definable—even though they may not be correctable in this decade or this century.

There is unity in the nature of markets in all sectors. There is also an underlying unity in the inner nature of public policies toward these markets. There is also a third unity, in the political economy that surrounds and shapes all such policies.

From these basic unities, this book tries to appraise actual and alternative policies toward industry. It draws on conventional economic tools, turning them upon familiar industrial facts and policy images. On many issues the jury is still out and may always be. Yet the basic ways to design good industrial policies can be widely agreed upon.

1 THE OLD PROBLEMS ARE NEW

Market power is an ancient, normal, and basic problem of human society.[1] It is sought in many forms and ways, and the selection of public

[1] See Adam Smith, *The Wealth of Nations* (New York: Random House, Modern Library, 1937); Joseph A. Schumpeter, *History of Economic Analysis* (London: Oxford University Press,

policies "toward" it (which are often also "from" it)—abating, breeding, arbitrating, controlling, hiding it—are among the biggest social decisions to be made.[2] Market power influences economic performance and social structure in many ways—most of them still imprecisely known—and the way a society regards and treats market power, and those who benefit from it, also defines much of its character.

These treatments are inherently controversial, because the market power they touch on is a major determinant of family wealth and status. And, through effective or mistaken use, these treatments can sharply affect the performance of the entire economy, and shape the structure of wealth. The real effects of the treatments are often misunderstood or literally not known; that indeed is true of the orthodox American treatments—antitrust, regulation, and others.

As concern has broadened in the last two decades beyond narrow allocational efficiency, the old problems of monopoly and its treatment have regained their priority as new problems. The image and the context of industrial policies have undergone a tidal shift; rather than secure, well-fitted treatments, they now often seem to be dubious ceremonials, which are ripe for revision or possible abolition.[3] Antitrust and regulation date back about 70 years, while others (weapons procurement and major subsidy programs) have been important for over 30 years. They are now being reexamined. There are several reasons for this new skepticism:

(1) The industrial structure has matured and stabilized, especially in the United States (see chapter 4).

1954); Karl Polanyi, *Primitive, Archaic and Modern Economies* (New York: Doubleday, Anchor Books, 1968); Karl Marx, *Capital* (New York: International Publishers, 1967); Fritz Machlup, *The Political Economy of Monopoly* (Baltimore: Johns Hopkins Press, 1952).

[2] This has been recognized both in economics and more widely. See Schumpeter, *Economic Analysis,* and his *Capitalism, Socialism, and Democracy* (New York: Harper, 1942); Alfred Marshall, *Principles of Economics,* 8th ed. (New York: Macmillan, 1920); J. K. Galbraith, *The New Industrial State* (Boston: Houghton Mifflin, 1967); and *Economics and the Public Purpose* (Boston: Houghton Mifflin, 1973).

[3] The new skepticism has several roots. One is a renewed faith in laissez-faire, focused in what is now called the Chicago school. Clear examples of this approach can be seen in various works by George J. Stigler and in the *Journal of Law and Economics*. This new Chicago school actually differs from the old Chicago school of Frank H. Knight and Henry C. Simons. The newer writers have a fuller faith that unfettered markets are optimal and self-correcting.

Radical critiques of capitalism have also challenged both the policies and the economic order itself. These critiques date mainly from the later 1960s, and they mostly express frustration with outcomes (imperialism, poverty) rather than a detailed understanding of the workings of the core financial and industrial markets.

(2) The tools for analyzing industrial organization have improved greatly, in many directions. Our diagnostic ability is now good, though still limited.[4]
(3) Certain costs of market power have been identified with more precision than had been possible. The cure or prevention of these costs is now on a more exact and reliable scientific footing (see chapter 4).
(4) The new skepticism about policy bred by the turbulence of the 1960s has spread to include industrial policies.
(5) The policies themselves have tended to grow conventional and rigid. Abroad, certain new forms and experiments have flourished, and they suggest a wider range of choices.
(6) There has been a quiet revolution in the methods and understanding of policy choice. The design of policy treatments is now partly a science rather than just an art or a set of legal categories (see chapter 3).

Also, it has grown apparent that the public fisc does not solve the equity problem. Knowing that taxes scarcely touch the inequality of wealth and opportunity, we may need to use industrial policies more firmly—if they can be used at all—for improving equity.

Specific disillusions—antitrust is ineffective, regulation is harmful, etc.—are part of this larger context, within which we need to rethink the nature of industry and policies toward it. Fifteen years ago, many of my colleagues regarded the whole topic as pretty much settled: policies were assumed to be reasonably well suited to the character of industry, as then imagined.[5] Actually, this new orthodoxy was less sophisticated than the views of many earlier analysts, who knew the danger of reducing the problem to a few mechanical concepts.

Now the neat framework has come unstuck, as it should, and the issues are more open. What forms does market power take? What is its scope? Its durability? Its effects? What constraints are antitrust and regulatory agencies really applying—if any? With what effects and yields—if any?

[4] See chapters 2 and 4. See also J. S. Bain, *Industrial Organization,* rev. ed. (New York: Wiley, 1969); F. M. Scherer, *Industrial Market Structure and Economic Performance* (Skokie, Ill.: Rand McNally, 1970); W. G. Shepherd, *Market Power and Economic Welfare* (New York: Random House, 1970) and "The Elements of Market Structure," *Review of Economics and Statistics,* February 1972, pp. 25–37; and L. W. Weiss, "Econometric Studies of Industrial Organization," in *Frontiers of Quantitative Economics,* ed. M. Intriligator, (Amsterdam: North-Holland, 1971).

[5] Attorney General's National Committee to Study the Antitrust Laws, *Report,* U.S. Government Printing Office, 1955; Donald J. Dewey, *Monopoly in Economics and Law* (Skokie, Ill.: Rand McNally, 1959); A. D. Neale, *The Antitrust Laws of the United States,* rev. ed. (Cambridge: Cambridge University Press, 1970); and S. N. Whitney, *Antitrust Policies,* 2 vols. (New York: Twentieth Century Fund, 1958).

A central folk belief has been that the competitive enterprise system in the U.S., and the policies that guide it, are unique and superior. Now the system and the policies are in question, among those who are most expert and informed. This is not ignorant nihilism or shallow dissent. As understanding has deepened, doubts have multiplied. About the nature of monopoly and its treatment, we have entered a healthy crisis of identity which is likely to bring large changes. Our task here is to rethink the answers and the questions *and* also the methods for formulating them.

2 THE OBJECTIVES OF ANALYSIS AND POLICY

The traditional goals of economics are efficiency and equity, but other social goals also matter: the value of work, opportunity, and others to be noted shortly. In practice, these goals are partly defined by the conditions to be treated. The raw material with which we must work is the character of enterprises and markets, and that is what must first be understood. A brief summary of the market process follows; chapters 2 and 3 give fuller detail.

These are the main points. Firms maximize within market opportunities, under supervision and constraint by financial units. This supervision is usually intimate but informal. Firms gain, hold—and often lose—market positions *over time*. The markets themselves evolve, often through predictable phases. Among the several elements of market structure, the primary one is usually the firm's market share (see chapters 2 and 4). Appreciable effects of market power occur when market shares rise above about 25 percent.

In most firms, management has a degree of discretion in its choices and performance.[6] When market shares are high and supervision by the board of directors and by bankers is weak, this discretion is often large. It permits inefficiency to arise and persist. The firm's profitability can be under- or overstated by the selection of accounting and other tactics, and diversified firms are especially insulated from outside review. Managers themselves usually have brief tenure, while major actions have long duration. Therefore

---

[6] The extent is debatable but surely not trivial. See E. S. Mason, ed., *The Corporation in Modern Society* (Cambridge, Mass.: Harvard University Press, 1959); O. E. Williamson, "Managerial Discretion and Business Behavior," *American Economic Review,* 1963, pp. 1032–57; W. J. Baumol, *Business Behavior, Value and Growth,* rev. ed. (Englewood Cliffs, N.J.: Prentice-Hall, 1967).

responsibility for the firm is often diffused. Managers also have a hyperconcern with secrecy of company data, present and past.

Accordingly, a knowledge of financial markets—with their supervisory and supportive role toward firms—is central to understanding and treating market conditions. Treatment needs to focus on the market shares of firms. The information needed to understand markets and to prepare treatment will often be lacking or biased. Treatments must be designed to *anticipate* future changes rather than simply to fit static conditions. Preventive treatments are more efficient than restorative ones, and treatments which apply incentives aligned with the firm's motivation will be more efficient than those which impose changes directly opposed to the motives of managers, banks, and owners. In medical terms, therapy and medication may usually be superior to surgery and controls.

Social performance also includes the content of enterprise activity, not just the narrow profit and efficiency aspects. Content includes the social structure of the firm, the character of work, and certain other social factors to be defined in chapter 2. These are less familiar in economic analysis, but they are likely to be important in total performance. A minor improvement in the whole content of work, for example, can outweigh even major increases in allocational efficiency.

Within this context, the proper objective of policy is to design treatments that optimize: whose total net benefits are maximized and whose marginal benefits are just equal to their marginal costs (see chapter 3 for details and sources). Such a cost-benefit approach is merely a way of putting good sense and logic in explicit form. It brings out for inspection what the sound treatments have always done: pursue actions just as far as they are "worth it," and avoid "harmful" ones. Making it explicit will, we shall see, help us to identify a variety of traditional biases and gaps, and it will enrich our choices among new alternative treatments. But cost-benefit thinking is no magic wand, and we shall take care to note its defects and to be aware of how the policy environment may cause the treatments themselves to become pathological.

The cost-benefit elements in the appraisal are often complex and difficult to measure, and the method itself can easily be honestly mishandled or contrived to mislead. One therefore needs to use logic, a sense of proportion, and plain caution in applying it to cases. The technique is in part purely scientific—to define and measure elements of an objective reality—but it also requires art and skepticism, for the evidence is often weak and biased. Above all, the really important conditions must be included, even though they may not be easily analyzed or measured. The problems are not impossibly difficult, but they require much care and maturity of judgment.

The problems and criteria are complex, and a complete study would tax an encyclopedist. To give structure to the analysis, the book adopts a set of simplifying assumptions (which are further discussed in chapters 2 and 3):

1. Efficiency is reached when the costs of production are minimized and production is at least roughly in line with the conditions of efficient allocation (with long-run marginal cost equal to price).
2. Equity involves shifts of wealth, income, and opportunity toward more equality than presently exists (see chapter 2). As we shall see, the shifts now available through industrial policies would move only a moderate degree toward full equality, and therefore they can be treated in a first approximation as being largely positive.
3. A good content for enterprise activity can usually be defined with reasonable clarity. It will minimize command powers, and provide for variety and interest in work, and for a sense of contribution and identity (see chapter 2). This can often be evaluated at least ordinally, so that content can be used as a policy criterion.

The book tries to clarify cost-benefit analysis on this basis, using such information as is available. The exercise is experimental and the policy lessons are tentative. Alternative assumptions and sets of data will no doubt be tried by other researchers. But some such cost-benefit comparisons are at the heart of a rational attempt to reach sound public policies toward markets.

3 IN DARKEST POLITICAL ECONOMY

But to define optimum policy conditions may—even if it is possible—be only of intellectual value. To develop optimum policies, one must understand the forces that actually create policy units (agencies, courts, commissions, etc.), govern the selection of "decision-makers," and then may shape their "decisions."

The political economy—that is, the setting of policy—may generate "solutions" that only reflect and perpetuate (or intensify) the underlying structure of power and wealth. In its extreme version, the hypothesis would be that actual policies are controlled by—or merely reflect—the underlying power structure, which favors established firms and wealthholders. Such a set of policies may diverge widely from the economic "optimum" and be quite impervious to change. This extreme hypothesis conflicts with our folklore of faith in democracy and a competitive economy, but it may nevertheless hold. The hypothesis has not been put to a clear general test, but we shall see that some industrial policies are consistent with it.

Policy choices in the United States and many other countries appear to be made by a democratic process. Such processes have imperfections. Recent decades, however, have erased the old realism about office-holders—recall Pickwick at the county election, and Boss Tweed—and bred a belief that our democracy will indeed optimize. It is true that a largely competitive democratic process does have great optimizing power, as analysis has shown, both for short-run detail and for searching out the best major long-run policy lines.[7] Such a process is incremental, and it optimizes along marginal conditions. The virtues seem even greater in comparison with other known systems of government.

Yet there are four basic limitations. (1) The distribution of wealth and advantages is skewed (partly from the effects of past monopolies). By nature, the process and its policy outcomes are likely to reflect this inequality, not to alter it. (2) There are serious imperfections in the process, even beyond the underlying inequality. The participants are of unequal skill and advantages in using the process, or even in understanding it. Irrational attitudes can be created or manipulated, and attention can be diverted. In parts of the system there is little political competition at all, and money can buy the skills and resources to sway elections and policy choices. Finally, the management of agencies often is detached from the political control process, operating in contrived obscurity.[8]

(3) The process usually acts slowly and with extended debate on actions to reduce inequality (e.g. "tax reform") or any other major change in structure. This gives time and tactical opportunities to forestall action. As it functions, the process prevents major, rapid, equalizing actions. Instead, change is usually by inches, possibly even slower than the structural and distributional changes injected by "natural" forces.

---

[7] Anthony Downs, *An Economic Theory of Democracy* (New York: Harper, 1957); Robert A. Dahl, *A Preface to Democratic Theory* (Chicago: University of Chicago Press, 1956); Robert A. Dahl and C. E. Lindblom, *Politics, Economics and Democracy* (New York: Harper, 1953); but see also K. J. Arrow, *Social Choice and Individual Values,* 2d ed. (New York: Wiley, 1963).

[8] See K. C. Davis, *Discretionary Justice* (Baton Rouge: Louisiana State University Press, 1969), and sources cited there.

(4) Information about the policy alternatives is crucial, but in practice it is subject to bias and suppression. Public-information agencies (the Census in particular) operate under politically set rules, which prevent disclosure of much information that could guide specific policy choices toward industry. Indeed, many of the data needed even for a research understanding of the general relationship are withheld or not collected at all. Therefore, as a natural outcome of imperfect democratic choice, there is a cultivated ignorance among the populace and the experts on precisely the most sensitive and significant questions. In general, the greater the social sensitivity of a subject, the less reliable official data will be on it. The corollary is that if there are excellent data on a subject, it is likely not to be significant (not, at least, in the form taken by the data).

The range of possible policy results is illustrated in Figure 1.1. Imagine that a certain effect is claimed by a policy, *e.g.*, "to increase competition." The actual treatment that follows may (as shown in Figure 1.1) (1) do just that, immediately, (2) do a little of it, slowly, (3) have no effect, (4) slowly cause some opposite effect (*e.g.*, reduce competition), (5) immediately prevent other possible policy steps which would give the effect, or directly cause the opposite effect.[9] A null hypothesis (number 3 above) may be adopted as a general expectation, rebuttable only by good evidence: under it, formal treatments are assumed to have no real effects, unless shown otherwise. The actual effects can be either positive or negative. The political economy may bring the outcomes to fit or accentuate the prior configuration of power and interests; this may have no relation at all to a genuine social optimum. Evidence about the real effects can be *deductive*—based on reasonable expectations maturely considered. Or, it can be *factual,* but usually without firm proof. Instead, one must often judge the net probability of effect by using weak and disparate indications. In doing this, one treats the formal statements of policy and the assertions by interested parties (including, of course, the policy managers themselves) only as a starting point.

The general lessons for policy are two. Past policy choices are likely to contain serious biases and possibly negative social yields. And for the future, one cannot rely simply on "enlightened democratic processes" to generate optimal choices. Those processes may have caused choices in the past

---

[9] A small example: Cigarette advertising on television was banned in 1970 to discourage smoking. But the banning also removed the free access of *anti*-cigarette advertising, which the fairness doctrine had required. The net effect was a shift toward a more *pro*-smoking mix of messages on all media taken together.

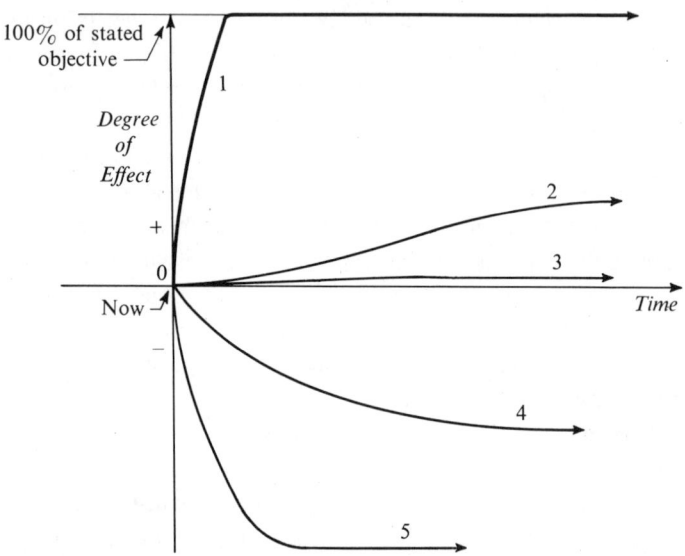

Figure 1.1 Actual effects may be unrelated to formal objectives.

which actually created the present problems. Nor can one rely on the old scientific aim "to inform the public, so it can act," to shine kleig lights on the facts and then watch the citizenry enforce a solution. For change to occur, power must be exerted, and power requires self-interest, activated. Therefore the analyst must think ahead to the mechanisms and incentives by which a seemingly optimal move can be triggered or enforced. Otherwise, one merely defines utopian schemes. Utopia is valuable, but schemes for it always run the risk of being diverted in practice against their own stated objectives.

In short, the conditions of political economy require one to be skeptical, to allow for—to harness—power and self-interest, and to think at least three moves ahead. The ideal "treatment" is a rule or constraint which is simple, cheap, and not in need of administering; or rather, which can succeed even when it is administered with an average degree of competence. This book offers few such ideal rules, but it does try to avoid vacuous or ponderous schemes which are likely to be turned against the public interest, and it conveys a method of appraising policies which could improve the results.

This book is also reformist, not radical; it uses conventional analysis to define optimal policy adjustments within the present setting. More basic changes are examined only briefly, in chapter 11. There we consider: What if power were radically altered? What scope and forms of treatment for industry would be suitable? How do they compare with the reform tool kit?

In chapter 11 we note that there are strong analytical reasons why a rapid shift in wealth and power toward equality is not likely to occur. Therefore, we are rational to direct this book mainly to treatments within the present context, with all its biases and inherent blocks to optimality. That is the road trod by most specialists, but it too has risks.

4 CONVENTIONAL CONCEPTS AND TOOLS

In this light we can outline the present conventional (1) concepts of markets and (2) policy treatments for them. They have grown orthodox and routine.

(1) The standard analysis of industrial organization envisages four levels, summarized in Figure 2.[10] Each market is regarded as a distinct entity, in line with Marshallian partial analysis.[11] The context of the market is considered to be extraneous. There are basic determinants that shape structure. The market's structure influences—how closely is debated—the behavior of firms in the market and the whole performance of the market.[12] Causation is virtually unilateral, though some observers have noted reverse causations and interactions. Structure is usually regarded as a matter of concentration or of barriers: each has its advocates. Behavior is narrowly perceived, primarily as matters of pricing and interfirm strategies. Performance criteria are matters of minimizing costs and prices; there is usually little attention to content or equity.[13]

[10] Their origin as a formal scheme is usually attributed to J. S. Bain (see *Industrial Organization*). See also E. S. Mason, *Economic Concentration and the Monopoly Problem* (Cambridge, Mass.: Harvard University Press, 1957), and Scherer, *Industrial Market Structure,* ch. 1.

[11] This tradition derives primarily from Marshall, *Principles of Economics.* See also E. H. Chamberlin, *The Theory of Monopolistic Competition,* 8th ed. (Cambridge, Mass.: Harvard University Press, 1962). Schumpeter had a more inclusive view and, to a degree, so did J. M. Clark, *Competition as a Dynamic Process* (Wash., D.C.: Brookings Institution, 1962).

[12] Among determinists, one would usually include J. M. Blair, *Economic Concentration* (New York: Harcourt, Brace, Jovanovich, 1972), W. F. Mueller, and Bain; those stressing a wide range of behavior variations include Stigler, J. F. Weston, and John McGee.

[13] This can be seen clearly in Bain, *Industrial Organization,* and Scherer, *Industrial Market Structure,* but it is common. I am here defining the approach, not belittling it. This narrowing of focus has helped to clarify and advance the analysis.

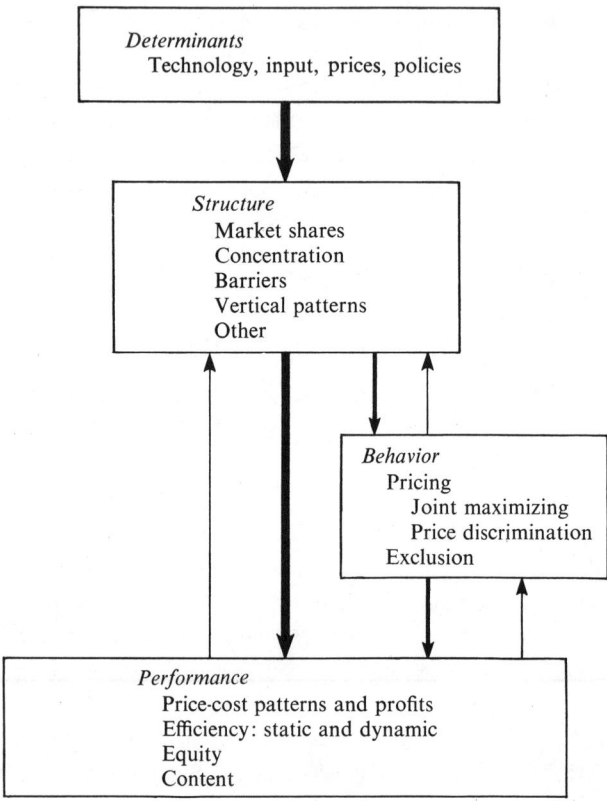

Figure 1.2 Basic concepts of industrial organization.

The standard format achieves some clarity by excluding some important elements and by assuming one-way causation. We shall see in chapter 2 that it can be usefully modified.

(2) Conventional policy tools in the United States have become antitrust for "the competitive sector" (which is primarily industry and trade), regulation for "utilities," and public enterprise for certain intractable cases and large parts of the social infrastructure.[14] There have also been a wide range of special cases—farming, oil, shipping, health, sport, weapons, etc.— whose scope and variety have recently been growing.

[14] See Bain, *Industrial Organization,* and Carl Kaysen and Donald F. Turner, *Antitrust Policy* (Cambridge, Mass.: Harvard University Press, 1959).

These policies are summarized as of the middle 1920s and middle 1970s, in Tables 1.1 and 1.2. This summary is meant only to convey the main outlines, and to compare the scope of policies over the 50-year period. The reality they represent is a matter both of legal domains and simple usage. Thus, for example, the Antitrust Division has legal standing in some industries but does not exercise it, while it has influenced bank merger policy by custom rather than strict law. There are many such debatable marginal cases, but the main outlines are clear enough.

Table 1.1 Estimates of Policy Coverage by Sectors, U.S. Economy, 1974

	Percent of National Income						
Sector	Total	Subsidy or cartel support	Public purchases	Exempt	Antitrust	Regulation on other control device	Public ownership (% of national income)
Finance, etc.	11.4	6.5		4.2	.7		1.4
Manufacturing	26.5	1.0	3.5	11.5	9.5	1.0	.9
Utilities	4.2		.5	1.5		2.2	.7
Transport	3.8		.2	2.2	.3	1.1	.9
Government	16.0		16.0				16.0
Wholesale and Retail	15.0			11.0	4.0		0
Services	13.1	3.0		9.1	1.0		2.0
Construction	4.6		.7	3.9			0
Mining	1.6			1.6			0
Agriculture, etc.	3.0	2.5		.5			0
Rest of World	.8						
Totals	100.0	13.0	20.9	45.5	15.5	4.3	21.9

SOURCES: Estimates are based on a wide variety of sources, including especially W. Adams, ed., *The Structure of American Industry*, 4th ed. (New York: Macmillan, 1971); F. M. Scherer, *Industrial Market Structure and Economic Performance* (Skokie, Ill.: Rand McNally, 1970); A. E. Kahn, *The Economics of Regulation*, 2 vols. (New York: Wiley, 1971); and *U.S. Survey of Current Business*.

Table 1.3 summarizes the public funds used directly in each policy type. It understates, because some of the costs (such as for court hearings of antitrust cases) are indirect, though real. Table 1.3 also offers estimates of the *private* resources employed in responding to, or anticipating, the public policies. Some figures in Table 1.3 can only be rough estimates, but they do suffice to show the main lines.

There are three basic impressions from these summaries: (1) there have

Table 1.2 Estimates of Policy Coverage by Sectors, U.S. Economy, 1924

		Percent of National Income					Public ownership (% of national income)
Sector	Total	Subsidy or cartel support	Public purchases	Exempt	Antitrust	Regulation on other control device	
Finance, etc.	15.1	2.0		13.1			0
Manufacturing	21.9			9.9	12.0		.4
Utilities	3.3			1.3		2.0	.5
Transport	7.5			3.0		4.5	.7
Government	9.6		9.6				9.6
Wholesale and Retail	13.6			9.6	4.0		0
Services	11.6		.6	11.0			0
Construction	4.4		.4	4.0			0
Mining	2.5			2.5			0
Agriculture, etc.	10.5			10.5			0
Rest of World	0			0			0
Totals	100.0	2.0	10.6	64.9	16.0	6.5	11.2

SOURCES: See Table 1.1 and U.S. Bureau of Census, *Historical Statistics of the United States,* U.S. Government Printing Office, 1957.

been changes in sectors and in the extension of policy coverage to some new sectors, yet (2) the original coverage of the traditional policies has been little changed. Meanwhile (3) the range of exceptional, ad hoc cases has risen.

Antitrust has three main parts:[15] it attempts to reduce cooperation among competitors; it screens mergers between firms and stops some of them; it copes with existing market power. Though its main focus is in industry and trade, it has been reaching recently into certain "regulated" sectors.

Regulation involves ratifying a firm as a utility and putting it under some degree of constraint by a commission.[16] Price changes must be approved by the commission. The criteria are (1) the profit rate is to be "fair," and (2) the price structure is to be "just and reasonable."

Public enterprise has spread to a variety of sectors, but it is least exten-

---

[15] See especially P. Areeda, *Antitrust Analysis: Problems, Text, Cases* (Boston: Little, Brown, 1967).

[16] See I. R. Barnes, *The Economics of Public Utility Regulation* (New York: F. S. Crofts, 1942); J. C. Bonbright, *Principles of Public Utility Rates,* (New York: Columbia University Press, 1961); A. E. Kahn, *The Economics of Regulation,* 2 vols. (New York: Wiley, 1971); and W. G. Shepherd, "Entry as a Substitute for Regulation," *American Economic Review,* May 1973, pp. 98–105.

Table 1.3 Policy Resources Under Selected Programs, United States, 1970–71

	Estimated Levels of Resources Used in 1970–71 ($ million)	
	Public agencies	Private units
Antitrust [a]		
Antitrust Division	11	150 +
Federal Trade Commission	8	
Regulation		
Federal Commissions [a]	108 [d]	350
State Commissions [b]	28 [e]	150
Public Enterprises [a]		
Postal (deficit)	1,583	
Federal Courts	40 [c]	
Bureau of Reclamation	149	
Federal Prison Systems	79	
Veterans Administration Medical Care	1,633	
Public Purchases [a]		
Department of Defense	21,584	
NASA	3,367	
Atomic Energy Commission	2,501	
Subsidies [f]	48,240	

[a] See U.S. Government Budget for 1970–71.
[b] See C. F. Phillips, Jr., *The Economics of Regulation,* rev. ed. (Homewood, Ill.: Irwin, 1971), ch. 3; and various state commission annual reports.
[c] This represents a minority share of the costs of Federal Courts.
[d] The raw total is $270 million; 60 percent of it is assumed to be applied to functions other than economic regulation.
[e] The total is $80 million; 65 percent of it is assumed to be applied to functions other than economic regulation.
[f] See Table 5.2, chapter 5.

sive in industry, finance, and utilities.[17] The U.S. is unique in its reliance on regulation of utilities in place of public ownership. The public corporation has become a standard form for public enterprises, but other varieties are now being tried.

The evolution of these policies helps to explain their present character. Antitrust growth since the Sherman Act of 1890 has been uneven. The Antitrust Division has had two main waves of major actions, during 1907–1920 and 1937–1951, plus possibly a third beginning in 1966. In between, the

[17] Clair Wilcox and W. G. Shepherd, *Public Policies Toward Business,* 5th ed. (Homewood, Ill.: Irwin, 1975); and W. G. Shepherd, "Public Enterprise," in *Corporate Power in America,* eds. R. Nader and M. J. Green (New York: Grossman, 1972).

Division has been static—"consolidating," perhaps—with its resources growing moderately and its active jurisdiction receding. The FTC has moved irregularly, with clear low points in the 1920s and 1960s. Yet its resources have been more than double the Division's since World War II. Hence, there is a real but only loose short-run relation between the level of antitrust resources and the scope of activity. During most periods, the agencies have had surplus resources.

The 1900–20 period also saw the first experiments in regulation. The ICC at last began to acquire real, not just formal, capacity to get data and apply constraints.[18] The first state commission emerged, and an embryonic Federal Power Commission was created in 1920. Yet real control has been extended more slowly. Most state commissions are passive, and the Federal Communications Commission—created in 1934—was largely acquiescent for over two decades, not beginning formal public proceedings on rates and structure until in 1965. For 90 years the formal scope of regulation has been expanding, in numbers of agencies, in resources, and in sectors "covered"; but the severity of constraint has varied widely and, in most cases, is still unknown.

The proliferation of public enterprise has been slow and peripheral but relatively steady. By 1900, there was a wide scattering of municipal gas and light utilities, but little more.[19] Certain social enterprises were in formation—schools, a few hospitals, some libraries—but charitable and private units were common. By the 1930s certain federal projects were added to the steady growth of urban enterprises, and by the 1960s a wide range of public enterprises had evolved. Compared to other "mixed" economies, the U.S. has relatively little public enterprise in finance, industry, and utilities. Yet even in these sectors there is more of it than is generally recognized. And abroad, the variety of public enterprises is greater and also growing.

Meanwhile public purchases and subsidies had both reached high levels. Purchases made a quantum jump with World War II and—supplemented by the space program and growing social programs—have continued growing.[20] Subsidies have a checkered history, rising in selected industries (housing, shipbuilding, airlines, etc.) and occasionally fading out. The

---

[18] I. L. Sharfman, *The Interstate Commerce Commission,* 4 vols. (New York: The Commonwealth Fund, 1931–37); Barnes, *Public Utility Regulation.*

[19] Barnes, *Public Utility Regulation.*

[20] M. J. Peck and F. M. Scherer, *The Weapons Acquisition Process* (Cambridge, Mass.: Harvard University School of Business, 1962).

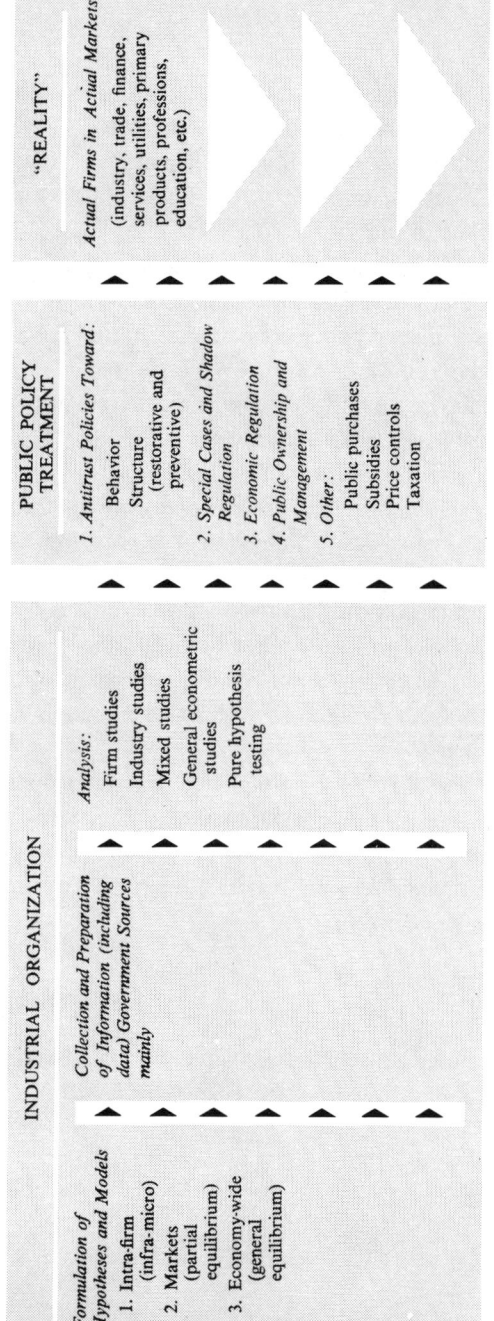

Figure 1.3 The interrelated world of industrial organization, public policy, and reality.

growth of federal taxation has brought a rise in tax subsidies as well, so that since World War II the total of subsidies has been much larger and more complex than even expert opinion has recognized.[21]

Altogether, these industrial policies are full-grown experiments, whose nature and coverage have matured. Only in the last 15 years have their economic effects begun to be studied skeptically. Some of them remain scarcely known, much less evaluated, yet the grist for the analytical mill is there, often of seven decades' standing or more.

The content of these policies will be analyzed in chapter 5 at some length. At this point, one notes that they are rooted in the standard concepts of industrial organization. Therefore they avoid dealing either with the *context* of the firm or the *content* of activity inside the firm. Even under public ownership, the model for behavior has commonly come to be the private firm with the usual cost-minimizing goals and patterns of authority.[22]

The concepts and policies are actually, of course, influenced by the real world, as outlined in Figure 1.3. Information, as controlled by the enterprises, limits the ability of (1) analysts to form correct images of markets and to test them, and (2) policy agencies to recognize the true problems. Therefore, bias is likely to occur both in the images and the policies. This problem permeates all discussions—in this book and others—about optimal policies. It can go very deep; the very neglect of context and content in U.S. industrial policies arises partly from our ignorance about who controls firms and what is going on inside them.

One result is that the American tolerance for high degrees of monopoly is remarkably great, as long as they are thought to be "put under"—and therefore validated by—a public agency of some sort. Along with the more intellectual features of the problem, this national habit of mind gives good grounds for skepticism about the outcome.

5 FORMAT

First we need to derive accurate concepts of markets and of the social performance criteria they may affect (chapter 2). Then (chapter 3) we can

[21] Joint Economic Committee, *The Economics of Federal Subsidy Programs*, 92d Congress, 1st Session (U.S. Government Printing Office, 1972).

[22] W. A. Robson, *Nationalized Industry and Public Ownership* (London: Allen & Unwin, 1961); W. G. Shepherd, *Economic Performance Under Public Ownership* (New Haven: Yale University Press, 1965); and R. Pryke, *Public Enterprise in Practice* (New York: St. Martin's, 1972).

analyze the conditions for reaching optimal policy choices. We also explore the different methods by which policy treatments may induce or compel the desired outcome.

The actual nature of markets and their policy yields are outlined in chapter 4, with attention to future trends in the more policy-sensitive markets. The existing set of policy treatments is explored at some length in chapter 5, to show what the treatments really do and what their effects probably are.

The rest of the book takes up the main choice situations which appear to offer high future yields. Financial markets and connections are treated in chapter 6; remedial treatments for existing market power are analyzed in chapter 7; preventive policies toward the formation of new market power are considered in chapter 8. Chapter 9 covers "utility" sectors, and the next two chapters move to less orthodox areas, where market structure and competitive behavior are more germane than is commonly realized. Chapter 10 treats the purchasing of weapons, chapter 11 considers treatments that would be consistent with an equalizing of wealth. The main lessons of the book are drawn together in chapter 12.

I have focused on the main sectors and policy tools, rather than trying to be encyclopedic, with the risk of being merely diffuse. The strategy is to give the mainstream cases their due, while also exploring certain boundary areas in the field. There will be international comparisons, and a certain amount of econometric information will be presented in (as much as possible) the English language.

At the least, this book codifies and revises parts of the oral tradition in the field, offers certain new information, and knits together some of the emerging critiques of the various policy tools. With the whole range of industrial policies—and their supposed economic rationales—presently in flux, a genuine crisis in policy choice has come into being. Even if this book is much less novel than I hope, it may help in the effort to rethink and revise industrial policies. Revisions there will be. The fundamental task is to develop a basis for making them along rational lines.

PART ONE

Concepts for Policy Choices

CHAPTER TWO
Defining Structure and Performance

OUR TASK is to understand the sources and criteria of "good" market performance so that we may define its benefits and costs. We must begin with valid images of firms in markets. We shall look carefully at what market structure is, how it changes, and what its effects are. Such an examination is in the "industrial organization" tradition; in addition, it makes better sense if we first clarify the surrounding context of the enterprise, and also the inner content of activity in the enterprise. Otherwise our cost-benefit policy criteria are likely to be rather narrow and mechanical.

So we begin by positing the familiar concepts of market power: that it may exist and cause inefficiencies or benefits of various sorts—depending on what economies of scale, Schumpeterian processes, and managerial motives there may be. These are too well known to need elaboration here.[1] Having said that, we shall first consider the *context* in which firms may hold such market power, next explore the inner *content* of behavior and choice inside the enterprise, and finally turn to the more orthodox analysis of what market

---

[1] W. G. Shepherd, *Market Power and Economic Welfare* (New York: Random House, 1970); J. S. Bain, *Industrial Organization* (New York: Wiley, 1969); and F. M. Scherer, *Industrial Market Structure and Economic Performance* (Skokie, Ill.: Rand McNally, 1970).

structure *is* and how it evolves. From all this we can then derive the nature of benefits and costs for industrial policies, so that chapter 3 can put them together in a connected framework for evaluation.

With this basis, we might ideally predict the course of each industry over time, so that policies could be predesigned exactly to the future optimal patterns. However, such precision is not yet within reach. The concepts need more refining, measurement of the relationships has been imprecise, and the most important issues may be the hardest to include. After 40 years of theory and testing, we are still only beginning to learn about the nature of market power, its setting, its evolution over time, and its effects.

We can aspire only to get the concepts in balanced and consistent form, and to be aware of the main areas of ignorance. Market structure in industry *X, Y,* or *Z* will be seen as being knit into the economic fabric; it cannot be understood or properly treated in isolation. For example, to restructure an industry without knowing banking connections and the industry's trends would be superficial, possibly futile, and probably harmful. The same holds true for franchising and regulating a "utility" without knowing its trends and financial setting. To ignore content is to risk omitting perhaps the most important outcome. The urge to treat market power as strictly a matter of market structure, of its "concentration"—an urge we all share because it simplifies the problem and seems "scientific"—is therefore to be resisted. Only if we understand the whole setting and the inner content can we work with "nature" rather than against it.

1 THE CONTEXT OF ENTERPRISES

Each firm is embedded in financial ties, as well as in the structure of its input and output markets. We consider this financial setting first, because it is the immediate context that supervises and affects its behavior. Then we shall note the broader distributional setting in which market activity takes place: the distribution of wealth, opportunity, and income.

Capital is the key input. It involves many firms in intimate supervision by external financial groups. Capital can buy any of the other inputs (including superior management), and it can even buy market positions outright by paying for whole firms or branches. It funds strategic behavior: with an ample line of credit at low interest costs, a firm's range of choice is wide; without funds, the choices are narrower, perhaps too narrow to permit survival. Also, the availability of funds in itself affects the degree of risk borne by the enterprise.

The structural analysis must therefore be set in an understanding of the conditions by which firms obtain capital. These conditions affect the structure itself and its yields. The general proposition that will emerge in this section can be called a "replication" hypothesis: banking structure tends to replicate itself throughout other markets. This would have cardinal policy implications if it were true and important, for financial ties would then be one cause of industrial monopoly. Accordingly, to change industrial structure or behavior, one would also need to treat the links to financial markets.

Capital suppliers are of many sorts, ranging from commercial and investment banks to insurance firms and other large portfolio buyers of equity capital. For brevity they are called "banks" here, but this is in recognition that commercial banks supply only a portion of funds.[2]

The importance of capital supply lies in the mutual reliance between capital suppliers and their clients. The mass of owners do not individually supervise managers in any meaningful sense (although the larger investors routinely gain closer information than others). Firms do however rely on their "bankers" for funds, and with these funds comes advice. Most corporations have long-standing and intimate relations with their bankers, in which senior banking officials know in detail about company performance, prospects, and strategies. These officials decide the availability and terms of loans, often counselling and limiting company decisions in detail. If one's banker won't "go along" with a project, often it cannot (and should not) be done.

In short, access to capital is by a variety of sources, some of which involve close mutual ties with specific bankers or other capital units. Because these ties go so deep, they are not quickly changed.[3] They are often reflected by directorships for bank and other officers (see sources in chapters 4 and 6). But usually such ties are only on the surface; it is the underlying mutual reliance and intimacy of the "banking relationship" which is the real stuff of financial influence.

The banks are also maximizing profitability, often with a rather greater

---

[2] On these institutions and their basic role, see the various studies by the Commission on Money and Credit, Paul M. Horvitz et al., eds., *Private Financial Institutions* (Englewood Cliffs, N.J.: Prentice-Hall, 1963) and any of the several leading texts on business finance and capital theory.

[3] See L. L. Werboff and M. E. Rozen, "Market Shares and Competition Among Financial Institutions," in *Private Financial Institutions*.

emphasis on the security element. They prefer secure, lucrative clients to risky low-profit ones, and so their ties to the "better risks" involve a degree of mutual reliance. After all, they are protecting their own loans by counselling on company decisions. In seeking "good risks," banks inevitably offer favorable terms to the more attractive clients.[4]

Yet there is circularity: the favorable terms—i.e., a longer line of credit at lower interest rates—themselves improve the security, profitability, and prospects of the client firms. Banking factors can therefore both reinforce and create disparities in market position and profitability. Getting good

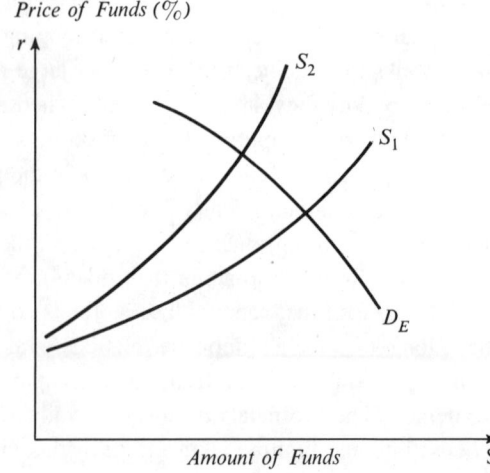

Figure 2.1 Supply and demand for funds.

banker support is often critical to founding or expanding a firm, to entering a market, or to adopting a strategy against rivals; or equally so to *preventing* any of these. And the terms themselves can determine the outcome in advance.

All of this would be strictly academic if capital markets were perfect. All seekers of funds would be fully evaluated by many alternative suppliers, and capital sources would be irrelevant to market position.[5] Yet this cannot be safely assumed, for capital markets frequently have very tight structure and banking relationships are not fluid (details of this are given in chapter 4). Therefore we need to consider how the imperfections might take effect.

[4] See Shepherd, *Market Power*, ch. 6, plus standard texts on corporate finance.
[5] See George J. Stigler, *The Organization of Industry* (Homewood, Ill.: Irwin, 1968).

First, consider all banking factors to be absent or neutral. Then an industrial monopoly may occur and have effect. But it would have good chances of lasting only if it had economies of scale or other specific protection. If the cost curve were flat and there were no entry barriers, then a dominant firm would have to decline or forego supernormal profits. It would be a mere shadow of a monopoly, of the kind mentioned by J. B. Clark and stressed by recent writers.[6]

Now to the other extreme. Let banking be a monopoly. The lone banker now has loans to the dominant firm, and is the only source of capital for smaller firms or possible entrants. The supply curve for funds to a smaller

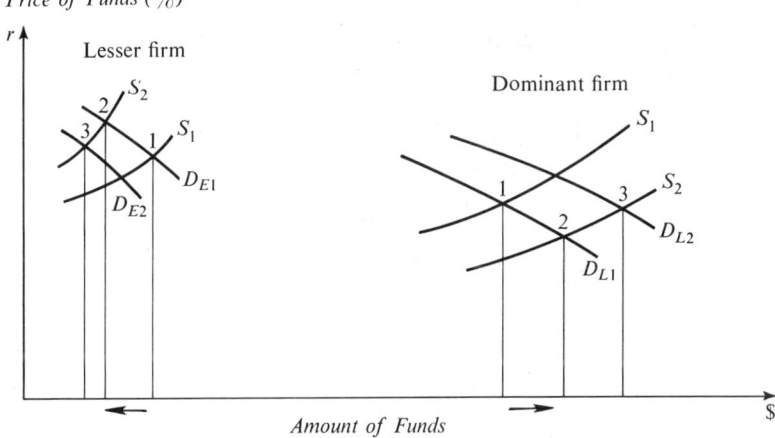

Figure 2.2 Borrowing conditions may differ for dominant and lesser firms.

firm or an entrant will be affected as in Figure 2.1. As the smaller firm or entrant succeeds, it cuts the leading firm's profitability and, thereby, the bankers' own profit-security results on its loans. Recognizing this, the bank operates along a higher offer curve, S_2. The entrant therefore borrows less, and at a higher cost of capital. This shift permits the dominant firm to attain excess profits without sacrificing market share. The static effects are shown in Figure 2.2, for a "large" and a "small" firm. The bank's preinvolvement with the large firm has the net effect of shifting the offer curves as

[6] J. B. Clark, *The Control of Trusts* (New York: Macmillan, 1901); Donald J. Dewey, *The Theory of Imperfect Competition* (New York: Columbia University Press, 1969); see also sources cited in Scherer, *Industrial Market Structure*.

shown. The result is a greater disparity in the interest rates paid and in the market shares held.

Also, the large firm's choice of strategies is widened, while the smaller firm's is narrowed. This has the effect of shifting out the large firm's demand for capital, while the small firm's demand curve shifts in. The final quantities, labeled 3, are farther apart, but the difference in r is lessened, in Figure 2.3 to a small amount indeed. Therefore, the observed r values understate the true degree of discrimination between the firms in the terms upon which funds are supplied to them.

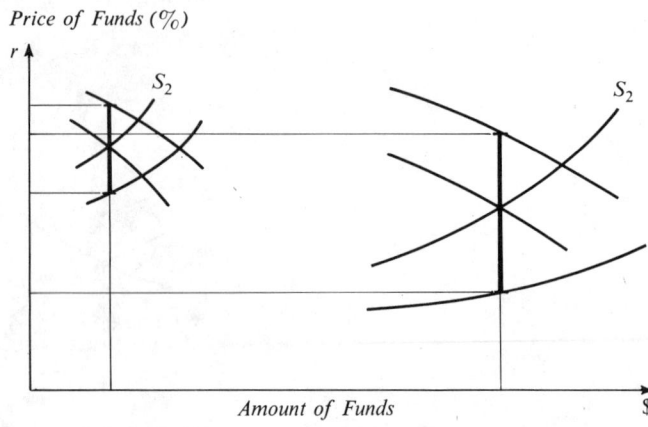

Figure 2.3 The resulting amounts and terms of loans and net profits earned.

For completeness, note that these supply and demand curves for capital are respectively the marginal cost of capital and the marginal return to capital curves for the firm. Each has an average cost or return counterpart, as shown in Figure 2.3. These determine the average profit rate to be earned by each firm during the planning period. Evidently the elasticities of both demand and supply of capital affect this profit rate. Note that the small firm can earn a significant average rate of return even though its capital supply (and growth potential) has been limited. Therefore, neither the interest rate differential nor the comparative profit rates are reliable guides to the underlying effects of financial structure upon market structure.

If the effects are significant, they will tend to maintain market power and to deter lesser firms and entrants. They will also create corresponding gains to bankers from arranging mergers between two or more competing firms. In all this, it is primarily the preexisting small firms that matter, not potential entrants. The resulting market structure is, like a suspension bridge, under tension from opposed forces. Technical diseconomies of scale may be traded off against the pecuniary economies of scale which imperfect capital markets inject. Any other limit on the ability of small firms to increase their market shares than simply further raises the larger firm's security and optimal longrun share.

Banks therefore influence structure: tight banking-market structure would be sufficient to create tight industrial structure even if all other causes were absent. More precisely: banking structure tends to replicate itself throughout other markets. If competition is to be increased, it must have additional support from capital suppliers. To analyze industry in isolation is to ignore a basic determinant, which would also have to be a primary target for any policy action.

These financial effects are not "entry barriers" so much as they are pressures against rises by small firms. Their effects are primarily upon the differences among market shares, causing them to be greater and to stay that way. The literature has recently regarded "capital barriers to entry" as a factor, perhaps a major factor, in structure.[7] Instead, this analysis suggests that imperfect capital markets are likely to influence the market shares of *existing* firms steadily and strongly. Such an influence could be large even if there were no potential entry. Or, at least, it could be more significant than one which merely deterred an occasional outsider from trying to add to the numbers of existing firms. In any event, banking factors appear to accord with a primary role for market share in structure. They operate on, and through, market share.

The *equity* setting is usually ignored by those evaluating industrial policy, on the premise that it is already satisfactory or, if not, is a matter for public tax and spending programs, but this is not wise, for several reasons. (1) The distribution of wealth is in fact highly unequal and appears to be staying so;[8] (2) much of the wealth traces back to earlier industrial monopolies which escaped effective industrial policies—the same effects may be recur-

[7] M. Hall and L. W. Weiss, "Firm Size and Profitability," *Review of Economics and Statistics*, 1967, pp. 319–31; Bain, *Industrial Organization;* and Dewey, *Imperfect Competition*.

[8] R. J. Lampmann, *The Share of the Top Wealth-Holders in National Wealth, 1922–1956* (Princeton: Princeton University Press, 1962); F. Lundberg, *The Rich and the Super-Rich* (Secaucus, N.J.: Lyle Stuart, 1968); and James D. Smith and Stephen D. Franklin, "The Concentration of Personal Wealth, 1922–69," *American Economic Review,* May, 1974, p. 162–67.

ring now; (3) tax and expenditure policies are increasingly being recognized as unlikely ever to alter the basic structure of wealth, opportunity, or income; (4) it is possible to define, if only roughly, an equity standard favoring greater equality. In short, greater equality is an unidentifiable, important, and workable element in designing industrial policies. (Or, at least, we can proceed with analysis here as if it were.)

The presence of sharp inequality needs no extended proof here, and we need not demonstrate that it arises partly from monopolies and tends to persist among generations. It has only recently begun to be recognized that public taxation is inadequate to equalize wealth. Instead, the tax laws can be regarded as if they were designed to *avoid* significant equalizing; the hypothesis—that they reflect, not alter, the structure of wealth, has not been refuted—nor can it be.[9] Therefore, a presumption in favor of reducing the inequality of wealth, opportunity, and income can validly be included in policy analysis.

Equity in distribution has several parts: patterns of present wealth and income, and of future opportunities. Equality is, of course, only one of many possible criteria of equity, and it must be defined carefully. Nonetheless, I shall posit a greater degree of equality as the basic criterion of equity. There are economic as well as social and ethical grounds for this.[10] Although certain deviations from it may be needed for practical reasons, no other single basic criterion, such as inheritance or efficiency, dominates it. It provides a reasonable organizing basis for policy choice.

Redistribution via industrial policies cannot be very drastic, as we shall see in chapters 4 and 7, in relation to the full structure of family wealth.

---

[9] See various volumes in the Brookings Institution (Wash., D.C.) Studies of Government Finance, including J. A. Pechman, *Federal Tax Policy*, rev. ed., 1971; R. Goode, *The Individual Income Tax*, 1964; A. C. Harberger and M. J. Bailey eds., *The Taxation of Income from Capital*, and G. R. Jantscher, *Trusts and Estate Taxation*, 1967. See also B. A. Okner and J. A. Pechman, "Who Paid the Taxes in 1966?" *American Economic Review*, May 1974, pp. 168–74.

[10] See John Rawls, *A Theory of Justice* (Cambridge, Mass.: Harvard University Press, 1971), and "Some Reasons for the Maximin Criterion," *American Economic Review*, May 1974, pp. 194–46, and references cited in these works: and Abba P. Lerner, *The Economics of Control* (New York: Macmillan, 1944). Henry C. Simons notes: "A substantial measure of inequality may be unavoidable or essential for motivation; but it should be recognized as evil and tolerated only so far as the dictates of expediency are clear." *Economic Policy for a Free Society* (Chicago: University of Chicago Press, 1948), pp. 51–52. Recent studies have indicated that the motivation case for inequality is very weak; see, e.g., R. Barlow, H. W. Brazer, and J. N. Morgan, *Economic Behavior of the Affluent* (Washington, D.C.: Brookings Institution, 1966).

Therefore, we can proceed as if moderate equalizing shifts—which are all that are available via industrial policies—are beneficial. Any clear exceptions to this rule can then be treated individually. The gains from such equalizing shifts are finite and may need to be traded off against other goals (chapter 12 explores these further).

2   THE CONTENT OF ENTERPRISE ACTIVITY

In standard analysis, activity inside the firm is not considered. The firm is regarded as a little black box: inputs come in, outputs go out. How this is done, under what regime or conditions of work, is regarded as irrelevant (or rather, as a management science topic). Managers are assumed to arrange working conditions that are not only privately efficient but also socially optimal. It is, in any case, their legal prerogative to do so, and society is not to interfere with that prerogative. Economists have therefore fitted their images and analysis to this premise. Owners and/or managers control and direct; employees acquiesce—and the content of their employment is immune from economic or social evaluation.

But consider how artificial this is. Assume that economic functions are basically three: production, consumption, and investment. Then, as in the standard analysis, only the owner-manager's utility is considered as relevant to production. Even then, it is relevant only as a determinant, not an outcome. The utility of others is considered only in analyzing consumption activity.[11] This achieves the breathtaking result of holding irrelevant for utility what most people spend most of their time, ambition, and effort on: their work. Indeed, one's work (career, status, skills, etc.) is in our culture the primary source of identity, as well as of economic status. To regard work as only a means to attain consumption of goods and services is to engage in fantasy. Both are important. Indeed, much consumption takes place on the job. At the upper levels, the job is often "reward enough," conferring prestige, power, and a variety of interesting experience.

Therefore, production and consumption mingle. This simple point has basic implications which redefine much of the conventional analysis of efficient allocation. In our context here it requires us to put content firmly among the elements we include in any cost-benefit analysis of policies. It

---

[11] It enters the work choice only in the individual's decision of which job to take. The chooser is assumed to take the wage levels as given.

requires also that policies deal with it as a genuine social issue. And it requires us to define—virtually for the first time—what content is, as the first step.

Content is presently an important but neglected scientific frontier in the field of industrial organization. It has been studied for some time by sociologists, industrial psychologists, and others, and it awaits a rigorous formulation.[12] The root factor is of course the degree of utility gained by the worker from the whole of "the job." Different people draw satisfaction from differing kinds of effort, responsibility, variety, and cohesion.[13] Therefore, one would not posit any form of work as a single optimum type. Modern technology does require a degree of specialization in work. Yet variety can be arranged in many ways, some pleasurable to few, others to many. Repetition is universally a source of disutility. Therefore, firm organization can usually be of many kinds, consistent with given cost levels. That is already clear from Yugoslav, Japanese, and Chinese economic performance, where firm content differs from what is customary in the U.S. The main elements in firm content appear to be: [14]

1. Variety in individual choice among tasks, both in the given "job" and in the ability to shift among jobs within the firm.
2. A sharing in responsibility, rather than being overseen by a command hierarchy with unilateral control powers.
3. A recognized personal effect from one's effort. This can be from direct contact with the users of one's work (compare an auto assembly worker with a craftsman), or from a sense that one's efforts contribute socially (or at least avoid harming society, e.g., by pollution).
4. A sense of local identity. This can arise from local control, local operations or local service of various kinds. It involves content, not off-the-job charity work.

[12] See D. Katz and R. L. Kahn, *The Social Psychology of Organizations* (New York: Wiley, 1966); R. L. Kahn and E. Boulding, eds., *Power and Conflicts in Organizations* (New York: Basic Books, 1964); and R. Likert, *The Human Organization* (New York: McGraw-Hill, 1967); and J. S. Coleman, *Power and the Structure of Society* (New York: Norton, 1973). See also J. Vanek, *A General Theory of Labor-Managed Market Economics* (Ithaca: Cornell University Press, 1970).

[13] This reflects their true differences in personality and character. Some seek responsibility, others security. Some wish to belong, others to exceed the rest. The orthodox image of the aggressive, individualist managerial type is actually quite a specialized personality category among the whole range of human attributes.

[14] Again, this can only be a rough approximation of the main elements, pending further study.

These elements are "soft" and so the science of content is soft, compared to the apparent precision in such orthodox concepts as minimum cost and Pareto efficiency.[15] The possible elements of content are hard to put in analytical form, and it is not clear what priority ordering of importance they should follow. Further discussion can be expected to alter the list. Still, the utility of work is of great importance in any evaluation of industrial performance, and its inclusion in industrial policies is in order.

Here we are merely extending the beachhead which the analysis of managerial motivation, and of discrimination by race and sex, has already established. In fact, economists have been edging content into the analysis since the late 1950s. But their concepts have been highly abstract, and, true to the old tradition, they have looked mainly at what the managers—the authorities—are doing. The study of managers' motives and discretion traces back to Berle and Means, but it has flowered only in the 1960s with Baumol's, Cyert's, Williamson's and Marris's work.[16] Even this flowering has barely touched the core problem of content, because it assumes that managers hold all control. A full analysis would include the possible diffusion of that control, rather than assume that it is exerted from the top down.

Leibenstein's concept of X-efficiency has crystallized the older notions of organizational slack and bureaucracy.[17] But it too assumes the older control structure, and—*ex definitio*—it does not try to define what X-efficiency contains or how it relates to content. Therefore, it can be regarded as an important early effort to legitimize the analysis of content, without carrying the analysis into detail.

More recently, discrimination by race, sex, etc. in large firms has been

---

[15] Yet, of course, these precise concepts are usually hard to measure in practice. Therefore they are quite soft *in use,* as distinct from mere manipulation of images.

[16] A. A. Berle and G. C. Means, *The Modern Corporation and Private Property* (New York: Macmillan, 1932); W. J. Baumol, *Business Behavior, Value and Growth,* rev. ed. (Englewood Cliffs, N.J.: Prentice-Hall, 1967); and "On the Theory of Expansion of the Firm," *American Economic Review,* 1964, pp. 1078–87; J. G. March and H. Simon, *Organizations* (New York: Wiley, 1958); O. E. Williamson, "Managerial Discretion and Business Behavior," *American Economic Review,* 1963, pp. 1032–57; R. Marris and A. Wood, eds., *The Corporate Economy* (Cambridge, Mass.: Harvard University Press, 1971), and Marris "Is the Corporate Economy a Corporate State?" *American Economic Review,* May 1972, pp. 203–15.

[17] H. Leibenstein, "Allocative Efficiency and 'X-Efficiency,' " *American Economic Review,* 1966, pp. 392–416; and "Organizational or Frictional Equilibria, X-Efficiency, and Rate of Innovation," *Quarterly Journal of Economics,* 1969, pp. 600–623.

tested in several studies.[18] These raise a basic issue of content, because exclusion is a central part of inferior content. But these studies are only preliminary so far, and they don't address the more general process of exclusion, such as the career (see below).

Therefore, the time is ripe for general analysis of content. There is precedent and preliminary work toward it. It is not just a matter of labor economies but relates, also, to the structure and behavior of the firm. It appears to be in the same realm of importance as the other features and effects of industrial organization, if not even more important. It also restores balance to the field, by widening the scope of what has increasingly appeared to be a technocratic orthodoxy. Therefore content is an appropriate and necessary subject in the field of industrial organization.

A basic component of content is the career. It needs some analysis here, even though (or because) it is so familiar.[19] The career is a cumulative process, a trajectory from initial to mature phases. Each firm can be seen—oversimply but validly—as a microsociety run by a small group of such careerists: managers and professionals (lawyers, accountants, financial experts, etc.). Their decisions control the rest of the employees, most of whose jobs are essentially repetitive rather than cumulative. Once one is off the career track, it is difficult to regain it.

Basic attributes of the career are: (1) It starts at a young age. Those coming late or from outside are excluded. (2) It is narrow, requiring intensive specialization during ages 20–35 at least. (3) It is normally full-time and cannot be interrupted or done at half-speed. This has eliminated most women. (4) Many career skills are simply acculturation, "learning the ropes." This is not inherently productive, and it is partly for excluding others.

Accordingly, members of the career group are subdivided and regimented among themselves in several ways, and are also protected from entry by noncareer people. The career system does not permit transferrals and restarting, and it also limits competition among generations (juniors do not chal-

[18] G. S. Becker, *The Economics of Discrimination* (Chicago: University of Chicago Press, 1957); W. G. Shepherd and S. G. Levin, "Managerial Discrimination in Large Firms," *Review of Economics and Statistics,* November 1973, pp. 11–22 (and other sources cited there); and W. S. Comanor, "Racial Discrimination in American Industry," *Economica,* November 1973, pp. 363–78.

[19] I am preparing a more detailed analysis, "The Economics of the Career." There is little economic work on the subject, and the sociological research is mostly on other attributes.

lenge senior officials; they work for them, biding their time until promoted). There is specialization by age, by subject and skills, by health, by upbringing, and by sex. The sorting process is (1) thorough, arranging participants into stable, small-group situations; (2) mainly irreversible; (3) a basis for disparities in rewards among participants, and between them and the rest.

The career operates by creating long-time (even lifetime) partial-monopoly situations of "specialists," on a detailed micro basis as well as among whole groups. It does not necessarily elicit the maximum in productive or creative efforts even from those who are in it. The best and most creative minds often stay outside it. It affects many participants so thoroughly that by age 35 they are capable only of narrow technical activity for the next 30 years. It evidently conflicts with certain criteria of "good" content, on two planes. On one plane it consigns the noncareer majority of workers to repetitive jobs, many of which provide little responsibility or sense of personal value. On the other plane, it eliminates much of the flexibility in the pace and content of the careerists' work during their lifetime.

Further, the career system adds to the authoritarian and elitist tendencies of enterprises. These tendencies achieved full sway during the 1870–1920 period of immigration and doctrinaire private-property beliefs. Their origins are indeed a major topic for research. Whatever these origins were, the career system has helped preserve them.

In short, optimal industrial policies may need to affect the career system and its allied tendencies. There are other elements of content, but the career system is a basic factor in the mingling of consumption and production activities within the firm.

Content can be represented crudely in standard cost functions for the firm. The usual shape of the boundary of the average cost set is illustrated in Figure 2.4, with a long stretch of nearly constant costs beyond some minimum efficient scale (MES). Such observed costs must be adjusted to filter out the pecuniary gains with size that arise in some industries (see chapter 4). This yields a cost curve AC_T reflecting technical factors alone. A priori, this curve will diverge increasingly from the observed AC curve at higher output levels.

In allowing for content, one adjusts the cost boundary once more. Let us assume—as seems likely—that content is lost (*i.e.*, is inferior) as the firm's size increases. Then the adjusted social cost curve AC_C will diverge from AC_T, as shown in Figure 2.4. We now have a choice: this divergence can be represented either by subtracting the additional content utility at low size, or by adding the "cost" of lost utility at highier size levels. In either case, the social cost boundary reaches its minimum at a lower output level and displays even steeper diseconomies of scale than AC_T.

Chapter 4 will discuss the content adjustment. Here we can only note that, on balance, it is likely to run in favor of smaller size. This cost analysis poses a possibly basic conflict, between competition and content. If the private costs of production are lower when content is poor, then competition can enforce such cost minimizing upon the firm as a condition of survival. Then the low-content firms will drive out those with better content. Indeed,

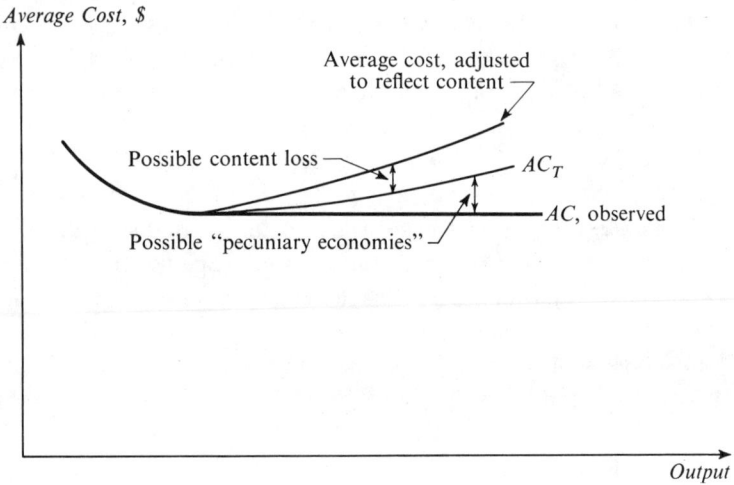

Figure 2.4 Average cost conditions.

this appears precisely to happen in the treatment of, for example, migrant farm labor, much as in the Shaftesbury revelations about British industry in the 1830s. Therefore good content may not be viable under competition and the drive for efficiency.

Yet there are reservations to this. First, content has several elements, some (or all) of which may reduce private costs or be neutral to them, rather than raise them. Example: greater worker responsibility on the factory floor or in decisions at other levels may *increase* productive effort and results. In fact, all of the elements of content may operate in this way. Second, workers may be willing to trade in some portion of wages for better content, if given the chance as part of the wage bargain. At present, the rules of authority and job limits (standard times, fixed tasks, etc.) all but rule this out for most employees except those toward the top, some of whom can vary their effort and accept lower career results.

Therefore, there is no presumption that good content means higher costs of production.[20] The net effect may go either way, depending on specifics of the industry, locale, and social setting. Good content may be entirely compatible with competition, if the crust of custom is broken and new choices are tried. Thus, if Figure 2.5 represented the true role of content in costs, it

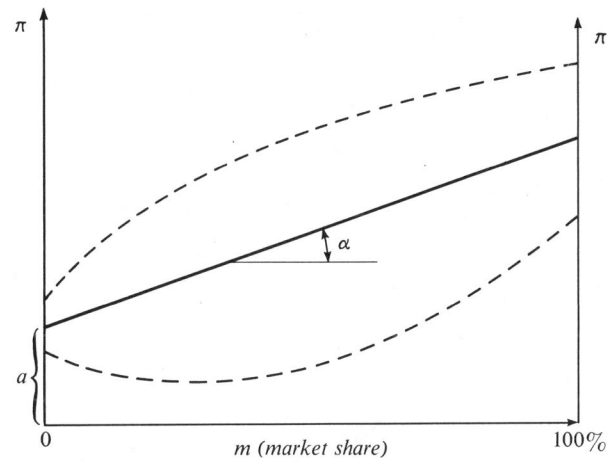

Figure 2.5 The basic relationship between market share and profitability.

would simply cause an evolution of market structure toward smaller firms, as they outcompeted the larger ones.

One therefore posits a neutral content hypothesis: Content tends to be neutral to the level of average costs in the firm. This could be rejected for individual cases and, perhaps, for whole classes of conditions. But it is a reasonable working hypothesis, and it will be adopted in the rest of the book as a rebuttable presumption.

In any case, we have enlarged the analysis to include content as a significant element. This does run a risk of injecting complex issues that cannot yet be conceptualized or measured with simple precision. But the gain from

---

[20] That is why many analysts have recommended "better working conditions" solely in order to raise productivity.

Defining Structure and Performance

adding such "soft" factors is a large one. It restores the subject to its true scope and character.[21] As standard industrial organization has become more exact and mechanical in its concepts, there has been increasingly a risk that it excludes major problems. One sign of this has been that the policy lessons have seemed increasingly narrow and peripheral—and unrealistic.[22] The answer is to add back the missing substance, not to harden the orthodoxy. In fact, the members of our trade have gone about as far as they can go in developing the traditional static notions of market structure. One new direction is therefore to extend concepts of structure to include those parts of the inner structure of firms which affect content.

3 CONCEPTS OF MARKET STRUCTURE

We next turn to the now-conventional subject area of market structure—apart from its context and from the inner content of firm activity. The analysis begins in a static vein. What, in this perspective, *is* market structure? Because the answer has grown confused in recent years, an attempt should be made to clear it up—to indicate which elements of market structure logically are foremost. I shall make this attempt, and then briefly discuss how the inner structure of the firm may relate to content.

The term "static" here refers to the workings of equilibrium processes, in which there are causes and effects. "Structure A causes performance X during the current period" is a static hypothesis. This discussion becomes fairly complex, but it boils down to basic causal ideas about how market structure takes effect.

The *firm* is the decision unit—the locus of motivation, behavior, and performance, and the target of any public policy. Although in some situations it is useful to think of oligopolists as a collective decision group, it will be seen that the firm is the logical building block for analysis.

We are concerned with modern enterprises of some size and complexity, the kind that raise the significant policy issues. Such firms can be assumed to be primarily motivated toward maximizing their profits in the long run.[23]

[21] It also helps to fill the gap in Marxian analysis, connecting the nature of modern enterprise to the experience of workers within them.

[22] The familiar example of this is the apparent inability of antitrust to resolve the core problems (see chapters 5 and 7).

[23] This is basically consistent with the newer motivational analysis; see Baumol, *Business Behavior;* Marris, "Corporate Economy a Corporate State?"; Scherer, *Industrial Market Structure.*

At each point, and for a given amount of invested capital, the expected rate of return (π) is maximized. There is also another dimension of profitability: the degree of security, or risk-avoidance.[24] For a given profit rate, the level of risk is to be minimized. Security is usually less important to firms, and to capital-market choices, than is the rate of return. But in special situations (utility regulation, for example), it can become more important.

To maximize profitability, firms strive to gain and exploit favorable market positions, and market structure is the result of such strivings. The firm's market position is defined by three possible elements: *market share, barriers to new entry,* and *the combined share of the leading firms,* which is usually called "concentration." We shall consider these separately below. Here, we shall appraise the nature and the likely importance of each element according to its effect on attainable profits. (Their actual importance is tested quantitatively in chapter 4.)

These appraisals are necessary. Each element could be the most important one—and indeed such claims have been made for each, on eminent authority. Yet they all cannot be. Furthermore, the policy treatments differ sharply among the elements; if barriers, say, rather than market share are the source of market power, the antitrust or regulatory treatments will be quite different.

The three possible elements are of different vintages. As an historical matter, pre-1930s neoclassical discussion was based on market share, and treated only the polar cases of pure competition and monopoly. Partial degrees of monopoly were not treated explicitly in terms of market share, but were implicit in the literature.[25]

The Chamberlin-Robinson breakthrough in 1932 into partial-monopoly cases was quickly diverted to multifirm analyses of interdependence and group behavior.[26] That is, the context shifted immediately from a *company* basis to an *industry* basis, where it has stayed for nearly 40 years. This shift was accentuated by the focusing of empirical research upon concentration ratios after 1939, and by the postwar advent of games analysis. The data

[24] F. H. Knight, *Risk, Uncertainty and Profit* (Boston: Houghton Mifflin, 1921); I. N. Fisher and G. R. Hall, "Risk and Corporate Rates of Return," *Quarterly Journal of Economics,* February 1969, pp. 79–92; F. R. Edwards and A. A. Heggestad, "Uncertainty, Market Structure, and Performance in Banking," *Quarterly Journal of Economics,* August 1973, pp. 455–73 (and sources cited there).

[25] Alfred Marshall, *Principles of Economics,* 8th ed. (New York: Macmillan, 1920).

[26] E. H. Chamberlin, *The Theory of Monopolistic Competition,* 8th ed. (Cambridge, Mass.: Harvard University Press, 1962).

were there, as was also the dazzling promise of game theory.[27] Despite Stigler's misgivings, the analysis of individual partial-monopolists continued in relative neglect until Baumol's analysis of growth-oriented, non-interdependent firms.[28] By then Bain had brought entry barriers to the forefront, still squarely in the context of *industry* structure, behavior, and performance.[29] Though welcomed with enthusiasm as a concept, barriers have been more slowly assimilated into the mainstream of theoretical and econometric literature. Indeed, they are not yet part of the core of microeconomic theory. Still, in 1967 there appeared two major articles stressing size and advertising as elements of structure, primarily on empirical rather than conceptual grounds.[30] It is now customary to frame analysis in terms of oligopolists' joint maximizing strategies toward limit pricing, which is governed by the height of entry barriers.

Each successive new element has seemed to be substitutable for, as well as complementary to, the previous ones. But their relative importance and mutual relations have remained uncertain, and each element has enthusiasts who regard it as the main one.

Market share derives directly from neoclassical theory of competition and monopoly. It ranges from pure monopoly down to *de minimis* or atomistic shares. Monopoly makes high profit rates possible—just how high depends on a variety of circumstances. No excess profits are attainable in equilibrium under pure competition. The yields for intermediate market shares presumably are interpolated in an intermediate range, but neoclassical sources say little about them. Let us focus now on the rate of return (π) alone, holding aside the risk aspect for the moment.

The general hypothesis is that there is a relationship between market share and profitability

$$\pi = a + bM$$

[27] Concentration ratios were first published for 1935. For successive census-year sets of ratios, see Annual Survey of Manufactures, *Value of Shipment Concentration Ratios,* 1970, M70(AS)-9, U.S. Census Bureau, U.S. Government Printing Office, 1972. The *locus classicus* of game theory is J. von Neumann and O. Morgenstern, *Theory of Games and Economic Behavior* (Princeton, N.J.: Princeton University Press, 1944). See also M. Shubik, *Strategy and Market Structure* (New York: Wiley, 1959).

[28] G. J. Stigler, *Five Essays on Economic Problems* (New York: Macmillan, 1949); Baumol, *Business Behavior.*

[29] J. S. Bain, *Barriers to New Competition* (Cambridge, Mass.: Harvard University Press, 1956).

[30] Hall and Weiss, "Firm Size"; and W. S. Comanor and T. Wilson, "Advertising, Market Structure and Performance," *Review of Economics and Statistics,* 1967, pp. 423–40.

where a is the competitive rate of return and b defines the marginal profitability yield of market share. We shall call this the "share-profit" relationship. A priori, b can be linear, or nonlinear with either convexity or concavity. Figure 2.5 illustrates the basic hypothesis, assuming a linear relation. A wide variety of industrial and commercial evidence attests to the importance of market share as a conscious focus of motivation and as an influence on profitability.[31] Therefore both theory and practical opinion identify market share as at least a significant element of structure.

The slope and shape of the share-profit relationship will reflect three underlying determinants. These are market power *(MP)*, technical economies of scale *(TE)*, and pecuniary economies of scale *(PE)*. Each of them can be hypothesized to have a specific relationship to π. Figure 2.6 shows likely forms for them. The *MP* function could rise linearly, reflecting the extreme returns frequently gained by pure monopolists, owing in part to the increasing latitude for price discrimination as share approaches 100 percent. Price discrimination is usually possible and extensive by dominant firms in large industries, even those regarded as homogeneous. Every large industry contains a diversity of demand conditions, so that optimizing the mix of products and discrimination among them is a complex and lucrative process for the dominant, "full-line" seller.

Such price discrimination arises primarily in line with single-firm market share, rather than with oligopoly concentration. Four equal firms together holding 80 percent of a market will be capable of far less price discrimination than will one firm holding 80 percent. The design of the price structure and the pooling of profits must be done internally. Among several firms the joint maximizing problems becomes complex and unstable.

Yet *MP* may taper off, for two reasons. First, as Dewey and others have noted, the net cost of acquiring more market share usually rises sharply as one's own market share approaches 100 percent.[32] To this extent, gains from the monopoly position are mortgaged in advance, and the true net marginal yield of high market shares is reduced.

Second, a general form of potential competition may normally constrain even those firms which approach full monopoly shares. Firms are usually surrounded by a gradation of actual, partial, and potential competitors, in

---

[31] Including A. D. H. Kaplan, J. B. Dirlam, and R. F. Lanzillotti, *Pricing in Big Business* (Wash., D.C.: Brookings Institution, 1958); Baumol, *Business Behavior*.

[32] D. J. Dewey, *Monopoly in Economics and Law* (Skokie, Ill.: Rand McNally, 1970), pp. 25–31.

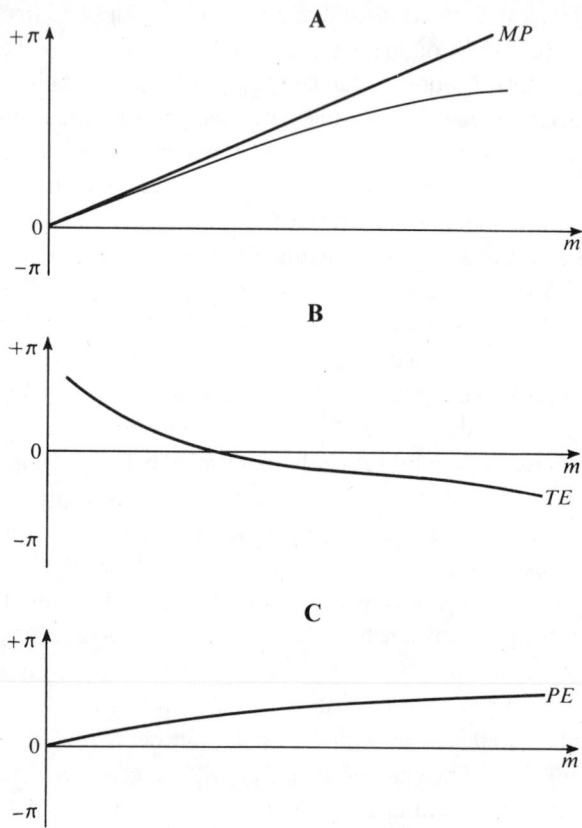

Figure 2.6 Components of the market share–profitability relationships. *A*. Net effect of market power. *B*. Net effect of technical economies. *C*. Net effect of pecuniary economies.

the markets and submarkets where they operate. This *firm*-based concept of potential competition (for industry-based concepts, see below) has been suggested by J. B. Clark and more recently by Allen, Kaplan, and Gaskins, among others.[33] It accords with the actual gradation of contacts impinging on most significant firms. To simplify, one may say that such firms will find

---

[33] Clark, *Competition as a Dynamic Process* (Wash. D.C., Brookings Institution, 1962); G. C. Allen, *Monopoly and Restrictive Practices* (London: Allen and Unwin, 1968); A. D. H. Kaplan, *Big Enterprise in a Competitive System*, rev. ed. (Wash. D.C.: Brookings Institution, 1965); D. W. Gaskins, "Dynamic Limit Pricing: Optimal Pricing Under Threat of Entry," *Journal of Economic Theory*, 1971, pp. 306–322.

it difficult or inadvisable to sustain a high excess profit rate in perpetuity, even where they hold a near or full monopoly.

The *TE* function is by definition high in the below-MES range, but then tends toward constancy at zero over most of the range, reflecting the constant costs observed in many industries. It could rise at high market shares, if the monopolist achieves economies of coordination and an avoidance of standoff advertising,[34] but it is under counterinfluences—especially if X-inefficiency increases to substantial levels as competitive constraints on costs weaken in the upper range.[35]

Therefore the net relation between market share and technical efficiency could be either upward or downward sloping. Economics of scale may exist, possibly even being steep throughout the full range of market share. But they may be offset by X-ineffeciency at middle and higher market shares.

Pecuniary economies are likely to be gained mainly in the lower range of market share, as the firm rises from a tiny to a significant size relative to the whole market. This is represented in Figure 2.6c; whatever its shape is, the *PE* function is likely to be upward-sloping. Where monopsony power enables the firm to drive down its input prices sharply, the *PE* function may slope upward fairly steeply.

On balance, the share–profit relationship is expected to be upward-sloping and possibly convex. By contrast, Cournot-type analysis (especially by Worcester) suggests a low or zero slope for the relationship.[36] If there is passive dominant-firm behavior, then the degree of profitability ultimately tends to be invariant with market share. Dominant firms yield up their market shares over time, until in steady-state equilibrium all firms in the industry tend to have identical profit rates. These profit rates are determined primarily by the industry's entry conditions. An observed positive π would solely represent short-term disequilibrium conditions; this is the opposite of the equilibrium context of the share–profit relationship.[37]

---

[34] Dewey, *Imperfect Competition*.

[35] Leibenstein, "Allocative Efficiency"; W. S. Comanor and H. Leibenstein, "Allocative Efficiency, X-Efficiency, and the Measurement of Welfare Losses," *Economica,* August 1969, pp. 304–9.

[36] D. A. Worcester, Jr., "Why 'Dominant Firms' Decline," *Journal of Political Economy,* 1957, pp. 338–47.

[37] The boundary version of such behavior is "umbrella pricing," in which the leading firms in undifferentiated, asymmetric oligopolies bear the brunt of upward price leadership and of output-restriction during recessions. This could actually yield a negative slope for the share-

A high market-power effect on profit rates is entirely compatible with any role for technical economies. The market-power effect is usually—perhaps always—present in some degree. By contrast, positive net technical economies may or may not occur; negative effects on profit rates are quite possible. Even if technical economies of scale do exist, one needs to ask how large they are. Market power effects may still be much larger.

The Leading-firm Group. It is possible (in some minds, probable or certain) that the role of the leading-firm group modifies or supersedes that of the individual firm's share.[38] At its simplest, the group's share (as indicated by, e.g., a concentration ratio) affects the average profitability of all its members. This relationship is likely to be continuous but to possess a range of indeterminacy, since the variety of internal-group structures will enlarge the variance of group-profitability outcomes throughout the range of four-firm concentration. Or there may be a critical degree of concentration, above which effective coordination can be established regardless of the group's internal structure.[39] The result would then be a step function relating concentration and profitability in industries, though a sharp step is implausible. This step function would be consistent with convexity in the firm's market share–profitability function, though it would not strictly require it.

There are three main difficulties in expecting "the group" to be a major determinant of profitability. One is that normally no distinct "group" exists in industrial markets, as opposed to theoretical models. The typical market structure is a gradation of firm sizes, not a series of distinct tiers.[40] The second problem is that the group, if it exists, may matter, but only trivially. Nothing in

---

profit relationship, except perhaps at extremely high market shares. Though most pronounced in recessions, the negative slope could be observable in any condition short of full-capacity operations. If it occurs in long-run equilibrium, it would be most evident in mature, homogeneous-goods industries with slow growth and cyclical shifts, such as the steel industry. It would not be expected in differentiable consumer-products industries, where cross-elasticities of demand among firms are relatively low and passive behavior by leading firms is implausible.

[38] Chamberlin and Fellner explored oligopoly choices in detail, but its treatment as the main element of structure is more recent. See Carl Kaysen and Donald F. Turner, *Antitrust Policy* (Cambridge, Mass.: Harvard University Press, 1959); and W. J. Fellner, *Competition Among the Few* (New York: Norton, 1949).

[39] J. S. Bain, *Industrial Organization,* rev. ed. (New York: Wiley, 1969).

[40] D. A. Worcester, Jr., *Monopoly, Big Business and Welfare in the Postwar United States* (Seattle: University of Washington, 1967); and W. G. Shepherd, *Market Power and Economic Welfare* (New York: Random House, 1970), ch. 7.

the massive literature of interdependence and intragroup behavior has established the probable scope of their effect on long-run profitability, and some give persuasive reasons to regard it as slight.[41] One may test it as an independent determinant, or one may test for a greater expected degree of variation of profitability for firms with intermediate—that is, oligopoly—market shares.

The third problem is that the group's *internal* structure may be the main influence. For the firm, the critical attribute would probably be its position within the leading firm group, or more specifically its share relative to the share of the entire group. This can be estimated by the four-firm concentration ratio minus the firm's own market share; here this is labeled G.[42] Its net effect on profitability could be hypothesized as negative, if dominant or leading firms normally fare better at the expense of their lesser rivals. The orthodox Chamberlinian hypothesis would instead be that the group's benefits are shared by all members; G would then have a positive coefficient. A zero observed association could reflect poor measurement, the offsets of differing intragroup patterns from industry to industry, or a strict irrelevance of the variable.

In summary, tests for the possible role of the group are a concentration variable, a concentration-minus-share variable, and extra variance in the middle range of the market-share–profitability relation.

Entry Barriers. What role does this leave for entry barriers into the firm's industry? Extending suggestions by Chamberlin and Fellner, Bain modified J. B. Clark's general notion of potential competition for *firms* into a purely *industry*-based concept. By this usage, "entry" to an industry means a substantial and unexpected creation of new capacity by a firm previously outside the market altogether.[43] Such entry may be forestalled by the industry's basic "conditions of entry," including scale economies and product dif-

---

[41] Baumol, *Business Behavior,* and Stigler, *Organization of Industry.*

[42] This is only an approximation, since "leading-firm groups" in many industries contain more or less than four firms. Also, it leaves unspecified the internal structure of the remaining 3-firm group. If the firm is not one of the leading firms, of course, the value of the variable approaches the concentration ratio itself. One alternative estimator is the ratio of concentration to firm share. Another is the rank of the firm, but that is less precise and tells little about the actual group structure.

The concentration-minus-share variable is valid primarily for firms among the leading group and in industries whose concentration is significant (e.g., above 25 percent).

[43] Bain, *Industrial Organization;* Dewey, *Imperfect Competition.*

ferentiation, or by the practice of "stayout" or "limit" pricing by the established firms, whose maximizing strategy is directed toward entry *probabilities*. At the extreme, these barriers can be regarded as determining the attainable profitability for all, or possibly only the dominant, firms in the industry. Where barriers are low, long-run excess profitability is negligible, even if market shares are high; with high barriers, profitability may be high even if market shares and concentration are low. An intermediate hypothesis is that barriers are only necessary; profitability will then vary both with them and with other determinants. A variable representing barriers in the firm's industry would therefore be directly related to profitability; if it supplants market share, the extreme barrier hypothesis is supported.

Yet in the context of firm activity as developed here, substantial entry may be only a borderline case, normally of little concern. One must first define it precisely; it involves a net addition to industry capacity by a firm previously not in the industry.[44] This firm's addition must exceed the sum of exit by other firms, which its entry may cause. If that exit is by many small faceless fringe firms, while the entrant is a single large entity, its whole share may be regarded as "net" entry by the leading firms.[45] But that point leads one to redefine entry as entry *into the leading-firm group* rather than entry into the whole industry, and such "entry" into the leading groups is, strictly, turnover rather than market entry. It could also occur by rapid growth of established small firms (possibly branches of large diversified firms), or by strategic intrusions by middle-range firms. In fact, the impact on each leading firm from strategies by other leading firms (*e.g.*, new-product innovations, advertising campaigns) would be essentially the same as from such "entry."

Entry to an industry has at least three main dimensions: extent (*e.g.*, the market share acquired or believed to be the entrant's target, minus the actual or expected exit by identifiable competitors), speed of occurrence, and distance (or degree of surprise).[46] Only a case that has high values for these at-

---

[44] Bain, *Industrial Organization; Barriers to New Competition*.

[45] Entry would then be inversely related to the number of firms in the market, reversing the usual belief. Note also that the net effect of net entry must allow for the previous force of potential competition. If there are several known strong potential entrants, the net effect of converting one of them to an actual competitor may be vanishingly small, even if the entry has high values for speed and extent; see also Roger Sherman and Thomas D. Willett, "Potential Entrants Discourage Entry," *Journal of Political Economy*, August 1967, pp. 400–403.

[46] Bain notes the first two of these, and defines entry as cases with extremely high values for them. The literature contains no further treatment of the conceptual problems in defining entry

tributes can be regarded as a significant entry; lesser values are indistinguishable from the host of marginal moves by established firms that shade into the cumulative competitive constraints on the firm.

Yet the probability of occurrence is inversely related to these values. Net entry out of the blue, rapidly and on a large scale, into a firm's market area is by definition improbable, as are all the other possible calamities. Moreover, entry's significance for any firm varies directly with its share, from high for monopolists to vanishingly small for loose oligopolists.[47] To this extent, *market share is itself the operative variable of the entry phenomenon,* and the independent significance of entry (and of the barriers that may affect it) is diminished. The critical impact of entry is the short-run reduction of the firm's market share (and future profit expectations). In this context, "limit pricing" relates to the share-maintaining price strategy of the firm (see Gaskins, and the comparative-static analysis below), rather than to pricing joint pricing strategy of leading firms toward possible entry into the industry.

Entry to the industry, therefore, tends to be indistinguishable in concept from other competitive constraints on the firm, and large instances of it are normally of second-order likelihood.[48] As for the "conditions of entry," or barriers, they have tended to be amalgams of specific influences, which are not easy to formulate or measure. The main sources are probably scale economies, specific absolute cost advantages, and produce differentiation. Each is relevant to certain industries (or firms within them), but each is important only to relatively few, and these are generally not overlapping sets.

---

to industries and distinguishing it from other competitive conditions. On the element of surprise or distance, see Dewey, *Monopoly in Economics and Law,* and B. P. Pashigian, "Limit Price and the Market Share of the Leading Firm," *Journal of Industrial Economics,* 1968, pp. 165–77.

[47] Contrast the effect of large entry (say, at 20 percent of the market) on a pure monopoly and loose oligopoly. The monopolist must expect to undergo the full reduction in share. The oligopolists (each with market shares of, say, 5 percent each) may lose 1 percent each, but this impact is not individually certain. Moreover, such an impact is likely to be smaller than other competitive dangers such a firm routinely faces. Both of these points derive from the firm's market share.

[48] An exception to this is local trades, where entry "from outside" is often clearly definable, must be at scale which does have a significant impact, and has a large element of surprise. Moreover the established firms in local markets often have little adaptability in the short run, so that the impact of the reduction in market share can be very sharp.

I am not denying that probabilities of entry do condition behavior, as Dewey suggests, but these probabilities are only one among many hazards faced by the firm and may normally not be of paramount importance.

Other ad hoc barriers have also been suggested, such as patents and *R & D*, and still others could be offered. Attempts to weld such instances into objective measures of barriers have yielded interesting but rather vague and unrebuttable classifications;[49] and the extent of actual entry in the past may influence the appraisals of the "height" of barriers, even though the causation should run the other way. The alternative in a static analysis is to introduce the possible barrier factors separately and precisely (as with size and advertising–sales ratios) in analyzing the firms for which they are likely to be relevant.

Firm size is one possible source of entry barriers. Yet the whole net effect, if any, of size on profitability may be either positive or negative. The possibilities are complex, and several simple hypotheses have been adduced. But no strong theoretical basis has yet been derived. Firm size relative to the total size distribution of firms (often loosely equated with "bigness per se") has long been held to increase attainable profitability, and it may raise "capital requirements" barriers to entry.[50] Baumol's analysis of constrained sales-maximization may be construed to imply that, in the long run, size and potential profitability are positively related.

Yet size may raise average costs even if competitive constraints are tight.[51] Also the constrained sacrificing of profits in Baumol's model implies a succession of short-run profit rates lower, and size levels higher, than would otherwise occur. A succession of such short-run choices would tend to lower the general observed size-profitability relationship.

The net effect of these opposed factors cannot be derived a priori, and so either a negative or positive relation between size and profitability is possible. The literature has favored a positive relationship. Theory does suggest that the relationship will be proportional to size, not in relation to absolute size. Therefore, the logarithm of size may be an appropriate variable to use in statistical analysis.

Another possible impediment to entry is product differentiability, of

---

[49] Bain, *Barriers to New Competition;* H. M. Mann, "Seller Concentration, Barriers to Entry and Rates of Return in Thirty Industries, 1950–1960," *Review of Economics and Statistics,* 1966, pp. 296–307; and Shepherd, *Market Power and Economic Welfare,* ch. 8.

[50] C. D. Edwards, *Maintaining Competition* (New York: McGraw-Hill, 1949); Bain, *Barriers to New Competition;* Hall and Weiss, "Firm Size."

[51] This is distinct from internal slack and nonpecuniary maximization, which may arise in firms with market power. It arises instead from control loss and added managerial costs stemming from sheer size.

which one source is high advertising-intensity. This may be primarily a means of reducing the firm's demand elasticity and making excess profits possible, an investment that in the long run yields no excess net return, or a mixture of both.[52] In any event, a positive long-run partial relationship between advertising-intensity and profitability would be observable across all firms, and particularly those in consumer-goods industries. But in the small subset of highly advertising-intensive industries, the intraindustry relationship between advertising-intensity and profitability is likely to be negative, because the larger firms achieve scale economies in national advertising. This intraindustry relation reduces the expected fit of the interindustry positive relationship, but it need not wipe it out entirely. Both hypotheses can be tested separately, in any event.[53]

In short, entry barriers are not so much a unified concept as a residual category in which many specific items can be included. Therefore, they are less than likely to be a central element in a general theory or explanation of market power. With a more adequate definition of barriers and entry, the notion may eventually achieve a solid status. But that is premature.

This lengthy analysis suggests that market share may be the primary element in structure. The other two elements—oligopoly group and barriers—are likely to modify, but not supplant, the basic effect of market share from case to case. Differing values of G and B may cause π to diverge from the share-profit relationship—upward where G is low and B is high, downward when the reverse is true. There are individual cases where a specific barrier (a crucial patent, for example) matters, though even here it tends simply to create a high M, which *then* is the direct factor. However, we can expect that market share will remain the core element. The distinction may seem to be a fine one, but it has a surprisingly deep effect on many research and policy issues.

Next we ask if the inner structure of firms relates to content. If so, then the structure-behavior-performance triad should be extended to include firm structure as well as market structure. The answer is that firm structure does relate to content, but at this stage one cannot derive strong and precise con-

[52] W. S. Comanor and T. Wilson, "Advertising, Market Structure and Performance," *Review of Economics and Statistics,* 1967, pp. 423–40; L. Telser, "Advertising and Competition," *Journal of Political Economy,* 1964, pp. 541–46; L. W. Weiss, "Advertising, Profits and Corporate Taxes," *Review of Economics and Statistics,* 1969, pp. 421–430.

[53] W. S. Comanor and T. Wilson, *Advertising and Market Power* (Cambridge, Mass.: Harvard University Press, 1974).

nections. The firm's structure is only a partial determinant; many other matters of personality, behavior, history, and chance also operate.

These structural effects seem likely to remain important after a decade of future thought and testing:

1. Size per se reduces content. It increases the degree of hierarchy and regimentation, while it reduces the sense of individual contribution, responsibility, and local identity. It usually sharpens the division between career and noncareer people. (Indeed, market share also tends to have the same effect as size.)
2. Decentralization of operations and control to lower units enhances some elements of content.
3. Worker participation in upper level decisions and ownership is likely to enhance content. This adds to the sharing of responsibility and of the rewards for success. This participation could take formal shape in a variety of ways.

There is much else in a firm which is not structural and yet does affect content. Here we are regarding those other influences as ad hoc, outside the analysis, and not amenable to direct policy treatments.

4 EVOLUTION OF MARKET STRUCTURE OVER TIME

The context now shifts from these static hypotheses to the causes of *changes* in market structure over time. This is necessary, first, for intellectual completeness; the motivations and conditions under which high market shares are gained and lost may closely influence the seeming static "effects" of market power at each point. In fact, structure may best be understood as *in passage,* rather than in being. The second reason to analyze structural change is that most policy choices have to deal with it. How fast a high market share would diminish naturally is a key variable for, e.g., antitrust and regulatory policies. Consider a market share of 70 percent at one point. If it dwindles quickly under market forces, then its potential effects are slight and may disappear before antitrust treatments can take effect. But if it is likely to remain, then the policy yield from causing it to fall may be much greater. This question is the test that distinguishes the "Chicago" view from the rest. Transient market power is trivial (or at least endurable) market power— if treatments are remedial and slow rather than preventive.

Theories about structural change have come in three main sorts: industry life-cycles, random processes, and optimum firm strategy toward market share over time. Each will be considered in turn. Each is still formative.

Life-cycles of industries. If industries normally proceed through regular phases of birth, growth, maturity, and decline, then structure and pending change at each point would be predictable. Such a stage theory is attractive, but the occasional efforts to make it rigorous have had little success. No structural evolution is universal or even close to it: some industries are "born" competitive, others as monopolies. Some evolve toward monopoly, others away from it. This evolution is likely to be influenced by capital suppliers, whose differential support or specific efforts to merge firms may determine the trends. The evolution can also be decisively influenced by patents or other devices for monopolizing the industry at the start.

One can define two contrasting paths, one with patents or arranged mergers at the start, the other without them. I shall first consider "normal" industries and then "utilities." There are three phases (illustrated in Figure 2.7):

> *Phase 1.* Demand rises rapidly and cost curves shift down and to the right. Minimum efficient scale increases but demand rises faster.
> *Phase 2.* Technology standardizes on roughly a constant-cost basis, and demand continues rising.
> *Phase 3.* Demand stabilizes and then declines, becoming more elastic as substitute goods emerge.

Technology would therefore prescribe possibly significant market shares in Phases 1 and 3, but not in Phase 2. The observed patterns are commonly as shown in Figure 2.8. The rates of change differ from case to case; the general forms may be valid.

For "utilities," a key influence is commonly the social decision to regulate them as a "natural monopoly." Often this occurs even though technology does not require it, with optimal scale well below 100 percent. The contrasting paths—with and without regulation—are illustrated in Figure 2.8.

Most "utilities" have a clearer life-cycle than do most conventional industries. The natural-monopoly phase for utilities is rarely permanent, in any event. This is explored more fully in chapter 9.

Random processes. Industrial structure is probably not more determinate than other human affairs, and so it reflects considerable randomness. This may be sufficient to cause structure to evolve from loose to tight oligopoly.[54] Moreover, random luck may explain some fraction of the correlation

---

[54] Scherer, *Industrial Market Structure*, ch. 14.

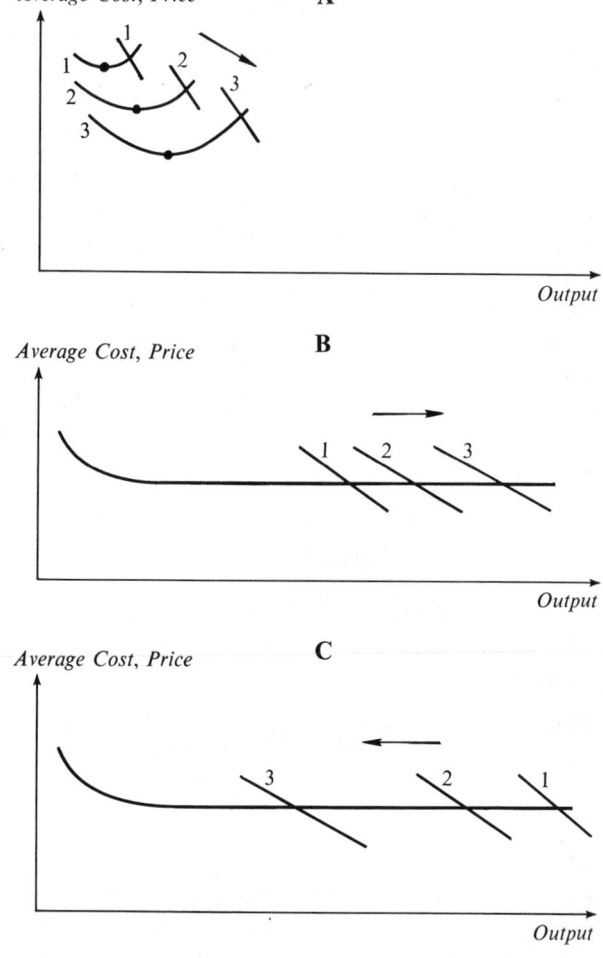

Figure 2.7 Typical evolution of cost and demand conditions.

between market shares and profit rates: "lucky" firms grow to have high shares and show high profit rates, while "unlucky" ones experience the reverse.[55]

To the degree that randomness explains how high market shares arise, it should equally cause them later to fall. This too we shall try to test.

---

[55] R. B. Mancke, "Causes of Interfirm Profitability Differences: A New Interpretation of the Evidence," *Quarterly Journal of Economics,* 88, no. 2 (May 1974): 181–93.

Market-share strategy over time. Rises and falls in market structure are also matters of choice. The firm may at any time adopt costly strategies to increase its share, so that future profitability will be greater, or it may cash in on present profits, so that its market share will slip. The optimal choice depends on several conditions. Analysis can clarify both the creation and the subsidence of high market shares. The subject is presently a frontier for theory and estimation, and alternative approaches to it are being tried. The following analysis tries to include the main elements. It tries to define the basic relationship between the firm's profit rate and the deliberate

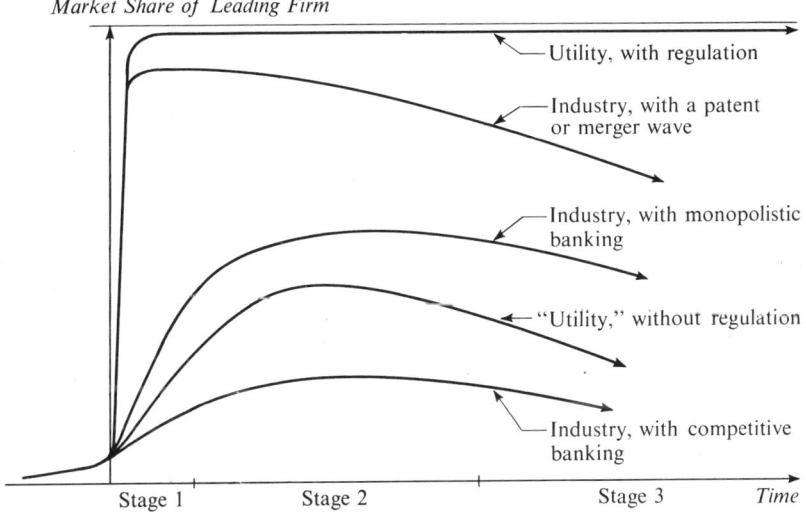

Figure 2.8 Alternative trends in the market share of the dominant firm.

change in its market share, during an interval of time. If such a relationship exists, it would affect a variety of policy yields.

Consider a firm in equilibrium, with a given market share *(M)* of M_1. The firm expects to gain a profit rate (π) *ex* tax of π_1 during the next planning period, if its present market share remains unchanged. The planning period is of "medium run" length, corresponding to 5 to 10 years in the main U.S. industries. Assume that attained equilibrium levels of π are related positively and linearly to M in most markets (recall section 3). Assume also that oligopoly elements—including G, the combined share of other leading firms, and entry barriers—are of second-order importance so that they can be ignored here.

Defining Structure and Performance   53

Now, the firm also considers its future possibilities for π and M, both of which it can influence in degrees. The hypothesis is that, *ex ante,* its prospective π and ΔM values—ΔM is the change in M during the planning period just ahead—are related. In its most general form this boundary of the possibility set for π and ΔM would be negatively sloped and linear, as represented by the line $\pi \Delta M$ in Figure 2.9. Sample curves for higher and lower initial market shares are also shown. We shall call this the "share-time" relationship.

Why the downward slope? The firm can add to M by strategies that sacrifice profits. Such strategies would include "investments" in price cuts, advertising campaigns, process innovations, etc. Alternatively, the firm can liquidate part of its M by taking high temporary profits while tolerating the predictable erosion of its market positions. By abstracting from disequilibrium cases—in which lucky firms get both ΔM and high π concurrently, and unlucky ones get the reverse—we are bringing out the normal facts of business life: in equilibrium the firm faces a tradeoff between future profitability and changes in market share, and the struggle for market share is a central concern to the firm.

The firm's preference function relating π and ΔM then determines its choice for the planning period. With the sample indifference curve in Figure 2.9, point A is chosen and M does not change. A more "aggressive" management would select some point such as B; a more "passive" management would choose C. The preference functions reflect managers' rates of time preference (since the new M level will influence the π that will be attainable in the *next* period), predictions about future opportunities, and management psychology. Managements differ in all three of these.

The diagrams are merged in Figure 2.11, to show that at each M level the firm has a tradeoff. By sacrificing π during one period, the firm reaches a higher M level, which subsequently yields higher π. The relative slopes of πM and π are important in determining the outcome of the choice process. The more α exceeds the absolute value of β, the more will firms "aggressively" seek higher share-profit values in each period. By contrast, if α is low and β highly negative, attempts to raise M would not pay: firms instead would tend to yield up M while reaping high current profits. For each pair of α and β there will of course exist a time discount rate, which equalizes the net current costs and future gains from raising M.

The share-time curve is the main interest here. The tradeoff it describes has several interesting attributes: negativity, form, position, and slope.

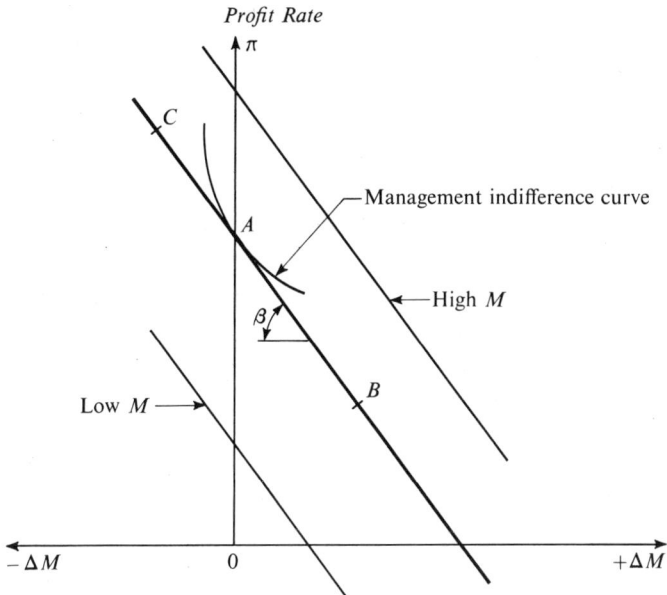

Figure 2.9 The comparative-static tradeoff between profit-rate and change in market share.

That the share-time relationship has a *negative* slope is intuitively obvious, in an equilibrium framework. If $\pi \Delta M$ were horizontal or upward sloping the situation would be unstable. A maximal ΔM would be chosen, leading to a complete monopoly. At that point the share-time relationship *must* slope down. Also, the possibility that more than one firm could attain a monopoly share is absurd. Therefore, the curve must slope down at some point. Normally, we may believe, the portion in the range of the initial share will have negative slope.

As for *form,* linearity is the simplest and most plausible assumption at this point. Upward convexity is also possible, if strategies encounter diminishing returns. The curve might have a maximum to the left because very rapid shrinkage might cause demoralization, which reduces efficiency and therefore profitability. Although linearity appears to be a reasonable first approximation, the question is open for testing.

The *position* of the curve will vary, as was noted. The height of the intercept will vary directly with the initial value of M. A "competitive" M value (of .05 or less) provides a minimum or "normal" π value. At high M values, the intercept π value would be much higher. It is possible that the inter-

Defining Structure and Performance

cept also varies with the "height" of barriers to new competition. Such barriers are, however, highly related to M itself, and their independent causative role may be quite limited, as we have noted in section 3.

The *slope* of the share-time relationship (that is, β) is of special interest, since it affects the basic outcome of the choice process. The most interesting and general possibility is that β is invariant among industries, at least to a first approximation. Such a general relationship would have much normative and predictive power. Industries do differ in many respects, which may affect the share-profit relationship, but there is no logical basis for rejecting a

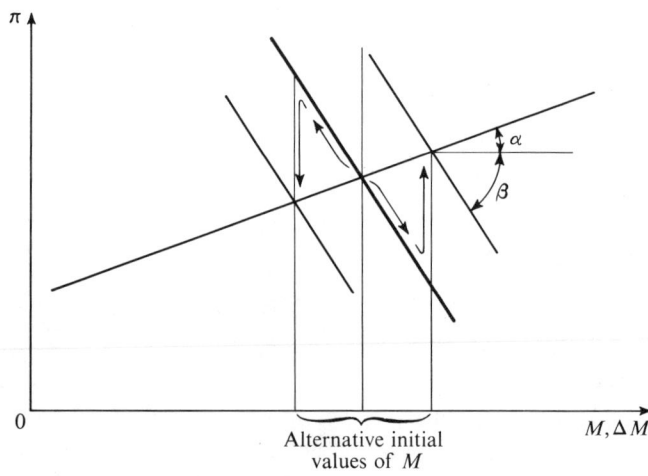

Figure 2.10 Combined analysis of market share and profitability over time.

priori the null hypothesis of a common slope for the share-time relationship. Exceptional cases can, of course, be identified, or at least conjectured. Highly advertising-intensive markets will perhaps have lesser slope than mature, homogeneous-goods industries. And monopolists will necessarily have a relatively steep slope. Yet such cases of high advertising-intensity and pure monopoly may be unusual.

For the mass of firms in the mass of markets, M values range between .05 and .60. They can be hypothesized to share similar values of β, even though the exceptional cases differ in predictable ways. Alternatively, β might differ systematically among basic categories of industries—producer and consumer goods, growing and shrinking, etc. If this were so, a consistent set of parallel values would exist.

To sum up, the share-time slope relating π and ΔM is of greatest interest, for it represents the conditions of choice that cause structure to change spontaneously. The greater β is relative to α, the more likely it is that high market shares—whatever their origins—will quickly be given up.

5 CRITERIA FOR PERFORMANCE

The social optimum for industrial performance includes three main attributes: efficiency, content, and equity. These three economic goals require some scheme for weighting, to combine them in their proper relative importance. There has always been much disagreement about this. One borderline view is that the problem is unresolvable other than by fiat, by the "planners' preferences" of whoever is presently in power. At the other extreme, criteria may be simply "what the competitive democratic process yields," judging purely by current end results.[56] Neither of these agnostic extremes is acceptable, since each counsels abandonment of the problem. Moreover, there may exist a broad consensus on social goals that is both reasonably consistent and not unworkably complex.

In this section we proceed as if efficiency, content, and equity are all that matter. Efficiency will be defined to include both static and dynamic efficiency (technological change), content is defined in line with section 2, and equity in distribution is premised on equality of opportunity and wealth for the rising generation.

These definitions are debatable, but they do provide a definite, simple basis for organizing the problem and for making first approximations. The basis is close to the mainstream of social views in this country. Special cases require special variations in evaluation and treatment, as we shall see, but the main dimensions for most cases can be usefully defined this way. No other single approach seems so obviously preferable for demonstrating the technique. One must begin with the simplest parts before adding on the broader elements.

Efficiency. Static efficiency is in the conventional terms of optimizing output levels and patterns for given levels of inputs. It has several components: allocational efficiency among markets, operating efficiency within enterprises, and the avoidance of specific "wastes." These efficiency effects

[56] Anthony Downs, *An Economic Theory of Democracy* (New York: Harper, 1957); Robert A. Dahl, *A Preface to Democratic Theory* (Chicago: University of Chicago Press, 1965).

often have to be measured indirectly, with a degree of uncertainty and conjecture.

As the literature has long recognized, the net loss from *misallocation* is approximated by the triangle A_{1-3} in Figure 2.11a (we assume for simplicity that costs are constant, so that marginal costs equal average costs). In this simple case, P_c is the competitive price and P_M reflects the exercise of market power. Here, A_{1-3} is drawn to look large; but it is often drawn to look small. It is also often said to include only triangles A_1 and A_2, on the ground that industries with intermediate degrees of monopoly (at P_I) are a rough second-best criterion; [57] but this is an extreme view, valid only if market power cannot be abated. If it can, then the whole A_{1-3} triangle—which is twice as large as $A_1 + A_2$—is the correct one to use.

In an open economy some fraction of inputs, including labor, are available from foreign sources to substitute for domestic ones. The higher the elasticities of supply of inputs and imports, the larger the fraction of B that will be a deadweight loss. Rectangle C is the redistributive flow from consumers to the seller. Normally this flow increases inequality. Its capitalized value represents, of course, a redistribution of wealth.

If monopoly induces slackness in management, *operating inefficiency* will raise costs, as illustrated by $MC' = AC'$ being above $MC = AC$ in Figure 2.11b. Price will now be at P_M, the A' triangle will be about as large as A_{1-3} was before, and the direct inefficiency loss will be rectangle D. Even if A' is small, D can be large. Indeed it is evident that the smaller A' is, the larger D will *relatively* be.

D also represents specific wastes, which raise costs. One possible example is "persuasive" (as distinct from "informative") advertising. The loss is a direct one, incurred for each unit of output.

These are the main static-efficiency losses which policies toward market power may aim to prevent or recoup. Their actual size will vary from case to case. If *MC is rising*, A will tend to be smaller but D will be unaffected.[58]

---

[57] A. Harberger adopted this premise in "Monopoly and Resource Allocation," *American Economic Review*, May 1954, pp. 77–87.

[58] Of course, if we also include producer surplus, then the sum of consumer and producer surplus may not shrink.

In practice, of course, d_i is difficult to measure: see John W. Kendrick, ed., *Output, Input and Productivity Measurement*, (Princeton: Princeton University Press, for the National Bureau of Economic Research, 1961). In fact, a truly comprehensive index of total productivity by sectors does not yet exist.

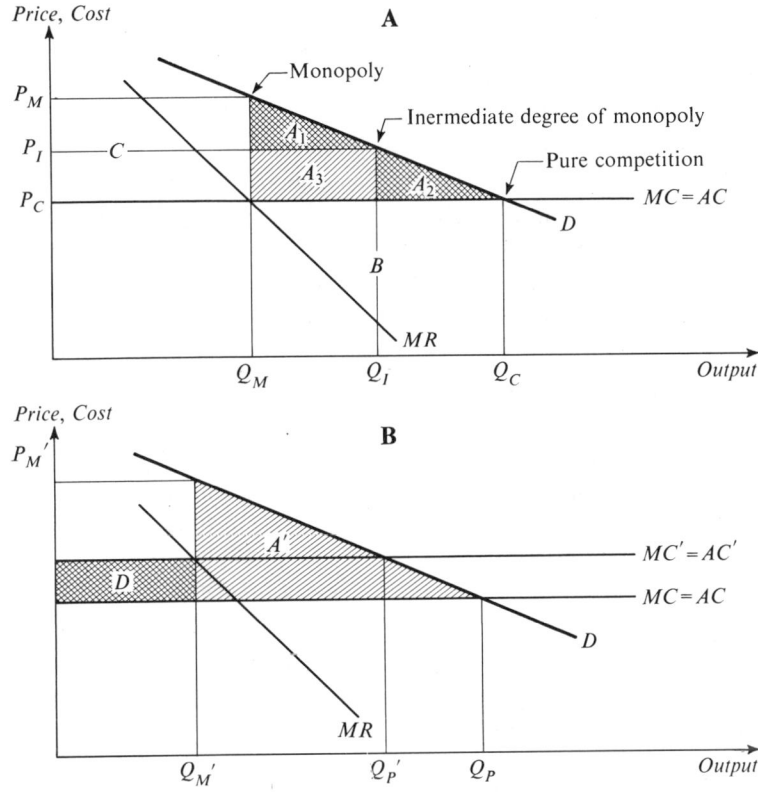

Figure 2.11 Effects of market power on allocative efficiency and X-efficiency.

"Dynamic efficiency" is in terms of rises in the ratio of outputs to inputs over time. This rise occurs because of innovations in the state of technology. Innovations are primarily of two types: in *processes* of production and in new *products*. The policy objective is to optimize these rates. In many cases, this involves maximizing the rate of innovation (but not in all cases, despite common impressions to the contrary). Because technical advance commonly requires resources for inventing and innovating, the problem can be regarded as one of optimizing the static allocation of such resources at each point in time. Here we treat it in terms of rates of change.

Let us label the increase in dynamic efficiency as Δd_n, where d_n is the rate of increase in the ratio of total outputs to total inputs for any *specific* process or product set n. A rise in d_n may or may not be permanent. Permanent shifts can be regarded as unusual and difficult to achieve, despite the tendency by some observers to treat them as normal. This is because most gains can be achieved by alternate means, so that any specific innovation may be a only slight gain on what otherwise would have occurred. Thus, the "gains" from nuclear power and satellite communications have been closely paralleled by further improvements in "conventional" technology, so that the *ex post* innovation gains have been much less than the early predictions. Moreover, if new technologies generate unexpected external diseconomies, these must be netted out. The automobile exemplifies this; so do jet airplanes, detergents, nuclear power, and the disposable bottle. Furthermore, the mingling of causes and events over time makes it difficult in practice to factor out the real gains of any specific innovations from the process of related changes.

In most cases Δd_n, and its capitalized value, will not be open-ended. Rather it will usually be on the same order of magnitude as the other effects. This applies equally to possible negative Δd_n which may occur. In any case the estimates of Δd_n must be made conservatively.

Equity and content have been discussed earlier at some length. Here we shall be brief.

Equity in distribution is defined in terms of relative equality of wealth, opportunity, and income. These three are often related in practice, and—as noted earlier—in the present context the equalizing shifts available through industrial policies are likely to be unambiguous gains. Therefore it may be possible to judge the equity effects approximately, even though they elude precise tests.

Content is defined by several aspects, and so it is no mere mechanical item. As was noted in section 2, workers' utility may derive from a sense of self-direction, contribution, local identity, variety of tasks, and choice among opportunities. Abating the career syndrome will usually be a major criterion of improved content. Subtle shades of these will often be hard to measure or even perceive, but big differences will be quite apparent, sufficient to include in policy choices.

6 SUMMARY

Evidently the subject—embracing context, content, the nature of structure, how it evolves, and the criteria of performance—is not an easy one.

We have concentrated on some of the more difficult points, because they can sharply affect the policy yields. The results are not wholly satisfactory, but they do add depth and a sense of priorities to the conventional analysis of industrial structure and its effects.

The main conclusions are:

1. Context and content are important parts of industrial organization and performance. The core of conventional analysis needs to be extended to include them, even if they are less rigorous during this early stage of study. Without them, the analysis tends to be technocratic: narrow, mechanical, and possibly peripheral to social performance.

2. Capital-market imperfections tend to be replicated in other markets.

3. The apparent permanence of inequality justifies treating greater equality as a social benefit.

4. Content has several elements, among which the career system is an important cause of social loss.

5. Market share is probably the central element in market structure. Barriers and the oligopoly group are probably secondary.

6. Several factors may cause market shares to change over time. These include industry life cycles, random forces, and deliberate optimizing choices.

7. The share-time relationship, if it exists, can be decisive for the rate at which high market shares will "naturally" decline. The relationship, and the rate of decline, are therefore key targets for empirical tests.

These points amount to a modest revision of the scope and content of the conventional analysis of industrial organization. They are meant to help us to think clearly about market structure and its effects. They will have much more value if we can measure their properties in the real world, but first we must develop a modest framework for using real-world yields to guide policy choices.

CHAPTER THREE
Evaluating Industrial Policies

POLICY CHOICES reach across so diverse a range of market types and policy tools that the task of deriving unified treatments may appear unmanageable. The custom has been to divide the subject into separate sectors and policies, each with its own apparatus of agencies, rules, and techniques.

We need instead to identify the common content of these choices. All policies involve degrees of public cost and public control. They can be tested by some form of cost-benefit analysis, as a basis for optimizing the level and allocation of scarce policy resources. When it is done well, the method is little more than explicit common sense. Many policy choices are already made using some version of it, primitive or implicit, to find if the policy is "worthwhile," but many other decisions ignore it; and the method is often used carelessly, incorrectly, or with biases. The proper aim is to use it explicitly and completely, to make the quantities known, and to leave out no essential part.[1]

---

[1] Benefit-cost techniques and difficulties are examined in Alan R. Prest and Ralph Turvey, "Cost-Benefit Analysis: A Survey," *Economic Journal,* 1965, pp. 683–735, and Peter O. Steiner, *Public Expenditure Budgeting* (Wash., D.C.: Brookings Institution, 1970). See also Alan Williams, "Cost-benefit Analysis: Bastard Science? And/or Insidious Poison in the Body Politick?" *Journal of Public Economies,* August 1972, pp. 199–226.

Now, policies presumably change things. The proper focus of analysis is the *net* change caused by any policy, compared with inaction or with specific other actions. Often the status quo would change radically if left alone, so that what looks like a drastic policy move will in fact yield only small real net effects.

Moreover, analysis must deal with the *future* effects of policies. This prepares us to judge which new policies to try and which old ones to change. The analysis can also be used to test choices that were made in the past. Indeed this is one aim of the book: to learn from the past so as to avoid repeating its errors, and to extend such wisdom as it has accumulated. We wish especially to identify preventive treatments, which anticipate problems and have higher yields than restorative actions. It will also be seen that all rational policy criteria reduce to some version of benefit-cost analysis.

In section 1 I note several basic points about the nature of industrial policies. These give background for the abstract cost-benefit methods that occupy the rest of the chapter. In section 2 I define the kinds of benefits public policies toward markets seek and the costs they incur. Then a simple model for evaluating them is set forth, fitted to the main conditions common in industrial cases. I discuss discounting of benefits and costs, as well as the cost-benefit choices *private* firms make in *avoiding* enforcement. I also define the conditions of optimal choice. I identify specific biases in public agency choices in section 3 and biases in choices on the private side in section 4. Incentives and side-effects of policies are treated in section 5, alternative criteria are noted in section 6, and section 7 is a summary.

1 BASIC POLICY CONCEPTS

First we define the nature of industrial policies. The conventional image begins with a pure market economy. Most of its sectors have conditions of demand and supply that will sustain competition, under antitrust policy. In utilities, technology dictates monopoly: average cost declines in the relevant ranges. This "natural monopoly" is then put under regulation or public enterprise. Antitrust is the basic policy; regulation and public enterprise cover well-defined utilities.[2] And all three policies are constraints imposed on

---

[2] See J. S. Bain, *Industrial Organization,* (New York: Wiley, 1969); R. E. Caves, *American Industry: Structure, Conduct, Performance,* 3rd ed. (Englewood Cliffs, N.J.: Prentice-Hall, 1972); L. W. Weiss, *Economics and American Industry* (New York: Wiley, 1961); F. M.

private firms—constraints intended to force behavior and performance toward the social optimum. Finally, in certain other sectors, special conditions call for social enterprises (schools, hospitals). The sectors define the policies, and the policies exert control.

This image is simple, powerful, and distorted. First, and obviously, policies do not necessarily do what their wording claims, and they often do other, costly things. Second, the policies often shape the technology and market structure. More fundamentally, the policy tools are *not* the traditional triad of alternatives, and what they do has to be carefully analyzed. Consider four propositions about policy treatments.

1. There are two policy spectrums: One is the degree of private or public enterprise, the other is the degree of regulatory constraint on profitability. These are illustrated in Figure 3.1. Public enterprise is not a substitute for antitrust or regulation. It is a substitute for private enterprise and is in many cases neutral or a complement to antitrust and regulation. Public enterprise is not in principle limited to "utility" sectors. It has functions and effects— e.g. on content—different from the treatments along the constraint-subsidy spectrum.

There are other dimensions to policies, including the following: (a) cost, in terms of public resources (agency costs, subsidies, etc.); (b) the degree of "publicness" of control: some controls are very responsive to the public interest, broadly conceived, while others strictly serve narrow private interests, in line with the hypothesis given in chapter 1; (c) the degree of equalizing effect, on wealth, opportunity and income; (d) the effect on the market shares of the dominant firms (raising or lowering them). There are also other surface "dimensions," which often are trivial; these include the supposed severity of the constraints as claimed in formal rules, and the asserted degree of public benefits. Instead of such formal items, one needs to analyze the real properties of policies. The "intent" of a policy can be irrelevant to its nature and effects.

2. Policies often accomplish more than one thing. These components are often counterpoised and tilted unexpectedly. For example, "antitrust policy" in the U.S. has at least three main parts: preventing collusion, preventing certain mergers, and abating existing market power. The policies' net effect—as they are in fact enforced, with checkered emphasis—may be to

Scherer, *Industrial Market Structure and Economic Performance* (Skokie, Ill.: Rand McNally, 1970).

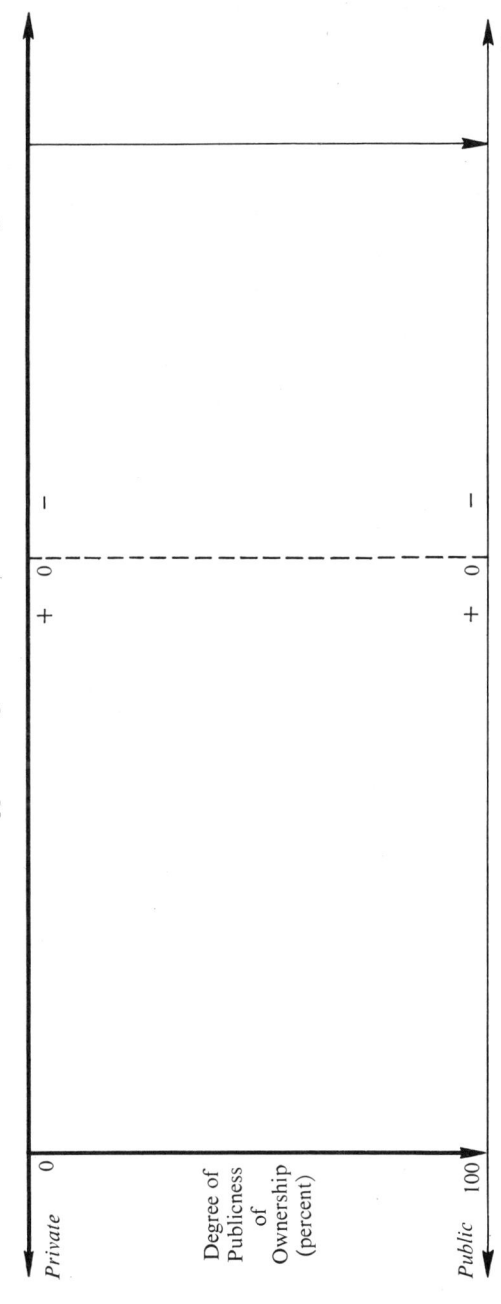

Figure 3.1 Two dimensions of policy choice: degree of constraint and public ownership.

harden structure and to benefit dominant firms, which is just the opposite of the supposed effects.³ Regulation has two main elements: authorizing a franchise and constraining profit rates. The one raises profitability, the other reduces it; the net effect also is indeterminate (we shall try to understand it in chapter 9).

Often the separate policy elements can be—and indeed are—managed independently. One must therefore know the elements, their actual and potential yields, and their side-effects before one can understand and evaluate them.

3. Sectors change over time, so that the effects—and appropriateness—of given policy tools also change. For example, utilities go through phases that commonly end back in competitive status (chapter 9); and cities grow in size and complexity, so that new policy treatments (e.g., transit systems) are needed. There are few fixed points or boundaries, and the rate of change can exceed the rate at which policies are adjusted. Some changes are predictable, but all require looking ahead and aiming at moving targets.

The best example of this is the natural rate of decay of market power (recall chapter 2). Virtually all monopoly will eventually dwindle, unless fortified by extraneous devices. But is the rate of decay fast or slow? Figure 3.2 illustrates that monopoly may be virtually permanent, or it may fade immediately. If it lasts even slow treatments may have high yields, but if it disappears quickly, any but the speediest treatments will be superfluous. The rate of decay is therefore central to optimal policy choice—in antitrust, regulation, and others.

4. Policies also evolve and cause adaptive responses in markets. This evolution is, in some cases, contrary to the optimum direction; utility regulation is an example. In other cases, the adaptive response wholly anticipates and deflects the "intent" of the policy; the financial sector offers numerous examples of such flexibility and speed.

In any event, the policy choice must often be dynamic—or at least time-related—on at least two planes. It must recognize the inner complexity and time-lags of actual policy tools, and it must be based on an understanding of the basic effects of policies.

It is also intrinsic in policies that they apply incentives: they either con-

---

³ That emerges in chapters 5 and 7. Or, possibly, it may limit market power and encourage innovation; see J. Markham, "Market Structure, Business Conduct and Innovation," *American Economic Review,* May 1965, pp. 323–32.

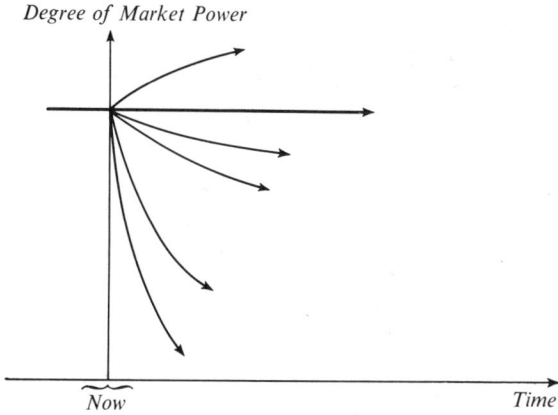

Figure 3.2 The rate of decay of market power can vary widely.

strain or subsidize; frequently they do both. The marginal incentives may be deep, even where their average effects are not. The firms "affected" (which often also help to design and enact the policy in the first place) then either have reduced or increased profit opportunities. Subsidizing obviously absorbs public resources directly, either in cash or in kind. Constraining is also costly, in a variety of ways. There is probably no significant industry or firm that is not both constrained and subsidized by public policies.

Policy treatments require (1) information and (2) rational analysis. Each is necessary but not sufficient. Most policy resources are used up in trying to gain information—by processing, hearings, investigations, etc. Information is critical, and the processes for gaining it may themselves contain biases. Rational choosers will err if their information is incorrect. Worse, they will fail even to consider problems if they—or the political process that guides their activities—are kept unaware of them. A recurring theme in this book is that information biases distort present policies, and that these policies must be offset by alternative treatment.

Public-policy resources come in several main varieties. The most fundamental of them is the scarce ability of the political process to evaluate and to exert control in "the public interest." Information is costly, and the ability of citizens to acquire it, weigh it, and act upon it has high opportunity costs in time, energy, and attention.[4] Each task taken up for public action

---

[4] Anthony Downs, *An Economic Theory of Democracy* (New York: Harper, 1957); Robert A. Dahl, *A Preface to Democratic Theory* (Chicago: University of Chicago Press, 1965); G. J.

diminishes the accountability and control that can be applied in others.[5]

Moreover, the control process itself is often biased, toward the interests of those with wealth and other strategic advantages. Therefore an abundance of accurate public knowledge, although necessary, may not be sufficient in itself to ensure effective public treatments. Moreover, knowledge is often *not* perfect or abundantly available, but deliberately hidden or falsified. The social control process, such as it may be, is of course the only one we have. It must be used sparingly, and in ways that fit its strengths.

Staff and funds are the other two main types of policy resources. Staff talent ranges from the highest orders of creative professional and strategic skills down to routine clerks and typists. Some of these people are entrepreneurs managing public enterprises; others are financiers, or civil servants, lawyers, engineers, theorists, economists, jurists, and technicians. Note that the career system is present here too, and it may influence the policy outcomes.

Public "funds" are also of several sorts. Most obvious are the budget levels of expenditure; $12 million for the Antitrust Division, $1.6 billion in postal subsidies, $12 billion in R&D grants, etc. Another cost is tax abatement to specific cases, such as to oil-well owners and drillers. This too is as real a cost as is direct spending of public funds. Less obvious but equally real is public absorption of private risks, such as loan guarantees to housebuyers, international corporations, farmers and small businesses (and numerous large firms, too). These burdens on public credit have a real economic cost.[6]

Certain other control devices do not entail costs in the same sense. Legal powers of compulsion—such as eminent domain to condemn land or the powers contained in the Sherman Antitrust Act—can simply be written into law at relatively little direct cost. The courts and ultimately the police and military stand ready to enforce these, but they are not often required to do so. Yet even here opportunity costs are often larger than they seem. Getting Congress, state legislatures, or even city councils to act on one problem often causes less action, or possibly a counteraction, in other areas. Further-

---

Stigler, "The Optimum Enforcement of Laws," *Journal of Political Economy*, May–June 1970, pp. 526–37.

[5] More precisely, it has rising marginal costs, per unit of "supervision."

[6] See Joint Economic Committee, *The Economics of Federal Subsidy Programs*, 92d Congress, 1st Session (U.S. Government Printing Office, 1972) and sources noted there.

more, the enforcement of existing laws often requires large flows of public resources. For example, industrial monopoly and racial discrimination are flatly illegal, but momentous enforcement resources are required to reduce them, let alone eliminate them.

Finally, the nature of those who manage the courts and agencies also influences the outcomes. They are mostly lawyers, trained to advocate and to decide issues by rules and points of law, by "rights" rather than in terms of optimality.[7] This slights economic analysis and a balanced evaluation: and in some cases, it leads to the opposite extreme of accepting economists uncritically.

In the courts, conservatism arises in several ways. The emphasis is upon attaining "perfect justice"—that ample time be given for preparation, that all sides be heard fully, that mistakes be avoided at virtually any cost.[8] Further, judges are commonly drawn from the legal-commercial strata. Therefore, they are schooled in free enterprise and private property rights, and so are often easily awed by business expertise and the "dangers" of disturbing the existing order. This conservatism is stronger in the lower courts, but during some periods it is evident at all levels.

In the agencies, a universal constraint is the brevity of tenure. In antitrust, the top positions have recently been held less than three years, on average; in regulation, average tenure on the most active and important commissions is about the same. But it usually takes at least five years to start a new treatment, develop it, apply it and carry it through, even within the existing laws. Major innovations often take 10 or 15 years. Therefore, most decision-makers are neither well prepared nor motivated to understand or press basic actions. This leads to shallowness and lack of continuity in policy.

2 THE BASIS OF CHOICE

The criteria for evaluating policies were worked out in chapter 2. Now we derive a simple method—or framework, or model—for such evaluations. This leads to a cost-benefit type of analysis to define the optimum conditions both for public and private choices.

---

[7] This is preeminently evident in regulation, but it is also important in antitrust enforcement. See C. Donahue, Jr., "Lawyers, Economists, and the Regulatory Process," *Michigan Law Review*, 1971; R. A. Posner, "A Statistical Study of Antitrust Enforcement," *Journal of Law and Economics*, 1970, pp. 365–420.

[8] M. Fleming, *The Price of Perfect Justice* (New York: Basic Books, 1973).

There are two parts to the optimizing problem: (1) to get the right level of total policy resources, and (2) to maximize the net public benefits yielded by any given level of policy resources, across the range of markets and policy types. Each policy is to be pursued quantitatively to the point where its marginal returns in net benefits are equal to the marginal returns on alternative actions. Each policy is also to be designed qualitatively so that the benefit-cost surplus is as large as possible for every given level of expenditure.

Specific policy choices can be framed in two ways.[9] Where there is a straight choice between types of policies, then the one with the highest ratio of total benefits to costs is to be chosen. Alternatively, and more generally, one may regard policy resources as investments, and seek to optimize their allocation in terms of internal rates of return on the resources committed. In that case, each policy would be pursued to the point where the net internal rate of return on its resource investment just equals the marginal opportunity cost of public-sector funds. Normally these approaches will yield similar policy choices. In either case, the analysis must include *all* benefits and costs of each choice.

Stated so simply, such rules are truisms—as economists have long been aware—but they can have great power. They are a consistent basis for organizing an evaluation, and they correctly require choices to be made among multiple alternatives, not just for or against a single policy tool. Further, we shall fit on to the analysis several elements that give it more substance; and by looking both at the *public-agency* choices and at the choices made in response by *private firms*, who are trying to alter or remove the constraints, we obtain a more complete basis for understanding the whole process of public action and reaction.

Every public agency has certain *tools*—in the form of (1) resources and (2) legal powers—and *problems,* defined by its (3) jurisdiction and (4) the severity of problems in it. Its effectiveness requires that these four be at least reasonably in balance. A large jurisdiction, embracing severe problems, requires large resources or powers. Resources and powers are often substitutable in some degree; with wider powers (e.g., to have final power of decision), an agency may need fewer resources (e.g., trial lawyers to persuade an outside court). With larger problems, both the

[9] On problems of methodology, see Steiner, *Public Expenditure Budgeting;* E. J. Mishan, *Cost-Benefit Analysis* (New York: Praeger, 1971); and R. Turvey, ed., *Public Enterprise,* rev. ed. (Baltimore: Penguin, 1970).

resources and the powers usually need enlarging. An agency with large problems and small tools will usually be ineffective; worse, it is also a bar to other, better treatments. At the same time, however, resources and powers can be wasted if an agency is inefficiently operated (e.g., it makes the wrong internal choices and develops internal "bureaucratic" slack). At first we shall assume such internal inefficiency to be zero (or of "average" degree) and inspect the conditions of optimum policy choices. Some questions of policy design and internal inefficiency are explored later in the book.

A GENERAL PUBLIC CHOICE

We begin with a single, simple case. Consider a public decision-making agency whose tools and problems are balanced. Suppose that setting a specific policy j at a level λ will incur certain direct costs C_a (a = agency) and probably yield certain benefits by changing efficiency, content, and equity. For brevity, we shall label efficiency as E, content as Y, and equity as D (for distribution). These costs and benefits will occur over time t, from the present to some distant horizon n. The general expression for determining the economic returns to this policy level is the present-value expression:

$$\text{Net Benefits}_j = B_j = \sum_{t=1}^{n} \frac{\Delta E + \Delta Y + \Delta D}{(1+i)^n} - \sum_{t=1}^{n} \frac{\Delta C_a + \Delta C_p}{(1+i)^n} \qquad (3.1)$$

where i is a rate of time discount. C_p is the private costs imposed by agency action, for example from an antitrust restructuring of firms. The agency has other policy tools to use its resources on, and it can also vary the levels of each tool. An optimum is reached when all policies are adjusted so that their net marginal yields are equal to the true opportunity cost of the agency's resources, defined by some social rate of return (r_s). A necessary condition for efficiency is therefore

$$\frac{\partial \Delta B_j}{\partial \Delta C_j} = b_j \geq r_s \qquad (3.2)$$

Thus if policy j at level λ yields a marginal return greater than r_s then its level should be increased; and vice versa.[10]

---

[10] There are various finer points to this. Thus, if there are certain time patterns of costs and benefits, it may matter in marginal cases whether one uses a present-value, internal-rate-of-re-

One does not envision precise figures being inserted in the equation. These are only predictions, in a world full of blurs and guesses. Judgment will be needed; cost-benefit analysis faithfully carries out the mistakes of those using it. Yet is does clarify the elements of choice directly, in contrast to the natural effort of policy-makers hide the key decision points.

Figure 3.3 shows the basic results for a specific treatment. Its efficient level varies with r_s, the cost of public funds. There will be a surplus of average returns over r_s. If the *MR* function is flattish, the choice of r_s may strongly affect the levels of optimal treatment.

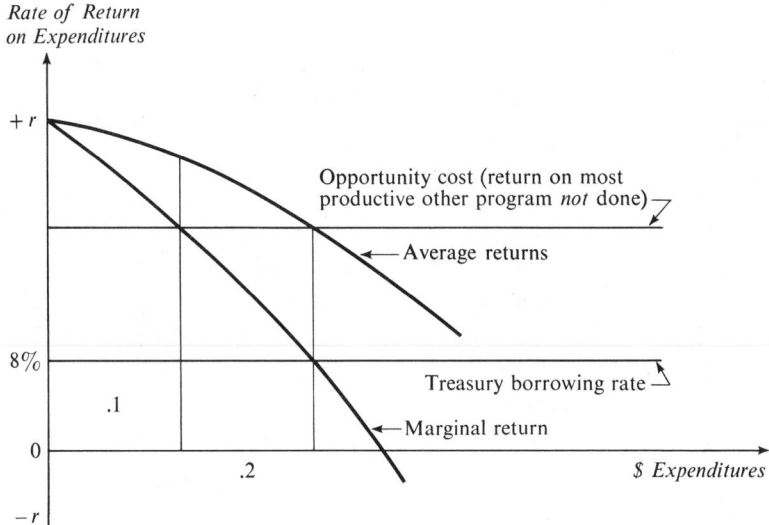

Figure 3.3 Typical yields and costs of policy resources.

Treatments are assumed to have optimal *design*. Otherwise outcomes may be as at points 1 or 2, inside the *MR and AR* possibility frontiers. Here the design, not the level, is inefficient. Also, we assume that benefits and costs are included completely and measured without bias.

The components in this simple model need discounting in three ways:

Time. The usual sequence is costs first, benefits later. To that extent, policy resources are investments. Where resistance by private interests

---

turn, or discounted-cash-flow method. But for the present level of precision, such questions are secondary.

lengthens the investment period, it reduces the present value of the benefits. This in turn normally reduces the efficient level of the policy. A correct choice will be free of any such time bias. *A neutral treatment also avoids putting time "on the side of" either the agency or the firm.* Otherwise, the ability to postpone action may be decisive.

The "correct" discount rate is not easy to specify exactly, as an extensive literature attests.[11] Higher i values shrink the benefits from actions that take a long time to run their course. A higher i may reflect a true government-wide, high rate of time preference on social expenditure, but short-run fluctuations in i (as "urgency" comes and goes) are assumed away.

Probability. Future outcomes are always uncertain in some degree, and so the cost and benefit magnitudes need adjustment to reflect these probabilities. Two inherent causes of uncertainty are involved, both relating to time.

1. Economic effects are not certain. Research has established several broad relationships between elements of market structure and performance, which chapter 4 will survey. But these are soft relationships, not clad in iron certainty. Also, each specific case at hand may deviate from the general rule, for some special reason. In extreme cases, a predicted beneficial effect could turn out instead to be negative; most private briefs against public actions make precisely that claim.

Social science proceeds by hypothesis-testing, which can never be conclusive. In the absence of repetitive controlled experiments, statistical analysis of recent data can seek whether or not to confirm the patterns theory suggests; but it can never finally prove or reject, never give tight answers. Worse, serious practical research problems are common. Crucial facts are hidden, the data for testing are usually inexact, the reality itself often changes. For example, profits and innovation are extremely tricky to measure, and econometric patterns in the 1950s could be rejected as invalid for the 1970s.

In short, *any* policy choice contains a weighing of *probable* effects on both sides. *A correct weighing procedure will poise the burden of proof evenly.* This neutrality is often difficult to achieve. For example, courtroom standards of proof for criminal cases will be inappropriate for settling the optimum structure of an industry, since the courtroom burden of proof—"beyond reasonable doubt"—is one-sided. The law of private property ordi-

---

[11] See the sources in note 9 and others they cite.

narily sets the burden of proof against changes in the status quo; this is true also of much recent regulatory law. Yet, in principle, this will lead to incorrect decisions. Stated more generally: *policy choices not to make changes should have as robust empirical support as any other choice.*

2. Even where economic effects are probable, their *normative* yield may be doubtful. Choice A may make benefit X sure to happen, but X might come about even without A. For example, steps to reduce a monopolist's market power will often seem to offer significant benefits. Yet that firm's market power might be eroded almost as rapidly by "natural" processes, so the net real gain from trying to force the change may be slight or zero. This is the question of natural rates of decay—recall chapter 2 and section 1 above—and it is of course precisely the defense offered by most targets of policy actions: that the goals are, or will be, gained as well or better without policy step.

The Schumpeterian amendment is that the market power arises from innovation and can be powerfully beneficial while it lasts, by stimulating further innovation.[12] Yet the issues are complex. Innovation *per se* shows nothing about policy yields, for an innovative industry may have had unusually rich opportunities for innovation, or may have innovated at *more* than the optimum rate.[13]

Correct policy choices will therefore be prospective, time-discounted and porbability-adjusted, and will *make comparisons with the results that could otherwise be reasonably expected to occur.* The performance criteria are partly conjectural and need to be set neutrally. The policy yields of any policy are the *net* changes from these alternative levels. Yet these alternative levels are themselves estimates, subject to probabilities.

These two uncertainty factors—about effects and normative standards—can be included by adjusting the "best estimate" values by probability factors. These will be set between 0 for impossibility and 1 for certainty. For simplicity, the notation here will include all such factors in a single summary multiplier p attached to each element of net benefits. Thus an estimated net benefit of $10 million at a p of .4 (a 40% chance) would have a value of $4 million. This is the simplest factoring scheme and it omits quite

---

[12] Joseph A. Schumpeter, *History of Economic Analysis* (London: Oxford, 1954).
[13] Recall K. J. Arrow, "Economic Welfare and the Allocation of Resources for Invention," *op. cit.;* Scherer, *Industrial Market Structure;* and see E. Mansfield *et al., Research and Innovation in the Modern Corporation,* Norton, 1971.

a few subtleties about risk preferences and related elements.[14] Still, it is a good starting point from which later refinements could be made.

Obviously p is itself a matter for subjective estimate, and in most cases it cannot be known precisely.[15] But large differences in the odds can usually be perceived, and rough estimates of p will often be in line with the inexactness of the other data in the decision. And, again, there is value in making these factors explicit. That, at least, enables the arguable to be argued clearly.

Precedent. Each policy choice may set precedents that decide other cases. A single decision may therefore have an additional policy yield which, in "landmark" instances, can go very high.[16] In such cases, an evaluation of the case's own yield is too narrow; a precedential multiplier m should be applied. In routine inframarginal cases, based on settled law, m will approach 1 (standard price-fixing cases are now of this sort). In marginal cases, which extend or retract the law, m may be large and either plus or minus. A minus holds if a case withdraws precedents that previously yielded net benefits or if extension of the law causes net costs in other cases. Such negative precedential effects—from economically mistaken decisions—are not rare at all; in some areas and periods they are common. Positive multipliers are more frequent when the law is developing, by covering new ground or new practices. A special twist is what lawyers call estoppel. Bringing an action at one point often gives a period of grace during which the action cannot be brought again. For example, IBM Corporation was regarded as free from further antitrust action for at least a decade after the 1956 consent decree settling an earlier case. Therefore the estoppel effect amounts to an internal precedent factor which is less than one.

One must bear in mind, however, that precedents frequently arise from the structure of the law, which can be revised. For example, FCC decisions

---

[14] These include the classic questions about risk-return choices, discussed in M. Friedman and L. J. Savage, "The Utility Analysis of Choices Involving Risk," *Journal of Political Economy,* 1948, pp. 279–304; D. D. Hester and J. Tobin, eds., *Risk Aversion and Portfolio Choice* (New York: Wiley, 1967), and H. Markowitz, *Portfolio Selection: Efficient Diversification of Investment* (New York: Wiley, 1959).

[15] Most of these are one-time events, and the basis for judging probabilities is often soft and arguable. See F. H. Knight, *Risk, Uncertainty and Profit* (Boston: Houghton Mifflin, 1921). One must rely on experience and inference, and individual versions of these may differ.

[16] L. W. Weiss, "An Analysis of the Allocation of Antitrust Division Resources," in J. A. Dalton and S. Levin, *The Antitrust Dilemma,* Southern Illinois University, in press, 1974, offers a pioneering effort to incorporate precedent in an evaluation.

on cable TV can be superseded by new laws on the matter. In certain cases, *m* itself is subject to a probability factor, if revision of the law is in prospect.

The general model of agency choice now takes the form:

$$\text{Net benefits} = m \sum_{T=1}^{n} \frac{\Delta E \cdot p_e + \Delta Y \cdot p_y + \Delta D \cdot p_d}{(1+i)^n} - \sum_{T=1}^{n} \frac{\Delta C_a \cdot p_{ca} + \Delta C_p \cdot p_{cp}}{(1+i)^n} \quad (3.3)$$

In terms of rates of return on policy resources, the efficiency condition at the margin is

$$b_j = m \frac{\Delta B_i \cdot p_b}{\Delta C_p \cdot p_{ca}} \geq r_s \quad (3.4)$$

The objective is still to reach an equimarginal set of optimizing conditions, of marginal yields among all policies. Roughly speaking, those with high benefit probabilities and precedential multipliers will be favored over others.

The "final" evaluations will be made at any one of several levels: agency staff members and advisers, at the grassroots level; or agency head officers; or upper-administration officials; or the courts at various state and federal levels. The focus differs, in practice: agency staff members usually deal primarily with the benefits expression, while their head officers focus more on costs and precedents. In the judiciary, higher courts are usually more concerned with precedential aspects than are the lower courts. Yet at each level, all elements in the evaluation should in principle be included.

B PRIVATE-FIRM CHOICES

While agencies are choosing among possible constraints or subsidies to firms, the firms affected are also arranging their strategies. The result is commonly a sequence of choices and moves on both sides, with occasional resolutions but no real terminus. Issues are rarely "settled"; there are usually compromises and partial changes, and underlying conditions often change further. Therefore, an analysis of choices by firms is complementary to our treatment of public agency choices.

We start with the conventional assumption that firms generally maximize profit *(P)* for a given investment *(I)*. For the entire firm, for period *n*

$$P_n = TR_n = TC_n \quad (3.5)$$

For any specific project or direction of expenditures, the expected yield (π) on funds committed must equal or exceed the opportunity cost of capital (r_c) to the firm:

$$\pi_n = \frac{R_n - C_n}{I_n} \qquad (3.6)$$

and

$$\pi_n \geq r_c \qquad (3.7)$$

One such direction of company expenditure is on efforts to anticipate, prevent, or mitigate the constraints public agencies choose to apply (or to increase the subsidies obtained).

Generally, any public policy that would reduce profits will be resisted up to the point at which the marginal rate of return on resistance expenditures just equals the opportunity cost of capital. At its simplest extreme, the excess profits at stake will all be used up by the firm in resisting the public agency, since otherwise they will be lost to the firm in any event.

Imagine a frictionless economy with no externalities, no equity problems, shared expectations about future events, and a "perfect" political process. Under such ideal conditions, both policy and resistance choices might turn out to be optimized, with the private and public opportunity costs of funds just equal at every margin:

$$\pi_n = r_c = r_s \qquad (3.8)$$

This optimum could occur even though the firms' evaluations are narrower than the agencies'. Thus a firm's concern with equity extends only to maximizing its own shareholders' wealth. The firm is oblivious to precedential effects that will impinge on other firms, and its efficiency concerns exclude any gains to other firms (especially actual and potential competitors) or any other external effects.

3 POSSIBLE BIASES IN PUBLIC-AGENCY CHOICES

Agencies operate within real constraints of their own. Their budgets and powers, the quality of their leaders, and the current range of "politically acceptable" actions are usually controlled from outside. Agency managers must pursue actions within given legal systems and rules. Traditions and the technical nature of their treatments always limit what they can do and how fast they can do it.

It is possible to identify several resulting biases in public-agency choices, which often distort choices among industrial policies. These are familiar to skilled practitioners of private-firm resistance but not, in many cases, to public agency officials and external observers.

Information bias. Public agencies need complete and timely information on sensitive variables (market shares, prices, costs, innovation choices, competitive tactics, and alternative treatments), both past and future. Such information is known intimately by firms, and when it influences profits it will inevitably be secreted. Because of the conditions summarized in the hypothesis about information, official fact-gathering agencies are often virtually useless as vehicles for access to such specific information. Their uselessness not only biases specific policy choices, but also excludes research efforts to clarify the general effects of market power and to provide a firm basis for general formation of treatments.

Both the degree of possible effects and the probability level at which we discount the effect are therefore affected. Until recently, we could measure market power mainly with concentration ratios, which are riddled with defects. Therefore the "effects" of market power appeared to be both slight and uncertain; that is, the regression coefficients and the goodness of fit were both biased downward because our data were incomplete and contained error.[17] Until disclosure rules are dissolved and a much greater range of company data are disseminated, this bias will make us continue to underestimate the general role of market power. And yet, since industry largely controls disclosure policies, a shift in information access is unlikely to occur.

Meanwhile, the costs of treatment are more directly measurable and, in contested cases, are fully asserted by the target firms, often with a degree of exaggeration. Therefore, bias is likely to be present in specific cases as well as in the general setting of policy lines. The effects of these biases are four. First, industrial policies are less firm and complete than they would otherwise be (because the problems and potential yields are underestimated). Second, whole problems, areas, and cases are ignored (because of ignorance). Third, agency resources have to flow much more into mere fact-gathering than a neutral information state would require. Fourth, actions are delayed and less complete. These biases are often cumulative.

Therefore it may be important to behave in accord with a full information hypothesis: Let all information about enterprise operations and structure be

---

[17] See Shepherd, *Market Power and Economic Welfare* (New York: Random House, 1970), and "The Elements of Market Structure," *Review of Economics and Statistics,* 1972, pp. 25-37.

available to external observers, competitors and agencies. This will then induce behavior such that market performance and policy treatments will both tend toward optimality. This hypothesis would hold generally, since it averts important biases which affect global and specific treatment decisions (see chapters 6–11). Valid exceptions to it might include costs of preparing information. Some complex information requires assembling and processing on a large scale (e.g., an analysis of marginal costs in a range of Bell System services or IBM products). This could limit the fineness of influence of the principle, but it would not affect its validity. Another exception might be certain strategic information which, if instantly available, would neutralize efficient behavior. For example, suppose a small firm's new product innovation is instantly overwhelmed by a dominant firm because of instant disclosure. Yet such problems will usually be less severe than they are claimed to be, and the optimal delay for them will usually be relatively short.

In any event, these provisos should bear the burden of proof against the rebuttable presumption favoring the principle.[18] An optimal information rule would require, as a minimum, a broad disclosure by all firms with significant market shares (such as 20 percent or more), either currently or after delays of no more than two or three years.

A more basic exception is that full information may not touch the context or the content of enterprises, so that neither content nor equity is induced toward optimal patterns. In short, the deviances may be too deep-seated or routine to respond to individual choices, *given* the underlying maladjustments. If so, more direct policy treatments will be needed.

Time bias. Several time biases are frequently observed. When one side can impose delay and also gains from the delay, then time is biased in its favor. This bias can be decisive, as we shall see when we examine merger, restructuring, and regulatory actions. The bias often flows from specific procedures or rules, which can in principle be altered.

Time bias also arises from the brevity of most policy-makers' tenure. New policies usually require at least three years to prepare and at least 10 years (often 20 years) for benefits to be fully harvested. Most antitrust and regulatory decision-makers are in office less than four years. And their inexperience often neutralizes them for the first year or two. They commonly

---

[18] At this writing an FTC effort to get line of business data from large firms appears likely to escape the usual prohibitions. Yet even it is a modest proposal, not touching context, content, nor several major items of firm behavior and performance.

apply a high rate of time preference, and this myopia favors quick, shallow steps rather than basic ones. It also makes the advantage of having time on one's side particularly strong.

Probability bias. Two important biases in the probability factors are recurrent—procedural bias and the burden of proof.

The outcome may be *procedurally* uncertain. For example, a restructuring case will require a court to find a firm guilty of monopolizing and order a basic remedy; the odds on either or both actions may be low and imprecise. A price-fixing conviction and remedy may, by contrast, be nearly a sure bet. Regulatory and other outcomes are also often subject to such uncertainties. (We here assume the procedures to be fixed, but if their odds clash with the economic magnitudes, then the procedures themselves may be changed. Thus an agency, or other group, may propose new laws, precisely to reduce procedural bias.)

An aspect of procedural uncertainty is that the passage of time raises political uncertainty. As elections come and go and governments change, the direction of policy may be reversed from above. Long-term actions are liable to be stopped in midstream, even though the conditions justifying them are unchanged.

An uneven *burden of proof* will permit one side to prevail even though its costs—evenly weighted by probabilities—exceed its benefits. As noted earlier, Western laws and traditions of private property rights normally set the burden of proof against changes in the status quo. Such a standard of "proof" is—in social research terms—a clear bias. An even burden of proof presumes, of course, equal access to sensitive data. Inequality of access will compound the bias created by lopsided requirements concerning the degrees of probability about benefits and costs.

As an illustration, Figure 3.4 compares hypothetical yields from two lines of antitrust treatments. The "true" basic yields are higher for restorative treatments than for conduct actions, but if restorative yields are discounted by the biases, they appear to be too low throughout to qualify. The true optimal levels are O_R and O_C; but it appears that restorative treatments should be zero. Such conditions as these would lead to a marked imbalance in antitrust policy (as Chapters 5 and 7 indeed will note).

Private costs. Public policies often lead to private resistance costs, as when an antitrust suit evokes defensive efforts. Should public agencies include these private resistance costs as part of the real costs of their actions? Plausibly, yes; the costs are real and often predictable. Yet they are often fully discretionary with the firm, so that any knowledgeable firm will threaten large or unlimited resistance purely in order to slant the agency's choice toward weaker actions. (Indeed, its delaying tactics alone will cause such a slant.) To this extent, the firms themselves could control public policy. This being obviously unacceptable, one could compromise by including only the "nondiscretionary" resistance costs in the public agency evaluation. But is this a practical distinction? The best answer appears to be to

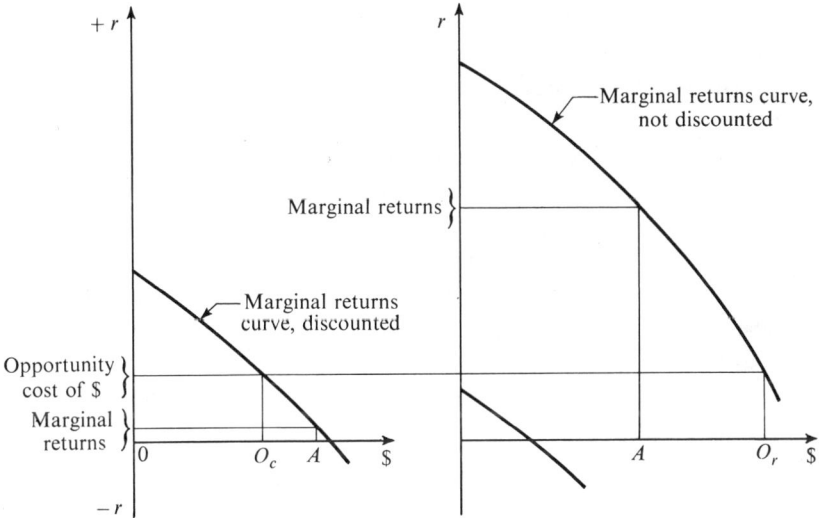

Figure 3.4 Discounting of the policy yields can be decisive.

leave private costs out on first-round evaluations and then put them in only if nondiscretionary costs are large, highly probable, and identifiable.

One final note: any policy action will help some and hurt others. This is true both of efficiency and innovation changes, and of distribution. In particular, any policy act or nonaction will redistribute income and capital in unforeseen ways. Therefore, that a policy will have a redistributive impact cannot validly serve as an argument against that policy (other than as an entry for ΔD). Otherwise policy choices would be paralyzed. A requirement that policies be distributively "neutral" is inappropriate. A "neutral" policy (i.e., one that leaves inequality unchanged) contains per se a judgment that the present distribution is the best possible. That might conceivably be true, but that implicit feature of neutrality must be fully recognized.

4 BIASES IN PRIVATE-FIRM CHOICES

The narrowness of the firm's evaluation will not necessarily cause bias, under ideal conditions. But lapses from the ideal can be frequent and important. Therefore bias will arise from private firms' indifference to precedential effects and external effects.

Private firms will often apply rates of time discount different from those of public decision-makers—higher in some cases, lower in others. Often firms will rate the probability factors quite differently from the public agency.

Bias may also occur when firms depart from strict profit-maximizing toward such other maximands as sales, risk-avoidance, or market share. The normative effect will vary from case to case, depending on the direction in which public policies are pressing.

Two other biases are quite systematic: taxes and speed of action. Tax bias is embedded deeply in the system. Resistance costs ordinarily are tax-deductible, so that the opportunity cost to the firm will usually be well below the true cost of the real resources absorbed. If the corporation income tax rate is t, then the profit-maximizing marginal condition of resistance costs (C_p) and after-tax profits at stake (P) is

$$P \geqq \frac{C_p}{1-t} \quad (3.9)$$

The present t of about .50 means that resistance costs would be extended until they are at twice the level of the marginal profits at stake. If, for example, the profits at stake (P) are $1 million per day (as they are in some cases—see chapter 7), then the rational firm will spend up to about $2 million to achieve each day of delay. A significant t therefore enlarges the resistance to policy constraints, perhaps well beyond a neutral outcome, because it makes resistance dollars "cheaper."

The general private-firm basis for a decision about resistance to policy i is

$$\pi_j = \frac{R_j - [C_j/(1-t)]}{I_j} \quad (3.10)$$

Firms benefitting from the *status quo* (and its continuation in the future) will devote resources to retarding any change caused by public policy. If the time yield of delay is high, the stalling effort may be large, again possibly absorbing the whole sum at stake.

As for the difference in speed of action, public choices are often made at slower rates than are private ones. This reduces the range of public choice. The lags may cause the public actions, *when they take effect,* to stray far from the optimum levels. The classic instance of this is an antitrust restructuring case which, after many years of trial and appeal, is finally won *after* the industry has changed. Another is the stoppage of bank mergers after dominant banks have already been formed. Strict optimizing requires that public actions be as rapid as private ones, even if they are not immediate. Strict optimizing is therefore often impossible.

These two dynamic elements are critical to a preventive treatment. Unless they can be overcome, the choices will be confined to remedial actions, which tend to have higher costs and lower benefits.

In combination, these biases on the public and private side can be strong. Occasionally they may offset each other, but that would be an oddity. Frequently they reinforce each other, causing divergences from the optimum. Such deviations are often not even recognized because essential information is lacking. And there are ironic departures; for example, firms often achieve valuable delay by providing an agency with *too much* information, which its staff can assimilate only at a snail's pace.

The reader can derive cases in which the biases would cause severe welfare loss, or nicely balance each other out. The essential fact is that the biases are numerous and can be powerful. Correct policies must allow for them explicitly.

5 OPTIMAL DESIGN

Treatment with "optimal" design will anticipate the biases in data, time, etc., and will apply incentives so that each party (firms and agencies) is induced to move toward the correct solutions. Design can be even more critical than policy *levels,* and optimizing it requires more than just making it bias-free, though that too is necessary.

First, it requires identifying which actors have the information and power to bring about the appropriate changes. These may be managers, shareholders, directors, workers, competitors, or a range of public officials—and their roles are not obvious. Thus, to induce managers to alter behavior or structure, it may be best to induce shareholders or directors to *make* them do it, not try to induce the managers directly.

Second, the efficient incentives need to be designed and applied. This requires knowledge of the motives of the actors, of the tradeoffs among the costs and benefits, and of the ways to get treatments applied.

In general, treatment should make it so that market power pays less without making efficiency and innovation pay less. Treatments will then fit the motives of the key actors, not run square against them. This will turn out in many cases to favor *therapy* (or behavior modification) over *surgery* (or enforced restructuring and penalties). It will also fit the general rule that preventive treatment is preferable to restorative actions.

Policy devices range from negative punishments to positive inducements (including subsidies). Optimum policies often involve inducements rather than negative, coercive remedies. These can use taxes and expenditure devices, rather than agencies' controls and rules. Coercion breeds costly resistance, as later chapters will show, and it often imposes transitional costs (as in dividing a monopoly into parts). Incentives shorten the time to remedy, and they can often improve the quality of the change, by rewarding the firms for developing it. Incentives have their costs too, either in the form of cash compensation or in favoring one group over others; incentives for some may mean penalties or exclusions for the rest. An incentive payment that exceeds the discounted social gains will rarely be optimal. Therefore incentives must often be combined with constraints.

In any event, policy choice must be preceded by searches for high-yield incentives, which maximize the inducement to comply for any given degree of loss to others. This principle is well known but hardly ever applied in utility regulation; it has rarely even been perceived in the antitrust literature.

6 ALTERNATIVE CRITERIA

Benefit-cost analysis is evidently an essential framework for rational choice. It is subject to abuse and biases, but it is also the proper analytical basis for identifying those biases and defining ways to correct them. Other policy criteria are often presented as alternatives to benefit-cost analysis, but on inspection, these turn out to reduce to benefit-cost form. Such criteria often do contain valuable offsets to benefit-cost biases. But they are still in the benefit-cost context, not alternatives to it.

Consider several such criteria (or articles of faith):

   a. *Incipiency.* Monopoly should be stopped at the earliest possible point in its growth. This is an important criterion used in preventing certain horizontal mergers. It embodies the benefit-cost evaluation that the discounted benefits from preventive action against increasing market shares via merger exceed the discounted costs sufficiently to justify drawing the line at low market shares (see chapter 8).
   b. *Competition* is the objective pure and simple, even apart from its economic results. Actually, this means that the total discounted benefits of competition are likely to be very large—so much so that there is a rebuttable presumption against market power.
   c. *Laissez-faire.* Let markets work freely to erode monopoly and virtually all public efforts to restore or supplant it will be unnecessary or harmful. In benefit-cost form: market power decays so rapidly that policy measures to reduce or constrain it have little or no net benefits.

Other criteria fit in the framework too. Some of them provide efficient rules of thumb or other consistent techniques. But their validity derives ultimately from a correct fit to the basic benefit-cost conditions; and validity can only be assessed in that context.

7 SUMMARY

We have now derived a way of designing optimum policy choices for correcting deviations in private market structure and performance. Such optimizing choices will neither overexpand nor underprovide public actions; nor will they cause deviations themselves (a real possibility, frequently observed to occur). Such a policy set need not require large amounts of resources for the state; on the contrary, certain modest and lean policy tools (such as some antitrust treatments) can often eliminate the need for other larger programs. And certain large programs with negative yields need to be pruned down, as we shall see.

All rational treatment criteria can be reduced to a benefit-cost form. But benefit-cost analysis is easier said than done well. Biases may permeate both the making and the carrying out of decisions. It will be only too easy to exclude important categories of costs and benefits, because they are controversial or unknown. Some items will be hard to measure, as chapters 4 and 5 show. Probability factors are inherently difficult to appraise. Getting the burden of proof poised evenly will often be a delicate and difficult exercise. There are other, lesser dangers about benefit-cost analysis, and so one must use the approach with due care.

The hope is to rough out the dimensions of the clearest and most important cases, rather than to mount a vast empty exercise in numerical speculation, embracing all industries. Such a focused treatment is entirely practical on an experimental basis. We shall see in later chapters that in certain cases the results are so one-sided that the lessons for policy choice are reasonably clear.

The search is for both the optimum levels and the efficient designs for policies. Often policy design is more critical than levels of policy budgets. The hope is to avoid large errors and omissions rather than to reach perfect, comprehensive answers. The number and extent of required evaluations may seem impossibly large, but that is partly an illusion. The evaluation process, once it has been developed by a learning process, requires only marginal adjustments from period to period, focusing on the more obvious changes. Brand-new evaluations will be needed only for the unanticipated, major, new market conditions, and these will usually be few. The process is not an easy one and will pose difficult choices, but the complexity of the evaluations is not a valid reason for not doing them and acting on their lessons. Otherwise, one is deliberately letting the choices be made in ignorance and, often, with intrinsic biases.

CHAPTER FOUR
The Basic Policy Yields in Actual Markets

THE ACTUAL RESULTS of policies are set by the conditions in real markets. These yields were defined in chapters 2 and 3 in terms of efficiency, content, and equity. This chapter tries to indicate their magnitudes. The primary objective is to set forth the relationships that exist and evolve in normal markets, in order to indicate the tradeoffs among policy choices. This helps to identify sectors that will probably offer relatively high policy yields in the future.

The exercise must be inexact. Our concepts and measurements of relationships are still in a formative stage, even after decades of research, and the research findings so far are rather soft. To identify the sensitive sectors requires even more speculation. Still, one must try to make the most reasonable estimates possible, in order to organize the problem and set priorities. In fact, the main lines can be set out with some clarity.

Our scientific analysis and "knowledge" depend on the available data and the amount of resources for studying them. We see through a small glass, darkly. The setting for research is not neutral, for two main reasons. One is that the subject under study has some influence over the data used for study. Most of the critical data are secreted by firms and by the U.S. Census

Bureau (whose advisory boards are mainly firms and industry associations), the Securities and Exchange Commission, bank regulatory bodies, and others. These agencies collect little or no data on many key facts about market position, financial ties, and performance, and what data they do collect are kept secret, permanently. Only four-firm aggregates of relatively insensitive data are released for us to try to use in objective study. And the secrecy is spreading, to newer data (e.g., on minority hiring), which are being put under the census iron curtain. Rather than casting light, these agencies on balance are suppressing—the word is not too strong—the key data, while seeming instead to purvey information. Such secrecy could conceivably be justifiable for three or five years, but to extend it back beyond the 1907 Census—as is the case—is scarcely credible. In cost-benefit terms, the costs of full disclosure would be slight, while the probable gains would be substantial. The following findings about market power and its effects probably are permeated with downward bias because of this methodological problem. The data contain error because public fact-gathering agencies are instead fact-hiding agencies.

The state of knowledge is also affected by the scarcity of researchers. With but several exceptions, there have been only scattered studies on most of the key relationships. Even now, after some growth in econometric studies during the 1960s, there are only one or at most a few people doing advanced work on most aspects, and on some points there is virtually no past or current work at all. This scarcity is puzzling. Perhaps it arises from a contrived scantiness of data. In any event, it helps to ensure that our knowledge of the basic relationships is incomplete. What follows must therefore be evaluated with art and sophistication, as well as hard-headed pragmatism.

We first consider context, using such data as there are. Then we reexamine the basic character of market structure, testing the relative importance of the various structural elements. In section 3 the return and risk components of profitability are dissected, while sections 4 and 5 assemble information about how market shares evolve. The effects that market structure appears to have—including those on content—are summed up in section 6; section 7 draws the findings together.

1 CONTEXT

We shall consider the banking context first, and then the structure of distribution.

The Financial Setting. Banking relationships are stable and important. The matter is regarded by those involved as sensitive, and so the facts are kept secret: no official agency reports them, or even collects them. Still, the folklore is definite, and there are some pieces of evidence.[1] Moreover, the economic reasons for stable, binding banking relationships are strong (as chapter 6 will show). Therefore, the correct image is of each firm being involved in a close, continuing relationship with one bank (or, in unusual and very large cases, two or three).

Banking structure itself tends toward tight oligopoly, especially in the medium-sized and smaller cities.[2] Even on the national and international levels, financial markets devolve into traditional sub-areas and specialties, spheres of influence, etc. These are not wholly fixed or rigid; but they do exist. Oligopoly patterns reflect complex determinants—which are not yet well sorted out by research—and a large degree of randomness.

Given that financial market structure tends toward tight oligopoly, the replication hypothesis does appear to hold: financial markets induce other markets toward tight oligopoly. This is consistent with the evidence about the supply of capital. In repeated major studies, the cost of capital varies inversely with the size of the firm.[3] There are also other widespread indications that capital costs vary inversely with market shares and, where they exist, with the "height" of specific entry barriers.[4] As chapter 2 noted, those observed differences will understate the underlying differences between the financing conditions for firms with large and small market shares.

The other critical condition in capital markets is the degree of insiderism, with layers of access to the key information needed to make capital gains by anticipating market moves. Here the informed consensus is unanimous and

---

[1] L. Werboff and M. E. Rozen, "Market Shares and Competition Among Financial Institutions," in *Private Financial Institutions,* Paul M. Horvitz et al., eds. (Englewood Cliffs, N.J.: Prentice-Hall, 1963); *Interlocks in Corporate Management,* Committee on the Judiciary, House of Representatives, 89th Congress, 1st Session (U.S. Government Printing Office, 1965); *Commercial Banks and Their Trust Activities,* Vols. I and II, Committee on Banking and Currency, House of Representatives, 90th Congress, 2d Session (U.S. Government Printing Office, 1968).

[2] Federal Deposit Insurance Corporation, *Accounts and Deposits in All Commercial Banks: National Summary, June 30, 1970* (Washington, D.C., 1972) gives a complete set of concentration data by cities. See also *Private Financial Institutions,* and J. M. Guttentag and E. S. Herman, *Banking Structure and Performance* (New York: New York University Press, 1967).

[3] See W. G. Shepherd, *Market Power and Economic Welfare* (New York: Random House, 1970), ch. 6 and sources cited there.

[4] This emerges from inspection of financial ratings on bonds and stocks, interest rates actually paid on bonds, and other common indications in the financial and business press.

in line with the observable structure and outcomes.[5] Sharp differences in access to timely information do exist; they are used, and the resulting gains closely reflect these differences. The small investor is at the end of the grapevine, using delayed, third-hand information and naive concepts of reality. He cannot, as a rule, properly anticipate events better than can professionals with closer access. There are exceptions, of course: good and bad guesses occur on all sides. But the average outcomes clearly and strongly favor those with better information.

The Structure of Distribution. The best studies show that the inequality of income is sharp and scarcely changing.[6] But they deal only indirectly with the main elements of inequality. One must look at wealth and opportunity, not just income, and one must look at cohorts and intergeneration transfers, not just crude cross-sections.

We cannot review here the mass of information about basic inequality (more is said about it in section 6), but the underlying patterns of inequality are consistent, along the following lines. The inequality of wealth within cohorts is more marked even than income inequality.[7] It too is not receding. Direct inheritance is a significant factor in inequality among successive cohorts.[8] This is accentuated by the passing on of skills and access to financial careers for the children of wealthy families. Though we lack comprehensive studies, it is a safe preliminary conclusion that the social structure of family wealth is highly unequal and slow to change.[9] It is not eroded by taxation, despite formal appearances to the contrary.[10] Indeed, given the political economy of tax legislation and enforcement, it is reasonable to assume that taxes are neutral to the larger structure of holding and passing on

---

[5] The fact is a staple in the financial press; see also H. Manne, *Insider Trading and the Stock Market* (New York: Free Press, 1966).

[6] R. J. Lampmann, *The Share of Top Wealth-Holders in National Wealth, 1922–1956* (Princeton: Princeton University Press, 1962). Lundberg's polemical account also gives useful indications and sources; see F. Lundberg, *The Rich and the Super-Rich* (Seacaucus, N.J.: Lyle Stuart, 1968).

[7] See E. C. Budd, "Postwar Changes in the Size Distribution of Income in the U.S.," *American Economic Review,* May 1970, pp. 247–61, and sources cited there.

[8] See F. L. Pryor, "Simulation of the Impact of Social and Economic Institutions on the Size Distribution of Income and Wealth," *American Economic Review,* 1973, pp. 50–72, and sources cited there.

[9] Recall also Lundberg, *Rich and Super-Rich.*

[10] See R. Musgrave, ed., *Essays in Fiscal Federalism* (Wash., D.C.: Brookings Institution, 1965) and J. A. Pechman, *Federal Tax Policy,* rev. ed. (New York: Norton, 1971).

wealth. The tax laws, as enforced, are as likely to accentuate inequality as to abate it.

The magnitudes involved are large. Aliquot portions of the total national portfolio wealth would average on the order of $200,000 per "families"— on an intergeneration basis (see section 6), which translates into a large income stream. And the process is cumulative—above a portfolio level of about $300,000, one need not work for a living at all, and this wealth increases by itself. The income stream more than exceeds the average family income, and the law of compound interest applies to the surplus saved. Those with larger portfolios engage the talents of professional investment managers who normally can supply superior information and judgment. Although obvious, these points need stating here, because they do define the setting in which industrial wealth is created and may continue.

In fact, much of the structure of family wealth in the U.S. and elsewhere derives from market power in various forms. A recent conservative estimate puts the effect of monopoly on wealth at roughly a third of the observed disparity.[11] A fuller analysis would focus on the 1870–1930 period, when much of the present structure of family wealth was formed. It would measure the rate of further growth and transmission of this wealth, and its relation to the rise of newer fortunes. However, such analysis is still to be done—another research frontier—and so one can only note that market power has been a major source of wealth inequality, much of which now persists by inheritance of money and other advantages. Furthermore, as monopoly has grown more institutionalized in recent decades, the degree of turnover and fluidity in the upper wealth structure has probably declined.

This affects the degree of inequality of opportunity also. While inherent "talent" and other abilities are distributed virtually at random in the population, the opportunities for applying and benefitting from those talents are not. This is part of the great social problem of our era, in which the racial problems are but a tip of a much larger iceberg of social disadvantage. The career system is a large part of this problem, but only part. Opportunities may be more equal than in most other cultures, but they are nonetheless skewed. Therefore, greater equality of opportunity via industrial activity is an important objective, because it is not provided by the rest of the system.

[11] W. S. Comanor and R. H. Smiley, "Monopoly and the Distribution of Wealth," *Quarterly Journal of Economics,* 1975 (in press).

2 THE MAIN ELEMENTS OF MARKET STRUCTURE

We shall now try to form a correct image of market structure. The main elements were laid out in chapter 2. Here we shall try to place these elements in their true proportions.

The starting point is the link between market power and profitability. Profits are the test of company success—the payoff to each part of the firm's market position. It has seemed increasingly clear in recent years that market power does give rise to higher profitability. Until recently, research on the matter has mostly been applied to concentration ratios and to average rates of profit in whole industries. The findings have been very "soft," partly one suspects because it has not been possible to introduce other structural elements with any real precision.[12]

A more direct route is to measure the market shares of individual firms, and then relate them—and other elements—to their profitability. I have done this to some 245 of the largest U.S. industrial firms, using information for the 1960–69 period. They are not final data, as I have explained more fully elsewhere; nothing can be final in this field. But they do provide as good a set of detailed estimates as we now have available, to show the relative importance of the various elements of market structure.[13]

The model does not explore life-cycle and profits-growth choices (see sections 4 and 5). It assumes them to be randomly distributed among the firms in the panel. The analysis then gives first approximations for the yields for each firm. These could then be modified in light of life-cycle attributes of the industries.

Although I shall give here only the gist of the findings—enough to show the common patterns—even that involves some tedious technical detail. The model "explains" each firm's average 1960–69 profit rate on equity by several variables representing the firm's market position: the firm's own average market share (M), the combined share of the rest of the leading-firm group (G), its asset size (S), its advertising-intensity (A), and its growth rate (E). S and A are possible causes of high entry barriers protecting the firm from new

---

[12] Shepherd, *Market Power;* L. W. Weiss, "Econometric Studies of Industrial Organization," in M. Intriligator, ed., *Frontiers of Econometric Research* (Amsterdam: North-Holland, 1972).

[13] The earlier presentation of this model is in Shepherd, "The Elements of Market Structure," *Review of Economics and Statistics,* February 1972, pp. 25–37; a companion treatment on an industry basis is Shepherd, "The Elements of Market Structure: An Inter-Industry Analysis," *Southern Economic Journal,* April 1972, pp. 531–537.

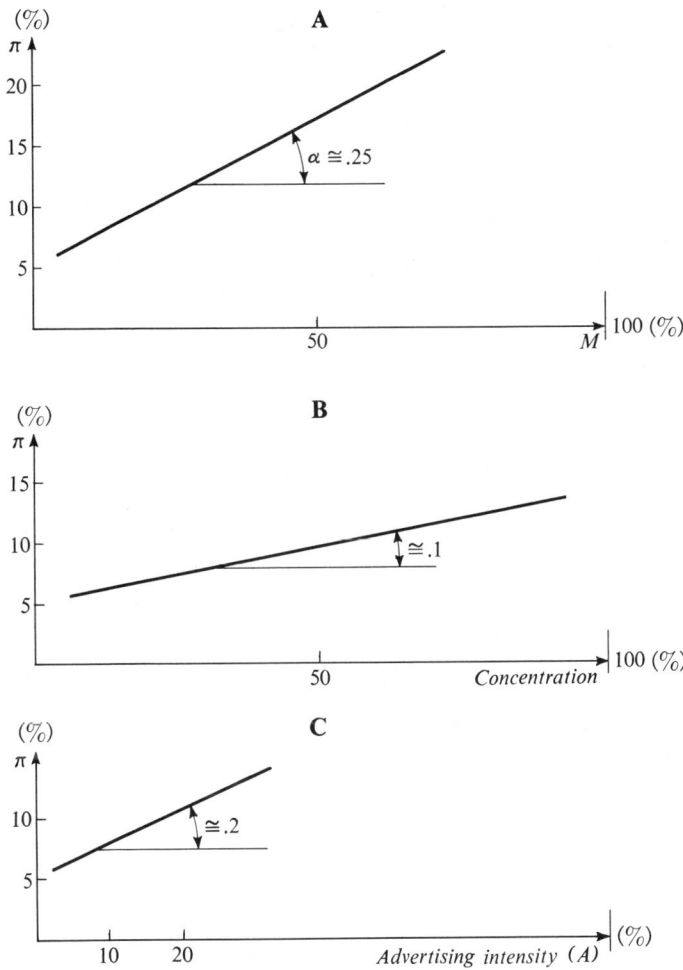

Figure 4.1 Estimated relationships between profitability and market share, concentration and advertising-intensity.

competition. The "height" of entry barriers can also be estimated in a general way, and so, like others, I will make use of dummy variables representing high barriers *(HB)* and moderately high barriers *(MB)* to the firms' main markets. The methods are explained further in Appendix A. The research is being developed further, but the basic patterns are already fairly clear. They are summarized in Tables 4.1–3 and Figure 4.1.

The strongest lesson is that the main element of market power is the

Table 4.1 Basic Analysis of Profitability of Large U.S. Industrial Firms, 1960–1969

Dependent Variables	Constant term	Market share M	Concentration C	Group G	Size (log of assets) S	Advertising intensity A	Growth E	R^2
Profit rate, 1960–69	5.13 (5.92)[a]	.250 (12.19)		.028 (1.60)	−.182 (1.34)	.021 (4.39)	.792 (3.93)	.554
Profit rate, 1960–69	4.38 (4.22)		.105 (5.57)		−.175 (1.06)	.024 (4.04)	1.28 (5.31)	.344

[a] *t*-ratios are in parentheses.

firm's own market share. The α coefficient is about .25, which means that there is on average a 2.5 percent higher rate of return on equity for each added 10 points of market share.[14] Our data cover shares only up to about 70 percent of the market, but the same pattern would be likely to hold through 100 percent. The .25 value for α persists even when subsets of years and firms are tested. Therefore the .25 coefficient appears to be an important general rule of thumb.

Now, four-firm concentration is also related to company profits, though much less tightly than is market share. Its coefficient is about .10, with a lower goodness of fit.[15] This may seem to show that oligopoly has at least

[14] The importance of market share is also confirmed by more recent work, using confidential company data: see S. Schoeffer, R. D. Buzzell and D. F. Heany, "Impact of Strategic Planning on Profit Performance," *Harvard Business Review,* March–April 1974, pp. 137–45.

Bradley T. Gale has tried to factor out the possible interaction between market share, concentration and barriers. "Market Share and Rate of Return," *Review of Economics and Statistics,* November 1972, pp. 412–24. Yet his results are statistically faint (with low values for the key R^2 and *t*-ratios). Also his data on market shares and concentration appear to be on a national basis, thereby involving error and possible bias from ignoring regional and local markets in many industries. The possibility of interaction clearly invites further research. Note that Figure 4.3 explains some of the scattering of observed M values around the fitted functions (even apart from measurement errors and purely random shifts). In any given period, some firms with an observed M value are in transit up or down, in line with their $\pi \Delta M$ choices. Their observed π values will diverge from the πM function, even though they will conform to it when they come to rest. In this sense, the closeness of fit that would obtain for constant-M equilibrium conditions is understated. Therefore, the true πM relationship is closer than empirical tests shown. Moreover, fitted α values will be biased below the actual α levels, because of this transitory element. Still, we may take .25 as the best presently available estimate of α, even though I expect that improved testing would find it closer to .3 or .35.

[15] This is closely consistent with findings by Collins and Preston, Weiss and many others; see L. W. Weiss, "Econometric Studies."

Table 4.2 Analysis of Profitability: By Subgroups of Firms

Dependent Variables	Constant term	Market share	Concentration	Group	Size	Advertising-intensity	Growth	R^2
125 Producer-Goods Firms								
Profit rate, 1960–69	6.41 (6.01)[a]	.155 (6.00)		−.010 (0.50)	.141 (0.97)	.046 (1.61)	.705 (3.73)	.459
Profit rate, 1960–69	6.33 (5.11)		.038 (1.82)		.147 (0.87)	.077 (2.36)	1.03 (4.91)	.276
120 Consumer-Goods Firms								
Profit rate, 1960–69	3.20 (2.53)	.323 (10.74)		.069 (2.61)	−.592 (2.40)	.010 (1.58)	1.99 (4.34)	.649
Profit rate, 1960–69	2.03 (1.28)		.171 (5.83)		−.548 (1.77)	.005 (0.65)	2.75 (4.89)	.448
50 Firms in "old industries"[b]								
Profit rate, 1960–69	3.70 (0.87)	.524M (2.09)	−.010M^2 (1.36)		−.285S (0.97)		.152E (2.88)	.420

[a] t-ratios are in parentheses.
[b] The industries are steel, meat-packing, glass, rubber, oil and copper.

some influence; perhaps, as some believe, leading firms set high profit rates for the *entire* industry. But that is probably an illusion. The role of the "rest of the oligopoly group"—variable G—turns out to be quite weak statistically, as Figure 4.1c shows. Variable G shows the role of the leading-firm group after the firm's own market share has been filtered out. A clear example of this is the automobile industry. General Motors ($M = 45$) had a rate of return at 17 percent; Chrysler's ($M = 16$) rate of return was 9 percent. To treat them as mere comembers of the oligopoly group ($C = 88$ percent) would mask the sharp differences between them in their market power. Therefore concentration, or oligopoly, is not to be regarded as a major *cause*

Table 4.3 The Role of Entry Barriers as an Element of Structure

Dependent Variables	Constant term	Independent Variables					
		Market share	Group	High barrier	Medium barrier	Growth	R^2
All 245 Large Firms							
Profit rate, 1960–69	4.58	.251	.001	2.45	1.55	.925	.528
	(4.60) [a]	(11.81)	(0.05)	(2.84)	(2.64)	(4.36)	
202 Firms with Medium or Low Barriers							
Profit rate, 1960–69	4.49	.239	−.001		1.69	.881	.518
	(5.16)	(10.65)	(0.03)		(3.03)	(4.29)	
71 Firms with Low Barriers							
Profit rate, 1960–69	5.39	.175	.019			.807	.461
	(4.20)	(5.14)	(0.68)			(3.80)	

[a] *t*-ratios are in parentheses.

of market power. It is merely a summary of the shares of the leading firms, each of which seeks monopoly profits primarily on the basis of its *own* market share. Market share is a determinant of market power, while concentration is only a descriptive statistic. The distinction is critical for certain policy choices (see chapters 6 and 7 below).

What about the notion that 50 percent is the key threshold level of concentration, the dividing line between tight and loose oligopoly, between excessive market power and effective competition?[16] The basis of three major proposals for deconcentrating U.S. industry has been to restructure those

---

[16] Recall this from Bain, *Industrial Organization;* Carl Kaysen and Donald F. Turner, *Antitrust Policy* (Cambridge, Mass.: Harvard University Press, 1959).

markets with concentration above 50 percent.[17] Yet here there is little econometric support for the threshold concept. Several tests with curved functions and analyses of low- and high-share groups were tried, with little result. The partial concentration-profitability relationships are linear, not with a stairstep at 50 percent concentration. Nor indeed does there seem to be even a moderate bend in the 40–60 percent range; curved functions had lower goodness of fit than linear ones. Better data might possibly change this, but for now the threshold simply lacks an empirical foundation with this general set of data.[18] This lack, too, has lessons for policy choices.

If bigness adds to market power, as seems likely, then asset size would show a positive sign in this analysis. Instead, its coefficient is weakly negative in Table 4.1, and in other studies too it is near zero.[19] This could mean that size is quite irrelevant to market power. Alternatively, it may be that size adds to market power, but also creates management difficulties big enough to soak up the excess profits. Further, it could reflect that the reduction in content with greater size leads to higher costs. This would depart from the neutral content hypothesis (in chapter 2) and comport, instead, with the possibility that improved content yields lower costs. Lacking better data, we simply cannot factor out these influences, but the net negative effect on π appears to be real. Still, we can use the working hypothesis that bigness per se does not sharply raise the degree of market power held by a firm.

Advertising, by contrast, appears definitely to be related to market power, or at least to high profits.[20] Actually, only rather few firms do really inten-

---

[17] Kaysen and Turner, *ibid.;* the "Neale Report," Report of the President's Committee to Study Antitrust Enforcement, released 1969; and Senator Philip A. Hart's Industrial Reorganization Act, filed in July 1972, which would establish a commission to investigate and arrange changes in seven major industries.

[18] The only hint of such a pattern is in an FTC study, *Food Manufacturing,* Technical Study No. 8, U.S. Government Printing Office, 1966. But it is weak and limited to certain food industries.

[19] See sources cited in Shepherd, "Elements of Market Structure"; also R. B. Mancke, "Causes of Interfirm Profitability Differences: A Reinterpretation of the Evidence," *Quarterly Journal of Economics,* May 1974, pp. 181–93.

[20] This is consistent with Comanor and Wilson, *Advertising and Market Power* (Cambridge: Harvard University Press, 1974), and L. W. Weiss, "Advertising, Profits and Corporate Taxes", *Journal of Political Economy,* 1969, pp. 421–30. However, when the panel is divided into producer and consumer goods industries, the advertising coefficient in the consumer goods panel fades markedly, to a barely significant level. This may reflect the negative *intra*-industry association in extremely advertising-intensive industries, but it does dilute the apparent robustness of advertising as an element in structure.

sive advertising, mainly in rather peripheral industries: cereals, soaps, toiletries, drugs, and beer. In these, advertising-intensity ranks as a potent element of structure. Yet its punch is limited, as its coefficient shows. Even at high degrees of advertising-intensity (say 20 percent of sales revenue), it goes with only a four-point rise in profit rate. This is much less than the 18 percentage points a 70 percent market share appears to add to the rate of return on equity.

Entry barriers need especially careful testing. To some (recall chapter 2), they are the critical element of structure, on which antitrust and regulatory policy should both mainly focus. Indeed, nearly all of the few antitrust "restructuring" efforts in the U.S. since 1913 have tried simply to open up entry, rather than to change market shares. Is this sound? Are barriers the main element of structure?

The answer appears to be that barriers are significant but secondary. High barriers go with only a two-point rise in profit rates (Table 4.3). This may understate, if barriers have not been estimated well. Still, the acid test is the difference between lines 1, 2, and 3 in Table 4.3. If entry conditions really control profitability (and market power), then market share will exert less influence among low-barriers firms than among all firms. Instead, the M coefficient is relatively constant regardless of entry conditions. Therefore, provisionally, the role of market share is not controlled by entry conditions. The M coefficient is slightly lower in line 3 of Table 4.3 than in line 2, suggesting that low barriers go generally with slightly lower profit rates than do higher barriers. This accords with other indications that barriers play some role. Also market shares may be causally related to barriers (recall chapter 2).

Yet market share remains as the primary element which embodies market power. Any separate role of barriers appears to reside mainly in the medium and low barrier range. Put oversimply: if market power is to be reduced much by cutting barriers, one must reduce barriers quite sharply, all the way down to "low" levels. Reducing them from high to moderate will make only a modest difference, unless one also changes market shares directly.

Next, do entry barriers shield high market shares? And conversely, where barriers are low, do high market shares tend to dwindle more than they do in high barrier markets? The 245-firm industrial panel again provides a relatively clear and broadly based set of data for testing these possibilities for the 1960–69 period. Some 88 of the 245 firms appear to have had significant changes in market share during the period. The analysis tests whether the height of entry barriers is related to these changes, both in simple regressions and in multiple regressions including other possible influences on market shares. As before, the entry barriers can only be represented by dummy variables, so that the answers are by no means final.

The results are in Table 4.4. A simple regression (number 1) shows no perceptible association whatever between barriers and market-share changes. In regression 2, initial-year market share is added, since there are strong indications from other analyses that initially extreme shares (high or low) do regress toward the mean over time. That is, unusually high market shares

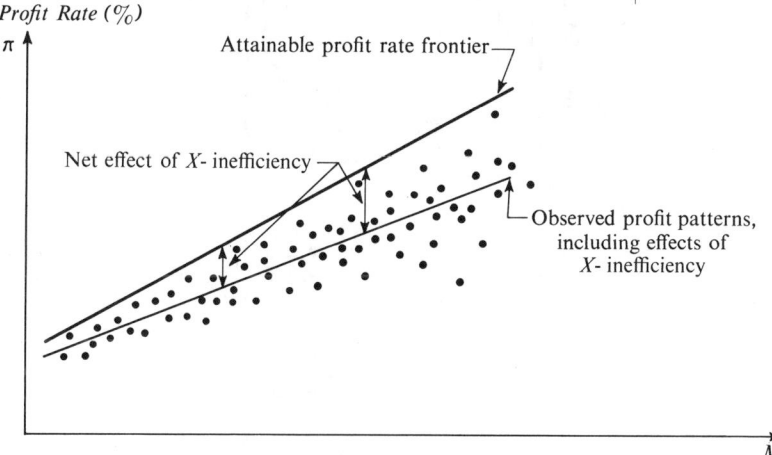

Figure 4.2 **Observed relationships may understate owing to X-efficiency.**

exhibit a "natural" tendency to dwindle. This tendency emerges here too, but it leaves unchanged the apparent irrelevance of entry barriers.

A fuller analysis is needed (see regression 3), since at least two other measurable influences may be present. One is initial-year profitability; where it is high, it may attract more intense competitive efforts by other firms, causing the firm's own market share to recede. The other is profitability during the rest of the period, which has been shown to have a strong positive association with changes in market shares. This association strongly suggests that firms strive to maintain market shares, rather than yield them up voluntarily over time as part of a long-run profit maximizing strategy (see below).

Table 4.4 Analysis of Changes in Market Share, 245 Large U.S. Industrial Firms, 1960–69

		Independent Variables						
Dependent Variable	Constant	High barrier	Medium barrier	Rate of return 1960	Market share 1961	Logarithm of asset size 1961	Advertis- ing sales ratio, 1961–68	Rate of return 1961–69	R^2
Change in market share	.586 (.53) [a]	−.265 (.35)	−.44 (.78)						.003
Change in market share	2.622 (1.77)	.347 (.43)	−.233 (.40)	−.002 (.42)	−.039 (1.63)				.021
Change in market share	−2.864 (1.49)	−.158 (.21)	−.523 (.97)	−.032 (6.45)	−.125 (5.43)	−.120 (.94)	−.006 (1.12)	.70 (9.42)	.299

[a] t-ratios are in parentheses.

In this expanded analysis (regression 3), barriers are still not associated with market-share changes. There are slight negative coefficients where positive ones would be expected, but they are not close to being significant either statistically or substantively.

On this evidence, barriers are apparently not related to the stability of market shares. Such a null conclusion can never be definitive, since we may simply have failed to measure either variable accurately. Yet it is the most reliable scientific indication we now have, judging both by the breadth of the interindustry coverage and the completeness of the model. Put another way: there would have to be startling changes in the underlying data in order to alter the results enough to suggest a powerful influence of barriers upon market-share stability. Pending that, it seems reasonable to presume that high and moderate barriers do not affect the vulnerability of the market shares of established firms, across the range of large-scale industries in the U.S..

The strong partial association between profitability and change in market share also indicates that changes in market share are a powerful determinant of company success. To the extent that it reduces market shares, entry will exert a strong influence on established firms' behavior. Trivial or slow or peripheral entry will scarcely affect established market shares and therefore behavior.

If it is important, entry should be a clear event, distinct from small-firm growth, intra-oligopoly shifts, or product innovation. It is *net new* capacity added by a *new* firm. An extensive search of industrial sources was made, to identify the main cases of such entry in U.S. industries since 1955.[21] Remarkably, only a small number of clear, significant entry cases emerged, despite common rhetoric about dynamic behavior among large corporations.[22] As Berry shows, most "entry" is so incremental as not actually to be entry—clear, rapid, substantial, by *new* firms.

---

[21] A wide range of trade, financial and general business press sources was used. Since these are not primary data, and because subjective judgment about the degree of "entry" was necessarily involved, this survey is tentative. For example, many cases of "entry" into chemicals markets are seemingly mere product extensions. See Jules Backman, *The Economics of the Chemical Industry* (New York: Manufacturing Chemists Association, 1970).

[22] These included Wilkinson's entry into razor blades with the stainless steel blade; Armour's entry into soaps with Dial soap; Proctor and Gamble's entry into paper markets; IBM's entry into copying equipment; and the rise of imports in steel and automobiles. The point is that these are included among the main identifiable cases, and that even if we have underestimated by an order of magnitude, the flow of entry is still an order of magnitude less than it is often believed to be.

The apparent scarcity of known cases of major entry in the last 20 years is more striking than one would have expected. The "entrants" were usually either established firms or imports, although the pure newcomer did occasionally occur. Entry can cause a sharp drop in profit rates and stock prices, but this does not always occur.

No definite lessons can be learned from this search, but several impressions may be worth noting.

1. Markets usually experience a series of small entries, exits, and shifts among fringe members, as well as moderate adjustments among the larger firms. Even the large cases of "entry" are often indistinguishable from the flow of small changes during a long initial period. Most cases of supposed "entry" are instead just rapid rises of smaller long-established firms.

2. Firms with high market shares frequently do become sluggish, thereby inviting both kinds of entry. However, the leading firms in the very largest markets (oil, automobiles, steel, computers, electrical goods) appear to have become virtually exempt from entry by takeover.[23]

3. Dominant firms commonly do not respond to entry until it is large and rapid, in the range of 15 to 25 percent of the market. The trigger is the perceived loss of market share. Often the entry has proceeded for many years before it is adequately perceived and responded to by the prior firm.

4. Only entry on a large scale (15 to 25 percent of the market) is sufficient to erode systematic price discrimination.

5. The "entrant" commonly must offer a different product, as well as a cheaper one, in order to gain market share. Successful entry by offering a homogeneous product at (or just below) current prices is rare, except for gradual entry by imports. In short, entry is normally combined with product innovation, and it is therefore more difficult to achieve.

6. Entrants tend to join in tight-oligopoly behavior and other devices to exclude further entry, rather than remaining as outsiders.

7. Large-scale entry is rare, but it does yield very high profits during the period of rising market share.

For a further test, we may ask how important entry has been in cutting concentration across the whole range of manufacturing industries. We take the 90 four-digit industries that are "large" and have "high" concentra-

---

[23] This was evident during the conglomerate merger wave of 1964–69, when second-level firms were under takeover threat. At no point were the very largest and market-dominant firms affected. Among the economic reasons for this, their great size was probably paramount.

tion.[24] Of these, 13 had significant declines of concentration during 1954 to 1970 (a drop of 5 concentration points or more). Data on these 13 are listed in Appendix A.

Six of these 13 industries appear to have had no important new entry during 1954–67, judging by a survey of industrial, trade, and financial sources. A seventh, metal cans, reflected the workings of an important antitrust consent decree, and was therefore man-made.[25] Moreover, the entry was primarily done vertically, by established can users. In the remaining six industries, significant new entry probably occurred. These accounted for about 5 percent of the total shipments in the panel of 90 "large" industries. But even in these, entry was not always a clear cause of the drop in concentration.

Therefore new entry cannot be said to have been a strong depressant on concentration in major industries. Rather one can say: in a few cases it is associated with a dwindling of the leading firms' market share, in other cases entry occurs without clear effect, and in still other cases entry does not occur even though inducements for it are very strong.

Some colleagues find these points difficult to accept, since they go against the effort in the last 20 years to put barriers in a central position. Yet some such revision is in order, for reasons that were explored in chapter 2. The whole concept of barriers and entry requires that entry be distinguishable from other threats to the firm, and that barriers and entry also be clearly defined and measurable. Neither of these hypotheses can be said, after 20 years of testing—indeed, after 75 years of theorizing about potential entry—to have strong support in logic or fact. Also, the attempt to attribute arcane notions of joint oligopoly strategies to possible entrants appears merely to direct attention toward secondary and vague elements.

Perhaps the study of entry and barriers is still so embryonic that their general role—if any—in market power is merely undefined. Of course, there are many *specific* cases of important barriers: drug patents, control of scarce ores, sales networks, copyrights, intensive advertising, and strategic loca-

[24] Large is defined as a value of shipments above $1.0 billion at any time between 1954–67. "High" concentration is a 4-firm ratio of 40 percent or more in 1954. Defense industries and heterogeneous catchall "industries" were excluded as being nontypical. Where data were not available for all of the 1954–67 period, the 1963–67 "trend" was extrapolated backward in line with information from a variety of other sources.

[25] See C. H. Hession, "The Metal Container Industry," in *The Structure of American Industry*, ed. W. Adams, 4th ed. (New York: Macmillan, 1971) and sources cited there.

tions are examples. Specific cases of actual entry, too, can easily be found. But these are special cases, not the basis for a general theory—and that general theory remains to be defined and tested out.

We can now sort out the relative importance of these structural elements as targets for policy treatments. Market share holds center stage. Advertising may be important in a special group of advertising-intensive industries, but its causal role is unclear. Oligopoly concentration—or leading-firm concentration—is relatively unimportant, once market share is taken into account, and its "critical" value of 50 percent lacks firm support. Entry barriers—to the limited degree that we can conceptualize and measure them—are also secondary in general, and they may operate mainly via high market shares. In short, concentration and entry barriers are not the proper general focus of policy treatment; high market shares are. Further research may modify the details of this picture, but it is not likely to change the basic patterns.

There is one proviso, long recognized in the literature: high profit rates may reflect a firm's higher efficiency or innovativeness, rather than monopoly gains. So our measures of "market power" might instead really measure certain aspects of "performance." [26] Indeed, in some cases this is no doubt quite so. But across the whole range of firms and industries that is probably not the case, and we are safe in relying on the econometric tests as first approximations. The best objective research indicates that the economies of scale in production are not strong in most industries (see below), and innovativeness too appears to taper off as market share rises above modest levels.[27] Also, X-efficiency may vary with market share,[28] but it probably varies directly (as in Figure 4.2), not inversely, so that the observed coefficient *understates* the effect of market share upon attainable profitability. Finally, the random component in the πM relationship appears to be small.[29]

To anyone not dedicated to finding economies of scale under every stone, it seems apparent that market power and pecuniary economies provide most or all of the observed πM relationship. This comports with good sense as

[26] That is, of course, the Chicago view and the contention of the leading firms themselves.

[27] F. M. Scherer, *Industrial Market Structure and Economic Performance* (Skokie, Ill.: Rand McNally, 1970); E. Mansfield, et al., *Research and Innovation in the Modern Corporation* (New York: Norton, 1971).

[28] H. Leibenstein, "Allocative Efficiency and 'X-Efficiency,' " *American Economic Review,* 1966, pp. 392–416; Scherer, *Industrial Market Structure;* Shepherd, "Economic Structure."

[29] This is shown in some detail below, in Section 5.

well as straightforward analysis. If reflects the wide importance of price discrimination by dominant firms. Such discrimination is often subtle and hard to discern. Yet it can yield remarkably high profit rates and also help retain market shares against competitive erosion. Therefore, the econometric analysis probably does show the general patterns of market power with reasonable fidelity.

One word of caution. The data and "model" may be defective. Also, they have tested only those elements which are presently testable. Other elements may matter but be unmeasured as yet, and so be wrongly slighted. One such possibility is the banking relationship. Another is vertical bargaining power. As is conventional, we have implicitly assumed purchases to be fragmented, which may not be generally true. Another possible element is "conglomerate" ties to firms outside the industry. These and others are simply untestable now, since the Census Bureau keeps the necessary data secret. Unless that limit is removed, one cannot be sure that the elements of structure have been analyzed adequately. But our grasp of them is improving.

Finally, note the clear apparent distinction between near-monopoly and oligopoly. They emerge as largely distinct problems, inviting different treatments. Admittedly they do shade into one another, over the range of industries. And near-monopolies often evolve into oligopolies, although one can identify at least 12 to 15 clear exceptions whose positions appear firm.

Yet a near-monopoly has a clear focus, on just one firm. Reducing its market share may yield clear performance gains and slight sacrifices of scale economies. Also, high market shares usually have high actual or potential profitability, and such cases usually are of higher policy priority than oligopolies.

By contrast, oligopolies offer less scope for restructuring, without running against minimum efficient scale. Their behavior is often inefficient and non-innovative. Fluctuations between high and low profitability frequently occur, and there is some tendency toward chronically low profit rates.

Therefore, near-monopoly is likely to invite *structural* changes as the policy goal, while oligopoly will instead need a change in *contraints* on management security and choices. In the twilight zone—of dominant firms with market shares of 40 to 50 percent—the policy choice is not clear. Indeed, we shall see that this ambivalence has paralyzed antitrust treatments in the past, especially in the United States.

3 RISK AND RETURN

We now consider a second possible element of profitability: risk. It could be important enough to affect many policy questions in this book, for differential risk is literally everywhere. Are profit rates "excessive"? What patent rewards are appropriate for the "risk" of invention and innovation? What would "comparable earnings" be under regulation? An understanding and measurement of risk could help answer these questions.

The hypothesis that risk is an important element of profitability, along with the rate of return, is plausible on logical grounds.[30] Yet risk-return relationships are proving elusive to define and measure. This is partly because a firm's risk and profit rate are both likely to be influenced by the market structure within which it operates.

The main body of research on risk and return, by Fisher and Hall, Cootner and Holland, and Conrad and Plotkin, has omitted structural elements altogether.[31] More recently, Caves and Yamey have noted that oligopoly interdependence is a possible determinant of risk, and in reply Fisher and Hall have added certain structural information to a regression.[32]

From this beginning, the natural next step is a more inclusive analysis, with a wider econometric coverage. First I shall discuss concepts of risk and market structure and derive testable forms. Then I shall consider several tests based on large U.S. industrial firms.

The basic premise is that rate of return and risk are both major components of total profitability. Investors adjust in response to both of them, so that equilibrium in capital markets is reached with equimarginal risk-adjusted returns obtainable from all securities.

Yet differences in market structure and other determinants may cause the appearance of differences among both the average and the marginal risk-ad-

---

[30] F. H. Knight, *Risk, Uncertainty and Profit* (Boston: Houghton Mifflin, 1971).

[31] See I. N. Fisher and G. R. Hall, "Risk and Corporate Rates of Return," *Quarterly Journal of Economics*, 1969, pp. 79–92, and sources cited there; P. Cootner and D. Holland, "Rate of Return and Business Risk," *Bell Journal of Economics and Management Science*, Fall 1970, pp. 211–26; and G. R. Conrad and I. H. Plotkin, "Risk/Return: U.S. Industry Patterns," *Harvard Business Review*, March/April 1968, pp. 90–99.

[32] R. E. Caves and B. S. Yamey, "Risk and Corporate Rates of Return: Comment," *Quarterly Journal of Economics*, 1971, pp. 513–17. F. M. Scherer has also noted that monopoly power and leverage may affect the Fisher-Hall results; see *Industrial Market Structure*, p. 205.

justed returns of firms. To evaluate such differences in true profitability, one must know both the rate of return and the degree of risk; high but unstable profit rates may offer a lesser degree of true profitability than do lower stable ones. The difference can be crucial in appraising the degree of market power held by firms, and the issue has become a staple in antitrust and regulatory proceedings and in broader debates over the ethical basis of the distribution of wealth.

The contrasting null hypothesis—that no risk premium exists either positively or as a normative criterion—can also be maintained. If risk-lovers balance out risk-averters in volume of funds on the market, that will make a premium unnecessary.[33] Also the intensity of risk preferences in the various groups may vary, perhaps enough to affect the premium. Thus several major plungers in the market may outweigh millions of small, risk-averse investors. Therefore, the existence of a positive risk premium is possible but not, a priori, certain.

But let us begin by hypothesizing that there is a positive risk premium. The core hypotheses state in combination that enterprise rates of return on capital reflect risk exposure as well as market structure, growth, and scale economies.[34] The partial risk-return relationship, in the presence of the other determinants, is what we wish to define and measure. Since the general process operates via investor choices among the whole universe of enterprises, interindustry patterns are only one aspect. Two firms in the same market can differ as freely in risk-return conditions as do two firms in different markets. Therefore the framework is general, not partial, equilibrium. Interindustry patterns are of interest (see Table 4.7), but they are only aggregations of the risk-return performance of the individual firms.[35]

We also wish to test directly the possible influence of market structure on risk, as suggested by Caves and Yamey. It is likely that a firm's profit insta-

---

[33] Recall D. D. Hester and J. Tobin, eds., *Risk Aversion and Portfolio Choice* (New York: Wiley, 1967), and H. Markowitz, *Portfolio Selection: Efficient Diversification of Investment* (New York: Wiley, 1959).

[34] Other determinants are possible but less plausible. Leverage in the firm's capital structure is one such possibility, but a recent study suggests that it has no causal role; see G. J. Hurdle, "The Relationships Among Leverage, Risk, Market Structure and Profitability: A Firm and Industry Study," (PhD dissertation, Ann Arbor: The University of Michigan, 1972).

[35] This is also discussed and given a preliminary test in Shepherd, "The Elements of Market Structure."

bility will be related positively to those elements of its market position which underlie market power.

The two basic equations are therefore:

$$\text{Rate of return} = f(\text{Risk, Market structure, Growth, Scale Economies}), \quad (4.1)$$

and

$$\text{Risk} = f(\text{Market structure}).$$

Even with perfect data it might be impossible to unravel the possible collinearity among the determinants. In fact—once again—the data are incomplete and imperfect. For a pooled analysis across industries, reliable measures of scale economies are not available. I assume that the net role of these is nil, as a first approximation, in this context. There is empirical support for this assumption (see below). Moreover, most of the firms included here in the empirical tests are likely to be above minimum efficient scale, owing to the method of selection (see Appendix A). Omission of scale economies might therefore not bias the results seriously.

Risk presents serious measurement problems. It is represented here by the variation of the profit rate over time (V), following Fisher and Hall.[36] True uncertainty risk in the Knightian sense is the uninsurable probability of default, an attribute that has various possible dimensions: default on dividends, or interest, or capital repayment. Fluctuation in profit rates over time is likely to vary with all of these, but it is only one element of total risk exposure. Admitting that it is an imperfect variable, we hope that it does not introduce bias.

The market structure (or power, or position) of the firm consists of several

---

[36] An alternative is the variation of profit rate around its trend during the period. Since trends are ordinarily not predictable, and a downtrend is itself a "risk" *ex ante,* it seems preferable not to factor out the trend when measuring profit variation. Regressions were run on both bases; variation around trend showed consistently less robust results than unadjusted variation.

A third alternative is to include the "Beta" coefficient—a normalized measure of covariability between the return on an asset or portfolio and returns on all risky assets as a whole. "Beta" has become popular in analyzing the risks and returns of securities in the stock markets; see Michael C. Jensen, ed., *Studies in the Theory of Capital Markets* (New York: Praeger, 1974). Beta may reflect company risk, but it does so at one remove; it also reflects shifts in investor appraisals and other secondary stock market factors. Variability in π is probably a more direct and simple estimator of the basic economic risk of the firm. Further research may clarify the issue.

possible elements, as already clarified in section 2 above. They make up the basic model to be tested.[37] The equations for estimation are:

$$\pi = a + bV + cM + dG + eS + fA + gE \qquad (4.3)$$

$$V = aC + bS + cA \qquad (4.4)$$

For comparison, estimation is also done with C interchanged for M and G.

Now to the tests. In their second paper, Fisher and Hall included firm size and eight-firm concentration to represent structure in an equation roughly parallel to equation 4.3, with data from 88 firms. These inexact structural variables turned out not to be statistically significant; a sharp rise in R^2 came almost entirely from the growth variable.

By contrast, the present analysis (see Tables 4.5 and 4.6) confirms the importance of market structure in whatever risk-returns relation may exist. The key result in Table 4.5 is that the partial association between profit rate (π) and variation (V) is nil or possibly negative, rather than positive. The structural coefficients conform closely to the patterns from earlier tests, with M and G more informative separately than when they are combined as C. Fisher-Hall's "risk premium" is conspicuously absent, apparently because the structural determinants are now more fully represented.[38] The seeming irrelevance of concentration in their model probably arises from two causes. First, their sample is more weighted toward producer-goods firms, for which concentration is a relatively weaker determinant (see line 4, Table 4.5). Second, their 1950–64 period included more recession years—during which the C coefficient will be further depressed—than the 1960–69 period.

The correct interpretation apparently is that "risk premiums" estimated in the past appear to have reflected, instead, structural differences.

This is further attested by Table 4.6, where several structural relations with profit variability are estimated. The primary influence is—as Caves and

---

[37] Fisher and Hall also include as an independent variable the price–earnings ratio of the firm's common stock, to reflect "among other things, investors' appraisal of managements' competence and effectiveness." Since in fact it may reflect so many characteristics interrelated with expectations, profitability and structure, it seems preferable to omit it in analysing objective structural elements.

[38] For similar conclusions from an alternative approach, see G. W. Douglas, "Risk in Equity Markets: An Empirical Appraisal of Market Efficiency," *Yale Economic Essays,* Spring 1969, pp. 3–45. F. R. Edwards and A. A. Heggestad, "Uncertainty, Market Structure, and Performance in Banking," *Quarterly Journal of Economics,* August 1973, pp. 455–75, suggest a more definite risk-return relationship, but again, the results are not highly robust.

Table 4.5 Analysis of Partial Risk-return Relationships, in the Presence of Structural Elements. Large U.S. Industrial Firms, 1960–69

		Independent Variables							
Dependent Variable	Constant term	Profit variation (V)	Market share (M)	Group (G)	Concentration (C)	Size (S)	Advertising-intensity (A)	Growth (E)	R^2
All 245 Firms									
π 1960–69	5.550 (5.57)[a]	−.016 (.71)	.249 (12.12)	.028 (1.63)		−.197 (1.44)	.205 (4.13)	.820 (3.99)	.555
π 1960–69	5.421 (4.52)	−.037 (1.35)			.110 (5.86)	−.252 (1.53)	.214 (3.57)	1.261 (5.21)	.352
125 Producer-goods Firms									
π 1960–69	6.219 (4.84)	.019 (.65)	.155 (5.99)	−.010 (.50)		.162 (1.08)	.049 (1.68)	.682 (3.55)	.461
π 1960–69	6.124 (4.12)	.018 (.55)			.038 (1.82)	.167 (.97)	.079 (2.40)	1.007 (4.71)	.278
120 Consumer-goods Firms									
π 1960–69	4.395 (3.12)	−.046 (1.40)	.316 (10.66)	.077 (2.81)		−.647 (2.66)	.007 (1.04)	1.992 (4.26)	.649
π 1960–69	3.748 (2.18)	−.084 (2.11)			.181 (6.34)	−.657 (2.22)	−.001 (.10)	2.674 (4.79)	.474

[a] *t*-ratios are in parentheses.

Table 4.6 Market Structure and Profit Variation, Large U.S. Industrial Firms, 1900–69

Dependent Variable	Independent Variables					
	Concentration (C)	Market share (M)	Group (G)	Size (S)	Advertising-intensity (A)	R^2
All 245 Firms						
Profit Variation	.242 (5.74)[a]			.184 (.41)	−.050 (3.05)	.134
Profit Variation		.186 (3.02)	.275 (5.49)	.158 (.35)	−.050 (3.01)	.127
125 Producer-Goods Firms						
Profit Variation	.256 (5.09)			.011 (.02)	−.023 (2.15)	.084
Profit Variation		.278 (3.37)	.245 (4.13)	.015 (.03)	−.024 (2.17)	.083
120 Consumer-Goods Firms						
Profit Variation	.210 (3.03)			.819 (1.02)	−.055 (2.48)	.133
Profit Variation		.102 (1.08)	.285 (3.47)	.768 (.96)	−.058 (2.63)	.106

[a] *t*-ratios are in parentheses.

Yamey suggest—the degree of oligopoly interdependence, as represented by C. The G coefficient is further confirmation: it reflects the relative instability of firms that face a relatively large and powerful group of other leading firms. The apparently positive M coefficient arises primarily in the producer-goods subset; this too fits conventional hypotheses about dominant firm responses to accelerator-induced fluctuations in homogeneous-goods markets. Advertising intensity, as expected, appears to insulate against profit instability; absolute size does not, by contrast.

In short, it appears that (1) true risk has not been measured by yearly shifts in π, and/or, (2) it does not in fact command the premium that has conventionally been assumed.

At present, both conclusions are attractive. The major implication is strong: no proven basis for allowing risk premiums in policy evaluations and actions yet exists. Until further—presumably different and better—research is done, the notion that a risk factor is profitability is purely speculative.

There is another more direct lesson for those who calculate risk-adjusted rates of return for industries. These will be subject to error unless the differing market positions of the member firms are allowed for. Unweighted averages, and regression-generated estimates which lack structural determinants (as do Fisher and Hall's), both may contain serious bias.

Large interindustry differences in average "risk-compensated" profit rates may exist and persist. Weighted averages for firms in the large-corporation analysis are shown in Appendix A; Table 4.7 briefly compares my results

Table 4.7 A Comparison of "Risk-Adjusted" Rates of Return

Industry	Risk-Discounted Rate of Return (π minus average yearly shift)	
	Fisher-Hall 1950–1964 [a]	Shepherd 1960–1969
Toiletries		25.0
Photographic		16.5
Drugs	16.6	17.1
Soft drinks		15.2
Office machinery	7.3	15.2
Automobiles	7.6	11.3
Tobacco		12.6
Electrical machinery	8.6	11.9
Soaps and detergents		12.1
Rubber	10.2	10.5
Grain milling		10.0
Petroleum	10.3	9.9
Containers		8.2
Glass		8.3
Steel	7.1	5.9
Meat packing		4.2

SOURCE: Table A.3.

[a] Fisher-Hall reported results for only 7 of the industries included here.

with those of Fisher and Hall.[39] A risk "premium" of $1/2\ V$ intuitively seems to be quite large enough, but adjusted rates based on V are used in Table 4.7. As expected, the "risk-adjusted" profit rates do not cluster; instead they fan out over a wide range. Two specific cases, automobiles and office machinery (which is mainly computers), show distinctly smaller risk-premiums and higher risk-adjusted profit rates than Fisher and Hall reported.

[39] The coverage of firms may differ from Fisher and Hall's, but the resulting error need not bias the comparison. Weighted averages are the appropriate basis because the Fisher-Hall estimates based on industry dummy variables are not statistically significant in most cases.

Concepts for Policy Choices

This reflects primarily the use of weighted averages to give weight to the dominant firms (Fisher-Hall weighted all firms equally). Differences in the time periods and in the companies included are less important.

These recalculated rates conform more closely than Fisher and Hall's do to specialists' appraisals of risks and returns. Thus, profitability in office machinery, automobiles, and electrical machinery is no longer rated about the same as in the steel industry, but about double or higher. Such a difference is, to oversimplify slightly, that between competitive and monopoly profit rates. These three industries are among the most sensitive and important cases for industrial policy. That Fisher and Hall's technique clearly misrepresents the probable profitability in several major industries shows once more that what we know about risk and return is still highly provisional and requires careful handling.

4 THE RATE OF DECLINE OF MARKET POWER: LEADING INSTANCES

Having gotten the elements in focus, we next ask how rapidly market power can be expected to fade away. The answer is decisive for many policy choices. A high rate of natural decay can reduce the net gains from policy steps while a low rate will correspondingly raise the expected yields. There have been wide divisions of opinion on the matter. Marshall, Schumpeter and, more recently, Stigler and others have regarded market power as transient, perhaps even yielded up voluntarily. At the other extreme, a variety of specialists have seen monopoly, once established, as virtually permanent or even likely to grow further.

There are two main ways to test these possibilities scientifically. First, one can test how fast the past cases of high known market power have faded. This is not easy, since antitrust and other policies have been at work on some of them (as chapter 7 will explore), and good data are scarce. Still, the main cases can be approximated for 1910, 1948, 1973. We shall try to determine if the rate of erosion has been rapid, and if it has changed as the decades have passed. Then we shall consider the relative duration of market power in the U.S. and Britain. The second approach is to estimate the general processes of change across a wide cross-section of industries (see section 5).

In tables 4.8 and 4.9 I have tried to include the known instances of dominant firms—with market shares of 50 percent or above—among the largest manufacturing industries and firms. This is a complex task, since good data are often absent and the extent of the market is often difficult to define. The sources, criteria, and basic calculations are discussed in Appendix B. I readily admit that further research may alter the measures, perhaps markedly in some cases, and expand or shrink the list of firms. It will surely refine these crude indicators. For showing the main directions and amounts of change, however, these estimates are perhaps a workable beginning. I have tried to cleanse them of any strong bias either way.

Table 4.8 Changes in Market Position, Leading Dominant Firms, 1910–1935

Firm	Degree of market power 1910 [a] (est. %)	Estimated assets, 1909–10 [b] ($ million)	Degree of market power 1935 [a] (est. %)	Change in market power 1910–35 (est. %)	Specific policy cause of change? [c]
United States Steel	22.0	1,804	17.0	− 5.0	(Informal antitrust effects?)
Standard Oil (New Jersey)	27.0	800	15.3	−11.7	1911 case
American Tobacco	27.0	286	13.3	−13.7	1911 case
International Harvester	25.5	166	15.0	−10.5	(Informal antitrust effects?)
Central Leather	21.0	138	6.0	−15.0	
Pullman	29.3	131	27.0	− 2.3	
American Sugar	21.0	124	14.7	− 6.3	
Singer Manufacturing	25.7	113	19.7	− 6.0	
General Electric	23.0	102	21.8	− 1.2	
Corn Products	21.0	97	17.3	− 3.7	
American Can	22.0	90	19.7	− 2.3	
Westinghouse Electric	20.5	84	19.3	− 1.2	
E. I. du Pont de Nemours	29.5	75	13.5	−16.0	
International Paper	18.5	71	11.0	− 7.5	
National Biscuit	18.5	65	11.0	− 7.5	
Western Electric	33.0	43	33.0	0	Exemption in 1913
United Fruit	27.0	41	27.0	0	
United Shoe Machinery	31.7	40	30.5	− 1.2	
Eastman Kodak	29.5	35	29.5	0	
Alcoa	32.9	35	29.5	− 3.4	

SOURCE: see Appendixes B and C.

[a] Based on estimated market shares and entry barriers: See Appendix B.
[b] Based on A. D. H. Kaplan, *Big Enterprise in a Competitive System,* rev. ed., (Wash. D.C., Brookings Institution, 1965), ch. 7.
[c] Based on Appendix C and other sources.

Table 4.9 Changes in Market Position, Leading Dominant Firms, 1948–1973

Firm	Degree of market power 1948 (est. %)	Assets, 1948 [a] ($ million)	Degree of market power 1973 (est. %)	Change in market power 1948–1973 (est. %)	Specific policy cause of change?
General Motors	22.0	2,958	21.8	− .2	
General Electric	20.5	1,177	20.5	0	
Western Electric	33.0	650	32.6	− .4	Exemption
Alcoa	28.0	504	17.0	− 1.1	Remedy of 1950
Eastman Kodak	27.0	412	27.0	0	
Procter & Gamble	19.5	356	19.5	0	
United Fruit	27.0	320	22.0	− 5.0	Remedy
American Can	20.0	276	14.8	− 5.2	Remedy of 1951
IBM	29.5	242	23.5	− 6.0	Consent decree?
Coca-Cola	22.0	222	19.5	− 2.5	
Campbell Soup	28.2	149	28.2	0	
Caterpillar Tractor	19.5	147	19.5	0	
Kellogg	19.5	41	18.3	− 1.2	
Gillette	24.5	78	24.5	0	
Babcock and Wilcox	22.0	79	19.5	− 2.5	
Hershey	25.8	62	23.5	− 2.3	
du Pont (cellophane)	30.5	65	22.0	− 8.5	Lapse of patent?
United Shoe Machinery	29.2	104	18.5	−10.7	Remedy

SOURCE: see Appendixes B and C.

[a] Sources: A. D. H. Kaplan, *Big Enterprise;* Moody's *Industrial Manual;* and G. W. Stocking and W. F. Mueller, "The Cellophane Case and the New Competition," *American Economic Review,* 1955, pp. 29–63.

For Table 4.8, the year 1910 is a better starting date than, say, 1900, because in 1900 many of the trusts were brand new and obviously fated for a sharp decline. By 1910 most of this transient shrinkage had run its course (e.g., in sugar and tin cans). Also, 1910 is squarely in the first wave of "trust-busting" cases, and so it is a good point for evaluating what was tried and achieved with those actions (see chapter 7). For Table 4.9, the logical date is 1948. It avoids the special conditions of the 1930s, and it is at the onset of the post–World War II "modern" industrial period. The 1910–35 and 1948–73 periods therefore provide two 25-year intervals for comparing early and recent industrial experience with market power.

The main lesson seems reasonably clear. The "natural" decline of leading dominant firms was much more rapid in 1910–35 than in 1948–73. I have used a single approximate index of market power in the effort to test this. The index is the predicted profit rate of the firm, based on estimates of its market share and the "height" of entry barriers into its markets. A 100 percent market share indicates an expected profit rate of 25 points; a high entry barrier adds two more points. This is based on the coefficients reported in section 2 above.

During 1910–35, four of the 20 firms in Table 4.8 were touched by strong policy influences. Three—Standard Oil, American Tobacco, and du Pont—underwent division, while Western Electric continued under its official antitrust exemption. The remaining 16 firms declined an average of 4.6 points in the "market power index." This is equivalent to a shrinkage of nearly 20 points in market share. Perhaps some antitrust attempts that failed in the courts (e.g., International Harvester, U.S. Steel) did in fact exert some downward effect, but that is difficult to appraise.[40]

During 1948–73, seven of the 18 instances can be said to have been reduced by policy. For the other 11, the decline of market power was only 0.8 index points on average, corresponding to a market-share shrinkage of 3 points. These declines were mainly among the lesser firms. The largest nine firms hardly changed at all, apart from specific policy effects.

During 1948–73, certain other firms rose to join the list, which stood in 1973 roughly as shown in Table 4.10. The newcomers are primarily IBM in computers, Xerox, aircraft, drug firms, and two major newspapers. Table 4.10 also indicates the relative permanence of these firms. This can be compared with the findings about the erosion of market shares and profit rates in the next section.

Finally, one can learn about the persistence of U.S. structural monopoly by comparing it with Britain, another advanced industrial economy.[41] One first identifies the main cases of high structural monopoly in each country and screens the two sets of cases down to equal quantitative importance, such as the same share of total manufacturing activity. Even if this can be done only approximately, it may permit one to note any gross differences in the newness or instability of structure in the two sets of cases. It is generally

---

[40] There are hints of this in S. N. Whitney, *Antitrust Policies*, 2 vols. (New York: Twentieth Century Fund, 1958), in his discussions of the various cases. It also emerges from more detailed sources.

[41] This passage draws on my "Structure and Behavior in British Industries with U.S. Comparisons," *Journal of Industrial Economics*, November 1972, pp. 35–54.

known that certain major British industries have undergone substantial structural changes in the last two decades, some of them still in process. Therefore the hypothesis is that leading British cases of high structural monopoly are newer and less firmly established than those in the U.S.

The two sets of industries are given in Appendix B. They reflect primarily concentration and also, in some cases, various specific entry barriers and

Table 4.10 Leading Dominant Firms and Their Background, as of 1974 [a]

Firm	Markets	Market share (%)	Barriers	Degree of market power	Present position dates back to about
General Motors	Autos, locomotives, buses	55	High	21.8	1927
IBM	Computers, typewriters	70	High	23.5	1954
Western Electric	Telecommunication equipment	98	High	32.6	1880s
General Electric	Heavy electrical equipment	50	High	20.5	1900
Eastman Kodak	Photographic supplies	80	Medium	27.0	1900
Xerox	Copying equipment	85	High	29.3	1961
Procter & Gamble	Detergents, toiletries	50	Medium	19.5	1940s
Boeing	Aircraft	45	High	19.5	1950s
McDonnell-Douglas	Aircraft	45	High	19.5	1968
United Aircraft	Aircraft engines	60	Medium	22.0	1950s
Coca-Cola	Flavoring syrups	50	Medium	19.5	1920s
Campbell Soup	Canned soups	85	Medium	28.2	1920s
Gillette	Razors, toiletries	70	Medium	24.5	1910
Kellogg	Dry cereals	45	Medium	18.3	1940s
Times Mirror	Newspaper	70	High	23.5	1960
New York Times	Newspaper	75	High	23.5	1966

SOURCES: Appendix B.

[a] A number of drug firms are omitted, for lack of reliable data, even though they are known to have high market power.

other elements of structure, drawing on a wide range of sources. The selections are not based on mechanical criteria for combining the various elements; no such basis exists. However the inclusions probably embody no substantial sample bias and can be regarded as reasonable consensus choices. Both groups account for about 25 percent of total sales in their respective manufacturing sectors.

The comparison lends support to the hypothesis. Nearly half of the British cases (accounting for three-fourths of the group's total sales) have had major changes in the 1960s. The U.S. cases are mostly of pre-1955 vintage; only two cases—steel and copying equipment—were altered during the 1960s (and Xerox now seems extremely well set as the dominant firm in copying equipment). The differences are most marked in the largest cases—automobiles, computers, electric equipment, telephone apparatus (a legally ratified monopoly in the U.S.) and oil. In several important U.K. cases (automobiles, tobacco and cement) the shares of dominant firms have shown a repeated tendency to decline over time. The major recent cases of rising concentration in major U.K. industries have tended to be subject to potential public-agency buyer constraints and detailed intervention (e.g., electrical and telecommunications equipment, steel, and computers). And there has been in U.S. industry nothing like the incursion of U.S. and other branches into major U.K. industries (e.g., in oil, automobiles and drugs).

To summarize, the British instances of high structural monopoly are newer, probably less stable, and potentially more subject to direct policy constraints than is the comparable U.S. set of industries. The U.S. monopoly problem does not appear to be less severe, either qualitatively or quantitatively. The leading U.S. cases appear to be more firmly established and freer from policy constraints than are their British counterparts.

Why has the predicted rate of decline for the major dominant firms gone down in recent decades? There are several possible influences, but none of them seems sufficient. One reason may be a lessening of flexibility in financial markets. Banker-firm relationships are now of long standing for the older dominant firms, and the capability of capital markets to foster aggressive new competitors may have declined. Banking markets now appear to be more stable than they were during 1900–1920, especially as the role of merchant banks has dwindled.[42] Only in the middle 1960s, during the brief run of the newer conglomerates, were certain banks willing to back newcomers. But that too has subsided, so the basic effects of financial markets on industry remain. As a result (recall chapter 2), existing dominant firms are favored. Though this favoritism may not affect the largest firms strongly, its tendency is to stabilize.

Another reason may be that antitrust limits on mergers may also have hardened market structure. Between 1958 and 1966, the limits became quite

---

[42] Banking regulation adopted in the 1930s has also solidified structure: see A. Phillips, "Competitive Policy for Depository Financial Institutions" in *Competition and the Regulation of Industry,* ed. Phillips (Wash., D.C.: Brookings Institution, 1974) and sources cited there; also chapter 6.

Concepts for Policy Choices 118

strict, so that mergers creating more than 10 percent of any significant market were likely to be stopped.[43] But informal limits came earlier, especially with the passage of the Celler-Kefauver Act in 1949. After the 1920s, few mergers with a large horizontal impact occurred (except in banking). Therefore dominant firms have become freer from competitive challenge via mergers among lesser firms. The rise of Continental Can and Bethlehem Steel by mergers is not possible today. Internal growth is now virtually the only source of change in industry structure. Admittedly, one should be skeptical that lesser-firm mergers to "challenge" the leading firm would in fact yield much of a "challenge." Still, the possibility is there. And now a strict antimerger policy virtually rules it out, and so market structures perhaps have been correspondingly made more rigid.

A third reason for retention of high shares may be economies of scale. The best evidence so far is that scale economies explain only a relatively small portion of most of the major dominant-firm positions. (The main reasons for our ignorance are the Census secrecy rules and the lack of policy actions toward these cases since 1952.) That is the clear lesson from survivor tests, despite their evident faults.[44] Bain (in 1950) and Scherer (in 1973), have made probes using "engineering" estimates and the existing size arrays to indicate the optimal sizes and cost gradients.[45] While these probes are not exhaustive, and they covered less than 30 industries,[46] they do tend to affirm that scale economies are quite limited in most industries. The cost gradients, especially, are low.[47] However, because Bain and Scherer did not look at some of the leading cases of market power, there is a

[43] They are reprinted in Clair Wilcox and William G. Shepherd, *Public Policies toward Business* (Homewood, Ill.: Irwin, 1975), ch. 8. I participated in the preparation of the final version of these guidelines. They were meant to codify existing practice, not to establish it anew.

[44] This is discussed in my "What Does the Survivor Test Show About Economies of Scale?" *Southern Economic Journal,* July 1967, pp. 113–22.

[45] J. S. Bain, *Barriers to New Competition* (Cambridge, Mass.: Harvard University Press, 1956), and F. M. Scherer, "The Determinants of Industrial Plant Sizes in Six Nations," *Review of Economics and Statistics,* 1973, pp. 135–45.

[46] The main possible bias is that each firm's officials regard their own plant sizes as best; and, alternatively, that they are guided by current fashions in international practice, even though their own specific national conditions may favor different approaches. This second factor might explain at least part of Scherer's puzzling finding that stated size preferences appeared to be virtually uniform even among a range of sharply differing economies.

[47] Thus, in F. M. Scherer, Alan Beckenstein, Erich Kaufer, and Richard D. Murphy, *The Economies of Multi-plant Operation: An Internal Comparisons Study* (Cambridge, Mass.: Harvard University Press, in press) even at a size level only one-third of the inferred minimum optimal scale, the imputed cost levels are only slightly higher than at the minimum optimal scale.

presumption (but not a proof) that the average cost curve flattens out at low sizes even in the main problem industries.

Finally, several specific kinds of barriers now exist, and might seem to cause an increasing rigidity of dominant-firm positions. Patents are important in drugs and photocopying equipment. Advertising-intensity influences soaps and cereals. Sales networks are important in automobiles, computers, drugs, and soaps. But, as noted in chapter 2, these are simply a series of specific conditions, not a well integrated set of general factors. Nor is it clear that they are stronger than in earlier periods; patents and sales networks, for example, have long been important. Therefore they cannot yet be regarded as general explanations of the trend in structural hardness, even though each one may need considering in specific treatments.

5 THE RATE OF DECLINE OF MARKET POWER: GENERAL PROCESSES

For a scientific understanding of why market shares do—or do not—decline, one must analyze the erosion process more broadly. The key question is the relation between profitability and change in market share. Put crudely: does it pay firms to yield up their market shares, liquidating their monopoly positions? We will tackle the issue from several sides, with a good deal of technical detail.

Dominant firms may deliberately yield up their market shares over time, taking profits *now* as part of a long-run profit maximizing strategy (recall chapter 2). If so, and if time-preferences are relatively high, then the deliberate decline might be rapid and widespread. The literature divides on the question. Worcester and Stigler expect a high rate of decay. Neoclassical theory and direct observation of business motivation suggest instead that high profits are normally made via gaining market share, and that market share itself is a maximand for many firms.

The specific relationship between change in market share and current profitability is the basic test on the issue. A negative sign would suggest voluntary yielding; a positive sign would suggest a low rate of voluntary market-share decay. Table 4.4 offers estimates of this, using the panel of large firms during 1960–69. The 1960–69 period is probably much longer than the strategy period of most firms (recall chapter 2). Therefore, the average for the period would reflect the more lasting yield of making the change and then harvesting the subsequent profits. In effect, it would reflect moves along the basic share-profit relationship, not just along the share-time relationship. The first four right-hand variables each allow for a factor likely to affect changes in market share. An initially high profit rate would invite increased competitive pressure. (The one year used—1960—may contain some error or business-cycle influence, but on careful inspection these do not appear to be great.) A high initial share would be expected to be subject to the basic regression tendency toward the mean. Entry barriers caused by size and advertising-intensity are likely to help shield the established firms against losses of market share. With these factors filtered out, the declining-

Table 4.11 Analysis of Changes in Market Share Over Time, 245 Large U.S. Industrial Firms

Dependent Variable	Independent Variables					R^2
	Profit rate, 1960	Market share 1961	Size 1961	Advertising intensity 1961–68	Profit rate 1961–69	
ΔM	−.348 (6.62) [a]	−.121 (5.36)	−.280 (3.46)	−.005 (1.07)	.781 (9.75)	.293

[a] t-ratios are in parentheses

firm hypothesis posits a negative partial relation between Change in Share $_{1 \to n}$ and Profit rate $_{2 \to n}$; The probable collinearity between Profit rate $_1$ and Profit rate $_{2 \to n}$ does not affect the validity of the test.

The possible mutual relation between profitability and market-share changes is, on its face, quite clear in Table 4.11 (which is only one of a number of tests, also using various subsets). The background variables are as expected. High initial-year profits are associated with later cuts in market share; roughly, an extra three points of profit rate points imply a later share drop of one point. The central tendency from initial-year share is consistent but weak. Similarly, size and advertising-intensity have insignificant coefficients, suggesting that they do not insulate the firm from reductions in market share. This fails conspicuously to confirm what is often regarded as their strong protective role (recall also Table 4.4).

The key indicator is the coefficient of profitability during 1961–69. It is positive and highly significant in repeated testing. This tends to affirm the neoclassical hypothesis rather than the hypothesis of voluntary yielding of high shares. One must tread lightly here, for cause and effect are at least partly entangled. Indeed, all of the variables may be jointly determined or mutually interacting. Still, the pattern seems clear. The positive general relation is, of course, consistent with the fact that, in many real cases, dominant-firm shares do decline. The correct interpretation apparently is that such declines usually occur involuntarily and under stress. This implies that managerial preferences are usually strongly toward keeping or increasing market shares.

The coefficient of M_{1961} implies that high market shares undergo a steady natural decline; for an initial M of 75 percent, the rate of decline is 1.35 points per year. This rate of decay is independently confirmed by more precise data on Japanese industries for the 1952–66 period. For M values in the 50–75 percent range, the yearly rate of decline is approximately 1.5 points.[48]

The Japanese data also provide the only available basis for measuring the variance of shifts in market share. For cases over the whole range of "dominant firm" shares, from 30 to 75 percent, $\sigma\Delta M$ is approximately 3.0 points of market share for each period. As the sequence of periods lengthens, this variance appears to be damped. The Japanese data suggest provisionally that the variance of ΔM for a long period reaches a value of approximately 3 times the yearly variance of ΔM, as the long period reaches and exceeds 10 years. Variance levels this high indicate that stochastic shifts could affect M and π strongly for any sequence of periods; the random changes in market shares and profit rates *could* be large.

What does this all show? Taken together, b and the variance estimates indicate that the maintenance of high market shares during a sequence of periods is indeed an improbable departure from normal outcomes. The prob-

---

[48] The analysis is based on a unique data set on 211 Japanese industries which give sequential yearly market-share data for individual firms during 1952–1966. See Japanese Fair Trade Commission, *Industrial Concentration Ratios of Principal Industries, 1963–66* (Tokyo, 1968) and *Industrial Concentration, 1938–62* (Tokyo, 1964).

If Japanese industries are more dynamic and open to stochastic changes from foreign competition, then the observed changes might exceed those in U.S. industries. That indeed is suggested by the higher value of ΔM observed for Japanese industries. Yet the difference is slight, and it would not alter the substance of the conclusions below.

For $30 < M < 50$, the yearly decline is as expected, approximately half of that rate, at .71 points. The more precise form is $\Delta M_i = -.035 (M - 0.2)$, where a = $-.035$ and .2 is an approximation of the average market share in both the U.S. and Japanese data. The ΔM equation indicates that $\bar{M}$ approaches .2 asymptotically.

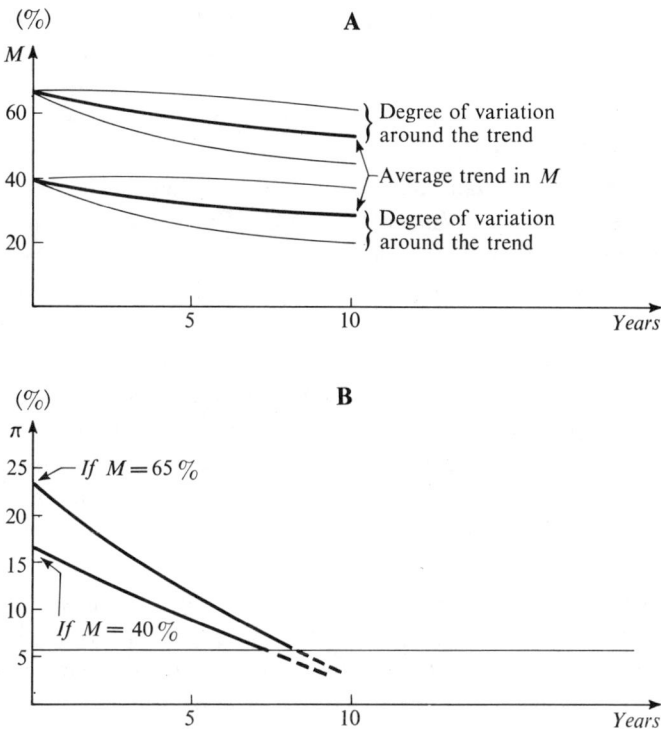

Figure 4.3 Estimated average trends in market share and profit rates, reflecting a process of decay.

abilities are portrayed in Figure 4.3, for initial market shares of 65 and 40 percent. After 10 years, expected market shares are down by 20 percent, and the probability of maintaining the original market share is less than .05. The process can be assumed to continue, and after 20 years the probability of M remaining at its original value through "luck" is vanishingly small.

The decline in profits is likely to be more rapid than this, as the vector of at least two effects. Successively lower market shares yield successively lower profit rates—as the basic static model has shown—and each decline in share itself causes a more rapid reduction in profit rate, as shown by the coefficient of Profits (1961–69). These static and comparative-static partial relationships are separately estimated, so it is not obvious what their combined effect on π over time would be. The direct effect of losing market share is likely to prevail during the onset of any sequence. Such a severity of the ΔM effect accords with common industrial experience, in which changes in market share (and absolute sales levels) cause sharp reactions in profit levels. Typically, a 10 percent change in sales causes a 40, 60, or 80 percent change in net income, etc., to which the financial press routinely attests every three months.

The simpler static relationship would eventually be expected to tend to offset it, as the sequence of ΔM effects on profit rate diverges—or plunges—increasingly below the static-equilibrium relationship. For example, a market share of 70 percent would be expected still to generate positive and perhaps high profit rates, even if market share has previously been declining slowly from 80 percent for a long interval.

These offsetting influences cannot yet be netted out with present data. A simple provisional hypothesis is that the ΔM effect operates until profit rate has declined to the bare competitive level, and then the profit rate will remain there until M stops declining significantly. On this basis, profit rate would normally decline to the minimum within 10 years for any initial M value within the range $.20 < M < .75$ (the panel of data does not extend above $M = .75$). The probability of maintaining an initial π value is, for any finite interval, even lower than the probability of maintaining the initial M value. This is axiomatically true if the ΔM effect operates to any degree.

The magnitude of this effect appears to be well above the possible loss of technological economies of scale caused by the decline in M (recall section 3). This can be verified for average conditions in manufacturing industries, with the Profit (1961–69) coefficient at .60 and the firm's ratio of invested capital to sales revenue at .5. If $-\Delta M$ reduces profits purely because of the loss of scale economies, then the implied elasticity of the average cost curve would be -3.0 (a ΔM of $-.01$ causing a 1.5 point reduction in π and a rise in average cost of .03). Recent studies indicate, by contrast, that the average cost gradient approaches zero at high market shares in the majority of markets. Even at low M levels, the gradient tends to be less than one-tenth of the imputed elasticity of -3.0.[49] The static long-run elasticity implied by α is lower, at $-.5$; this still exceeds the estimated cost gradients at high M values in most industries by an order of magnitude.

High market shares *are* usually eroded over time. The average decay process is strong enough to abate monopoly positions in the course of 20 to 30

[49] Recall Scherer, Beckenstein, Kaufer, and Murphy, *The Economies of Multi-plant Operation.*

years. Yet this rate is exceedingly moderate. And there are major exceptions, in which dominant firms maintain high market shares and profit rates for many decades.

In short, we have identified and estimated the tendency for high market shares and profit rates to decline. The implied declines in profit, in either a static or comparative-static analysis, are a multiple of the probable scale economies present when market share is high.

Provisionally and by default, the main component in α in *such abnormal cases* appears to be market power, as analyzed in chapter 2. The coefficients also provide a normative basis for evaluating, in real-world cases of continuously high M values, those parts of M and π which exceed "normal" values. Very roughly speaking, where high M and π values remain undiminished for 10 years, these excess parts approach the actual market share minus 20 percent and the actual profit rate minus the competitive profit rate. For a firm with $M = 60$ and $\pi = 20$ percent, the excess market share would be close to 40 points and that part of the profit rate which is excess would be about 12 percent (taking the competitive rate to be about 8 percent in recent years). Therefore we reach a strong conclusion: the more correct the "randomness" hypothesis is, the more it accentuates the abnormality of the familiar, long-standing dominant-firm cases.

This suggests that the value of the basic share-time choice coefficient—which was labeled β in chapter 2—is relatively low, compared to the static value of α. We can deduce the values of β that would be "neutral" to α, implying no net tendency either to sacrifice or seek market share.

To impute the most likely value of β from the estimated α, we reason as follows, using a declining market share to illustrate. During the transition period an additional margin of profit rate $\alpha \Delta M$ will be earned. But thereafter, π will be less by $-\pi = \alpha \Delta M$.[50] As r and the length of the planning period rise, the present value of the gain becomes relatively larger than that of the loss. Suppose for illustration that the rate of time discount (r) is 10

---

[50] The perpetual reduction in profit rate has a present value of approximately

$$PV_L = \sum_{2}^{n} \frac{-\alpha \Delta M}{(1+r)^n}$$

while the gain in π is, in present value, approximately

$$PV_G = \sum_{1}^{2} \frac{\alpha \Delta M}{(1+r)^n}$$

percent, the planning (or transitional) period is 5 years, and the terminal horizon is 20 years. On that basis, the β value which is neutral to an α value of .25 is .30. At r of .08, neutral β is .36; at r of .15, neutral β is .21. β just equals α at an assumed r of .13.

The imputed values of neutral β may appear to be sensitive to the length of the planning period, but in fact the sensitivity is less than it seems. A firm with a short period (say 2 years rather than 5) would also have a high r and a short terminal horizon, all because it is highly present-oriented. Such interactions between the three elements can be complex, but they would make the estimates less sensitive.

Therefore, a range of β between .20 and .40 is a plausible first approximation. Values far outside that would be unlikely, except possibly for special market types whose α may depart from the general value of .25. The comparative-static results suggest that β is in fact below the neutral range for many or most dominant firms. Losing market share is known to be associated with loss of profits (the direction of causation is not always clear). Therefore, it appears that in the normal case, managers attempt to maintain or increase market share.

It is not valid to use *ex post* measures of π and ΔM to estimate β, unless all disequilibrium elements can somehow be removed. Probably the only direct method for estimating β is to question managers directly about the tradeoffs they believe they face. These subjective values could differ from the objective tradeoffs, possibly with systematic biases, but they would still be perhaps the best possible estimaters. Whether they are feasible to obtain is another question, which can best be answered by practical trials.

In homogeneous-goods industries, β is possibly relatively high, because retaliation is easy and quick. This would accord with the sticky-price behavior often, if not always, observed in these markets. By contrast, β will be relatively low in advertising-intensive industries, because successful product differentiation is difficult for rivals and newcomers to reverse. Yet one may need to factor out the costs of advertising, as an "investment in goodwill," so that the "true" π during the planning period would be lower than it seems. Therefore the true β in advertising-intensive markets may not deviate from normal values.

The uses of this share-time relationship in guiding policy deserve a special emphasis at this point. Assume that it exists and can be measured, either in general form or as a set of values for industry types.

1. It would then establish a norm for evaluating actual profit rates and changes in market shares. The mass of firms will conform to the central pattern. The exceptional cases—especially those with high π and steady M values—will be more readily identified, and the degree of their divergence will be measured with some precision.

2. It will be possible to specify the degree of "excess" profits in high π values more accurately than has been possible. This relates to long-run profit strategy, often in conjunction with specific entry barriers and scale economies. Conversely, one can define "excess" retention of market share for any given M and π levels.

3. There are specific policy uses. The most obvious use is in evaluating candidates for antitrust action. In place of vague judgments about the "given" degree of market power and profits, the net costs and benefits of alternative actions would be more accurately estimated.

In addition, the functions help to analyze and predict the effects of policy constraints, as in Figures 4.4 and 4.5. Antitrust limits on market shares (implicit or not) are readily seen to induce firms to take higher profits. This in turn could cause a shift toward diversification by merger or internally, such as appeared to occur in the 1960s. Predatory pricing can be seen to be pric-

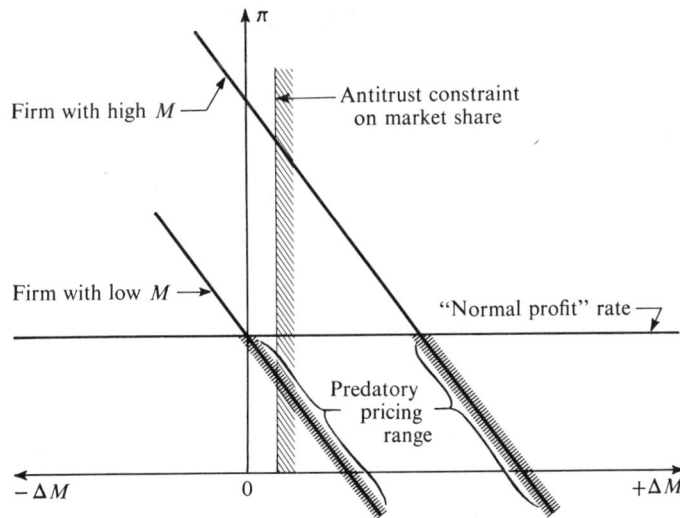

Figure 4.4 Antitrust implications of a relationship between profit rate and change in market share.

The Basic Policy Yields 127

ing in the range below normal profit, in order to gain more market share. The effects will vary according to the vertical position of the share-time function.

Under utility regulation, there are two effects (Figure 4.5). First, the service-area franchise given the utility is a large and absolute entry barrier, which will shift the share-profit curve (Figure 4.1) vertically upward. Second, the profit rate constraint cuts off the higher portion of the share-time curve, which in turn shifts the chosen point to the right. The utility is thus

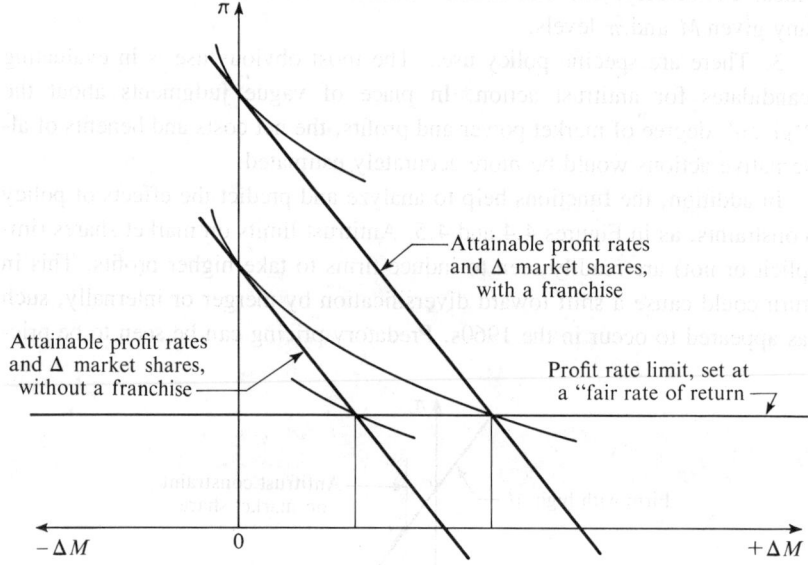

Figure 4.5 Regulatory implications of a relationship between profit rate and change in market share.

induced to intensify its efforts to control "its" market and related ones. It may do so by modifying its choices of technology toward more exclusive modes, and by developing positions in adjacent markets. This accentuation is double: the constraint alone would induce it, but the service franchise adds to it. This fits the observed fixation of most utilities (see chapter 9) on controlling their exclusive markets and selecting technology that tends to close access by potential competitors.

In short the share-time function is basic to understanding the process of structural effects and changes. If it exists in a general form, it would have great predictive and normative power. Even if it varies among certain industry types, it may be measurable and useful in evaluating behavior.

These points of analysis and evidence suggest that high market shares do tend to decay—but only at moderate or slow rates—and that this will continue to be so. This reflects a combination of rational managerial behavior and unexpected outside factors, in line with fundamental conditions of choice over time. There are exceptions, of course, but the general rule still holds. Moreover, other evidence suggests that growth does not tend to dissolve concentration, despite frequent optimistic hopes to the contrary. We may therefore approach the individual cases of high market power with the general expectation that they are mostly going to persist.

6 EFFECTS OF MARKET POWER

We need next to review the probable net costs of market power. These are of several sorts (mainly X-inefficiency, the misallocation of resources, retarded innovation, loss of equity, and loss of content—the same as were fitted into the benefit-cost analysis in chapter 3). Knowledge about them is still formative, but the general magnitudes are now reasonably clear.[51] I shall point out some details and special problems.

The misallocation burden is probably understated, because our data are too coarse to show the full range of specific monopoly positions. Averaging therefore reduces the apparent cost below the probable true levels. Even so, it is relatively slight.[52]

X-inefficiency is also probably underestimated. Cases of mismanagement are customarily neglected in the business press, so that outside evidence is incomplete. The large-firm econometric study of 245 firms provides new estimates of possible X-inefficiency. Each firm's market position (market share, size, advertising-intensity, etc.) gives it a *predicted* profit rate. As noted above, this is an index of market power. The firm's actual profit rates may differ from this, and the difference may be an excellent direct index of X-efficiency. Individual cases will draw varying interpretations;

[51] Shepherd, *Market Power;* Scherer, *Industrial Market Structure,* ch. 17. For zealous but largely ineffectual efforts to deny these effects, see H. J. Goldschmid, H. M. Mann, and J. F. Weston, eds., *Industrial Concentration: The New Learning* (Boston: Little, Brown, 1975), especially the papers by McGee, Brozen, and Demsetz.

[52] See the discussion and sources in Shepherd, *ibid.,* chs. 12 and 13, and Scherer, *ibid.,* pp. 400–404.

among the most intriguing are the possible effects of antitrust actions in the past that are believed to have been taken (Alcoa, American Can, Swift) or which were denied (U.S. Steel). In any event, this kind of information, as it is further refined, can be helpful in evaluating the gains in X-efficiency that public policies might yield. Though the information is soft, it seems likely that X-inefficiency commonly rises to the region of 5 percent of costs as market share approaches 100 percent.[53] Note also that much X-inefficiency may also arise under public programs, such as weapons purchasing, regulation, shipbuilding subsidies, and public housing.

On technical progress, there is now something like a consensus among the small group of experts that, at market shares above the 20–25 percent range, the marginal net productivity of research and development resources tends to decline.[54] As the market share rises toward 100 percent, the retardation probably is substantial. A rough working approximation would be that the rate of productivity increase is 1 percent yearly above the average at market shares of 25 percent, and then declines to 2 percent below the average at pure monopoly shares of 100 percent. In exceptional cases, mainly small industries, there may be economies of scale in research and development which offset the tendency of high-share firms to imitate rather than innovate. But as a rule, market shares above 25 percent and high entry barriers both tend—as a general rule, subject to exceptions—to reduce the rate of technical progress below the rate the industry's underlying technological opportunities would yield.

The equity impacts of market power are, of course, the most difficult to assess. The flow of excess profits raises stockholder income and wealth relative to customers' income, but there are three specific problems with this. First, high profits might reflect high efficiency and innovation rather than monopoly rewards. However, most researchers believe these elements to be slight or zero in most cases—even negative in some—so that supernormal profits are a good first approximation to the redistributive flow. In any event, these factors would not alter the actual incidence of the flow. This flow is disequalizing when—as in most firms—the customers have lower income than the shareholders.

The second problem is that the degree of disequalizing will vary from

[53] Shepherd, *ibid.*, ch. 13; Scherer, *ibid.*, pp. 404–8.
[54] Shepherd, *ibid.*, ch. 14; Scherer, *ibid.*, chs. 15 and 16; Mansfield, *Research and Innovation*.

case to case. Some transfers will be between near-equals: for example, between Cadillac buyers and GM shareholders. Other transfers are extreme, from the very poor to the very rich. The ΔD value in the cost-benefit equation will therefore have a wide range per dollar of redistribution. In principle, one could measure these exactly and arrive at precise estimates of the equity effects for individual cases. In practice, no such exactitude has ever been attempted. Even the simplest equity estimates are only embryonic, so far.

Third, some portion of the excess profits are often absorbed into higher costs through X-inefficiency. These can be regarded either as a dead loss or as a transfer from customers to input suppliers. Such transfers are usually less disequalizing than are those to stockholders, because input suppliers are mainly lower-middle-class workers. Still, the transfers are involuntary, and they do involve some degree of sheer waste. So it is reasonable to regard them as either a dead-weight loss or as part of the equity effect. In either case, they enter into the benefit-cost analysis as a cost.

Still, we can outline the broader equity patterns on the simple premise that all excess profits cause the same incidence of redistribution. A naive method is to assume all *actual* profits over some benchmark competitive rate of return—say 10.0 percent of equity capital—to be monopoly returns, and hence redistributive. This sweeps in lots of temporary high profits, caused by random shifts rather than market power. Therefore, a more precise measure is the level of *fitted* profitability for each firm, which is derived from the model of market structure. These can be regarded as best estimates of the equity effect of market power.

The basic effects seem to be reasonably clear, in the coefficients of the fitted model. The resulting redistributive flow is probably at least 2 percent of GNP yearly, even despite the constraints of antitrust and other public policies.[55] This capitalizes as a wealth redistribution on the order of at least $100–$150 billion—large but still only a moderate fraction of all private wealth.[56]

Yet these values do not go to the heart of the equity problem. That problem exists in terms of family wealth, ranging from near-zero net worth for most families up to a billion or more for some others. The amounts at

---

[55] Shepherd, *ibid.*
[56] See Shepherd, *ibid.*, ch. 14 and compare Comanor and Smiley, "Monopoly and the Distribution of Wealth."

stake are large, as we have noted before. It is true that strict wealth equality per capita in the U.S. would result in only about $20,000 per person, but the average would be $100,000 per household. A better basis for comparison is the intergeneration "family," viewed broadly. This is a more extended group, corresponding to the basis on which family fortunes are actually held and passed on. These would vary in scope from case to case, but one could reasonably estimate them at about half the number of households. Equality would therefore mean about $200,000 in wealth per "family," which is not a trivial sum. It would generate a risk-free income of about $10,000 annually. The wealth–equity issue—and the scope for redistribution—is therefore of a magnitude that deserves close attention.

In the past a large share of extreme family wealth did originate from the monopolizing of markets, especially before 1930. Yet most large family wealth holdings are now in diversified portfolios, and the stock market has discounted the monopoly returns from the remaining firms holding substantial market power. Therefore, abating present market power will not undo the past impact of monopoly, except for the few odd cases where tight family control continues. On the contrary, stopping the fortune-building from new monopolies might tend on balance to harden the present stratification and to retard social mobility.

The issue is complex and has been insufficiently studied. We need to know more about the relative importance of market power in generating wealth, and about the rate at which family fortunes decay.[57] Meanwhile, we can expect that antimonopoly policies—no matter how radical—will not greatly alter the existing structure of economic inequality. The inequity yields from most antimonopoly actions will probably be positive—and in some cases they may be very large—but each case will deserve specific study, to identify those with the highest equity yields.

The equity effect on opportunity is also significant, and it brings us into the domain of content. Opportunity is not a simple matter, because the policies of a number of exceptional firms run against the general tendency toward discrimination under market power. Some companies are neutral toward blue-collar workers but discriminate at the white-collar level, others discriminate against women but not blacks or other minorities, or vice versa. Moreover, the supply of "qualified" minority workers may be short.

[57] Pryor's simulation is one pointer toward methods for studying the process of wealth creation and diffusion.

Still, the general pattern is for market power to increase discrimination, among industrial, banking, utility, and other large enterprises.[58] Minority opportunity is confined mainly to competitive and nonprofit enterprises, and there are, of course, fewer such opportunities than in large and profitable private enterprises. The cost of such discrimination has been measured only to a first approximation so far, with data only on blacks and women. The broad tendency is for minority employment to be about 20 percent less—and lower in relative status—under high concentration than under low concentration. Women especially are excluded from top-level jobs in large enterprises. Thus, special motivation or outside pressure appears to be necessary to overcome the inherent tendencies toward discrimination in large firms.

In the "normal" large firm, the content includes strong discrimination against minorities and women, as the career process and other factors would predict. This can be taken as an indication that the other negative features of the career process are present in strength. This is suggested also by a range of other studies: The large firm is indeed managed along autocratic lines, with a relatively low degree of content; career and noncareer jobs are separated; there is little diffusion of responsibility or relation between workers and those they "serve"; local identity survives, where it does, only in spite of pressures to homogenize operations and suppress local factors.

Many large corporations foster habits that conflict with the criteria of good content. This has recently evoked a scattered reaction, in extreme cases of content reduction. The superficial alteration of assembly lines into "teams" scarcely touches the surface of the program. Nor does the doctrine that contented workers are more productive, as industrial sociologists have known for several decades.[59]

In general, there appears to be a negative relation between size and content. Bigness per se may have only tenuous relations to market power and its effects, but a variety of evidence suggests that size tends to reduce the content of activity within firms. This cost can be partially mitigated by efforts to decentralize, to foster content, etc., but the basic fact remains; and the con-

---

[58] Shepherd, *Market Power*, ch. 14, and W. G. Shepherd and Sharon G. Levin, "Managerial Discrimination in Large Firms," *Review of Economics and Statistics,* November 1973, pp. 412–22, indicate this. See also the sources cited there.

[59] D. Katz and R. L. Kahn, *The Social Psychology of Organizations* (New York: Wiley, 1966); R. L. Kahn and E. Boulding, eds., *Power and Conflicts in Organizations* (New York: Basic Books, 1964).

tent loss tends to raise production costs, rather than reduce them.[60] One would like to have precise measures of the effects on content, but they do not yet exist. Still, the general tendency seems clear, pending quantitative tests.

7 HIGH-YIELD SECTORS AND FIRMS

We can now try to discern the markets where the policy yields may be relatively high in the future. The exercise is inexact, because—as we have seen—the data are imperfect and the research findings about the effects of market power are soft. Still, first approximations are better than ignorance. I shall begin with industrial markets, and then move on to other sectors. The aim is not to derive firm policy guidelines. Rather it is to illustrate the estimating techniques and to suggest broadly where basic policy concern should be focused.

The main cases of market power among industrial firms in the U.S. were indicated in Table 4.10. These estimates are based primarily on general relationships, and do not reflect an exhaustive specific analysis of each firm. They are of course subject to error and to revision. Still, they are a consistent set of estimates based on some of the more thorough research now available.

They indicate the probable gross benefits that would result from abating the degree of market power held by these firms down to "loose-oligopoly" levels. This effective-competition target would involve long-run profit rates of about 10 percent—still moderately above the bare competitive minimum. These estimated benefits are not discounted (recall chapter 3) for probability, for time, for precedent, or for spontaneous change. Nor do they allow for economies of scale, which might be sacrificed in certain cases. These will be considered in the next chapters.

Table 4.10 indicates the cases of existing market power in the industrial sector that should draw the closest policy attention. This list is not complete, since the panel of large firms it is derived from did not include certain weapons suppliers, and other firms that may also offer high policy yields. These must be evaluated more subjectively, because there are special factors and less data to work with.

[60] *Ibid.,* and R. Likert, *The Human Organization* (New York: McGraw-Hill, 1967).

Note also that these estimates will understate the average costs of size in reducing content. By reasonable standards, the upper range of large industrial, banking, utility, and retailing firms are subject to losses of content, which may exceed the other costs of market power. They may be mitigated in exceptional cases—where personal efforts or specific policies overcome the normal negative effects—but the common run of large firms do exhibit content losses.

Among other sectors, major capital markets offer probably the highest policy yields. Indeed, capital market changes may be necessary in order to draw lasting gains in industrial markets. Banking and stock markets are the key parts, in their relations to market power in other industries. These relations are not just matters of local banking concentration, of interest rates on loans, or of stock exchange fees and membership. Rather they come to a focus in the mutual bank–company connections, in which banks are close advisers and companies rarely shift their accounts. In stock markets, the critical factor is the degree of insider information. The present structure of stock exchanges and regulatory policies tends to give greater access to company information to larger investors. This further skews the inequality of opportunity to gain wealth in capital markets.

Certain utility sectors are also ripe for policy change, as will be explained in chapter 9. Transport and telecommunications are the clearest cases, containing new areas where competition appears to be feasible. More generally, the public-regulation device itself may need to be revised and combined with other tools. The potential gains are primarily in efficiency, including allowance for external effects. Other sensitive sectors include certain labor markets, broadcasting, sports, performing arts, weapons supply, and certain agricultural products.

Taken together, these policy-sensitive sectors are an important share of the economy, but much less than one-half of it. Many of the sectors are of long standing; others are still formative. Their variety suggests that the treatments will need to be carefully fitted to specific conditions. Their limited extent suggests that policy attention and action can be focused.

PART TWO

Policy Alternatives in Practice

CHAPTER FIVE
Policy Instruments

WE SHALL now take an inventory of existing policies, to see how the more familiar devices are used and what their main effects are. This background will allow us to move in the next several chapters to consider the optimal policy choices in the main sectors.

For a variety of reasons, the design and effects of policies have been a neglected topic until recent years. Our survey will therefore be useful but inconclusive. We shall be able to suggest only the main lines of policy actions and results, while leaving a sizable margin for error and debate. We shall start with exemption and exposure, then consider antitrust, regulation, public enterprise, and finally summarize public purchasing, direct subsidy programs, and taxation.

1 EXEMPTION AND EXPOSURE

"Nontreatment," or delegation of power to industry groups, covers large areas of the economy.[1] It includes most intrastate trade, especially local ser-

[1] For estimates, compare Carl Kaysen and Donald F. Turner, *Antitrust Policy* (Cambridge, Mass.: Harvard University Press, 1959) and W. Adams and H. Gray, *Monopoly in America* (New York: Macmillan, 1955).

vices. Privately held companies are also usually exempt, because their activities are virtually secret. So are a variety of important cases of self-regulation, such as in the medical, legal, and accounting professions.[2] Certain sectors under state regulation—such as insurance and nursing homes—are virtually exempt from genuine economic control. Most aspects of international trade are equally untouched; airline rates, for example, have been essentially self regulated, with the CAB primarily ratifying the agreements.[3] Also exempt are labor unions, certain sports, agriculture and—in part—weapons, oil, shipping, stock markets, and banking.

Exemption as a pure case simply involves the absence of public disclosure or controls, beyond nominal items. Self-regulation goes further in most cases, by using the law or public agencies as a means of setting and enforcing controls on what the existing sellers may do and who can enter. Chapter 9 will show that some "public" regulation also verges on self-regulation. These conditions commonly tend to increase market power.

In some financial markets, certain forms of "regulation" also occur. In banking, the federal and state agencies do control certain aspects of entry, structure, and behavior; but profitability is not constrained, and the agencies publish virtually no useful information on banking relationships. The main effect is to limit competition rather than to constrain market power.[4] The Securities and Exchange Commission sets certain safeguards on securities markets, but this control is widely recognized to touch only certain acute abuses.

The SEC has recently tried to withdraw its *de facto* ratification of price fixing for fees in stock exchanges, and in May 1975 it finally succeeded. Some states formally "regulate" insurance firms, but the resources and powers are minimal and serve mainly to forestall federal regulation. Much

---

[2] Professions proliferate almost without bounds. Any group that can set qualifications and make them stick through an enforceable licensing procedure may be considered professional. The range is from physicians to embalmers, from accountants to hair dressers.

[3] See R. E. Caves, *Air Transport and Its Regulators* (Cambridge, Mass.: Harvard University Press, 1962); George Eads, "Competition in the Domestic Trunk Airline Industry: Excessive or Insufficient?", *Competition and the Regulation of Industry*, ed. A. Phillips (Washington, D.C.: Brookings Institution, 1975).

[4] See Phillips, "Competitive Policy for Depository Financial Institutions," in *Competition and the Regulation of Industry, ibid.*, and J. M. Guttentag and E. S. Herman, *Banking Structure and Performance* (New York: New York University Press, 1967).

Policy Alternatives in Practice

of this "regulation" is therefore pseudoregulation, tending to increase market power and to protect the established firms.

The basic complement to exemption is exposure, in accord with the full-information hypothesis stated in chapter 2. Where public control is absent, public information should naturally be maximal, to offset the clear chances for abuse. Instead, actual exposure is spotty and slight. If a general pattern can be observed, it is perverse: *Exposure tends to vary inversely with the degree of market power and directly with the degree of public control.* It is least where it is needed most, and even where it is most, it is small. Thus, public information about key variables of structure and behavior is virtually absent for banking and its ties to industry, for the major market-power cases, and for most of the other key areas noted at the end of chapter 4. This absence fits the negative political economy prediction—that policies will reflect underlying power rather than alter it—but, natural as it may seem, the absence still runs against the criteria for optimal policy.

2 ANTITRUST

The two U.S. antitrust agencies are the Antitrust Division of the Justice Department and the Federal Trade Commission.[5] Their policy positions are shown in Figure 5.1. The two agencies share jurisdiction over a broad range of markets.[6] In practice, the Division deals primarily with heavy industry (steel, oil, automobiles), the FTC with lighter, consumer-oriented industries (foods, clothing, furniture). The lines are not clear or permanent, and there are wide overlaps.

The basic antitrust law—the Sherman Act of 1890—has provided a limited and unsure legal base for treatment. Despite its categorical wording, it lacks the full enforcement provisions that were in earlier drafts. This has posed severe procedural blocks (see chapter 7) and left a wide range for

---

[5] There are no comprehensive histories or analyses of these agencies. Useful critical studies include M. J. Green et al., *The Closed Enterprise System* (New York: Grossman, 1972); and E. F. Cox, R. C. Fellmeth, and J. E. Schulz, *The Nader Report on the Federal Trade Commission* (New York: Grove Press, 1969).

[6] Other agencies also affect these markets, of course, including the Defense Department, the Atomic Energy Commission, the Securities and Exchange Commission, the Tariff Commission, the automobile safety and telecommunications groups, and various state and city agencies. Jurisdiction is, in practice, highly diluted in a variety of major and minor industries.

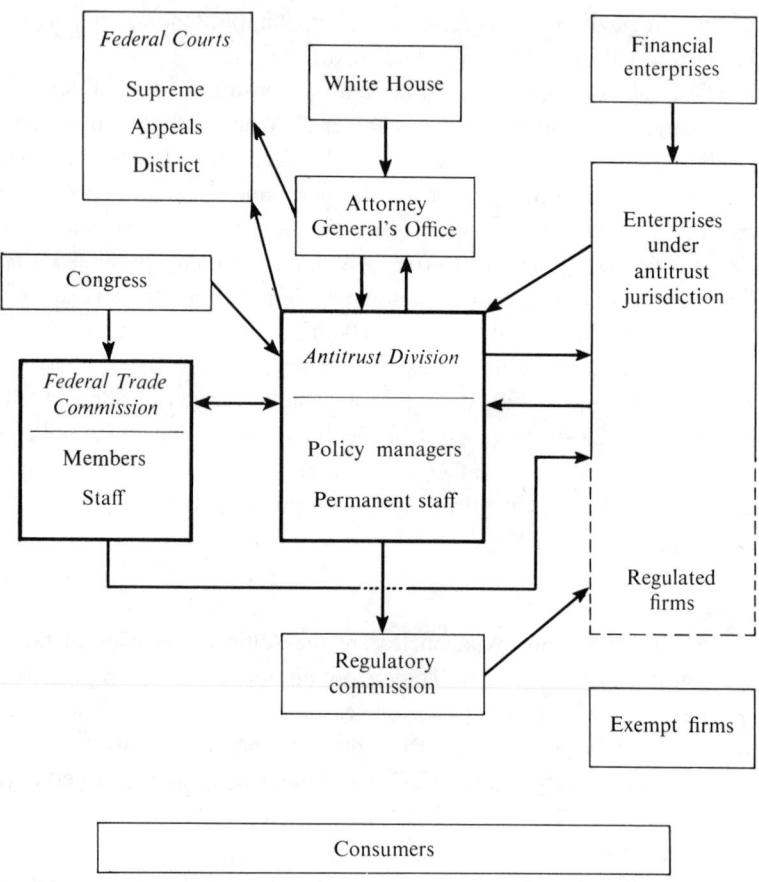

Figure 5.1 The setting for antitrust policy.

treatment to fluctuate in. Even at its peaks, antitrust has still been remarkably moderate, slow, and—in the end—of mild impact. As U.S. antitrust receded during 1953–68, certain treatments abroad began to approach the American degree of severity, in some directions going further. Compared to the scope of untreated market power, U.S. treatment cannot now be said to be more strict or optimal. The U.S. no longer has the only—or the most complete—antitrust treatment.

Conventional antitrust involves policing, remedies, and prevention. The laws forbid, basically: (1) *cooperating* to fix prices, divide markets, or restrain trade in other ways (Sherman Act, Section 1); (2) *monopolizing,* which raises problems of existing monopoly (Sherman Act, Section 2) and of *mergers* (Clayton Act, Section 7); and (3) several specific kinds of activities (Clayton Act and others). The two agencies have to discover these violations, proceed against them and get convictions in the courts, and then make sure the remedies are adequate.

Their performance has been mediocre on the whole and checkered in specific areas. Some of their tasks are hard, others quite easy. In cases against existing monopoly, they usually must prove that some new structure would be better than the existing or evolving one. The opposite extreme is price-fixing cases, where the agency lawyers need to prove only that an attempt to fix prices was made, not that it was successful or that the industry's conditions need changing.

The bulk of antitrust resources go to *policing* conduct, trying to stop or limit attempts at price-fixing, patent restrictions, predatory pricing agreements, and so forth.[7] Obviously, no exact measures are possible, but a reasonable approximation for the Antitrust Division in recent years is 40 percent to conduct, 20 percent to mergers, 15 percent to restorative treatment in regulated industries, 10 percent to restorative action in industry and trade, and the rest to miscellaneous others.[8] At the FTC, the shares are perhaps 60, 20, 5, and 15 respectively. Many of these are extremely detailed and complex matters, but most are relatively simple. The number of investigations is high, but even these may be only a small sample of the actual violations in real markets. Most of the cases are settled informally by consent decree or by a lower court decision. Most are of slight importance—worth doing, but not making new law.

Certain acts are illegal *per se;* price fixing, market sharing. Conviction requires only a showing that the act occurred or was attempted. Yet such strict rules are not so broad as they seem. Because of the many exemptions of sectors (see above) the *per se* rules cover only a minority of economic activity. And they induce efforts by businesses to attain, by similar tactics, the same results as they would have achieved by price-fixing or market sharing.

Preventive actions, which are mainly toward mergers, absorbed a rising

---

[7] See also R. A. Posner, "A Statistical Study of Antitrust Enforcement," *Journal of Law and Economics,* 1970, pp. 365–420.

[8] This is based on direct observation within the Antitrust Division during 1967–68 and on discussions with a variety of personnel at various times. It is of course meant to be illustrative, since the activities mingle and change from year to year.

share of resources in the 1960s as the merger wave rose and crested. Only a few mergers, among thousands each year, are intensively studied and even fewer are eventually opposed. In those which are opposed, the usual intent is to set precedent in marginal areas. These cases tend also to be quickly dispatched. As the rules against horizontal and vertical mergers have been tightened (see chapter 8), the more subtle issues of conglomerate mergers have come to the fore, especially since 1965. Here, the agencies are entering more marginal issues, different from those in horizontal mergers.[9] Also, the Antitrust Divison is increasingly involved in screening mergers by regulated firms, such as airlines, electric utilities, banks, and railroads. This requires convincing the regulatory commissions—and often the courts, on appeal—to disallow merger proposals.

Remedial (or restorative) activities toward existing market power deal with both regulated and unregulated sectors. Antitrust attempts to reduce monopoly and open up entry into regulated markets have grown recently, in such sectors as communications, transportation, and stock exchanges.[10] Other possible sectors are still untouched, as we shall see.

In the unregulated sectors, by contrast, remedial policies have dwindled since 1952 to a mere foothold. Restructuring of industrial market power has recently been sought in the computer, copying equipment, and cereals industries, but that is virtually all. Restructuring can occur only if action is initiated to prove that monopoly exists and to require remedies. This is usually a difficult and protracted procedure (see chapter 7). Yet the near-monopolies are often also informally *quasi-regulated*. Their market positions and profitability are reviewed indirectly, as possible triggers for restorative action.[11]

---

[9] See D. F. Turner, "Conglomerate Mergers and Section 7 of the Clayton Act," *Harvard Law Review*, May 1965, pp. 1313–95; and J. S. Campbell and W. G. Shepherd, "Leading-Firm Conglomerate Mergers," *Antitrust Bulletin*, Winter 1968, pp. 1361–82.

[10] See D. F. Turner, "The Scope of Antitrust and Other Regulatory Policies," *Harvard Law Review*, April 1969, pp. 1207–44.

[11] I participated in one important example of this. In 1968, a key part of an eventual Division suit against IBM was the degree and character of IBM's price discrimination. This required direct review of the core pricing practices of IBM on its 360 computer line, both vertically among computer types and horizontally among users of each type (see W. G. Shepherd, *Market Power and Economic Welfare* [New York: Random House, 1970], ch. 15). The critical data were quite definite, although they would not be made public unless trial of the suit, filed in January 1969, actually occurs. What matters here is that the data were reviewed and that IBM and other major near-monopolies are aware that such scrutiny is likely to occur as part of an antitrust review. Therefore, their behavior is likely to be influenced, at least in part, in the same way (and perhaps as strongly) as are utilities, which are part of a more formal review process. See also chapter 9 for comparison.

So the firms have—or believe they have—incentives to absorb some profits in costs, and to moderate their price discrimination. These are similar to conventional regulation (see below).

In short, the agencies have come to devote their resources primarily to certain types of behavior, to marginal merger issues, and to certain utility matters. Lesser duties also absorb resources—Congressional letters and legislative testimony, stopping of fraud and deceptive labeling, etc. The budgets usually rise by a small increment each year, with no attention to specific needs (such as a series of big cases or new problems). The FTC, funded directly by Congress, is frequently threatened with cuts.[12] Though the Antitrust Division's budget, as part of the Justice Department budget, is more insulated from such threats, its higher officials often believe that drastic enforcement moves could lead to retaliation, possibly to drastic reductions in the Division, or even outright abolition.[13]

Motivation of the agency heads reflects their legal background, the brevity of their tenure, and the slowness of procedure. In this setting, success is reached by maximizing the visible measures of action, particularly the number of cased filed and won, and the fines and other possible "savings for the consumer." These are yielded mainly by price-fixing cases and by stopping mergers. Longer-term, complex and subtle cases—where the defendants can assert possible disruption, loss of innovation, etc.—have low or negative yields from the current managers' viewpoint. Indeed, the defendant's skill in merely asserting dangers—real or imagined—will influence the policy managers; aggressive, skillful opponents are therefore able to define the terms of their own protection.

Consider now the process by which antitrust decisions are posed and made.[14] The basic actor is the staff lawyer, specializing in one or, more often, several industries. Large and old industries may be worked on by several lawyers, in each agency; small and new ones are often thinly covered or

---

[12] And certain specific projects of it are cut out; for example, a major study of the 1,000 largest firms was specifically prohibited in the 1960s.

[13] I have heard many such opinions from inside the agencies. One irony is that abolition or deep cuts are not live prospects, for private antitrust practice has become too prosperous and steady an activity for the small army of private antitrust lawyers, some of whom are politically influential.

[14] This is needed for evaluating the results and the alternative approaches. As I observed it at close quarters, it is little changed since Walton Hamilton and Irene Till's superb description of it in their *Antitrust in Action,* Monograph No. 16 for the Temporary National Economic Committee (U.S. Government Printing Office, 1940), especially pp. 23–100.

neglected. The lawyer has latitude to ferret out possible violations, on his own or on an assigned investigation or solely in response to a private complaint or lead. A "case" or investigation is usually triggered by a complaint or an important change reported in the press. Investigation may also involve staff economists and on occasion an outside consultant. The investigator or group does a research report (a "fact memo") on whether a violation of antitrust law has occurred and a suit against the offender is justified. The criterion is, of course, legal: can a violation of the law be established? If the attorney recommends suing, he also draws up a draft complaint. The fact memo and the complaint form the basis for the action, and then pass up through several higher levels for discussion, further work, and decision. In the Antitrust Division, the Assistant Attorney General for Antitrust ultimately decides, usually after more study, whether to approve suit. Then, *if* the Attorney General approves—often after wider consultation—the case is filed in a U.S. District Court. Trial may then take several years to begin (the 1969 suit against IBM has already taken more than six years to begin). After decision, appeals may take several more years, and in big cases, the Supreme Court may send the case back down at least once for practical remedies. At the other extreme, actions against planned mergers may have effect in a matter of weeks or even hours. With mergers, time favors the Division, since judges commonly prevent full consummation of the merger until the basic issues are clarified.

At the FTC, cases are brought before the Commission by the staff. In smaller matters, the Commission's decision is final, in effect. But where the stakes are big enough, cases are appealed all the way up to the Supreme Court, and the final outcome may take many years.

The sides favored by the burden of proof and by having time on its side can be summarized as follows:

Subject of Action	The Burden of Proof Favors	Time Delay Favors
Price fixing	Neither	Neither
Mergers	Agency	Agency
Restorative	Firm	Firm

The natural roles are for staff attorneys to make out the best possible case for suit. The policy managers then select from this portfolio those cases which "look best" in legal and perhaps economic terms. The courts then further select those cases which have merit, with the judicial procedure tending toward conservatism. Ultimately, the Supreme Court can also select the "correct" margins of policy treatment. In short, a "rule of reason" can be applied at all levels, but only if the agencies lean on balance toward strictness will the courts be given a range for selection.

Where agencies are inactive, suits or other actions by private groups often take up some of the slack. These have mounted in volume since 1960. But they are not a reliable or complete supplement, especially against dominant firms. The private outcomes may not coincide with the social optimum.

These are relatively low-budget agencies, with a clear need to allocate resources to the highest-yield cases. One result is that large areas of enforcement are routinely neglected; that is, nominal powers are simply not applied. Big cases that are brought are routinely accused—often with some justice—of being too episodic and unexpected, of singling out a few victims rather than treating all offenders evenly. Also the reliance on career lawyers means that newer industries tend to be neglected while the treatments for older sectors proceed, possibly in too much detail.

Also, the agencies' capacity to absorb key information is limited, especially in the Antitrust Division. Because the Census Bureau secretes all data on individual companies, the agencies lack direct and timely information, and they must conduct their own research, such as it is, from scattered sources. Even the FTC's large economic staff is capable of doing this for, at the most, several large cases at a time.[15] The Antitrust Division's economists have been capable only of providing simple data required by the staff lawyers; there is little chance of mounting thorough research on major industries, on the scale of the Bureau of Corporations during 1906–14. Therefore the Division's reach has automatically been limited to simpler cases.[16] It

---

[15] There are over 40 economists now at both the FTC and the Antitrust Division, but most specialize on a sector or a problem, and the level of training has been low. The complexities of researching a major Section 2 case, in the face of sophisticated company resistance and the lack of sound official data, are sufficient to deflect even the most highly trained specialist.

Recently the structure and status of the Economic Section at the Division have been formally improved, but the effect or that improvement is not yet evident.

[16] This could conceivably be changing. Also, from 1965 to 1973 there was a yearly appointee as Special Economic Assistant to the Division head, who provided for close contact and advice on many cases. The appointees were, in order, William S. Comanor, Oliver E. Williamson, William G. Shepherd, H. Michael Mann, Leonard W. Weiss, Kenneth Elzinga, George Eads and George A. Hay. But these well-placed advisors had neither powers nor sufficient research resources.

must rely on court trials to bring out full information. This means that in the broad range of major industries, antitrust choices are starved of thorough information, and the courts often lack means or procedures to carry out remedies, even when the need for change has been established.

The effects of the whole antitrust experiment are evidently likely to be complex, perhaps with unknown side effects too. Yet a few obvious effects can be identified here. First, early restorative actions have probably reduced market power in certain industries (oil, cigarettes, aluminum, tin cans: see chapter 7). But, second, as effort has shifted instead to policing conduct, the whole treatment could tend to constrain lesser firms relative to dominant ones. This is explored in detail in later chapters. In any case, such a shift is natural, in light of the motives and constraints on agency managers as they pass through. But it could fit optimal treatment only if there is a high rate of decline in dominant firms. If, instead, dominant firms tend to hold their positions, then the peculiar bias of antitrust would be perverse—and may even help to preserve those positions. In short, the rate of decline is critical: if the natural rate at which high market shares decline is low, then the combined net effect of current antitrust treatments could be to increase structural monopoly.

Also: antitrust would seemingly be inequitable, by ratifying dominant firms while restraining lesser ones.

In any event, antitrust may have had little or no economic effects, regardless of popular belief and propaganda.[17] How much effect, and with what costs and benefits, remains to be seen.

3 REGULATION

Regulation by public commission is an American device that has acquired standard forms and processes since the 1900–10 decade.[18] It is a 50-year-old

[17] Among the few economic opinions about its effects is Jesse Markham's "The Joint Effect of Antitrust and Patent Laws upon Innovation," *American Economic Review*, May 1966, pp. 291–30.

[18] The best reviews are A. E. Kahn, *The Economics of Regulation;* C. F. Phillips, Jr., *The Economics of Regulation* (Homewood, Ill.: Irwin, 1969); I. R. Barnes, *The Economics of Public Utility Regulation* (New York: F. S. Crofts, 1942); J. C. Bonbright, *Principles of Public Utility Rates* (New York: Columbia University Press, 1961); M. H. Bernstein, *Regulating Business by Independent Commission,* Princeton: Princeton University Press, 1955); see also sources cited in chapter 9.

experiment, which is still spreading to new sectors. There are several conventional federal commissions and some 50 state commissions, all focusing on "utility" sectors (power, transport, communications). The conventional commission (1) tries to constrain the economic behavior of a private firm that (2) holds a monopoly franchise in its service area. Also, there are a great variety of other "regulatory" bodies, in a wider range of sectors, many with conflicting jurisdictions, and some of them actually doing no genuine regulating at all. Furthermore, many state commissions spend heroic efforts on resisting federal regulation. In short, regulation is a complex and often irrational patchwork.

The common position of conventional commissions is shown in Figure 5.2. The commission has formal powers to direct or control; but in practice it usually negotiates and often merely acquiesces. In some cases, regulators are irrelevant or passive to company behavior, or even serve to legitimize it.[19]

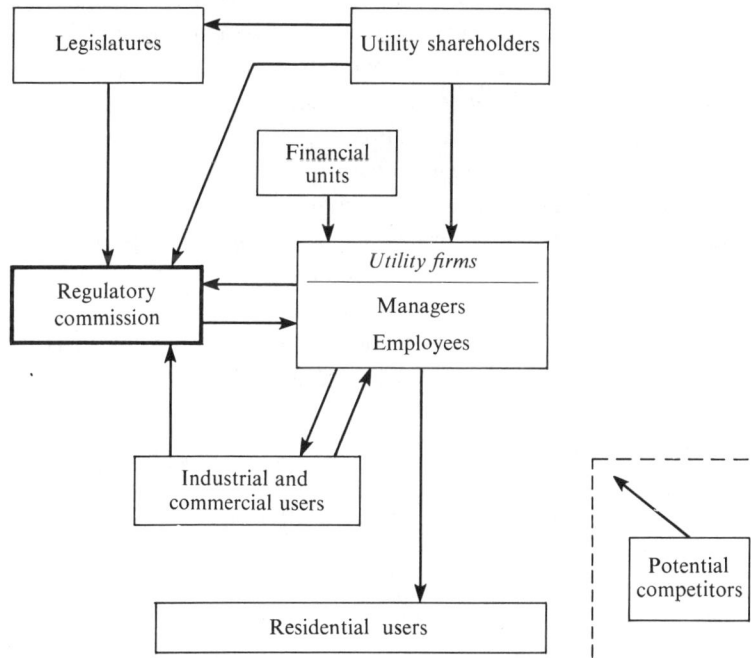

Figure 5.2 The setting for regulatory policy.

[19] See Kahn, *Economics of Regulation;* Bernstein, *Regulating Business;* W. G. Shepherd and T. G. Gies, eds., *Utility Regulation* (New York: Random House, 1966); Shepherd and Gies,

Only rarely, and briefly, does a commission freely control utility behavior (for reasons to be seen in chapter 9).

Consider first the regulators' motives,[20] which reflect the regulators' origins and brevity of tenure, as well as the narrowness of their controls. Most regulators are politicians—either young ones on the way up or older ones past their peak. The younger and more active ones especially are usually in office for relatively brief periods. The commissions' powers are confined—by law or custom—mainly to narrow issues of profit rates and prices (chapter 9 will show this narrowness more fully). Under these conditions, there are two main criteria for rational behavior by regulators: the formal reduction of utility prices increases below requested levels, and the avoidance of service breakdowns.

The two main questions actually posed for regulators are profit-price decisions and whether to permit new entry and competition. The regulators' motivation yields obvious solutions to these: profit-raising requests will be cut—but not severely[21]—and entry will be permitted only if it does not appear to threaten service breakdowns. These standard responses may, of course, stray far from what would be optimal.

The distinctive fact about regulation of private firms is that the utility firm issues equity stock *with voting control,* in addition to bonds. Directors and managers are creatures of these shareholders alone; no regulatory agency controls who is on the board or how the board members supervise their managers or how self-selecting and self-controlling the managers may be. The capital and management—and therefore the motivation—are private.

Yet the state partly creates the utility too, by approving it as the sole franchised supplier in its area. This hardens and often extends the monop-

---

Regulation in Further Perspective (Cambridge, Mass.: Ballinger, 1974). Even my experience as chairman of the Cablecasting Commission in 1973–74 in Ann Arbor, Michigan, fitted this practical mode.

[20] See also G. J. Stigler, "The Theory of Economic Regulation," *Bell Journal of Economics and Management Science,* Spring 1971, pp. 3–21; also Barnes, *Public Utility Regulation;* and H. M. Gray, "The Passing of the Public Utility Concept," reprinted in American Economic Association, *Readings in the Social Control of Industry* (Philadelphia: Blakiston, 1942), pp. 280–303.

[21] See Kahn, *Economics of Regulation;* and E. Troxel, "Telephone Regulation in Michigan," in Shepherd and Gies, *Utility Regulation.* The general tendency is for the ratio of permitted rises to approach 50 percent of the requested rise. This may reflect that the requested rise has been set at about double the needed rise, in anticipation of the conventional cut. Naturally, specific factors will influence the outcome away from 50 percent in many cases.

oly—both in space and time—and it excludes entry. Thus shielded from actual *and potential* competition, the private utility has an unusually tight monopoly. This franchise raises the value of the enterprise; the regulatory commission's constraints on profits and the price structure are intended to reduce the value. In all this, the management is under double supervision. These private and public constraints are not entirely divergent; both, for example, may induce managers to avoid gross inefficiency. But certain important divergences also occur.

The primary divergence is in the commission's efforts to restrain total profits to some proper, or "fair," rate of return on the utility's investment. The basic choice is in these terms:

$$\text{Rate of return} = \frac{\text{Total Revenue} - \text{Total Cost}}{\text{Capital}}$$

Capital is supposed to include all fixed assets actually used—and necessary to be used—in supplying the utility service. The rate of return includes the return to all investors, in both equity and debt. The normal range for "fair" ceiling rates of return is about 6 to 9 percent, or about 2 to 3 points above the rate on riskless Treasury securities. Normally the Commission attempts to find the "cost of capital," a weighted average of bond rates of interest and a rough-guess (10, 12, 15 percent) "cost" imputed to equity capital. The "fair" rate is then set just above this supposed "cost of capital." However, the process of decision often appears to be merely a compromise between the proposals of the company and the commission's staff, rather than an exercise in logic or basic optimization.[22]

The second task is to get an efficient price structure. Utilities supply many different types of consumers—in residences, shops, industry, offices, etc. The outputs also vary—in times, amounts, and terms of supply—and they are often supplied via direct physical connections to the users. The utility has wide discretion in price-discrimination—to set prices in line with demand elasticities. The regulators' task is therefore to prevent "undue" discrimination. This means setting prices in line with the true costs of service, which, properly defined, are marginal costs. The objective is:

[22] See D. J. Dewey's chapter, "Regulatory Reform?," in Shepherd and Gies, *Regulation in Further Perspective;* and Ben W. Lewis's and Roger Cramton's chapters in Shepherd and Gies, *Utility Regulation.*

$$\text{Price} = k \text{ (Marginal Cost)}$$

where k is some ratio that is both similar among outputs and as close to unity as possible.[23] The utility, of course, wishes k to vary with demand elasticity, and possibly with cost as well. The customers will press at hearings for lower rates. Caught between consumers and the utility managers, who know their own cost and demand conditions best (though not always very well), the regulators usually settle on compromises which reflect both cost and demand conditions.

These decisions are reached after hearings. A hearing is called normally at the utility's request, to consider a change in some or all of its prices. The issues and timing are therefore usually set by the company, not the commission. In inflationary periods, these requests come frequently. Stable and deflationary periods often pass with no formal hearings at all. The company often anticipates in its request the probable cut which the regulators will make. The utility puts on expert witnesses—company officials, consultants, and academics—to make its case. The commission's staff usually offers a countercase, designed to offset the exaggeration inherent in the utility's case. In recent years, a variety of other interests have also joined in, representing private and public consumers and, occasionally, input suppliers (such as labor unions). The testimony creates a wide range of plausible outcomes; among the variety of specialists with differing views, one or more can always be hired to make out a preferred case.[24] The commission then adjourns, works out a compromise, and announces it with a brief rationale.

In these adversary hearings on prices or on new competition, there are standard biases in the burden of proof and the advantage of delay:

Subject of Action	The Burden of Proof Favors	Time Delay Favors
Rate hearings:		
if costs are rising	Agency	Agency
if costs are falling	Firm	Firm
New competition	Firm	Firm

[23] See Kahn, *Economics of Regulation,* and Bonbright, *Principles of Public Utility Rates.*

[24] The choice of witness can be regarded as an interesting strategy question (which applies in other legal settings too). The tradeoff is between a prospective witness's eminence, effectiveness in the witness chair, and congruence of views with the interested party. The selection and reward process tends to evolve specialists with modest eminence but considerable experience and usefulness. This in turn leads the hearing process to contain much boilerplate testimony and arid adversary exchanges.

Utility officers have three prime motives. One is to raise the profit ceiling. A rise can have potent effects on shareholder capital, since a "mere" one-point rise in the rate of return can increase portfolio values by 10 or 20 percent. The second motive is to set prices in line with demand elasticities.[25] Such discrimination may be less than would occur if total profits were unconstrained, but it will usually be considerable. It is designed also to minimize long-run risk and enlarge the rate base upon which profits can be earned (chapter 9 discusses this further).[26] The third motive is to avoid, at almost any cost, a service failure, for that event endangers the utility's privileged status as no other can.

The regulators share the third motivation, for service failures call *their* role into question too. The other two motives are partially shared by regulators, for they provide a seemingly "high-quality" and "expensive" service. Certain consumer groups also share these motives, in varying degrees and patterns. The costs that regulation is likely to levy are mostly subtle rather than dramatic, and not clearly onerous to any influential group.

In short, the regulatory process creates shared interests among utilities, regulators, and major user and supplier groups. In the process of negotiation and compromise, commissions often behave like mediators. Their objective is to make regulation appear to work well, in order to minimize outside criticism. A resemblance between this and strict public control—with clear scientific decisions based on full knowledge and economic criteria, and having the force of directives—is not only coincidental but contrived.

As chapter 1 noted, the effects of regulation may be presumed to be zero until proven otherwise.[27] Yet a consensus has evolved on several probable

---

[25] There is a large but focused literature on price discrimination; see J. Robinson, *The Economics of Imperfect Competition* (New York: Macmillan, 1933); Kahn, *Economics of Regulation;* Fritz Machlup, "Characteristics and Types of Price Discrimination," in *Business Concentration and Price Policy,* ed. G. J. Stigler (Princeton: Princeton University Press, 1955), pp. 400–423, and A. C. Pigou, *The Economics of Welfare* (New York: Macmillan, 1920), pp. 240–256.

[26] The modern classic article on this is H. Averch and L. L. Johnson, "Behavior of the Firm Under Regulatory Constraint," *American Economic Review,* 1962, pp. 1052–69; see also W. J. Baumol and A. K. Klevorick," "Input Choices and Rate-of-Return Regulation: An Overview of the Discussion," *Bell Journal of Economics and Management Science,* Autumn 1970, pp. 162–190; and L. L. Johnson's 10-year retrospect on the issue in Shepherd and Gies, *Regulation in Further Perspective.*

[27] This possibility is more or less explicit in Cramton, "The Effectiveness of Economic Regulation—A Legal View," and G. J. Stigler and C. Friedland, "What Can Regulators Regulate?

effects: (1) inefficiency will often be permitted or induced, under the "cost-plus" regulatory situation, so that all resources are overused;[28] (2) capital will be particularly overused[29] (this arises as a side-effect both of the rate-of-return constraint and of the regulators' deep aversion to service failures); (3) the utility's monopoly will be extended and protected, rather than kept aligned with the basic "natural-monopoly" conditions of cost;[30] (4) modest constraints will be set on profits and price discrimination. But there has been a loose consensus that the benefits from these constraints are outweighed by the costs.[31] Once again, as with antitrust, the appraisal turns largely on the rate at which the monopoly is likely to dwindle on its own (see chapter 9).

4 PUBLIC ENTERPRISE

Public enterprise—a relatively unfamiliar subject—takes a great variety of forms. It includes nearly everything—apart from antitrust and utility regulation—public policy does or might reasonably do to affect market structure and behavior. It ranges from conventional utility cases, through industrial and service areas and certain subsidy programs, and into important "social" enterprises such as public schools and universities, mental hospitals, the courts, and prisons. We are surrounded with public enterprises of many sorts, from factories to specific controls. Yet in this country their true nature is rarely recognized.[32]

The Case of Electricity," both in Shepherd and Gies, *Utility Regulation;* also in Kahn, *Economics of Regulation;* Barnes, *Public Utility Regulation;* Bernstein, *Regulating Business.*

[28] See Kahn, *Economics of Regulation,* and sources cited there.

[29] Averch and Johnson, "Behavior"; and Kahn, *ibid.*

[30] See also R. A. Posner, "Natural Monopoly and Its Regulation," *Stanford Law Review,* 1969, pp. 548ff.; and Shepherd, "The Margin of Competition in Communications," in *Technological Change in Regulated Industries,* ed. W. M. Capron (Wash., D.C.: Brookings Institution, 1971).

[31] An attempt to compare costs and benefits is made by Paul W. MacAvoy in "The Effectiveness of the Federal Power Commission," *Bell Journal of Economics and Management Science,* Autumn 1970, pp. 271–303; Kahn, in *Economics of Regulation,* offers a more favorable appraisal, but in general terms. See also the debate among W. S. Comanor, Joseph C. Swidler, W. G. Shepherd, and R. A. Posner in *The Stanford Law Review,* February 1970, pp. 510–46.

[32] American economists have quietly let the whole topic fade, hardly mentioning it as a public policy toward business. See Richard E. Caves, "Industrial Organization and Public Policy," in *Economics,* ed. Nancy Ruggles, Social Science Research Council (Englewood Cliffs, N.J.: Prentice-Hall, 1970); L. W. Weiss, *Case Studies in American Industry,* 2nd ed. (New

They all share two of the usual basic policy dimensions: public *control* and public *sponsorship*. Table 5.1 informally arranges a variety of cases according to these two criteria. One also needs to look at the degree to which the public enterprise is national or local in scope, and its degree of market power. Some of the cases in Table 5.1 are "programs," not "public firms." I include them here on purpose, because they help to show how diverse the tactics of "public enterprise" are. They go far beyond TVA, British Railways, and the local municipal water works,[33] and there is wide variation among national economies in the scope of public enterprise.

The history of public enterprise is checkered. One line is autocratic, from ancient statecraft through to the Organic State of Italy, Soviet-type economies, and other nondemocratic political systems. Another is sentimental British and Continental socialism, which is embodied in national firms in certain utility and sick-industry cases. Still another line is the municipal utility common in the United States (there are over 1,500 municipally owned electric systems, at present).[34]

Public enterprises are best fitted for sectors where goals are multiple, hard to measure, transcend efficiency, and pose hard choices of equity, and pricing choices are discretionary and have a large effect on equity. So public enterprise suits "soft," complex, and culturally important sectors. This fits its richness of forms and tactics.

Yet, oddly, the public firm has been consigned instead to utility sectors, mainly in the form of the "autonomous public corporation." Furthest developed in Britain, it is found in utility sectors throughout Europe and, less frequently, North America. It is commonly regarded as *the* alternative to the regulated private utility. Normally it is similar to a private firm, except that its capital is all from the public treasury or backed by public guarantee, and

---

York: Wiley, 1970), ch. 7; F. M. Scherer, *Industrial Market Structure and Economic Performance* (Skokie, Ill.: Rand McNally, 1970). By contrast public ownership is treated extensively, though not analytically, in successive editions of *Public Policies toward Business,* 4th ed. (Homewood, Ill.: Irwin, 1971). My own *Economic Performance Under Public Enterprise: British Fuel and Power* is virtually the only monograph in the area.

[33] See W. A. Robson, *Nationalized Industry and Public Ownership* (London: Allen and Unwin, 1961); and Stuart Holland, ed., *The State as Entrepreneur* (White Plains: International Arts and Sciences Press, 1972).

[34] Richard Hellman, *Government Competition in the Electric Utility Industry: A Theoretical and Empirical Study* (New York: Praeger, 1972); and see Federal Power Commission, *Statistics of Electric Utilities in the United States,* annual (U.S. Government Printing Office).

Table 5.1 Selected Public-Enterprise Activities in the United States, by Approximate Degree of Control and Subsidy

	Full Control	Partial Control	Slight Control
No subsidy	Municipal utilities (water, sewage) AEC enrichment plants U.S. Government Printing Office Social Security Municipal parking facilities Municipal transit Federal courts Public law programs Child-care programs Primary education	State liquor stores National land management Amtrak SBA programs (including minority support) FAA programs Airports Highway construction and maintenance State courts Local courts Federal maritime program Mental hospitals State and local law enforcement agencies Prisons Corps of Engineers Census Bureau	Port of New York Authority Federal Reserve Board FHA housing program Tennessee Valley Performing arts centers Sports stadiums Public housing Medicare Medicaid Public universities SST program Military R&D contracting Veterans Administration hospitals Weapons purchasing and management
Full subsidy			

it is not formally regulated but "supervised" by a government department.[35] This is shown in Figure 5.3. Its board members are public appointees, but they and the managers are often indistinguishable from their counterparts in private firms. Indeed, they are normally drawn from the same population, move freely between public and private positions, and often hold directorships of both kinds.

As a first approximation, we may assume that public-firm managers' preferences are similar to those of private managers. The constraints on them differ, but they usually involve budgetary limits on costs and revenues, a definite profit target, and a degree of financial supervision akin to what actually occurs in large private firms.[36]

Such public firms cluster in utility sectors, and in certain other sectors with a special "social impact." They sell products or services, and are required to take in enough revenue to cover costs plus some degree of profit on capital. They are also usually burdened with a variety of "social" policies—to perform tasks the government is not willing to fund and operate directly. These social burdens can be heavy, so the firm's profit targets are often entangled in definitions of its "commercial" and "social" activities. Also, their capital usually comes at reduced costs, from the treasury or with a public guarantee, so there is some possibility that investment will exceed the margin at which its returns cover the true opportunity costs of capital to the state. This holds even for public firms that use private capital sources, because the guarantee increases their access and lowers the cost.

The conventional public firm unifies—i.e., monopolizes—its industry, backed by franchise and entry protections as ample as those of private firms under regulation. Its target or minimum rates of profit are set in the same range (6–10 percent) as regulatory *ceilings* on rates of return. This often leaves the price structure questions at least as indeterminate as they are in private firms under regulation. In fact they may be systematically less determinate in the public firm, for the managers are less constrained toward profit-maximizing per se. Instead, they may be strongly motivated toward

[35] See W. G. Shepherd, *Economic Performance Under Public Ownership: British Fuel and Power* (New Haven: Yale University Press, 1965); Robson, *Nationalized Industry;* and especially C. D. Foster, *Politics, Finance and the Role of Economics: An Essay on the Control of Public Enterprise* (London: Allen and Unwin, 1971).

[36] Foster, *ibid.;* R. Turvey, *Economic Analysis and Public Enterprises* (London: Allen and Unwin, 1971); and Robson, *ibid.* Foster reflects the now-common concern with private criteria, and the deemphasis of content and social effects.

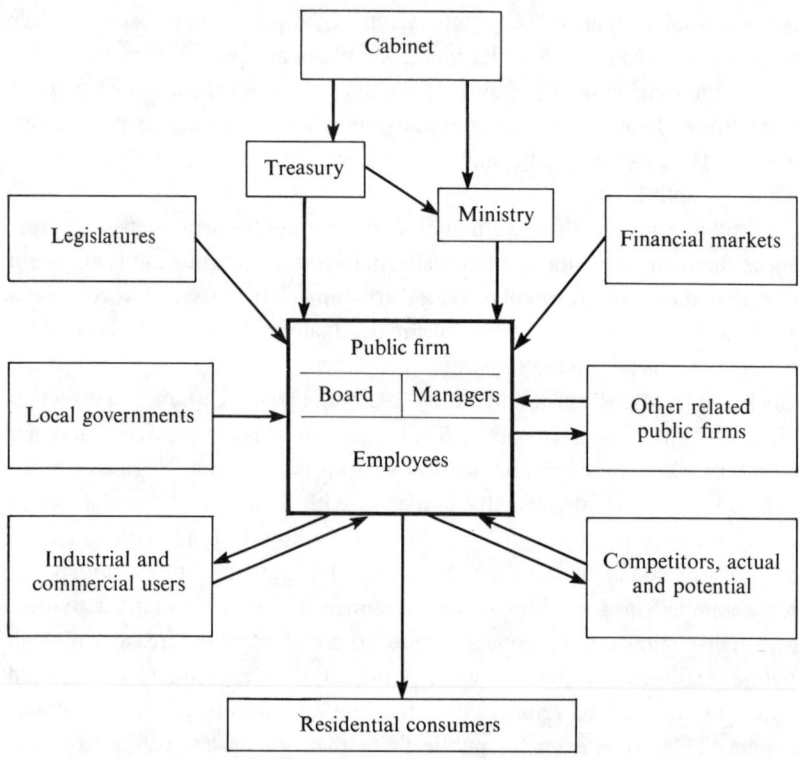

Figure 5.3 The setting for conventional public enterprises.

risk-minimizing and possibly sales-maximizing. In any case, in classical utility price structures public firms are potentially even less rational than those of weakly constrained private utilities.

The standard public enterprise has come in the last several decades to be firmly set under commercial criteria. The main weight of political pressure and economic analysis has forced most public enterprises to imitate private enterprise behavior. Improvement of content has been relegated to a distant secondary objective, now scarcely mentioned. Behavior to upgrade content typically has to be defended as being really commercial in intent and effect. The success of public enterprise is now rated in narrow commercial terms. In all this, economists have had little to add, and that little has conformed almost entirely to the orthodox images of control and goals. Because public enterprises have been cut into commercial patterns, it is possible to ask whether public enterprise matters at all.[37] But since the experience has been diverted from the main possible effect of public ownership—to raise content—the question itself is off the point.

This classic form may also tend to enlarge the public's commitment of capital and severely limit the public's control over what the enterprise does. Even so, it does not involve an outright public subsidy of all or most of the costs, as do the classic "public good" cases, such as schools, medical insurance, and prisons. These too are public enterprises; they have latent competitive and commercial aspects, yet they are commonly ignored. At the other extreme (see Table 5.1) are public enterprises with thorough control and no subsidy. Indeed, some public enterprises are operated to yield a large flow of funds for the public purse.

In short, "public enterprise" includes a variety of controls, pricing choices, degrees of subsidy or profit, internal structures, and degrees of monopoly. Many have been virtually thrust upon the public, because of commercial failure. Some are inefficient and costly, while others yield high net public returns. The objective is not to decide about public enterprise versus private ownership, or versus regulation or antitrust. Rather it is to learn of the variety in public enterprise, to identify the more efficient types, and to combine them with other strategies.

Evidently, "nationalization" and "public ownership," in the classic British and TVA style, are not representative cases. In no other Western economy is there nationalization comparable in scale to that in the large U.S. economy. Abroad, even the largest public firms are only on a regional and local scale by U.S. standards. Also, public ownership is only one device within the whole public enterprise toolkit.

Given this great variety, it is instructive to identify the two extremes of public-enterprise types: those whose yields are relatively low and, conversely, those relatively high.

Among the low-yield cases, there are at least four types. One is high sponsorship with low control. This shades into straight subsidies, often from poor to rich, often via state guarantees against private risks. A few possible examples are interest-free loans to military suppliers, the 1971 loan guaran-

---

[37] See Shepherd, *Economic Performance Under Public Ownership;* and R. Pryke, *Public Enterprise in Practice* (New York: St. Martins, 1972), for attempts to judge whether this has occurred in practice; also W. G. Shepherd, "Public Expenditure," in R. E. Caves and Associates, *Britain's Economic Prospects* (Wash., D.C.: Brookings Institution, 1968).

tee for Lockheed Aircraft, and portions of the U.S. maritime subsidy program.[38]

Another type is subsidy for activities used mainly by those with above-average income and wealth. Possible examples include certain subsidized programs for performing arts, much suburban commuter service, parts of the Amtrak system, and tax support of university education for children from upper economic levels. Because access to the best legal counsel is unequal, the several systems of courts can be regarded as public enterprises having primarily a regressive incidence—including their treatment of commercial matters. These examples include some of what are regarded as our finest institutions, in the arts, education, law, and the courts.[39] Their whole effects go well beyond the narrow economic impact.

A third type is the syndrome of the "sick" industry, often using large amounts of capital and often selling to (and buying from) large private firms. Since the "sickness" is often industry wide (with severe dislocations and intraindustry externalities that invite a "unified" treatment), the common strategy is a centralized monopoly financed partly by the treasury. The classic form is the U.K. public corporation, in coal, steel, and railroads; railroads are, in fact, in this status almost everywhere in the world.[40] British experience suggests that these cases should be handled differently. Many of the "social" impacts are external to the industry, but governments routinely fail to treat them directly, instead leaving them as a burden on the public firm, to be met by slowing down closures and by cross-subsidizing the losing parts. The public firm is also often prevented from raising its prices, and it is usually expected to raise wages rapidly. The main beneficiaries often are industrial users and equipment suppliers. The resulting financial losses, redundancy, and demoralization in the public firm are often interpreted as discrediting all forms of public enterprise. The drain from all this on public supervision, public funds, and public administration talent has been large, but the disillusion with public enterprise should be only with this specific form of it and with the special constraints on it.

The last type is the nationwide public firm in a "healthy" utility sector,

---

[38] See Joint Economic Committee, *The Economics of Federal Subsidy Programs*, 92d Congress, 1st Session (U.S. Government Printing Office, 1973) for a more complete listing of this kind of aid.

[39] See, e.g., W. J. Baumol and W. G. Bowen, *Performing Arts: The Economic Dilemma* (New York: Twentieth Century Fund, 1966); M. Fleming, *Perfect Justice*.

[40] See Pryke, *Public Enterprise in Practice;* Robson, *Nationalized Industry;* R. Turvey, ed., *Public Enterprise,* rev. ed. (London: Penguin, 1970).

such as electric power and telephones. "Health" means that revenues cover costs (often because of excess demand) and that there are few big external effects (such as pollution) or social impacts. Yet these enterprises still absorb large amounts of capital and administrative talent. The gains are often minor and (e.g., in the U.K., telephones) mainly taken by private firms and upper economic groups.[41] TVA's biggest customers now include aluminum firms, along with—in lesser proportions—the rural poor.[42] Moreover, the lack of competitive constraints can induce internal inefficiency. A switch to private bond financing can abate much of the reliance on public funds, but the other costs persist and the whole economic and social yields may remain small or negative.

These are categories of public enterprises that perhaps should—according to criteria of efficiency and equity—be revised in form and objectives. By contrast, certain other kinds of public enterprises have tight constraints (by competition or budgetary control), minimum use of public funds and talent, a progressive incidence, and flexibility in arrangements.

One such type is the public-firm competitor, with a quarter or less of the market and some mixture of private-public ownership and motivation. It can cause improved pricing and efficiency in tight-oligopoly markets. Its takeover threat to firms in other tight-oligopoly markets could indirectly induce increased efficiency in them, too (see chapter 7).[43]

A second group is the public entity as countervailer against private market power, which may be inaccessible to other constraints. An instance is the British national health service as a buyer of drugs from private companies.[44] It is paralleled on a small scale in the U.S. by the Veterans Administration and certain hospital groups. Purchases of weapons occasionally—but not consistently—are done on this basis.[45]

---

[41] See Shepherd, "Public Expenditure," in *Britain's Economic Prospects,* ed. Caves, and sources cited there.

[42] But see also Hellman, *Government Competition.*

[43] There is a pioneering study by W. C. Merrill and N. Schneider, "Government Firms in Oligopoly Industries," *Quarterly Journal of Economics,* 1966, pp. 400–412; see also Holland, *The State as Entrepreneur.*

[44] This is explored in the "Sainsbury Report," *Report of the Committee of Enquiry into the Relationship of the Pharmaceutical Industry with the National Health Service, 1965–1967,* Cmnd. 3410, Her Majesty's Stationery Office, 1967; see also Shepherd, "Public Expenditure."

[45] M. J. Peck and F. M. Scherer, *The Weapons Aquisition Process* (Cambridge, Mass.: Harvard University School of Business, 1962); J. R. Kurth, "The Political Economy of Weapons Procurement: The Follow-on Imperative," *American Economic Review,* May 1972, pp. 304–11.

Third are activities with high, progressive benefits spread throughout society. Among the activities are public libraries, good-quality legal services for the poor,[46] immunization programs, and universal primary schooling—if properly structured. The social-critic and innovator aspects of public universities also are of this sort.

Fourth are units whose outputs go mainly to wealthy groups and which maximize profits. Prime examples are state universities, performing arts programs, and high quality medical care, *if they were operated to gain large profits*. This can be done by using price discrimination—charging what the traffic will bear—on a means test or some other basis. This group is the mirror image of the second "worst" type above; the objective here is a progressive incidence consistent with the usual efficiency criteria.

Between these extremes lie many mixed cases. For example, the U.S. Social Security insurance enterprise yeields certain benefits of efficient allocation over time, but its financing is unnecessarily regressive. Hospital and health-insurance enterprises (Medicare, Medicaid, others) may be insensitive to inefficiency. Public housing projects have had negative effects—via isolation and poor design—which could be avoided. The three AEC uranium-enrichment plants absorb large amounts of public capital (and TVA electricity!) and yet subsidize a narrow group of large firms and utilities, which use their services. In these and other cases, it is primarily the policies that are nonoptimal, not the fact of public enterprise.

From such experience and from logic, one can posit a regressive shift hypothesis: The benefits of any public enterprise will normally tend to become less progressive over time.

The public firm is, like any other social device, a target for interest groups to use to their advantage. Large firms and affluent citizens will normally be able to adjust more quickly and fully to reap the benefits of public enterprises (e.g., low-price outputs). Over time, this means that the benefits will shift toward less needy groups. Examples: TVA at its creation had a variety of progressive effects on rural poverty. Now it primarily sells bulk electricity to large private firms and utility systems. The U.K. National Coal Boards' output has shifted primarily from households to industry and the generation of electricity.

With care the regressive shift can be avoided, but the tendency toward it

[46] Yet even these may not yield high net benefits in practice, because they are subject to the trend toward a regressive incidence.

is inherent, as it is with any public policy operating in the real political economy.

More broadly, the actual effects of public enterprise are even more obscure than are those of antitrust and regulation. There are evidently cases of social waste and inequity. But other cases have high social yields. In still others, the effects have probably been nil. Since many public enterprises have been trapped in narrow commercial criteria which ignore content, many of the past "lessons of experience" are incomplete and biased.

5 PURCHASES BY PUBLIC AGENCIES

Public-agency purchasing is also a distinct and important category. The buying of weapons influences many industries (see chapter 12), and other programs are also important—in purchasing R & D activity, nuclear development, construction of schools and highways, medical services, and many others.

The methods used in these purchases are various, but three of their features stand out. One is the frequent resort to cost-plus-profit as the basis for payment. Such cost-plus treatments have been known for over a century to lack incentives for efficiency. Yet they persist for much public purchasing, though often informally or in camouflaged forms.[47] Second, much purchasing is done noncompetitively, by preselecting the supplier without an open process of bidding and choice.

And third, where competitive bidding is used, it is commonly done by sealed bids, which minimizes the incentives for price-cutting by bidders.[48] Those who do underbid are directly exposed, and since the bids are sealed, any auction series of competitive price-cutting cannot occur. The result is rigidity before the decision, exposure afterward.

The whole effect has probably been to reduce competition and to redistribute wealth upward. Efficiency in several senses—internal, allocational, the form of national military policy, innovation—has probably been appreciably reduced, and mutual interest groups likely to maintain these conditions have evolved (see chapter 10).

---

[47] F. M. Scherer, *The Weapons Acquisition Process: Economic Incentives* (Cambridge, Mass.: Harvard Business School Division of Research, 1964); R. A. Tybout, *Government Contracting in Atomic Energy* (Ann Arbor: University of Michigan Press, 1965).

[48] G. J. Stigler, *The Organization of Industry* (Homewood, Ill.: Irwin, 1968), ch. 16.

6 SUBSIDY PROGRAMS

Among the range of all subsidy programs, an important share goes to specific industries. The exact extent cannot be defined, for many consumption subsidies are indirect subsidies to the suppliers of the service (e.g., to those who construct public housing). Still, the scope of direct subsidies can be shown, in Table 5.2. Some of the subsidies are direct payments; others are through cutting taxes; still others by guaranteeing risks.[49]

Table 5.2 Gross Budgetary Costs of Selected Major U.S. Federal Subsidies, 1970

Category	Cash payments [a]	Tax subsidies [a]	Credit subsidies [a]	Benefits in kind [a]	Total
Total, all major subsidies	11,801	38,480	4,183	9,245	63,709
Agriculture	3,879	880	443	1,109	6,311
Medical care	973	3,150	52	4,617	8,792
Medicare	0	0	0	1,979	1,979
Medicaid	0	0	0	2,638	2,638
Education	1,976	785	434	409	3,604
Loans	0	0	301	0	
International trade	106	420	623	34	1,183
Export financing	106	0	394	0	500
Housing	195	5,680	2,550	0	8,425
Commerce and development	2,041	15,635	59	1,518	19,253
Postal	0	0	0	1,510	1,510
Transport	300	10	0	362	672
Maritime	262	10	0	0	
Air transport	38	0	0	229	267

SOURCE: Adapted from Joint Economic Committee, *The Economics of Federal Subsidy Programs,* 92nd Congress, 1st session, U.S. Government Printing Office, 1972.

[a] $ millions.

Subsidies usually contain two inherent effects. First, they commonly apply negative incentives for efficiency. Such perverse cases are not rare. Only if the subsidy is tied to efficient performance or is explicitly temporary will it avoid some degree of negative effect. The second question is equity: subsidies commonly have a regressive incidence.

Yet there is variation among them, and the object is to find which actual or alternative programs will induce efficiency and avoid a sharply regressive incidence.

[49] Joint Economic Committee, *Economics of Federal Subsidy Programs.*

7 TAXATION

The one basic tax measure that touches on industrial structure and performance is the corporation income tax.[50] Apart from a few special-interest provisions to be noted, there is no specific use of tax incentives to alter market structure, context, content, or other dimensions of performance.

The corporate income tax affects primarily the incentives to merge and the extent of company response to public policies. The tax rate is formally at about 50 percent of net income.[51] Because the pooling of losses and profits is permitted, with carry-forward provisions, a whole class of mergers—involving firms with low or negative profits—is more profitable than it would otherwise be. Although the effects are not known, they would tend to increase size and market power.[52]

That the corporate profits tax is likely to induce higher resistance to public policies was shown in chapter 3. No one has yet measured how strong this effect is, and it might even tend toward doubling the resistance. We can certainly expect that it is not trivial.[53]

The more specific tax measures also tend to increase or be neutral to market power, but not to reduce it. The tariff on imports is an important and ancient tax, which excludes or reduces foreign competition from many industries.[54] It tends unambiguously to increase the market power and profitability of the domestic producers—often quite sharply. Special tax treatments for oil and other "wasting asset" industries tend more to reduce efficiency and equity directly than by altering structure,[55] but they definitely do not promote competition.

[50] See J. A. Pechman, *Federal Tax Policy,* rev. ed. (New York: Norton, 1971).

[51] It is presently at a nominal rate of 48 percent of net income. But in practice many provisions reduce actual taxes below this rate, in some cases toward zero or even negative. See Joint Economic Committee, *Tax Subsidies and Tax Reform,* Hearings, 92nd Congress, 2d Session (U.S. Government Printing Office, 1973), especially pp. 6–28, for a survey of such patterns among the largest industrial firms.

[52] But see also J. Lintner and J. K. Butters, *Effects of Corporate Taxation* (Cambridge, Mass.: Harvard University Press, 1948).

[53] The only exception would be those firms which have arranged under special tax provisions to have low or zero tax rates.

[54] It was one of Adam Smith's primary targets. Repeated studies have failed to show any relation between an industry's degree of monopoly and its rate of protection. This is partly because defining and measuring the degree of protection is difficult; see especially W. M. Corden, *The Theory of Protection* (London: Clarendon Press, 1971).

[55] See A. E. Kahn, "The Depletion Allowance in the Context of Cartellization," *American Review,* 1964, pp. 286–314. Recent events may alter this, moderately.

In short, present tax provisions tend to increase market power, its costs, and its resistance to treatment. There is no purposive use of taxation to abate market power or raise content. Taxes, we shall see, are one great unused set of treatments that may have power and precision.

8 PRICE-WAGE CONTROLS

The peacetime price controls that have been tried in the 1970s have had only slight effects, although some observers regard them as necessary for the "new" conditions.[56] These conditions include high market power in major industries (both of producers and labor unions) and structural problems in labor markets. If inflation arises mainly in major industries, then a set of focused price-wage controls may be both necessary and effective. Yet the optimal design of price controls is not likely to be adopted (see chapter 9).[57]

Wage controls have had equally mediocre results, for obvious reasons. Unless the gains of investors and managers are limited, controls on wages will be disequalizing. Such inequality will not only violate canons of fairness, but will also eliminate labor's willingness to accept the constraints. That is what has happened, in all western economies, for two reasons.[58] First, investor and managerial rewards are elusive to define and constrain (indeed, the presence of controls may cause the rewards to be exaggerated). Second, and more important, the political economy appears to be quite resistant to it. The outcome violates content, too, by altering the reward structure even further toward inequality than it already is.

Accordingly, optimal price-wage controls remain a thoroughly hypothetical matter. So far their use has been mainly for cosmetic purposes. Where constraints have had genuine force, they have tended to disequalize and to reduce content. On the whole, the recent experiments with price-wage constraints have demonstrated their ineffectiveness and costs.

[56] Among the advocates is J. K. Galbraith, *Economics and the Public Purpose* (Boston: Houghton-Mifflin, 1973).

[57] This has been equally true in Western European experiments with such controls. On U.S. experience, see R. F. Lanzillotti, M. Hamilton and B. Roberts, *Phase II in Review: The Price Commission* (Wash., D.C.: Brookings Institution, 1974).

[58] Only in 1973 were slight efforts made in the U.S. to constrain executive pay increases. But they were mild and relatively easy to avoid. No visible effect was to be seen in actual changes in remuneration. See also J. Sheahan, *The Wage-Price Guideposts* (Wash., D.C.: Brookings Institution, 1967).

9 SUMMARY

Conventional antitrust, regulation, and public enterprise have a variety of limits and internal biases. These cause the policies' scope, direct effects, and side effects to differ from their formal effects, and probably from the optimal results. The side effects in particular are possibly large, but are little known. None of the policies, as now used, deals effectively with context or content—not even public enterprise. Therefore, basic revisions or replacements of these treatments are probably in order.[59] The ultrapolitical-economy hypothesis—that the treatments reflect and serve the underlying power structure—cannot be rejected. Indeed, it is roughly in accord with reality, as best we can observe it.

Three policy tools—exposure, purposive taxation, and public enterprise—are underused, compared to their potential. Information policies are markedly defective, with official agencies causing or acquiescing in secrecy virtually across the board. Taxation tends to accentuate market power, though it could operate with precision to abate it (see below). And the recognition that content is important places the proper scope of public enterprise on a new footing. Nothing else in the policy toolkit deals so directly with content.

In short, the policy array in the U.S. is presently thin, erratic, and rigid—

---

[59] These policy defects are sufficient to make an abolitionist position plausible, even attractive. But we should keep in mind four basic points about laissez-faire in its Chicago-Freiburg and other versions.

First, selective abolition—*e.g.*, of regulation—may misjudge the alternatives. Each treatment may appear defective, but each may be no worse than the alternatives, including nontreatment.

Second, full abolition is like abandoning ship before the iceberg is struck. Ultra-political economy urges that policies reflect and protect the underlying array of interests and power and may therefore tend to harm rather than cure. But that is an extreme position, more definitional than either deductive or factual. Also it denies that policies can ever act upon the power structure, or be designed so that the special and general interests are congruent. The issue is not yet settled.

Third, abolition requires its own consistency. Piecemeal abolition may worsen the damage. The optimum strategy of abolition is in itself not obvious and may be quite complex, and abolition must exclude other monopoly-creating policies as well as antitrust and regulation.

Fourth, a careful and balanced appraisal of costs and benefits is needed. It is not sufficient to find one real or probable nonoptimality of a treatment. The whole effect must be estimated and compared with real alternatives.

In short, abolition may be as hazardous to the health of policy as naivete. Most of the hard choices are likely to be in the middle ranges; care and realism must be used in evaluating probable effects and alternatives.

and probably costly. The costs may not be vast, but they are large and chronic; and the policies are permeated with illusions and cynical deceptions. The old errors are, if anything, being repeated and extended, within a limited intellectual framework for understanding and correcting the problems. If chapters 2–5 have been reasonably correct in defining market reality, deriving a rational basis for choosing policies, measuring the yields, and evaluating the policies at hand, then we can perhaps begin to design treatments that may be genuinely close to optimal. Our cardinal principle will be to design treatments that recognize and perhaps even use the political economy rather than naively ignore it or run bravely against it.

CHAPTER SIX
The Financial Sector

THERE ARE several main sectors and several main policies to apply to them. A suitable format is to take the sectors one by one, outlining treatments that fit—even if only roughly—the criteria of optimality. Since the underlying conditions and criteria are unified, this sectoral treatment may seem more ad hoc than it really is.

Therefore, I shall begin by briefly recounting the principles governing the practical choices in all the sectors.

1. Draw on the same policy set for all sectors. Unify policies, rather than create separate policy sectors.
2. Use therapy rather than surgery where possible. Go with the grain, not against it; fit treatments to the natural motives, skills and information of the key actors.
3. Have complete disclosure of information, save only in exceptional cases where a strong basis for secrecy can be made.
4. Use taxation and related incentive devices freely. They can induce responses that could be coerced only at high or infinite costs. Several specific taxes will be explored.
5. Always tie monopoly grants (e.g., patents and utility franchises) to private costs, which induce a yielding up of market share.
6. Deal with content by using public enterprise, but do so in efficient ways which are sparing of public resources.

These points will recur, with some inevitable repetition. For example, a tax on market share comes up in finance, industry, and utilities (chapters 6–9) in basically the same form, and public enterprise recurs in several contexts. The basic benefit-cost method of choice is, of course, the same throughout.

Because financial markets are a main part of context, they are central to understanding and treating market power. One must have a policy for them—even if it is not totally sufficient—in order to optimize the outcomes in other sectors. We shall therefore take up the financial sector first, although the criteria for their treatment are much the same as those for the rest of the economy.

In the United States, capital markets may be moderately competitive and yet offer large unrealized policy yields. This is especially so because financial markets influence competition elsewhere in the economy. The basic problem is unequal access to capital and to information. This inequality of access arises from market power in banking, as well as from the broader problem of inside information. Part of the solution is to revise the treatment of banking, but broader treatments of the insider problem are also needed. As certain of these problems have grown in recent years and conventional policies have hardened, a wide variety of treatments have been proposed. It will appear that optimal treatments probably follow lines rather different from most of the familiar suggestions.

First we shall review the probable effects of banking structure in the present setting, after which we shall derive revisions that will lead toward an optimal treatment. Section 3 then outlines what the effects of this treatment might be.

1 THE EFFECTS OF BANKING STRUCTURE

To recall from chapters 2 and 4: banking markets are in several layers, from local to international. These layers are not entirely distinct, but one can speak broadly about the degree of market power in each. In each layer, the key activity is the same: to supply both credit and counsel to individual firms, usually via a "banking relationship." These relationships are often intimate and are not often changed.

Quite naturally, the larger firms tend broadly to have relationships with the larger banks. Firms also deal routinely, and on a long-standing basis, with other financial units—underwriters, investment banks, and institutional investors. But the banks have the primary supportive role in allocating funds and counselling on enterprise strategy. They also play a central role in supervising management performance, redirecting it where appropriate and, on occasion, participating in (or against) takeover efforts by individual firms.

This context of market structure tends to be rigid and noncompetitive, and it is therefore likely to cause a degree of inefficiency and inequity. There is near-unanimity among experts on these conditions,[1] and more recently it has appeared that these conditions may also be undermining the allocative efficiency of capital markets.[2]

The first condition is that banking structure is now stable and, in many parts, highly monopolistic. The structure grew out of a wave of horizontal mergers during 1950–63, which increased the market shares of leading banks in many metropolitan banking areas.[3] Concentration is reinforced by several "public" policy limits—against entry, rate competition, and takeover by non-banking firms.[4] Moreover, other semibanking units are excluded by law from competing directly with commercial banks. These limits were applied in the 1930s to assure banking security, but they have since come to avert competition almost as neatly as if the dominant banks had arrnaged them in their own interests. Even the new limits on bank mergers since 1963 have hardened banking structure; these restrictions were applied after the largest banks had already merged, and were not applied retroactively to undo them.[5] As a result, banking is now significantly monopolistic, and this market power has a very low rate of decline over time.

Second, "banking relationships" are important. They do not account for

---

[1] A. Phillips, "A Competitive Policy for Depository Financial Institutions," in *Competition and the Regulation of Industry,* ed. Phillips (Wash., D.C.: Brookings Institution, 1974); D. Alhadeff, *Monopoly and Competition in Banking* (Berkeley: University of California Press, 1954); J. M. Guttentag and E. S. Herman, *Banking Structure and Performance* (New York: New York University Press, 1967).

[2] See Irwin Friend, "The Economic Consequences of the Stock Market," *American Economic Review,* May 1972, pp. 212–19, and sources cited there.

[3] For one summary of bank mergers see P. M. Horvitz and B. Shull, "The Bank Merger Act of 1960: A Decade After," *Antitrust Bulletin,* Winter 1971, pp. 859–892; and see also Phillips, "Competitive Policy."

[4] See Phillips, *ibid.,* and Alhadeff, *Monopoly and Competition.*

[5] See Horvitz and Shull, "Bank Merger Act"; the critical case was U.S. v. Philadelphia National Bank, 374 U.S. 321 (1963).

all of the relative advantage that large and high-share firms have in the availability and cost of capital. Actually, as chapter 4 noted, the differences in observed interest costs probably understate the real difference in advantage. Still, the bank–firm ties do underlie part of the difference. They also allocate inside information and expert advice differentially. The actual ties and their effects are mostly secret, owing to commercial customs and the tight confidentiality rules banking agencies follow.[6] One cannot demonstrate them with precision, for that reason.

Why they persist is not intuitively obvious, for one might suppose that free choice would neutralize the bias and dissolve the relationships. Thus, a firm whose capabilities are genuinely superior should theoretically attract—on the basis of its prospects—equal capital supply from any and all banks, regardless of whether it is small and new or large and established. Yet this is not so, because banking competition is limited by structure, rules, and custom, and a shift in a banking relationship can be costly.[7] Large bank–firm relationships are stable because their combination of counseling and borrowing rates benefits both sides. Also, services are not priced separately but are instead lumped together. Specific cost and price alternatives are not offered or known.[8] To change banking relationships, small or new banks need ample capital, an ability to cut interest rates extremely sharply for long periods, and a capacity for inside information and expert counsel that is at

[6] Banking regulatory agencies follow tight secrecy rules, releasing virtually no useful data on individual bank behavior and performance. The only exception is the FDIC listings of 1-, 3-, and 5-bank concentration ratios for the larger cities.

[7] This cost can be seen with a brief example. Suppose that Large Inc. has total capital of $400 million, on which its customary profit rate has been about 15 percent. Its primary banking relationship is with Large Bank, from which it gets advice, inside information, and financial backing which add (or so the firm believes) .5 percent to its profit rate (that would be a gross understatement for many real cases). This is a yearly profit flow of only $2 million, but it would capitalize at 8 percent over 20 years into a present value of about $20 million.

Large Inc. has short-term capital needs of $50 million, which Small Bank would like to compete for. To make it rational for Large Inc. to shift from Large Bank, Small Bank will have to offer a cut in credit cost which equals in present value the $20 million which Large Bank's advice seems to be worth. That cut would have to be at least 4 percent—i.e., from 9 percent to 5 percent or from 6 percent to 2 percent—which is not only large but impossible in practice. Large Inc.'s interest costs will already be low because Large Bank values Large Inc.'s stability (and Large Inc. may also have gotten the low rate by playing off banks against each other).

[8] There are a few signs that this uniformity is being breached by a degree of separate pricing by several lesser banks (see *Business Week,* October 27, 1973). And a more competitive spirit is regularly said to be growing in banking circles. But this is embryonic so far, and it scarcely touches the core banking relationships.

least as good as the larger banks. This combination is normally well beyond the reach of new entrants and smaller banks, and so banking relationships are indeed stable. The only group capable of supplying the combination would be the leading officers in the large banks who would form a new bank, "taking the large company accounts with them." This is presently ruled out by the "public" policy rules on chartering, and by the unwritten code of banker behavior. In practice, it simply is not done.

Third, inefficiency is therefore likely to arise and persist within banks and within the firms they counsel. The incentive to discipline or turn out inefficient management is reduced, and takeovers are ruled out, both for banks and their client firms.[9] At the other extreme, the *best*-managed firms with market power are mostly not available as clients to new or maverick banks endeavoring to compete. As a result, the degree of monopoly and its effects are higher in both banking and industry because of the mutual relations between the two. This fact has been underemphasized by those who study industrial market structure alone and treat finance as a different subject.

Fourth, this effect has recently been increased by the growing role of large institutions in stock markets. It has always been true that large-scale, expert investors have gotten higher yields than small investors who rely on public information. That accounts in part for the decline during the last decade in participation in portfolio investment by small shareholders. This effect has been sharpened because institutions have recently tended to move in unison, which has destabilized share prices even in the leading issues.

The rise of institutional trading is also reducing access to investible capital by lesser firms. From a figure of 30 percent in 1963, such high-volume trading has risen beyond 70 percent of all trading on the New York Stock Exchange. By focusing their holdings in a relatively few leading firms—estimates range from 25 to 300—these large traders have reduced the access of lesser firms to investment capital. Many of these favored firms are those which emerged in chapter 4 as problem cases. The relative disadvantage of smaller firms is reflected by low price-earnings ratios, which have come to prevail over the broad range of secondary firms. Accordingly, smaller and newer firms have added difficulty raising new equity capital. Moreover,

---

[9] This is perhaps more marked in Britain. The clearing banks have undergone a relative decline partly because of their relatively passive and restrictive behavior. Some regard this as the core of the problem of entrepreneurial capacity in Britain during the last generation at least.

their managers' stock options are often rendered worthless, and new firms find it increasingly difficult to offer shares publicly at all. The net effect is to reduce the prospects for competition in a variety of industrial markets.

In summary, capital markets now appear to contain appreciable biases both against small portfolio investors and against small competitive firms. The efficiency and equity costs of such biases may be large and widely spread. They are a vector of many conditions of structure, habit, and rules, in several types and levels of markets.

These conditions define the main objectives for treatment: to provide access to capital on unbiased terms of cost and availability, to equalize access to financial counsel, market information, and support for competitive strategies, and to eliminate disparities in information for portfolio investors. Treatments will apply primarily to banking and stock markets, as they relate to nonfinancial firms. These treatments will be suited both to dominant firms which are inefficient and need rehabilitation, and to those whose profits are high and secure. In short, treatment will affect both banking and nonbanking markets.

2 ALTERNATIVE TREATMENTS

To be effective, treatment will need to address and correct imperfections in the very core of the modern economic system—conditions that have generated the largest personal fortunes and advantages in the present fabric of society. The stakes are evidently high and the capacity for resisting treatment—or capturing it—is great. Indeed, treatments in the past have largely conformed to the ultrapolitical-economy hypothesis. That is partly why the imperfections are now of such moment.

A treatment will need to reduce banking concentration, to abate the power of "banking relationships," and to reduce the insider problem. A wide range of tools is available, including public ownership for part or all of banking and stock exchanges, large-scale public supply of capital to lesser firms, deconcentration of banking, prohibition of certain banking relationships, stricter penalties for insider violations, deregulation of banking behavior and entry, limits on institutional investors.

I shall explore a more moderate and unified set of treatments here—treatments that rely mainly on designing appropriate incentives to modify behavior rather than on prohibitions and coerced structural changes. The treatments employ the self-interest of those affected by present conditions —rather than trying simply (and naively) to obstruct interests that are presently favored—and also resolve some of the serious conflict-of-interest situations that are now routinely acute in large areas of banking and management. On the whole, this set of treatments is less drastic than those proposed by several leading and thoughtful experts.[10]

Banking structure. It is probably too late and too difficult to undo the large banking mergers of 1950–63. Most of them would have been prevented if the treatment of horizontal mergers had been as rational then as it is now. For the future, most objective observers agree that entry and competitive behavior should no longer be appreciably constrained, either within commercial banking or between it and quasi-banking units.[11] The security of deposits in banks is already amply guaranteed by deposit insurance. A reduction in banking concentration would be induced by applying a graduated tax on each bank's profit rate on equity. This surtax would be scaled in line with the bank's share in its relevant SMSA market. The tax rates would be roughly the same as those for nonfinancial and utility firms (see chapters 7 and 9), ranging probably from 45 to 55 percent. Indeed, the gradient in the tax rate could be surprisingly small.[12] The tax would not foster inefficiency (see chapter 7). Depending on the net direction income and substitution effects, the tax would as likely as not induce *better* bank management.

This set of treatments could be confined to the larger banks, perhaps those with assets above $1.5 billion (there were about 60 in 1973), which would cover two or more banks in the ten largest banking metropolitan areas, plus leading banks in 12 other large cities.[13] Whatever the exact criterion might be, the coverage could be focused efficiently on those banks where the yields are relatively high.

Defining the true market will, as ever, be difficult. Yet it would be reasonable and effective to use the bank's share of its metropolitan banking

---

[10] Thus Phillips' preferred treatment ("Competitive Policy") is more drastic in several respects; he also cites a variety of concurring observers.

[11] Phillips, *ibid.*; and Alhadeff, *Monopoly and Competition.*

[12] It must be small, or else it will more than offset the rise of after-tax π as market share rises. A small gradient in t will reduce α sufficiently to shift choices toward a lower M value. Since α is based on after-tax profit rates, the t gradient can be higher than α without in fact offsetting it. The gradient suggested here, in fact, only reduces α by half.

[13] The cities with two or more such banks are New York, San Francisco, Chicago, Los Angeles, Pittsburgh, Detroit, Boston, Philadelphia, Cleveland, Dallas and Seattle.

market as the criterion.[14] Banks that deal in national and international markets could subtract from their local share loans to firms with headquarters in other cities. Banks would thus be induced to reduce their local share and to increase their share in other cities, which will lead toward an optimal solution. This market-share criterion for setting the tax rate is efficient and the only practical one.

The eliminated entry restrictions would be those against new banks and against branching within and among states, as well as those against takeover by nonbanking units, and against formation of new banks by existing bank officers. The bank's management and accounts would remain separate. There would be only three restrictions on takeovers:

1. The connection between banking and nonbanking firms would be temporary. A time limit, perhaps of 10 years, would be set.
2. The banks could not extend loans to its owner (or merger partner). This would prevent favoritism in banking terms and exclusionary conduct—a replication of Japanese and German patterns—that might otherwise occur.
3. A major share of the bank's stock would be left in public hands, to preserve access for alternative owners and to provide information to the market as a whole.

In short, the present laws limiting entry would be amended, not repealed. Only their anticompetitive and antiefficiency features would be removed.

Banking relationships. An efficient treatment would broaden these ties and make them publicly known in detail. A firm could borrow more than a given percentage of its total (15 percent would seem reasonable) from any one bank only if an annual tax of, say, 1 percent were to be paid on the amount of the loan that exceeded the threshold criterion. Actual borrowings would be made public at specified intervals. The threshold for borrowing might affect the very largest firms only moderately; most of them already have several sources. The constraint would be roughly inverse to size, and so it would need to be focused on firms that are larger and have leading market shares. In any event, these data would be assembled for related treatments (see chapters 7 and 8). The criterion by which industrial firms would be included in the treatment would be structural. For example, those firms with market shares of 30 percent or more in a market of $50 million sales or more, and all firms with over $100 million in sales, would be under the banking-relationship treatment. There are perhaps 70 or 80 such firms, and

---

[14] These are fully reported by the FDIC annually.

the main problem resides in them. Disclosures of borrowings would be by these firms, plus all others with over $100 million in sales. The added disclosure would not greatly extend the existing degree of financial exposure (on a confidential basis) by firms to the SEC and other agencies, but it would make available information having a significant element of public interest.

A Public Investment Bank. As a further supplement, some version of a public-enterprise investment bank is likely to be appropriate. It would add competition in banking markets and also supplement the takeover function for inefficient nonfinancial firms, which private financial units may fail to exert.

The basic form is simple: one or more public banks (with no voting stock outstanding) funded by the state and by its depositors, with branches in major cities.[15] Such a public bank would perform a hybrid of commercial and investment banking activities. It would be run by professional bankers of top level quality; it would add competition to the market for deposits; its investment strategies would be directed toward oligopoly firms with X-inefficiency (see chapter 7), and toward aspiring monopolists, which might yield large capital gains.

The public bank's objective would be to maximize its returns for the public purse, by performing competitive and supervisory functions. Within this objective, an operating rule would be to require improved content in the firms it comes to influence. This improvement would be as likely to increase profits as to reduce them. If so, no basic clash between social and commercial goals would occur. In any case, the public bank would go beyond narrow commercial goals, and not just imitate private banks.

The social yields of a public investment bank would tend to be reduced if the other treatments were fully adopted and effective. Yet such a banking unit would be an important supplement in any case, to ensure that the basic changes occur and to deal with inefficiency and content more directly.

Insider treatment. Here again an efficient treatment is relatively simple and focused: (1) All personal trading of a company's stock, either by its

---

[15] It would differ from the Italian IRI by being smaller and more deposit based; it would be more the merchant banker than are the several large publicly owned banks in France. There have also been experiments in Britain, Canada, and Sweden, among others. See Holland, *The State as Entrepreneur;* John Sheahan, "Experience in France and Italy," in W. G. Shepherd and Associates, *The Economics of Public Enterprise,* 1976 (in press); and D. A. Alhadeff, *Competition and Controls in Banking* (Berkeley: University of California Press, 1968).

directors, managers, and professionals or by officials of any financial unit that accounted for a significant fraction of the firm's loans or outstanding stock, would be prohibited.[16] (2) If such trading occurred, all holders who sold before a rise in stock price could claim full repurchase from the company at the early lower price. This could be strengthened by permitting class-action suits or awarding treble damages. The treatment might be confined to listed shares, or perhaps to firms over some given size level.

The prohibition would require aspiring managers and other upper-level white-collar workers to set their holdings in their own firm at the start and then stay with them.[17] Their choice among all other stocks and other assets would remain untouched, and so their deprivation as investors would be trivial. The treatment would, however, abate the bulk of the insider problem at one stroke. The only other change would be in the use of employees' stock options. These would simply have to lose their optional character. The manager, director, or professional would be able to exercise them only after leaving the firm's employ, or perhaps after a further period of delay. This would preserve their possible incentive value, while eliminating their obvious possible abuse on the basis of insider information.

Any weaker treatment than this permits inequity and acute conflicts of interest to continue.[18] The insider problem now erodes both efficiency and equity in capital markets, and it places high officials of nearly all banks and firms in chronic conflict-of-interest situations.

3 EFFECTS OF TREATMENT

This set of treatments is evidently a moderate one, relying primarily on private incentives and the elimination of the more obvious potentials for

[16] To a degree, a policy requiring full disclosure by firms of their divisional results could provide similar gains. But it would treat the insider problem only indirectly, and it could be manipulated by merging divisions and by other devices. Therefore a direct and adequate treatment is needed.

The threshold for banking connections would be perhaps 5 percent of the firm's loans (compared to the 15 percent threshold for the "tax" on banking connections). The threshold for stock holdings would be perhaps 3 percent. Since bank officials would be free to trade in all other stocks, the limit on their scope of choice would be minimal.

[17] Also, predesigned mechanical plans for adding shares could be permitted. Only trading that could be guided by inside information in this firm would be stopped.

[18] Again, present rules touch only a small part of the problem, and this problem is pervasive and often acute.

abuse. The probable effects on structure and behavior would also be gradual, moderate, and balanced. These effects can be outlined, to give an impression of the resulting financial sector.

Tax and deregulation. Assume that the tax rate *(t)* is defined as shown in Figure 6.1. This is a light gradient, rising merely to 55 as market share reaches 40 percent. Very few banks would be above this share, and even at the rare market shares of 50 percent, *t* would still be only 58 percent. In the largest cities, few banks have large market shares; of the 29 cities with deposits over $2 billion only nine have a bank above 30 percent, and only four

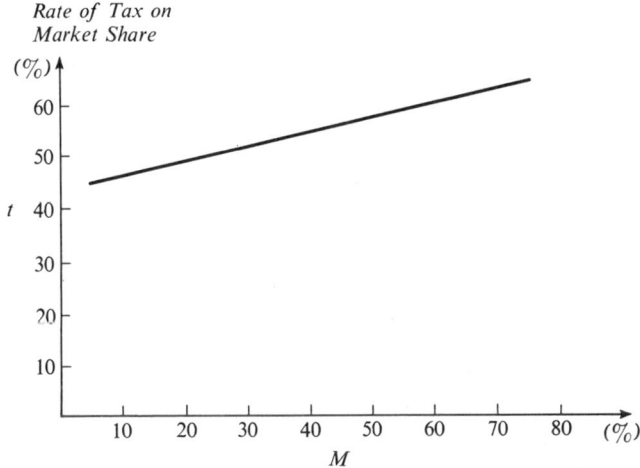

Figure 6.1 A progressive tax on market share.

have one above 40 percent.[19] The graduated tax rate would therefore have a relatively limited focus, and the larger banks in New York and Chicago—the two largest markets by far—would have average tax rates about at the present flat percentage (but marginal rates would still be steep). The profits of banks with market shares above 35 percent could be reduced significantly, but the profit rates would still mostly be above 8.0 percent, even if *X*-efficiency did not improve under this incentive structure. The extra taxes on these banks would be only a small proportion of all bank taxes now

[19] These are based on FDIC *Survey;* see also Fortune's *Directory of the 50 Largest Commercial Banks* (published yearly by Time-Life, Inc.) to identify the individual banks. The banks with shares over 30 percent in 1970 were in Buffalo, Phoenix, Pittsburgh, San Francisco, Minneapolis-St. Paul, Boston, Cleveland, Portland and Indianapolis.

paid. The total tax take from all banks would be approximately unchanged in the short run, since taxes on lesser banks would be slightly lower than at present. The higher market shares would probably decline, as this incentive and the other treatments take effect. Most probably, the decline would occur primarily by dividing out operations, rather than by a simple atrophy. This reduction would be gradual. Only the larger shares would decline by very much, but a wide range of lesser shares would probably also be slightly abated.

The added cost of deposit insurance for banks would be relatively slight, and the risk of bank failures with harmful wider effects would also remain small.

Takeover. Bank takeovers would be relatively few. There might perhaps be ten during the first several years, although some of them might involve large banks. The takeover threat would have to be taken seriously by all but the few largest banks, and the degree of efficiency in many of them would appreciably increase. The net effect on the profitability of most banks cannot be predicted a priori, because so many countereffects would be present. No clear presumption of lower bank profits would be justified.

There would be virtually no sacrifice of technical economies of scale in banking. These economies are mostly achieved at sizes well below those affected by the treatment, and the slope of the average cost curve is relatively slight except at very small scale.[20]

Banking relationships. Because information on banking relationships is almost entirely secret, the effects of the borrowing rule can only be conjectured. Possibly all firms with high market shares would be affected. Many firms would choose at first to pay the small excess-loan tax, but over time there would be a tendency to move down toward the loan limit. The tax take would therefore be both small and declining. The disclosure of banking relationships would increase competition among banks for clientele and reinforce this downward trend. The changes would focus on perhaps 10 to 15 firms and would be gradual.

Public investment bank. It is reasonable to expect that such a bank could be started with perhaps $300 million in capital and that it would attract on

---

[20] See Phillips, "Competitive Policy," and numerous references he cites. The economies appear to be real but relatively mild in degree.

the order of $4 billion in deposits.[21] As a medium-sized bank, it would have offices in perhaps the five largest banking cities. Within three years it would reach a steady-state position, with equity holdings at each point in perhaps 10 to 15 companies in a wide range of markets. These holdings would shift over time, and the bank would probably accrue total returns on its investments at least as high as the average profit rates in private investment banking.

Insider constraints. The rule against trading would be applied after a grace period, during which holders could trade in order to reach preferred long-run positions. At the point when it comes into force, the rule would of course have no visible effect. The total trading volume in such stocks would be little affected. Indeed, the elimination of most of the insider problem would probably cause public noninstitutional funds available for equity to increase appreciably. The penalty for violation is both severe and self-motivating. Aggrieved shareholders could be counted on to initiate and press action in hopes of substantial gain, although a class-action basis for suits might be optimal. There would probably be no net loss of managerial or directorial motivation, since holdings (as distinct from trading) would still be fully permissible.

4 SUMMARY

An optimal treatment of the financial sector would include: a profit tax scaled in line with market share; deregulation of entry, takeover, and chartering of banks, combined with full deposit insurance; a small tax on high loan shares from individual banks; a public investment bank operating in parallel with private ones, under certain conditions; a prohibition on trading in a firm's stock by all officials of the firm and by those in a banking relationship with it.

The exact coverage and details of these devices would be matters for further analysis. Altogether, the treatment would induce gradual changes toward a set of more open, competitive, and efficient capital markets. The more acute problems would be abated, primarily in those relatively few

---

[21] Its capital could be partly from public sources, with the majority from private deposits. It could also sell bonds in private markets to raise additional funds. A large range of financing sources could be tapped, consistent with its special "public" character.

markets and conflict-of-interest situations where they are now most serious. The elements of the whole treatment would be reinforcing, and the range of choice and potential profits would be increased for much the greater number of participants. Constraints would impinge only on units that now hold market power sufficient to cause inefficiency and inequity. The treatment would be perceived by those involved as both fair, workable, and—compared to the alternative treatments that may otherwise come to be necessary—moderate. No direct divestiture or reversal of banking mergers would be involved. No bank nationalizations would occur. No size limits would be set on banks or institutions. No single strategy, such as flat deregulation, would be regarded as sufficient to solve the whole problem.

While widening opportunity for a variety of talent, which is suppressed under the present tight system, the treatment would not generate a relatively few large windfall fortunes. Rather, capital markets would become more equitable; more than they have ever been before, and more than they could ever be under present rules.

Most of the elements in this set of treatments are matters of degree, subject to learning and revision with experience. But they are not highly sensitive to the exact standards that are first tried out. Their main value lies in applying incentives that are in the optimal direction. Therefore, it is not necessary to postpone this set of treatments until the optimal quantitative standards have been precisely derived. That derivation may be impossible to do abstractly, and so learning by experience may be necessary and appropriate.

CHAPTER SEVEN
Conventional Markets: Restorative Treatments

FROM CHAPTER 4, it appears that abating the prime cases of market power would yield positive net benefits. Yet the speed and efficiency of action is critical, and near-monopolies and oligopolies present distinctly different problems. Restorative policies are therefore both important and complex.

Several devices for causing the abatement can be tried, including actions taken under Section 2 of the Sherman Act. Our first task is to put Section 2 in correct perspective, to assess the past and prospective yields of Section 2 cases. We shall then turn to other approaches, ranging from incentive taxation to partial public enterprise. The aim is to illumine the general methods of choosing among restorative policies, but in doing this it will be helpful to consider some of the individual candidates for treatment in some detail. All of the detail is tentative, since we are barred from direct access to the facts.

Indeed, the first policy need is to arrange for full disclosure of information (recall chapter 2). Comprehensive data on firms' structure, context, and operations are to be collected and made public. We have discussed the types of information needed and have seen that the time lag in releasing the data should be minimal, perhaps a year or two at most. There would be a need for full divisional reporting, so that large market shares in individual markets could be known. This disaggregation of data would need to be standardized, so that profitability by division could be measured. This process raises interesting accounting problems, some of which will require somewhat arbitrary working answers. These problems are not insuperable, although some interested parties will assert that they are.

The new method of data reporting would require a revision, but not an increase, of Census and FTC activities. Any possible increase would have slight costs compared to the resulting gains. This full-information policy would be the most efficient among all the policies discussed in this book, and by stimulating competitive and other anticipatory actions it would make the other treatments less necessary.

The special role of content is set aside until section 5. Sections 1–4 are conventional in perspective, to give continuity with the mainstream literature. Actually, the treatment of content simply shifts the optimal degrees of public enterprise and firm size. Therefore, putting content in its own section makes the whole discussion more logical and clear.

1 ACTIONS UNDER SECTION 2

In recent decades Section 2 has become nearly a dead letter. Its language is unconditional:

> Every person who shall monopolize, or attempt to monopolize, or combine or conspire with any other person or persons, to monopolize any part of the trade or commerce among the several states, or with foreign nations, shall be deemed guilty of a misdemeanor. . . .

Every monopoly or attempt to monopolize is illegal.[1] There are no provisos about scale economies, good behavior, harm to innocent investors, or intent. Yet by now, and especially since 1952, application of Section 2 has become infrequent and unpredictable, even though many market shares in the "monopoly" range are known to exist.[2] Two conditions have been informally added to the law. The courts will now require proof of monopoly position,

---

[1] For discussion of the dilution of the bill before its enactment, see Walton Hamilton and Irene Till, *Antitrust in Action,* Monograph No. 16 for the Temporary National Economic Committee (U.S. Government Printing Office, 1940); H. Thorelli, *The Federal Antitrust Policy* (London: Allen and Unwin, 1954); and W. Letwin, *Law and Economic Policy in America* (New York: Random House, 1965).

[2] See Shepherd, *Market Power and Economic Welfare* (New York: Random House, 1970), ch. 7.

plus some evidence of intent to monopolize, and plus evidence that the monopoly can be abated without giving up important economies of scale or capacity to innovate.[3] If the defense can show that the high share arises from "superior skill, foresight or industry," or scale economies in any important direction, including innovations, acquittal will usually follow.[4] To convict would be regarded as either punitive against good performance or irrational, since no efficient remedy could ensue.

This judicial restraint has been further extended by the antitrust agencies. Potential cases against firms with high market shares are simply not prepared or brought, wherever scale economies are thought possibly to loom as significant; and by a perverse twist, the high market share itself often suggests to agency staff members that large scale economies are present or can, at least, be successfully alleged.[5]

The upshot is that the true conditions are not investigated in depth, either by the agencies or in court. If Section 2 were applied as it reads, no such paralysis would occur. Monopolists would be simply defined as such, as speeders are ticketed whether they are rich, or parsons, or polite, or busy making fast deliveries. The proper remedies would still pose intricate problems, but the law would apply as it exists. To those inclined to apply the law as it is written, the present status of Section 2 must be a travesty.

In this perspective, we can now assess the two major waves of Section 2 cases in the past, which were in 1906–20 and 1938–52. The efforts are outlined in Tables 7.1 and 7.2. Estimates of the effects of these efforts—if any—are given in Table 7.3 (based on calculations described in appendix C). The estimates are inevitably speculative, based on assumptions about the rate of decay in the absence of action, the average effects of market power, and the presence or absence of scale economies. Table 7.3 presents estimates that are probably close to the true values. The reader can prepare al-

---

[3] The first proviso has long been a conventional part of judicial interpretation; see A. D. Neale, *The Antitrust Laws of the United States* (Cambridge: Cambridge University Press, 1970); P. Areeda, *Antitrust Analysis: Problems, Text, Cases,* rev. ed. (Boston: Little, Brown, 1974). The second point has also been present and potent, though implicit in the choices made by antitrust officials as well as the courts.

[4] This was important in the du Pont cellophane case and United Shoe Machinery; a case against the General Motors near-monopoly in buses was withdrawn in 1965 on the second ground. See Neale, *ibid.,* and Areeda, *ibid.*

[5] This is based on a variety of experience and discussion in the Antitrust Division during 1967–68.

Table 7.1 Major Section 2 Cases, 1905 to 1920

Cases	Time between Monopolization and Remedy		Time between Beginning and End of Action [a]		Outcome
	Years	Interval (years)	Years	Interval (years)	
American Tobacco	1890–1916	26	1906–1912	6	Dissolution into three main firms
Standard Oil	1875–1918+	43+	1905–1912	7	Dissolution into about a dozen regionally dominant firms
du Pont gunpowder	1902–1913	11	1906–1912	6	Mile dissolution; reversed by effects of World War I
Corn Products	1897–1920	23	(1910)–1919	(12) [b]	Slight changes from a consent decree
American Can	1901–	—	(1909)–1920	(11)	No change
U.S. Steel	1901–	—	(1907)–1920	(13)	Acquittal. Informal limits on further mergers
AT&T	1881–	—	(1909)–1913	(4)	Compromise. AT&T retained its position; agreed to interconnect and avoid further mergers
Meatpackers (Armour, Swift, Wilson, Cudahy)	1885	—	(1905)–1920	(12)	Compromise. Packers agreed to stay out of adjacent markets
American Sugar	1890–	—	1908–1914	6	No action. American Sugar's position had slipped already
United Shoe Machinery	1899–	—	(1908)–1918	10	USM leasing restrictions were modified
International Harvester	1902		1906–1918	12	Compromise. Trivial divestiture

SOURCES: S. N. Whitney, *Antitrust Policies*, 2 vols. (New York: Twentieth Century Fund, 1958), and various other references in Appendixes B and C.

[a] Based on estimates of the start of official investigation and the end of official actions.
[b] Parentheses indicate estimates.

Table 7.2 Major Section 2 Cases Since 1937

Cases	Time between Monopolization and Remedy		Time between Beginning and End of Action [a]		Outcome
	Years	Interval (years)	Years	Interval (years)	
1938 to 1952					
Alcoa	1903–(1953) [b]	(50)	1934–1950	16	War plants sold to new entrants
National Broadcasting Company	1926–1943	17	1938–1943	5	"Blue Network" divested (became American Broadcasting Corp.)
Pullman	1899–1947	(65)	(1937)–1947	(10)	Divestiture of sleeping car operation. Manufacturing monopoly was not directly changed
Paramount Pictures	1914–1948	34	(1935)–1948	(13)	Vertical integration removed
American Can	1901–(1955)	(54)	(1945)–1950	(5)	Certain restrictive practices stopped, to foster entry
du Pont (GM holdings)	1918–1961	43	1945–1961	16	Divestiture
United Shoe Machinery	1899–1970	71	(1945)–1969	(61)	Share reduced to 50 percent
United Fruit	1899–1970	71	1948–1970	22	Moderate divestiture
American Tobacco	(1920)–	—	1938–1946	8	Conviction but no significant remedy
du Pont (cellophane)	1925–	—	(1945)–1956	(11)	Acquittal
Western Electric	1881–	—	1946–1956	10	Case effectively abandoned
IBM	(1925)–	—	1947–1956	9	Case effectively abandoned
Since 1968					
IBM (1969 case)	(1925)–	—	1965–	—	Trial begun in 1975
Cereals (1972 case)	(1950)–	—	1970–	—	In process
Xerox (1972 case)	1961–	—	1970–	—	Tentative settlement in 1975
AT&T (1974 case)	1881–	—	1965–	—	In process

SOURCES: S. N. Whitney, *Antitrust Policies*, 2 vols. (New York: 20th Century Fund, 1958); M. J. Green et al., *The Closed Enterprise System* (New York: Grossman, 1972).

[a] Based on estimates of start of official investigation and end of official action.
[b] Parentheses indicate estimates.

ternative estimates, using alternative assumptions. Following is a discussion of what appear to be the main lessons from these two sets of actions.

Scope. The first set of cases was extraordinarily complete. It touched virtually every major case of high market share at the time, including a majority of what were then the ten largest industrial corporations. Although conviction and restructuring were obtained in only a few cases, these led to major changes. Little direct relief was gained in most of the other actions,

Table 7.3 Estimated Benefits and Costs, Selected Major Treatments of Dominant Firms [a]

Company	Estimated costs [b]	Estimated benefits [b]	Ratio of benefits to cost
Standard Oil	45	3,021	67.1
American Tobacco	15	312	20.8
International Harvester	15	331	22.1
Corn Products Refining	6	46	7.7
United States Steel	27	636	23.6
Alcoa	25	470	18.8
American Can	13	96	7.4
United Shoe Machinery	20	93	4.7

Source and methods: see Appendix C.
[a] Adjusted to 1947–49 price levels.
[b] $ millions.

but implicit constraints were in effect on such firms as U.S. Steel and International Harvester.[6]

The second wave, during 1938–52, was confined to firms ranking lower in the national lists, but these firms still included nearly all of the major firms with markey shares over 50 percent. Several of these cases were successful legally, but others were inconclusive; and the two most important ones—IBM and Western Electric—were largely abandoned in the 1950s.

In both periods, oligopoly was barely touched. The major meat-packers were put under the 1920 consent decree, which placed adjacent markets off limits until it was modified in 1974.[7] The 1946 Tobacco case broke legal

---

[6] See S. N. Whitney, *Antitrust Policies,* 2 vols. (New York: Twentieth Century Fund, 1958) and sources cited there.

[7] The meatpacking firms did attempt to have the limits removed in the early 1930s and 1950s. During 1967–68 I helped to define an efficient partial relaxation of the decree. It would have let the packers into eight industries with high concentration. The change announced after 1970 (and still under final negotiation in 1974) was roughly along those lines.

Policy Alternatives in Practice 188

ground on tacit collusion, but to no practical effect. Therefore, past cases have covered near-monopoly fairly completely—but with limited effect—and tight oligopoly has been left virtually untouched.

Severity of Remedies. The severity of remedies was moderate even in the big 1911 cases; it abated sharply after 1911, and it has dwindled further since the 1920s.[8] Since 1913 there has been scarcely any dissolution at all in manufacturing industry, and the conduct remedies have been studiously moderate. Some of today's apparent weak performers in basic industry are firms that escaped conviction or other strict remedies in the 1913–35 period: examples are steel, meat packing, and glass. Note that major wars have played a strong role in forestalling severe remedies. World Wars I and II and the Korean War all interrupted the thrust of enforcement waves and softened judicial attitudes toward major firms. World War I nullified the du Pont Gunpowder remedy and generated resources for duPont holdings in automobiles, tires, and chemicals. In all, the end probability of achieving a full remedy under existing procedures has gone down, probably as far as .1 or .2.

Duration. The duration of actions—from initial study to remedy—has lengthened, from about 6 years to about 20. The average interval from the original monopolization to remedy, which was already over 20 years in 1911 (35–40 years for Standard Oil), has now grown much longer. In the two major 1911 cases, Standard Oil and American Tobacco, a "drastic" remedy was applied two or more decades after the momopoly was created, and only after the firm's market position was already weakening. In no case has an incipiency treatment been applied quickly enough to intercept a rising position of market power. The 1951 IBM case might have produced that effect on the emerging computer industry, but that possibility was excluded in the 1956 settlement.

Original offenders. In no case has the action removed much or most of the capitalized monopoly gain from the original monopolizers. The wealth of the Rockefellers, du Ponts, Dukes, and other major families was virtually untouched by the early antitrust actions, and the second set of actions during 1937–52 was even more remote from the original gains. In effect, there has been an amnesty for monopolizers.

Conditions for success. The two preconditions for bringing suit were a high market share, and a high degree of profitability. There were virtually

---

[8] The big 1911 cases—Standard Oil and American Tobacco—and the duPont gunpowder case in 1913 merely undid earlier mergers. Since then there has been little of such de-merging, and even less direct restructuring.

no suits against oligopolists or against firms with average or depressed rates of return. The elements of a legal victory in the two sets of cases were, in the main: (1) A well-conceived and thorough economic case for action, based on extensive research on the critical points. The old Bureau of Corporations supplied this in the first wave; it was often lacking during the second wave, partly because the Antitrust Division lacked adequate resources. (2) Grassroots support, both political and in the form of private and state suits against the target company. This was true of Standard Oil by 1911.[9] (3) Brilliant antitrust strategy, particularly to prevent delay by snowing the agencies with irrelevant documents and by procedural detours. This is helped if (4) The private side is caught by surprise, or is complacent or inept, or if it has displayed abusive actions and markedly excess profits.[10] (5) A specific, feasible basis for remedy must be available, lest its absence chill the case from the start.

An effective remedy was likely to be ordered if (1) there was a technical basis for dividing, such as decentralization and an origin in recent mergers, (2) the product was relatively simple and standardized, so that innovation or national military involvement were not major questions, (3) only a moderate weakening in the monopolists' total position was involved—so that potential competitors were active and expectations were not sharply reversed by divestiture (but not so severe a weakening as to make action superfluous)—and (4) the stock was closely held, so that the expected or actual impact was not widespread.

Yields. The net yields of actions appear to have been high, especially for the earlier moves. The results taper down markedly in the more recent actions. The estimation procedure may contain biases of several sorts (see appendix C). These are more likely to understate the yields than to overstate them. The estimates are not highly sensitive to the underlying assumptions about discount rates and weighting. The main sources of high antitrust yield are the size of firm, quickness of action after original monopolization, and closeness of control of the firm. The ideal case has been a large recent (or incipient) monopoly still in the original monopolizers' hands.

Tight oligopolies are not among the cases that offered high yields but were spared treatment. This fits theoretical expectation. It also fits the image

---

[9] See Letwin, *Law and Economic Policy* and R. W. Hidy and M. E. Hidy, *Pioneering in Big Business, 1882–1911* (New York: Harper, 1965).

[10] Standard Oil also displayed this attribute in extreme degree; see *ibid.*

of tight oligopolies in mature industries as residual cases that were not treated at an earlier stage, when there was near-monopoly.

2 PROSPECTIVE YIELDS

The present set of primary candidates for treatment is roughly as given in Table 4.10. The estimates of future yields were made, as before, on reasonable assumptions about natural rates or erosion, scale economies, and the effects of market power on performance.

A series of high yields appear to be available, especially from the near-monopolies. Even on the most conservative assumptions, the quantitative economic case for abating market power in at least a dozen major firms appears to be strong. This is true despite the several biases in estimation that we have discussed. The list does not exhaust the field of possible candidates, because many firms or divisions that hold high market power may have been passed over in preparing the panel of large firms. Moreover we have focused only on horizontal structure. There may be vertical elements that would offer high yields; petroleum products and steel are obvious possibilities of this sort.

In any event, there is an important set of major firms for which the economic case for abating market power seems to be rebuttably clear. The lack of actions to abate them during 1952–73 has probably caused net economic losses.

Four significant cases—IBM, cereals, Xerox, and AT&T—have been started since 1968.[11] Otherwise, little significant action has been taken since 1952 toward any of the firms in Table 4.10, and the IBM case has turned into a textbook case of delay, passive handling by the Division, and uncertainty about objectives.[12]

---

[11] I prepared parts of the economic content of the Division's case against IBM in 1967–68. The core of the case was highly focused and complete by mid-1968. The delay in bringing the case to trial has been remarkable. It has reflected extreme efforts and clever strategy by IBM counsel, a lapse in Antitrust Division handling during 1969–72, and passive behavior by the court. On the economic content, see Shepherd, *Market Power and Economic Welare,* ch. 15.

[12] The Division staff was vulnerable to such tactics as extensive tangential interrogatories and "snowing" via masses of irrelevant documents. These are among the classic devices for stalling antitrust processes. As noted, the core of the case was completed early and it consisted of a compact set of economic data. While the IBM case was thus permitted to slide, the Division was led into a large and spectacular effort to stop conglomerate mergers. Despite the public im-

The agencies have also studied several of the candidates, and in some cases specific actions have been prepared, but not started. These include automobiles, detergents, and the nuclear power equipment industry.[13] Yet no thorough economic study of the first two was possible, given the lack of agency resources. Filing suit would have been primarily a device for getting an exposure of issues and information via the trial process itself. The suits would have stated that a violation of Section 2 was probable and that the facts at trial would probably indicate the need for substantial relief. But neither prior conclusive evidence nor a complete plan for remedy would have been possible before the decision to file suit.

The rest of the candidates were scarcely studied. These include General Electric, Eastman Kodak, several pharmaceutical firms, Campbell Soup, Gillette, and newspapers.[14] For various reasons, the prospects of obtaining relief seemed too low to justify putting resources even into a significant study. These reasons became especially evident when in 1967–68 efforts were made to identify tight oligopolies that might merit treatment as shared monopolies, in line with the Kaysen-Turner position of 1959.[15] About 12

---

pression, the net effect of this allocation of resources was toward protecting established dominant positions from competitive or takeover incursions (see also chapter 8).

[13] I helped prepare a suit testing the status of the leading automobile firms; this was only one of several efforts to clarify the issue. A compact and well prepared suit seeking to reopen the Western Electric issue was ignored by Ramsey Clark from 1966 to 1969 (see M. J. Green, et al. *The Closed Enterprise System* (New York: Grossman, 1972); and W. G. Shepherd, "The Margin of Competition in Communications," in *Technological Change in Regulated Industries*, ed. W. M. Capron (Wash., D.C.: Brookings Institution, 1971). W. S. Comanor researched the role of advertising in the detergent markets for the Division in 1967–68. He established that the predicted relationship between advertising intensity, profitability, and market share did exist. But no action was then taken or even prepared, primarily because no adequate remedy available under antitrust processes seemed to exist. Finally an expensive ($385,000) study of the nuclear power equipment industry was commissioned by the AEC, with A. D. Little, Inc., the winning bidder. But the study was necessarily superficial, partly because no real effort was made to get the inside information on costs and pricing necessary for a thorough analysis.

[14] Some modest monitoring of some of these instances was continued, but no serious thought was given to adequate research or new actions. In general, the resources applied to the major cases were thin and often diverted into special legal angles. Even, or especially, on the major problem cases, the Division's resources are scant compared to those of the firms.

[15] This was the attempt to apply the position of Carl Kaysen and Donald F. Turner to tight oligopolies (*Antitrust Policy* [Cambridge, Mass.: Harvard University Press, 1959]). I helped organize this survey of priority candidates and the attempt to determine whether legal action against them would be successful. The prime candidates (apart from automobiles, which were given separate analysis) were electric lamps, tires and tubes, flat glass, steel ingots, metal con-

prime candidates were identified, but some were old and now unprofitable. Others stemmed mainly from patents or advertising, and so remedy would clearly have been difficult to bring about. It could have been argued that still others faced monopsony power—tires, for example. Several were relatively trivial cases. Finally, all were less promising legally and economically than such near-monopoly cases as Western Electric and automobiles, which at that time were not being brought. Therefore, there seemed little reason to put scarcer resources into these marginal cases, since even the obvious ones were blocked. Furthermore, as we shall see, the remedies for tight oligopoly require resources that are simply unavailable via section 2 and the courts. That the Kaysen-Turner proposals were not applied therefore had strong practical reasons.

Traditionally, Section 2 solutions involve a conviction for monopolizing, followed by a remedy negotiated among the firm, Antitrust Division lawyers, and the district court judge. Actual splits have nearly all been along obvious lines; reversing mergers, selling war surplus plants (Alcoa), or dividing out sub-units (Standard Oil). An aura of untouchability has arisen around more unified conditions, and some firms now centralize in order to immunize themselves against divestiture.[16]

It is widely believed that the courts will resist restructuring, on five grounds: efficiency gains are speculative, transitional costs would be high, innovation may be stopped, innocent new shareholders will unfairly suffer capital losses, and market power is fading away in any event. These are all prejudgments of amounts and probabilities, without a tested basis. The new-shareholder point also contains a dubious ethical decision that investors should be relieved of this source of risk. Such a prejudgment is beyond the competence of anyone to make, especially when it is based, as it is, on hear-

---

tainers, explosives, sulfur, primary batteries, carbon and graphite, cereals, auto rentals. Marginal cases were transformers, copper, trucks, and gypsum (see Green, *Closed Enterprise System,* pp. 305–7).

These tight oligopolies were quickly seen to be of lower priority than near-monopoly cases, and permeated with special legal and economic problems. The effort was soon set aside in the press of other business.

In 1973 the Division did sue leading tire companies, but on other grounds. The FTC action toward cereal firms is presently in process, and in 1975 the FTC also began action toward the three leading automobile rental firms, partly on shared-monopoly reasoning. Yet the tight oligopoly problem is mostly untouched, and problems of remedy have scarcely been reached.

[16] In 1969 General Motors was widely reported to have markedly recentralized its operations in order to forestall possible antitrust treatments. The corporation did not deny the reports.

say. Investors routinely absorb a variety of other, greater risks, as part of normal market choices.[17] The implicit risk-absorption by the courts—and, more broadly, society—on behalf of supposedly innocent stockholders needs a better justification than it has had in the past.

All of these supposed predispositions favor the efforts by defendant firms to resist. The biases also inhibit precedent; each case must go against the grain of a different judge's beliefs and firms' resistance. In short, the main features of the system skew the burden of proof and time, possibly by orders of magnitude. They clearly do not favor restructuring, and so the outcomes are likely to fall short of the optimum degree of competition.

The net result is a de facto repeal of Section 2. The law itself is total and sufficient, but in practice it has been milled away and encrusted with provisos, while the agencies have been left without sufficient resources to preresearch the cases and to carry out remedies. The very power to punish the defendant—via the treble damages conviction triggers—ensures total resistance and delay. The agencies lack resources to frame and carry out remedies, and other possible constraints, via other kinds of agencies, are simply lacking. The U.S. now has only one shot in its locker—Section 2—and it is an inadequate one.

Other countries have been more inventive. The British Prices and Income Board assessed profits, and on occasion management performance, while deciding on price increases during 1966–71.[18] In Italy and several other European countries [19] public holding companies own part or all of certain leading firms. Public buyers exert monopsony power against leading firms in some other industries, especially via public enterprises and national health programs.[20] Even "antitrust" strategies are being tried in interesting ways.[21] These efforts have often been unsuccessful or mishandled, but they

---

[17] Thus there have been drastic shifts in average stock market values during the last 15 years, and individual share values shift even more sharply, often dropping by more than half. In short, the market "confiscates" sharply and routinely. The possible effects of most policy treatments contemplated here are slight by comparison. In many cases, they would *increase* share prices.

[18] The Board issued about 150 reports, of surprisingly good quality and great value as factual sources.

[19] See S. Holland, ed. *The State as Entrepreneur* (White Plains: International Arts and Sciences Press, 1972); John Sheahan, "Experience in France and Italy."

[20] See Shepherd, "Public Expenditure," in *Britain's Economic* Prospects, ed. R. E. Caves and Associates (Wash., D.C.: Brookings Institute, 1968).

[21] See various reports of the U. K. Monopolies Commission, and C. K. Rowley, *The British Monopolies Commission* (London: Allen and Unwin, 1966); W. Pengilley, "Australian Experience of Antitrust Regulation," *Antitrust Bulletin,* Summer 1973, pp. 355–74.

do indicate some of the variety that U.S. policy does not have. In addition, there are tax devices which can go to the heart of the problem.

The causes of the Section 2 repeal are the same biases identified in chapter 3:

(1) The scientific basis for estimating costs and benefits has been diluted by the lack of general information for research about structure and performance.
(2) The agencies have mandates far exceeding their resources and powers to study, to prosecute, or carry out remedies.
(3) The candidates control most of the germane information, including the costs of remedy.
(4) The court process sets the burden of proof and of time against the agencies.
(5) A lack of deadlines further biases the time-structure of decisions against action rather than leaving them neutral.

The dual-agency system—for all its other merits—means that no one is responsible for a lack of effective action. The shortness of tenure of the agency heads accentuates this. Section 2 cases are believed in the agencies to have no precedential value. Though this is probably not true, it still influences current policy choices.[22] Meanwhile, candidate firms do routinely resist up to the margin at which after-tax gains equal the tax-adjusted costs of resistance.[23] All changes or remedies are forced upon defendants. There are no tax or internal incentives for the owners or managers of the firms to comply either after conviction or in anticipation of suit.

Finally the very infrequency of recent action has made it seem erratic. Therefore defendants can fairly assert that an action toward them is unfair—since like cases are escaping treatment—and injurious to innocent third parties (e.g., shareholders), since action is so unpredictable that it creates intol-

---

[22] This view emerged during extensive discussion and observation in the Division. It is not true, however, because major wins in one or more Section 2 cases would clearly change the odds for getting convictions in succeeding cases, and this—via the discounting process (see ch. 3)—would alter the expected values in both private and public choices.

[23] In the case of IBM, let the profits at stake under Section 2 be only one-fourth of all IBM after-tax profits, now at about $1.6 billion yearly. This is equivalent to over $1 million per day as a rough estimate of IBM's gain from merely delaying action, much less averting it. After adjusting for taxes, it is over $2 million per day. On either basis, it quite dwarfs the resources available in the public agencies or for objective outside study. This is only a prominent instance of the large flows and incentives at stake in many firms. Together they are several orders of magnitude greater than those available to the antitrust agencies and to the handful of outside researchers (recall ch. 2).

erable risk. These are persuasive points in court. Yet, a thorough and systematic program of treatment would automatically take care of them.

3 BASIC POLICY TOOLS

To sum up, large cases of market power remain from the past, even though some instances have been abated, mostly in earlier decades. And apart from mergers by newcomers (see chapter 8), new instances of monopoly, once established, need not seriously fear removal by public policy for at least 15 years, if at all. This leads to large economic losses in a range of identifiable cases. The costs of applying the direct structural remedies to these cases might be even larger: that could justify the virtual moratorium on restructuring since 1952. The irrationality in present policy is that these matters are not getting studied properly, if even at all, and that alternative treatments are simply not even being considered. These alternatives would add resources, powers, and tactics, rather than load new responsibilities onto the presently overstretched agencies. The key attributes of effective new alternatives would be to reverse or even up the burden of proof, engage private interests to force and optimize the remedies, and ensure that supporting resources are available to accomplish the changes. The treatments for near-monopolies and oligopolies would differ, as follows.

A NEAR-MONOPOLIES

The first need is for a way to measure market structure accurately and objectively. This would not involve the possible reasons for high market shares (e.g., scale economies, predation, intent, randomness) nor the remedy, if any, that may be appropriate. It would simply be a vehicle—with data, an agency, and a fair process—for defining reality correctly. The second need is to apply incentives for the firms to seek a lower market share.

I shall now outline two alternative strategies for inducing a reduction in market shares. Both apply a progressive profit tax based on market share. The first strategy assumes that precise data on market shares and profits will be available, the second that the data will be less precise and therefore more arguable, so that more direct tactics will be needed to get the optimal result.

First strategy. If precise data are available and out in the open, then a profits tax scaled in line with market share would be an efficient inducement. Presumably this would be the same as the treatment for banks and utilities (chapters 6 and 9). The tax rate might range between 45 and 60 percent, for most cases, in fixed relation to market share.[24] Since accounts would be disaggregated, the tax would reach down to apply different rates to company divisions with differing market shares (e.g., General Motors' bus, car, and appliance divisions).

The scaled tax would operate by shifting both the share-profits and share-time curves, as shown in Figure 7.1. There the tax is assumed to be constant

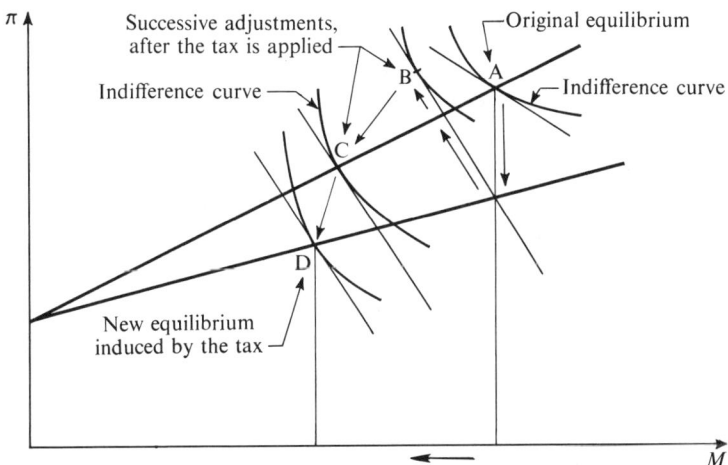

Figure 7.1 A progressive tax on market share would shift the conditions of choice for the firm.

up to shares of 10 percent, and then rise after that. Therefore, the π of a firm with a 60 percent share would be shifted down and its tradeoff between π and ΔM would be tilted as shown. This would induce a series of choices toward lower M levels than would otherwise occur.[25]

Second strategy. Suppose that disaggregation, cost allocations, and market definitions are debatable and need careful weighing comparable to what a court now tries to do in a Section 2 case. If so, a more involved process,

---

[24] The conditions and conclusions parallel those in chs. 6, 8 and 9.

[25] The tax would *not* induce X-inefficiency or give greater scope for it. This is because it is based on M, not on the profit level itself. This avoids the conventional point against the graduated tax on profits—that it induces waste. Rather it induces the firm to reduce M.

Analysis of the optimum gradient for t is important. It would relate to both α and β and to the economies of scale that may exist. Use of the surtax would not need to await derivation of an exact solution.

with more direct tactics to induce compliance, will be needed; but it can still avoid most of the procedural biases that now plague Section 2 actions. The key is to define market share without regard to intent, scale economies, etc., and then to induce restructuring by management.

The definition of a "monopoly" position can never be precise, since the boundaries of many markets are shaded. In all of the instances in Table 4.10, there are grounds for honest dispute over the product and geographical scope of the market. Therefore, an agency could aim merely to determine rough categories of market share. Tradition and economic analysis indicate 60 percent as a threshhold for near-monopoly. Chapter 4 also suggests that market share of 40–60 percent provide "dominant firm" status that affects performance. Above 80 percent, market share is very close to pure monopoly. These three categories, therefore—call them groups 1, 2, and 3, starting at the top—would be plausible bases for determining the approximate market position of firms, via an adversary proceeding in court. In an IBM case, for example, the Antitrust Division would allege 70 percent, and IBM would allege 30–35 percent, as is presently being done. The court might take the 40–60 class (group 2) as containing the probable market share. Or it might perceive separate markets—say for smaller and larger computers—and assign one to a higher group than the other.

If the court puts the market share below 40, action ceases. Otherwise, the case is transferred to an agency that supervises the application of financial incentives to all significant defined "monopolies" in the economy. The incentives would be of two main sorts, applied uniformly across the board on the basis of objective criteria.

1. A graduated tax on the rate of return on total assets would be applied. There would be three marginal rates, tied to the three market-share categories.[26] The optimum schedule of rates depends upon two sets of factors. One is the net disincentive for efficiency that a graduated tax might conceivably inject. Yet, no net disincentive at all need occur; income effects may overcome substitution effects. Second is the incentive the tax applies toward reducing the firm's market share, in order to get into a lower tax bracket. These two possible effects can be conjectured but not presently specified. This may not be a serious problem, since there are not likely to be negative effects from any moderate degree of progression.

[26] For example, the surtax rate on net income above the competitive rate of return (say 10 percent on assets) might be an additional 5 percent for each category, reaching a marginal rate of about 65 percent for group 1 firms.

2. The other type of incentive would be tied to voluntary moves by the firm to reduce its market share. A market share of 30 is roughly the point at which the effects of market power on performances begin to be significant, as chapter 4 noted. Let us suppose that the objective is to induce a reduction of M to 30 percent by some target date X months away.

The inducements apply ultimately to the managers, who are best able to accomplish an efficient division of the firm. Yet the managers' motivation needs to be reinforced by shareholder incentives, and so it is to shareholders' interest that the incentives must directly apply.

Among many possible types of incentives, one seems to fit efficiency and equity criteria especially well—to make all damages arising from the monopoly designation tax-deductible if the deadline for change is met. This feature will be strongest for firms with the highest marginal tax rates. For them, the damages will be largest and the tax savings will be most marked. This will presumably evoke strong stockholder pressure to achieve restructuring in time, if necessary by stockholder suits to force action or by takeovers by outside groups willing to tender for shares at prices reflecting the prospective tax savings.

If the firm's stock price suffers from the whole process of action, compensation might be provided to smaller investors. Large holders can presumably bear all risks, including those of public policies. Small holders are generally less informed and more vulnerable. An equitable, partial protection to such "innocent third parties"—if indeed they are innocent—would be for the public agency to stand ready to buy shares from small holders at a price midway between the present price and the price obtaining when the investigation was begun. The details are less important than the basic idea, which is to focus compensation—if there is to be any—on deserving parties.

The whole set of incentives presents a complex problem in optimizing among multiple policy tools. The primary elements are best stated in terms of the firm's profit choices. The strategic objective is to balance the firm's expected profit loss from the graduated tax rates with its potential profit gain from meeting the deadline for restructuring itself. This will then leave the firm neutral to the whole process and, concurrently, avoid a large net tax loss to the public fisc (apart from possible compensation to small holders). As a result the firm will not resist the process, as it now does.

The basic choice situation is:

Profits $= f($Market share, Economics of scale, Tax rates, . . . Length of $X)$

The graduated profit tax reduces the future profit stream. The prospective damages are, at maximum, treble the summed difference between the actual and "competitive" profit level for the past period of monopoly, *if* there are no scale economies present. If there are scale economies present—either part way or all the way up to the present level of market share—the damages will be smaller, and also the prospective profit of the restructured parts of the firm will be smaller (because they would have higher average costs).

Both proposals allow automatically for inducing the correct choices, by letting the firm choose to remain unchanged, with a high market share, if it regards that as more profitable, on balance. In the extreme case of scale economies accounting for all of the market share and all of the "excess" profit—that is, the case of a "natural" monopoly—the firm will remain a monopoly, as it should on efficiency grounds, but it will also be subject to surtax. *Assuming the incentive rates are at least approximately correct, the treatment will simultaneously induce the correct structure and apply constraints to minimize its effects.* It will therefore avoid the artificialities and costs which arise under both antitrust and regulation, when the definitions are made externally and then attempts are made to impose specific constraints or changes from outside, in relative ignorance. The key element in both systems is that they are self-operating. The firm makes the choices, and as conditions change—for instance, if scale economies abate—it will gain by initiating the reduction of market share during the following period.

The incentive structure is not likely to be highly sensitive and difficult to optimize. The general magnitudes seem intuitively within reason. For all but a few firms and divisions,[27] the surtax presumably would range no higher than 60 percent. The cost of compensating small investors would not, in any event, be a major item. The rates of tax and possible compensation could be adjusted with experience, and in any case the potential losses from missing the optimal incentive structure seem small compared to the accumulated social losses from the present impasse. We shall see that the system applies generally to "ultilities" (chapter 9), as well as to the incentives toward new market power (chapter 8). Therefore, it may offer gains over a wider domain than just the present core of industrial problem cases.

The important part is the incentives themselves, which neutralize the biases in the present system and make congruent those who choose among

---

[27] Recall ch. 6. Few cases of industrial market shares above 65 percent are likely to exist now, and these would presumably fade.

alternative changes with those who possess the information and the direct control over structure.

By these two key factors—an even burden of proof and instant rewards for change—the process will minimize its costs and virtually eliminate unanticipated arbitrary side effects. The remaining risks, costs, and impacts on share values would be quite within the magnitudes investors routinely face. Orderly action by all sides would be encouraged, in contrast to the erratic gambling situations Section 2 activities—and inactivities—now engender.[28]

B OLIGOPOLY

Because loose oligopoly is broadly the optimal form of market structure, the larger cases of tight oligopoly may offer high yields to restorative policies. And yet, despite a doctrinal venture in the second American Tobacco case of 1946, tight oligopoly has been exempt from antitrust as long as it avoids direct collusion.[29] This has evoked proposals for extending Section 2 to such "shared monopoly cases," but there is little chance that the proposals will be adopted.[30] An experimental FTC action against the larger cereal firms since 1972 is exploring the special role of advertising in that distinctive industry. Yet its outcome is quite uncertain, and the larger stable oligopolies—such as steel, glass, aluminum, copper, and basic chemicals—have been left aside.

On closer inspection, the yields from restructuring are surprisingly low in the several main tight oligopolies that have long been regarded as prime antitrust cases. The probabilities of net benefits are lower, especially for technical progress. Restructuring action would embrace several firms rather than just one, perhaps with higher transition costs. There are few "clean" cases: most tight oligopolies are now encumbered with special conditions, such as vertical integration, mineral rights, ingrained cooperative behavior, and indi-

---

[28] This discussion is in broad agreement with W. Breit and K. Elzinga, "Antitrust Penalties and Attitudes Toward Risk," *Harvard Law Review,* February 1973, pp. 693–713, who propose a sharp flat-rate surtax on convicted firms. That would massively increase the penalties attached to Section 2, but only after conviction on the conventional grounds. Therefore, it would not apply the direct incentive proposed here, and it would deter judges even more strongly from convicting in Section 2 cases. As a result, it is superior to the present situation but less effective than the systems proposed here.

[29] American Tobacco Co. *v.* United States (S.C. 1946); see Neale, *The Antitrust Laws of the United United States* and Areeda, *Antitrust Analysis.*

[30] As noted by Kaysen and Turner, *Antitrust Policy,* and the "Neale Report," Report of the President's Committee to Study Antitrust Enforcement, released 1969.

rect boardroom interlocks. Moreover, half-loaf antitrust treatments in the past have created estoppel problems for some of them.

This is clear from Table 7.4, which includes what are probably the main eligible tight-oligopoly cases, roughly in decreasing order of yield. Some of these are industries in which high yields during 1906–20 and 1938–52 were *not* realized—steel, oil, copper, aluminum, glass, and rubber. Now often permeated with a degree of X-inefficiency and cooperative habits, they are

Table 7.4 Major Tight Oligopolies, U.S. Manufacturing, 1970

Industry	Value of shipments ($ million)	Official 4-firm concentration ratio (%)	Imports (%)	Are there geographic sub-markets?
Petroleum refining	22,737	33	Slight	Yes
Iron and steel	9,328 [a]	47	~25	Yes
Flat glass	670	92	Slight	No
Electric lamps	892	92	Slight	No
Farm machinery	4,367	40	Slight	No
Primary aluminum	1,758	90+	Slight	No
Primary copper	673	75	Slight	No
Cigarettes	3,503	84	Slight	No
Fluid milk	8,253	20	Slight	Yes

SOURCE: U.S. Census Bureau, *Value-of-Shipment Concentration Ratios,* Annual Survey of Manufacturers, 1970, M70(AS)–9 (U.S. Government Printing Office, 1972).

[a] Value-added is given; value of shipments is not reported.

probably intractable to structural changes alone, and they do not engage in overt price-fixing which Section 1 action could remedy.

Yet these are industries with basic problems—primarily of inefficiency—which do not appear to be self-correcting and which do contribute to the national economic problems of inflation, unemployment, and foreign trade imbalance. The social yields from treating these problems would have parallel private yields, because an improvement in efficiency would generate higher profits and, for shareholders, capital gains.[31]

Efficient treatment of oligopoly therefore will rely more on takeovers and

---

[31] These shareholder interests are not small. In major tight oligopolies, a number of leading firms have recently accrued total returns (dividends minus capital depreciation) which are sharply below the opportunity cost of capital. Some of this relatively negative performance could have been avoided by better management. Much of it has not been at all attributable to general shifts in stock market averages. See *Fortune Directory of the 500 Largest U.S. Industrial Corporations,* 1972 (New York: Time-Life, Inc., 1973).

Policy Alternatives in Practice   202

other ways of changing managerial behavior, and less on direct structural changes. Poor management under market power can be cured most directly by boardroom action. Normally, severe X-inefficiency arises and persists only when there is boardroom passivity. The rules, customs, and power relations of most large corporations have made it difficult to apply external pressure on managers and directors, except where X-inefficiency has gotten visibly large.

Takeover is the classic ultimate remedy for this, and therefore conditions that trigger it as soon as X-inefficiency becomes appreciable are appropriate. Yet takeover also enlarges the size of the firm and may increase its market power. Optimum merger rules therefore need to be carefully drawn, so that they do not proscribe all mergers by leading firms. To prevent all such mergers would be to shield firms officially from takeover threats that may usually have net social benefits.[32] The optimum takeover was, in fact, roughly approximated by certain conglomerate mergers during 1964–69. A number of firms with leading market shares were taken over and revised by corporate outsiders, who were relatively indifferent to the gentlemanly codes that commonly inhibit such behavior. It was partly because such takeovers were touching on major firms and banking ties that they came to encounter fierce resistance by private interests and, ultimately, public agencies. The "tough" official antitrust moves against such major conglomerates as LTV and ITT in 1969 were in fact measures to shield established management in a range of oligopolies. When a broader rule against *all* sizable mergers by *any* of the 200 largest industrial firms was set out in 1969, the shielding effect was simply made more complete.[33]

Optimum merger policy is therefore necessary, even if not sufficient, in treating mature oligopolies (as well as near-monopolies). Only conglomerate mergers provide the takeover constraint on inefficiency while also minimizing the addition to market power from an actual merger. Horizontal and vertical mergers usually add appreciably to market power. Conglomerate mergers do provide some possible addition to market power, but only by increasing the firm's total size. And this "deep pocket" may be shallow.

[32] D. F. Turner, "Conglomerate Mergers and Section 7 of the Clayton Act," *Harvard Law Review*, May 1965, pp. 1313–95; J. S. Campbell and W. G. Shepherd, "Leading-Firm Conglomerate Mergers," *Antitrust Bulletin*, Winter 1968, pp. 1361–82; and P. O. Steiner, *Mergers: Motives, Effects and Policies* (Ann Arbor: University of Michigan Press, 1975).

[33] This was announced by then-Attorney General John Mitchell in June 1969 as a formalization of the program of Richard A. McLaren, then in charge of the Antitrust Division.

In short, limits on pure conglomerate mergers should be minimal. This accords with the efficient treatment for takeovers in financial markets (chapter 6) and in "utility" sectors (chapter 9). The only restrictions on such mergers would be:

1. All branches would be operated with separate accounts, and with a large share (perhaps 25 percent) of the shares kept outstanding.[34] This would minimize the likelihood of further entrenchment and inefficiency from the merger.

2. Firms that hold more than 40 percent of the market shares in their primary lines of business could not acquire smaller firms with market shares above 40 percent. This rule would avert the possibility of mutually entrenching market power, which Edwards and others have identified. The rule would still permit takeovers by a substantial number of the very largest corporations. Therefore it would treat the core problem of entrenchment without sacrificing the takeover discipline on efficiency.

Takeovers—partial or complete—could occur by the public investment bank as well as by private firms. Indeed, the threat—or the actuality—of public takeover would fill a big gap now present in private markets. The country's very largest firms are virtually immune from private takeover, because they are just too big and too closely supported by their bankers and other financial units. For these, only a large, outside entity could credibly threaten a partial or complete takeover. The bank would operate in accord with the functions outlined in chapter 6. It would have substantial capital of its own, and also be empowered to arrange consortia with other financial units in order to deal with larger firms. It would have free run in selecting firms for treatment. It would normally seek only "working control" (which requires less than 25 percent of shares in most of the firms in question here), rather than majority control. The degree of control would vary, however, in line with specific objectives and company conditions. Holdings would be accompanied by directorships and by an active role in guiding managerial changes and behavior. Holdings would normally be temporary, on the order of 5 to 10 years. This would be long enough to make changes, but short enough to avoid creating permanent mutual interests and acquiescence in the firm's affairs.

[34] The LTV Corporation did this extensively, and to good effect. It did preserve some degree of independence and openness and, of course, it reduced the capital which the parent company had to commit to the subsidiary. Other firms did not follow LTV's innovation.

In short, the public bank would operate as a large independent investment bank, specializing in changing management quality. It would engage talent and expertise comparable to that in other leading financial groups; it would itself be under competitive constraints in the markets for banking services and for corporate control; its activities would be more fully reported than a private bank's, in order to assure accountability. But it would aim to yield financial gains—in income and capital gains—from generating social gains. Related versions have been tried in Britain, Canada, Italy, and other countries. Their success has varied, generally being higher where the initial capital has been large, the management is expert, the focus is on lesser firms, and the experiment has lasted 10 to 20 years, not much more or less.

Judging by past experience, it may be optimistic to expect an objective environment in the U.S. for such experiments. Yet the program would be under close scrutiny, and its possibilities when compared to real alternatives—not ideal ones—are objectively favorable. In particular, it would probably be less drastic and more lucrative (and acceptable) to private shareholders than divestiture or complete public ownership. It would base accountability on economic power, and would itself be accountable.

The Bank would focus on leading firms with a degree of inefficiency which can be converted into increased profits, lesser firms which can be operated as pacesetters to put more competitive pressure on leading firms by taking away their market shares if possible, and new entrants needing temporary support. One of its prime criteria would be the level of content in the firm.

The practical scope and cost of such a program can be estimated with little difficulty. The main candidates presently are in five to ten tight oligopolies, whose identities are fairly well agreed upon among specialists. Assume that share ownership averaging 20 percent will suffice, and that firms ranking first to fourth are usually selected, one to an industry. On this basis and for these industries, only about $3 billion of share purchases would presently be needed, and a number of "public directors" would go onto boards of directors to represent these holdings. These are moderate amounts, compared to the problems and to alternative remedies. They would be smaller than the holdings of the leading investment banks and bank trust departments. Had the purchases been made in 1960, the subsequent capital gains for the public would have been substantial (see note 31). In two of the producer-goods firms, improved management might have avoided more than

$1 billion in private portfolio losses during 1960–73. Such cases should attract powerful private support for public shareholdings. The holdings would of course yield dividends for the public purse and also deliver competitive improvements.

This estimate is for a maximum program, assuming that there is little restructuring, incentive taxation, or any other policy actions toward these industries. Any use of other treatments would reduce the need scope of this policy tool. The mixture of private and public constraints does not guarantee benefits, as Italian and other experience suggests. In this country, the Reconstruction Finance Corporation provides only indirect evidence that investments can be managed without corruption and with competence. Yet the marginal gains may, after discounting, outweigh the risks and costs up to high levels of funding.

4 SUPPLEMENTARY TREATMENTS

Even at their best, these treatments would touch only the main core of problem cases. They would take time to work, and in no instance would they restore the disequalizing of wealth that originally occurred. However, they would at least be effective general treatments. We now need to consider several more specialized tactics, which might supplement the basic treatments. These specific tools, while useful, have a narrower scope than is normally realized, and all of them will be difficult to apply.

Reductions in Trade Barriers. This has been a staple proposal since Adam Smith's time, and of course it is attractive in principle. Tariffs were integral with the trust issue between 1880 and 1900 in the U.S., and in such trading economies as Britain, Japan, and Germany these levers could clearly be powerful. They already are powerful in many industries; indeed, a main rationale for Britain's joining the Common Market was to subject British industry to increased competition from abroad.[35] In the U.S., tariff reductions on a large scale are highly unlikely. Even if instituted, the effects of such a reduction would be limited and many problem cases would be unaffected.

Trade barriers go through periodic general shifts, as protectionism waxes and wanes. Occasionally specific barriers are added, such as the oil import quotas in 1959. What seems impossible to get are deliberate, specific cuts in

[35] In a few cases the British Monopolies Commission has suggested reducing tariffs as a means to increase competitive pressure. But it has not been done.

trade barriers in order to apply new competitive forces. The resistance to cuts is focused and effective; either the protected firms are profitable and have a large stake, or they are stagnant and so imports will cause extensive structural changes. Other causes might also be involved in the political economy of the issue, including the natural unwillingness of any nation to reduce trade barriers unilaterally. The political economy, therefore, makes the prospects for using this strategy remote, as is indicated by long experience in the U.S. and abroad. The tool is much admired but idle—probably forever.

How far the treatment might reach depends on the extent and incidence of existing protection. These are complex matters, requiring information on imported goods, on import substitutability, effective tariff rates, and nontariff barriers.[36] One must rely on rough estimates, using data on tariffs and other barriers and on import trends.[37] By any such appraisals, the possible scope of tariff cuts would indeed be highly selective, covering a limited range of industries and missing many of the problem cases.[38] In some cases (e.g., computers, film, oil, automobiles, copying equipment, soaps, drugs, and toiletries) already the leading U.S. firms are already the leading actual or potential importers, and so the effects of tariff-cutting would be diluted.

Import competition has been powerful in certain cases, particularly steel and automobiles. Yet others—such as computers, copying equipment, soaps, electrical equipment, glass, and telephone equipment—appear to be virtually immune. The causes of immunity vary from high transport costs for glass or soap to specific conventions or rules against buying imports (as in most telephone equipment, aircraft, and electrical equipment). Among the main problem cases, only automobiles, steel, aluminum, and copper appear sensitive to this treatment. In steel, for one, the recent direction has in fact been toward more protection, not less.[39]

In other economies—such as those of Britain, Japan, and continental

---

[36] See W. M. Corden, *The Theory of Protection* (London: Clarendon Press, 1971).

[37] See B. N. Vaccara, *Employment and Output in Protected Manufacturing Industries* (Wash., D.C.: Brookings Institution, 1960); and B. Balassa, "Tariff Protection in Industrial Countries: An Evaluation," *Journal of Political Economy,* 1965, pp. 573–94.

[38] They include primarily flour, liquor, cigarettes, various chemicals, certain nonferrous metals products, electrical equipment, batteries, ships, films, and specialized instruments.

[39] An informal international cartel arrangement to limit imports to the U.S. was created in 1968, with strong State Department efforts. These limits have not stopped import competition, but they have reduced it.

Europe—trade involvement is usually more extensive, and so there are wider possibilities. Many manufacturing industries are highly sensitive, so that the problem is primarily one of meshing selective changes with overall trade and currency balances. Thus, instead of leading to currency revaluation a rising exchange balance could lead to tariff-cutting for industries with high market power and X-inefficiency. This fundamental point of strategy (which has, for example, been ignored throughout the recurring monetary crises in Britain since 1945) must be understood before foreign trade can be used as a practical tool. Because it is not, trade barriers continue to protect many problem cases, and changes are not considered at these crucial times. For example, the postdevaluation 1968–70 surge in Britain's payments balance made possible a large array of tariff cuts, which probably could have affected British industries more, and earlier, than entry into the Common Market has. It would have focused the pressures where they were needed and avoided such losses as were caused by the side-effects of entering the Common Market.

In short, certain high-yield treatments of trade barriers are presently being underused abroad. The losses to Britain and certain other countries may be quite large. In the U.S., possibly significant gains are probably being sacrificed in only a few major cases.

Patents. Patents, mineral rights, and advertising are among the many possible causes of entry barriers (recall chapters 2 and 4). We shall consider possible limits on them, taking patents first. Here we shall consider restorative changes in patents, to abate existing market power. Preventive treatment of patents will be taken up in the next chapter.

Patents focus in certain industries. They particularly underlie market power in the drug, photocopy equipment, and photographic supplies industries. These account for 7 of the top 14 cases of market power in Table 4.10, with over $4 billion of capitalized "excess" market power. It appears from general analyses that shorter patent lives would not sacrifice substantial degrees of inventive and innovative activity.[40] The marginal benefit in induced innovation from additional years of patent life is of low probability, while the marginal restrictive effects are definite.

---

[40] See W. D. Nordhaus, *Invention, Growth and Welfare* (Cambridge, Mass.: MIT Press, 1969); F. M. Scherer, *Industrial Market Structure and Economic Performance* (Skokie, Ill.: Rand McNally, 1970); Scherer, "Nordhaus' Theory of Optimal Patent Life: A Geometrical Reinterpretation"; Nordhaus' "Reply," *American Economic Review,* June 1972, pp. 422–31.

Yet a general shortening of patent lives, even down to five years, would not soon touch the existing problems in these industries. The structure has now hardened sufficiently so that, as in many consent decrees which "open up" patents, little would happen from altering old patents.[41] Such a change is not likely, in any event. For these industries, a specific measure to shorten existing patents and constrain their use might be mildly effective. In drugs, especially, the equity effects—on top of the efficiency losses—from tight patent use mean that the net discounted benefits from altering patent usage toward shorter lives and compulsory licensing might be large. Drug firms would still have strong relative incentives to develop new drugs first, but the absolute level of drug prices and profits would simply be less.

Only in drugs and copying equipment are restorative gains from altering existing patents likely to be large. If all new patents were shorter-lived and subject to limits (see chapter 8), market power and its effects in these two industries might eventually decline. Yet this effect could well take decades, which suggests that patent changes can have only a slight effect on existing market power, and that it is especially important to design patents to fit preventive goals.

Raw Material Controls. Controls over mineral and land rights are important in certain metals, minerals, and forestry-products industries.[42] They appear routinely to have soporific effects on management. Certain major steel, copper, aluminum, and forest products firms, for example, have had periods of marked inefficiency, which would have been impossible without the security of exclusive materials controls. And these controls appear to help maintain market power at downstream levels.

The efficient treatment is not obvious or easy. One way is to transfer materials to a public or common-carrier basis if they are critical to entry or to competitive strategies. Holders would then be required to sell to all comers, on reasonably short-term contracts, at "reasonable" prices, which could be challenged formally in court.

Another approach would be to require the controlling rights to be spun off

---

[41] Thus the AT&T and IBM decrees in 1955 and 1956 provided patent access, but to little if any affect. By contrast, Xerox Corporation has now prepared a network of some 1,800 patents in its continuing patent and pricing strategy to maintain its near-monopoly in copying equipment. As the older patents die, the newer ones serve the same function. Whether the 1975 FTC settlement will reduce this effect sharply is doubtful.

[42] See D. R. Fusfeld, "Joint Subsidiaries in the Iron and Steel Industry," *American Economic Review,* May 1958, pp. 578–87.

into separate entities, in which the Public Investment Bank could take shareholdings. All sales would be on an arm's-length basis, and modest public holdings and directorships might then be adequate to ensure that access is open.

Both treatments would also create freer input markets so that established firms could also engage in more flexible competitive tactics. Much of the present rigidity of shares and of cooperative behavior in these markets over many decades has arisen directly from the straitjacket of materials; it has been literally impossible to change positions.[43]

Advertising. There has recently been much discussion of the possibility that advertising is an important entry barrier. This complex issue revolves around the ability of large advertisers to achieve increasing returns in nationwide selling activities. Moreover advertising is often a weapon for entering a market or establishing a new brand—in short a weapon for increasing competition. Therefore, only if advertising scale economies were not so genuine as other input economies and its anticompetitive effects outweigh its procompetitive role would restrictions on it be efficient.

Even then, designing optimal restrictions would be difficult. A blanket limit on advertising—restricting it, say, to 2 percent of sales—would penalize the lesser firms, since the leading firm already uses a lower percentage because of the "scale economies" of saturation advertising.[44] Also, many firms would easily adapt by shifting advertising expenditures into such forms as sales networks and promotional discounts. In 1968 these problems defeated the only direct antitrust attempt ever made to identify and constrain the role of advertising.[45] The issue had emerged from direct evidence that the advertising behavior patterns in a range of soap and detergent markets closely fitted the Comanor-Wilson predictions. Advertising apparently did operate to limit competition and enhance the leading firm's profit. Yet no effective remedy appeared possible, even if conviction under the antitrust laws

---

[43] *Ibid.* Also, joint-venture oil products pipelines play the same role, in mutually controlling the choices competitors can make. Colonial Pipeline—the "Big Inch" connecting Texas with New Jersey—is a premier example of this, but there are scores of others.

[44] This arises from the economics of advertising; see W. S. Comanor and T. Wilson, *Advertising and Market Power* (Cambridge, Mass.: Harvard University Press, 1974).

[45] This was the project analyzing market shares, advertising intensity, and profitability in detergents (see note 13).

were possible.⁴⁶ The current FTC case against leading cereals companies is also facing this dilemma.

This negative lesson actually has a limited scope, because only a handful of industries are strongly influenced by advertising in any event (recall chapter 4). Even if antitrust doctrine and strategic devices were favorable, abating advertising's effects would be a limited strategy.

Applying Monopsony Power. Public agencies and firms purchase from a wide range of industries. Where they have monopsony power, it could be exercised to constrain market power and to induce a more competitive structure. In the U.S. this tactic would affect certain problem industries, but only a minority. Abroad, the coverage is more complete.

The most obvious candidate is the drug industry, which sells in bulk to large public agencies, nonprofit groupings, and regulated buyers. Unified, aggressive purchasing may ultimately be the only practical way to abate market power in the drug industry. It works, to a degree and with some exceptions, under national health programs in Western Europe.⁴⁷ The U.S. system of medical insurance, with passive "regulated" paying groups such as Blue Cross, operates almost as if it were designed to minimize the effectiveness of such monopsony behavior. The possible gains from changed behavior, even with no changes in structure, could be large.

Other sectors are weapons supply and utility equipment. Past treatments have been erratic and often perverse. The tendencies toward passivity and mutual interests in these cases may be inherent in the given structure, so that other changes may be needed in order to improve performance (see chapters 9 and 12). Similarly, stockpiling of materials as a constraint device has tended, instead, to be operated so as to minimize the impact on industry pricing.

In short, public monopsony is an unfulfilled possibility, which may need a

---

⁴⁶ This partly reflected the inherent difficulty of the problem, and also partly the added limits of doing so under the narrow context of antitrust laws. The 1968 discussion of detergents was thorough and futile. It is not clear that the current FTC action toward major cereal firms can resolve the paradox any better.

⁴⁷ In Britain, the National Health Service has had moderate effect as a unified buyer, but it has not exerted its maximum monopsony power. Only the intervention of the U.K. Monopolies Commission 1972–75 secured drastic price cuts in the tranquilizers Librium and Valium, which Hoffmann-LaRoche had been selling at multiples of real cost. Once again, effective treatments may require combinations and overlappings of policy tools.

different setting or incentive structure from what has yet been tried. And its potential reach in the U.S. is not broad.

Price Controls. Direct controls on prices have been tried both in war and peace, and some form of control may be inevitable in modern economies.[48] Moreover, controls are commonly focused on the core monopolistic industries. In principle, this constraint could replace all the other policy tools.

In practice, the prospects are slight (recall section 7, chapter 5). Effective constraints would require reducing the rates of return to competitive levels, and even in wartime the purpose of controls has never been to reduce high profit rates, but only to keep prices from rising. It would be naive to expect the situation to change. The impetus for sustained, detailed administrative denial of powerful financial interests is not likely to exist.

Even if it did exist, the constraints could cause costly side effects. Rate-base regulation may induce general inefficiency, overuse of capital and predatory competition in adjacent markets (recall chapter 5 and see chapter 9). These costs could be greater in sum than the losses under unfettered monopoly. The issue has yet to be studied thoroughly, and no reliable estimates of these costs of regulation are likely to be made, because the effects are subtle and complex. Still, even discounting for uncertainty, the probable losses are significant, and they would presumably arise under controls of industrial prices.

The various practical and analytical problems with orthodox price controls seem sufficient to disqualify them as a general treatment for "nonutility" cases. The graduated profit rate tax would be more efficient and would avoid the side effects by preserving a degree of profit incentives. One hybrid price control treatment might, however, abate inefficiency in certain cases. It would make approval for price increases conditional on an outside efficiency audit of management. The audit would be published (thereby stimulating possible takeover), and its recommendations would have to be applied before prices would be raised. This process was tried with some success by the British Prices and Incomes Board during 1967–71.[49] It serves as a deterrent, since the threat of audit and possible takeover would induce firms to avoid the process altogether.

---

[48] This view has achieved some currency since 1970; see, e.g., J. K. Galbraith, *Economics and the Public Purpose* (Boston: Houghton-Mifflin, 1973).

[49] The PIB developed expert staff capability for direct appraisal of management performance, and it used this in several cases involving public firms.

In short, industrial price controls by themselves are much less effective than controls that would trigger more direct treatments. Yet even these hybrids would be incomplete, for they would touch only firms with rising prices. Many problem firms may have stable or falling prices, for a variety of technical and external reasons. They would be unaffected by this form of treatment.

5 TREATMENT OF CONTENT

If content is added to the evaluation, the main change in the treatments is in the optimal size of firms (and their operating divisions) and in the scope of public enterprise. The costs of bigness tilt the cost-benefit choices toward a smaller optimum size for the total firm and its divisions. Of course, exceptional steps can be taken by large firms to enrich content, to diffuse responsibility, to broaden opportunity, etc. Some steps may occur in any event, but the average conditions offer large rises in content from reducing the size of the firm. This will require a new set of studies to clarify the choices, since there is little systematic information. Possibly, these studies would show that the larger firms should be subdivided down to small fractions of present size, and that their operating units should be additionally decentralized. It is also possible that no major change would be indicated. More probably, the content criteria would suggest a marked reduction in size. Such a reduction could of course be accomplished in most cases by routine corporate revisions.

The optimal scope of public enterprise would also rise, to optimize content. How far this would go is not yet measurable, and it would depend partly on the reductions in size. Where scale economies or other factors favored the retention of large size, a degree of public enterprise would be needed in any case. To some extent, the prospect of such public ownership might preinduce firms to take extraordinary steps to improve content. This could be impressed on the public investment bank as grounds for minimizing the degree of public ownership.

Content therefore could call for marked adjustments in size and public ownership, and perhaps in other choices. The scope of these changes depends on further study of content itself, and on its relations to the policy devices.

6 IN SUMMARY

Past yields from Section 2 actions have been high, but biases against further such cases are now strong. A balanced set of treatments would include at least: a full information policy, including disaggregation of company data; a scaled profits tax linked to market share (perhaps with an agency to supervise changes and tax incentives to mobilize shareholders to press for restructuring); a public investment bank to treat cases with high market power and those with severe content problems; and a variety of secondary efforts to adjust tariff and patent conditions. Some restructuring efforts by the present agencies would still be appropriate. The inclusion of content as an objective shifts the choices toward smaller firm sizes and more extensive public enterprise.

The basic need is to focus on the main problem cases in the economy, and on the basic treatments. Without focus, one cannot establish priorities, and so policy choices have lacked direction and consistency. The recent Section 2 moratorium reflects this loss of focus and the inability to identify the net gains to be had. At its worst, it leads to perverse antitrust "toughness" in the wrong directions, which fortifies market power rather than abating it. At any rate, it diverts attention from the range of other treatments that are available.

Under present approaches, Section 2 has become virtually a dead letter. But with revised procedures and allied with tax incentives, a "new" Section 2 could be effective. Correct basic treatments can probably abate the main problem cases much sooner than they would spontaneously change, by optimizing public and private choices. Information, supervisory capacities, and public funds would be used efficiently. The damage to "innocent" parties would be minimized and it could, if appropriate, be compensated. Transitional costs would also be minimized, and the existence of sale economies would automatically be reflected in informed company choices which optimize among economies, tax incentives, and uncertainties about the future.

Other supplementary policy steps may fit individual cases, but they should not supplant the basic treatments. Tariff cutting, patent changes, price controls, etc., would not be widely effective, even if they were likely ever to be tried. Once again focus is essential if correct policy priorities are to be established.

There is added importance in applying these restorative treatments. The key long-run need is to treat emerging market power on an incipiency basis. Yet such preventive treatments are vulnerable, and indeed ultimately unfair, if they are not allied with thorough actions to abate existing market power. That is precisely the awkward and destructive bias now tainting antitrust policy. Effective restorative action is the fulcrum on which the rest of competitive policy must turn, if it is to turn at all.

CHAPTER EIGHT

Conventional Markets: Preventive Treatment

THE PREVENTION of new or "incipient" market power might be both a necessary and a sufficient treatment in the long run. At present, a tight limit on horizontal and vertical mergers is the only tactic being consistently applied. Ironically, that approach is part of a whole treatment that hardens market structure. Depending on other policies, therefore, individual preventive treatments may have either negative or positive yields.

I shall assume that restorative treatments are to be applied, as advanced in chapters 6 and 7. If they are, the main outlines of effective preventive treatments are reasonably clear. They are integral with the restorative policies.

The preventive treatments will need to fit the causes—as yet still unknown—of new market power. We shall review what is known about these causes in the next section, and try to define "incipiency." Treatments for the main causes will then be considered one by one.

1 SOURCES OF NEW MARKET POWER

There are many sources of new market power, including many ways in which the State creates, or is manipulated into creating, monopoly. Even in these official cases, however, one needs to look at the deeper economic determinants at work. Therefore our starting point is the economic origins of rising market power. If we can identify these, then we can define "incipient" market power and design efficient treatments.

A rise can occur when a firm increases its share of a given market (examples: U.S. Steel in 1901, General Motors in 1910–27) or when a monopolized industry grows faster than the economy (examples: IBM in 1956–73 and Xerox in 1962–73). Both instances may occur at once. To prevent rises, one must be able to predict when either of these will occur and apply treatments quickly (such as regulatory moves to avert new utility monopolies). Preferably, however, one should simply have disincentives in place to automatically deter the rise. Such deterrents would include the graduated profit-rate tax in chapter 7, or a flat rule against mergers whose share of the market exceeds a certain percentage.

The driving force for monopolization is of course the excess profits and capital gains that result, whether or not scale economies are present (and often despite the presence of diseconomies of scale). If scale economies are present, the rise of at least one firm's market share is accordingly more likely. This pressure can take several practical directions: collusion, merger, internal growth, or a resort to specific devices for exclusion. Putting one route out of reach merely transfers efforts to the other tactics, which may be easily substituted.

The "causes" operate within a larger process—the life-cycle of industries (recall chapters 2 and 4). A common sequence is that one firm gains a leading position in the new industry, either from a patent or from economies of scale, and perhaps by means of mergers. The industry then grows to large scale, while the leading firm retains all or most of its market share, even though the original patent or economies have been outgrown. A preventive treatment therefore needs to be applied early.

The sum of these possibilities at any time is embodied in the firm's share-time curve (recall chapters 2 and 4). The policy objective is to lower this curve to the right—so that the gains available from adding market share are less—but without reducing the performance of the firm. This then shifts the choice toward stable or declining market shares.

We need a priority ranking of the sources of new market power, so that the treatments can be focused on the most important ones. No definitive ranking is possible, in fact, because—as ever—data are scanty and past research has been embryonic. We shall summarize past research and look backward at some problem cases to learn what we can about their alternative sources.

The main specific sources of new market power are economies of scale, merger, rapid growth of the industry, patents, and official franchises of various kinds.

Economies of scale are an important cause of high market shares in many embryonic industries, but in most cases these are soon outgrown, so that in normal or mature industries a preventive treatment would not appreciably affect the level of costs (recall chapter 4). These are exceptions, of course, but they are relatively few and easy to identify.

Mergers have been a limited source of market power in large industries since 1901, and the present tight antimerger limits have virtually eliminated this source in major industries. Yet there are two gaps in this. First, large loopholes have been drilled in this constraint, by specific exemptions (e.g., the 1967 professional football league merger) and "special" cases (the McDonnell-Douglas merger in 1967 and the Penn-Central Railroad merger in 1968). Many sectors now lie at least partly out of antitrust reach; for example, utilities, shipping, airlines, banking, agriculture, sports. These exemptions are being whittled away by recent Antitrust Division efforts and Supreme Court rulings, but for now the horizontal merger limits are much looser in these areas. And even in conventional industrial markets, large exceptions are often made to permit major mergers.

Second, the really new industries are often too small and novel to attract antitrust attention. The critical mergers thus occur in obscurity, and their scope therefore remains virtually unknown. Ultimately it matters little for policy whether the early dominance comes by merger or internal growth, but a truly preventive policy would need to go beyond the present antitrust policies, to identify and treat these formative mergers. In short, merger limits—tight as they are—are not yet on an effective incipiency basis. The coverage is incomplete and the exceptions are numerous.

Rapid growth is clearly a major source of new market power. It has created most of the large near-monopolies of 1930–70 out of midget monopolies. This is evident for the aluminum, automobile, computer, oil, telephone equipment, and copying equipment industries, among others. The point is so obvious as to seem trivial, but it is nevertheless a cardinal factor for treatment.

Patents are another important source. They commonly arise at the very inception of the industry, as in lightbulbs, telephone equipment, drugs, and copying equipment. Their 17-year life often gives ample time to solidify the leading position well into the industry's maturity, frequently by the amassing of more and interrelated patents. In an important subset of industries, therefore, a preventive treatment must alter the nature and role of patents.

Finally, the State gives other kinds of support to aspiring monopolists. It permits professionals to cartelize and control entry into their service markets; banking, medical care, legal services, accountancy, and stock-exchange trading are leading examples of this. As a research sponsor, public agencies often limit innovation activity and growth to one or two firms. The Defense Department does this frequently with weapons markets, and so has the Atomic Energy Commission in supporting nuclear power development.[1] And as a regulator of "utilities," it may induce regulated firms to monopolize new adjacent markets at cutthroat prices; possible cases of this are numerous in telecommunications.

On the whole, the main sources of new market power appear to be growth, patents, and other State supports. This implies that preventive treatments will need to become quicker and more sophisticated. They will also need to reach into new areas and to cause changes in other governmental policies (such as patents, regulation, and agency R & D policies).

One should not expect to develop a fine-tuned definition of incipiency that would apply over the whole range of sectors. A reasonable working definition would be a 30 percent market share in a market of $100 million sales or more, which is growing at a rate above the national average. The size threshhold would roughly take in the 1,000 largest industrial firms. It would leave out several million smaller firms, many of them local, which no policy can hope to treat thoroughly. As for growth, it would take only a moderate judgment and research effort to single out those markets which are likely to continue growing most rapidly and rise soon to major status. Judgment would also be needed in estimating market shares; the markets often have blurred edges, partly because the product types are new and formative.

The main point is that some such working criterion of incipiency could be used to bound the problem and to guide treatments. Applying it to the main past cases, one would assign the incipiency periods very roughly as in Table

---

[1] See M. J. Peck and F. M. Scherer, *The Weapons Acquisition Process* (Cambridge, Mass.: The Harvard University School of Business, 1962); R. A. Tybout, *Government Contracting in Atomic Energy* (Ann Arbor: University of Michigan Press, 1965).

4.10. The main lesson is that incipiency occurred very long ago for nearly all of these instances. Some of them even predate the Sherman Act itself. And the 1904–20 actions, ambitious as they were, failed to treat the several major incipiency cases that then were ripe. If they had, they would have averted large-scale market power that has lasted, in some cases, for nearly 75 years.

A second lesson is that many of these cases were quite predictable at the time. The industries were clearly rising to major status, and the likelihood that the leading firm would recede back to a small share was small. Where patents were important (Alcoa, Xerox, drugs) or other barriers existed (Western Electric), the prediction could become quite accurate for most cases. This suggests that pinning down genuine incipiency may usually be quite feasible.

Altogether, preventive treatments appear to offer high yields, stretching out over long periods of time. They could be based on reasonable definitions and estimates. It is impossible—and in many cases unnecessary—to avert all or even most new market power, but the main cases probably can be foreseen and treated.

2 TREATMENTS

Collusion obviously should continue to be flatly prohibited. The practice imposes monopoly losses, while yielding appreciable social gains only under the most unusual conditions. I shall also assume in this section that restorative treatments (chapters 6 and 7) are applied. Beyond that, there are three main directions for treatment to take: toward growth, mergers, and patents.

Internal Growth. The optimum treatment often seems baffling when the firm's internal growth is the main origin of market power. Such growth appears more natural than mergers or patent-based monopolizing, and it may reflect superior "skill, foresight, and industry." [2] It is widely believed that limiting such growth will destroy incentives to perform or even to compete. That fear has forestalled strict remedies even when—as in Alcoa in 1945 and United Shoe Machinery in 1953—the monopoly was held illegal under Section 2.

[2] This is now the standard wording in Section 2 decisions when "good" performance is used to exculpate the firm. See P. Areeda, *Antitrust Analysis: Problems, Text, Cases,* rev. ed. (Boston: Little, Brown, 1974), and United States *v.* United Shoe Machinery Corp., 110 F. Suppl. 295 (D. Mass. 1953), and United States *v.* Grinnell Corporation, 384 U.S. 563 (1966).

Despite the belief that internal growth is always socially desirable, no cross-section analysis, case study, or controlled experiment has been conducted on this subject. The key question is whether the unity of the growing firm can be diluted enough to avert full monopoly behavior without also abating incentives for efficiency and innovation. The possibility that it can is indicated by at least two sets of facts. One set is the evidence summarized in chapter 4 that internal efficiency and progress are superior under competitive constraint. Firms presumably are aware of this and could perhaps be induced to act in accord with it. Second, many firms have deliberately diluted their unity by decentralization into distinct, semicompetitive divisions. General Motors is only one well known example.[3] There is a strong possibility that such separations can reach a socially optimal balancing of cooperation and competition.

A preventive treatment would therefore induce firms with market shares rising above some threshold (such as 30 percent) because of pure internal growth to create autonomous competing subsidiaries to hold less than 30 percent each. To some extent the profit-rate surtax (chapter 7) will induce this, but preventive policy needs to anticipate, in two other ways. First, it needs to identify without delay when the 30 percent share is reached. Second, it needs to define the extent of autonomy—in decisions, accounting, and ownership—that must be created. Accounts would be kept and reported separately, along traditional divisional reporting lines. And some divisional shares would be publicly held. All of these would accord with well-tried business practices, though their exact degrees would be a matter for research.

What matters is that internal growth as a source of monopoly can be treated preventively, along conventional lines. There is no scientific basis for immunizing it from treatment. The more sophisticated practices in certain large firms indicate, instead, that it should be directly treated, and the treatment would fit closely with the criteria and incentives of the restorative treatments in chapter 7.

Merger policy. The main lines of treatment are to extend the present constraints on horizontal and vertical mergers to incipient cases in all sectors, including those presently exempted from antitrust policy. One cannot show

[3] Management fashions come and go, and individual firms experiment with various degrees of decentralization. Still, a large degree of decentralization is now common. See also O. E. Williamson, *Corporate Control and Business Behavior* (Englewood Cliffs, N.Y.: Prentice-Hall, 1970).

conclusively that the present merger limits—which merely codify Supreme Court precedents—are optimal. That figure might be a few points lower or perhaps as much as 10 percent higher. The proper limit also depends on the ease of granting exceptions. Still, there is a broad consensus that the present limits are about right, and the burden of proof rests upon those proposing a change. True, the limits are probably slightly too tight if restorative treatments are lacking. But we are assuming here that they are present.

The incipiency criterion would simply focus more attention and enforcement effort on certain smaller merging firms than is now common. It would also provide a standard basis for reaching back to undo mergers where incipiency was not accurately seen at the time or action was mistakenly withheld. This would apply to both horizontal and vertical mergers. Exceptions would still be permitted in cases where economies of scale could be shown to be large relative to the future (not present) size of the merged company, but those asserting that scale economies exist would have to bear the burden of proof.

Patents. Patents inherently reduce the degree of risk, while also raising the attainable rate of profit. They also create market power, which may persist long after it has ceased to yield any net social benefit. This happens mainly with a relatively few major patents, which are the proper focus for treatment. Therefore constraints on both the profitability and the life of certain patents may properly be part of an incipiency treatment. It has become customary for established dominant firms to reach consent decrees which make patents available free or at a "reasonable" license royalty, but this happens too late to avert or erode the dominant position. Either a quicker tactic is needed, or the limits need to be built into the patent grant itself.

The most effective treatment would be careful shortening of patent life. The next best treatment would draw on competitors' interests to trigger and enforce constraints. It would avoid making public agencies evaluate the net costs and benefits of individual patents. A rational treatment would define the scope of reasonable returns and market share for major patents. "Major" could be determined by the willingness of any firm to make a binding offer of a substantial amount (say $10 million) for any patent.

A balanced approximate set of criteria would set a 30 percent market share for the patented item as the threshhold and would set a 20 percent rate of return on R & D and innovation costs as the maximum "reasonable" level. The treatment would then require unconditional licensing of the patent at royalties based on the ceiling of a 20 percent rate of return, and it would prohibit the firm from having a market share greater than 30 percent as long as the patent was in force. The firm could then choose to sacrifice the patent in pursuit of a market share above 30 percent.

Incentives to make the firm declare its choice would be applied by instituting treble damages for overcharging. A customer or competitor could then sue to recover treble the excess profits over the *competitive* rate of return (not the 20 percent royalty basis) for the period when the firm's market share in the patented good exceeded 30 percent and it had not declared its release of the patent. This would presumably be a self-activating device to prevent noncompliance. Alternatively the firm could retain the patent, hover at a 30 percent market share, and license others to supply the rest. They would of course be under the graduated profit surtax.

This strategy would prevent the future creation of patent-based dominant firms, mostly by making use of self-interest. Only in rare cases would court action be necessary. There would be little need for exhaustive efforts to decide the optimum life or social value for individual patents. The key choices would be made by the patent owners, who would best know the costs and returns involved. Altogether this approach would fit the guidelines of chapter 3, even though the specific criteria cannot be fine-tuned at the start. It would be possible to test the sensitivity of these criteria as experience grows, so that eventually the optimal treatment could be approximated. Meanwhile, these rough criteria are probably not far off optimal levels, nor are the results highly sensitive to them. Major inventions and innovations would still promise extremely attractive returns.

3 SUMMARY

Preventive and restorative treatments are integral; they apply the same types and directions of incentives. Full disclosure and graduated taxes are parts of both approaches. Merger and patent policy can be genuinely preventive if they are quick, tight, and aligned with private incentives. The treatments I have outlined would have averted a large share of the present problem cases. They would not have sacrificed much, if any, efficiency or innovation. On the contrary, performance would probably have been improved in the long run, and treatment would not have required great exactitude in the criteria applied.

What matters is having well-designed restorative treatments, and basing preventive treatments on the incentives of those who have information and a powerful self-interest in the outcome. Present merger and patent policies do not have these attributes. Because there is a lack of restorative policies, merger policies now tend to protect leading firms. Because they are based on ignorance about the incentives and benefits in innovation, patent policies tend to create and perpetuate monopoly beyond any known degree of net social benefits. These proposed preventive treatments would also require little new administrative effort or complex information.

Several other directions for preventive policies—in finance, utilities, and weapons—are covered in other chapters. The basic rule is that exemptions from antitrust (and from an incipiency treatment) should bear a heavy burden of proof. Rarely have they actually borne that burden, and the exemption commonly outlasts whatever original economic justification there may have been.

The political economy of the situation makes the rule especially important. The market is usually new, with overtones of innovation, and it is not regarded as conventional antitrust material. The firms fully realize the large, permanent stakes they are reaching for. Competitors are often few. In short, the situation usually contains biases toward exemptions. Therefore it is important to set the burden of proof correctly.

CHAPTER NINE
"Utility" Sectors

DURING MUCH of this century, "utility" sectors have been widely regarded as "natural monopolies." That has been the basis for such distinctive policy devices as conventional public enterprise and, in the U.S., utility regulation. This "naturaly monopoly" rationale has come increasingly under doubt in recent years, for reasons that will emerge in this chapter, and regulation itself has seemed increasingly to be a cause of inefficiency and a device to protect the utility (recall chapter 5). From this disillusion flowed, in the 1960s, a wide range of proposals for reforming or replacing regulation—complete deregulation, franchise actions, graduated profit constraints, "better" regulation, management audits, full public ownership, and incentive regulation, to name just a few.

Regulation reached a low ebb in the 1950s, but took on much greater substance, force, and clarity in the 1960s [1]—coinciding, ironically, with severe new criticism of regulation's economic effects. Therefore even the improved regulation is—quite properly—under strong doubts.

---

[1] Chapter 5 notes some of these changes. By the 1950s much regulation had sagged into ritualistic treatments of profit rates. It passively permitted utilities to extend their control of markets, and academic study had dwindled so that the situation and its effects were scarcely recognized. During the 1960s the FPC revived, and the FCC began open hearings and reversed some of its passivity about competitive margins. Scholarly research on certain issues has

The utility sector is not fundamentally different from other sectors. Therefore parts of the "utility problem" blend in with other restorative and preventive treatments. However, the optimal treatment combines several elements into a fairly complex system, which differs from the present one, and it needs to be presented as a unit.

I shall first outline the basic evolution of utility industries and of regulation. This will bring out the main lines of optimal structure over time, and of the lags that cause policy to depart from that structure. Next I shall assess the several constraints—on profits and prices—that regulation supposedly applies, and their effects. I then outline a revised treatment for utilities, designed to apply only during the phase when a "utility" really is a "utility," to apply only the correct constraints, and to induce choices that will terminate the treatment at the optimal time.

1 LIFE-CYCLES AND POLICY EVOLUTION

There is no permanent utility sector. There are industries that temporarily have "natural monopoly" attributes.[2] These constitute an evolving group, as industries move in and out of utility status. An optimal policy will adapt to these conditions.

The key to the topic is the regulatory contract between the firm and the State. This contract governs competition, often by custom and easement rather than by explicit clauses. This contract is more aberrant than has been realized, because it contains a series of absolute exclusions, which usually conflict with the routine evolution of the utility and of the optimum policy treatment for it.

I shall define the regulatory problem with a series of eight brief propositions.

1. *Utility sectors commonly proceed through four stages.* A regulated utility is usually a system providing many services to a spectrum of users, whose levels and elasticities of demand vary greatly. The network has per-

---

grown. See A. E. Kahn, *The Economics of Regulation*, 2 vols. (New York: Wiley, 1971); W. G. Shepherd and T. E. Gies, *Regulation in Further Perspective* (Cambridge, Mass.: Ballinger, 1974).

[2] On these attributes, see J. C. Bonbright, *Principles of Public Utility Rates* (New York: Columbia University Press, 1961); Kahn, *Economics of Regulation;* Posner, "Natural Monopoly and Its Regulation," *Stanford Law Review*, 1969, pp. 548ff.

manence, often uses public facilities, and often is attached physically to the user. The utility's technology can change or be supplanted by rival modes.

Most utilities can be regarded as passing through four stages, as follows (in skeleton form).[3] In *Stage 1*, the system is invented, often leading to control by patents. This phase is usually brief but decisive for the form of the system. During *Stage 2*, the system is created and grows, often displacing a prior utility. Cross-subsidies among users, and a separation of creamy and skim markets, become embedded in the price structure. The new service seeks regulated status, for permanence, legitimacy, and market control, and the regulators act as promoters, to make the service available to all households.

In *Stage 3* the system becomes complete as a matter of technology and market saturation. It now shifts from offense to defense. Competing new technologies arise beyond the utility's control, to substitute for it in basic and peripheral markets. Physical layout and pricing structure fit evolving city patterns less well than before. Users in creamy markets challenge the prices they face, and traditional external impacts (e.g., pollution) are less acceptable. The utility finds itself increasingly trying to obstruct new technology or to modify it to fit its private optimum structure. Finally, in *Stage 4*, the systemic monopoly attributes yield to these pressures of competition and technology, and the sector is economically capable of reverting—no longer a "utility"—to conventional competitive processes. Or, in certain cases where externalities and equity are peculiarly important, a unified public enterprise solution is superior.

Table 9.1 estimates very roughly the stages for a number of present and past "utilities."[4] During these stages the technology prescribes different optimum structures and policy treatments. The set of utilities in 1924 differed sharply from those of the present, and those in 2024 probably will dif-

---

[3] These stages are only crude summaries of complex interactions among several technological and demand conditions, with interesting dynamic properties. Some of them were touched on in chapter 2. They await a complete formal analysis.

[4] Table 9.1 is highly approximate because the topic has scarcely been broached in the literature. Evolution is clearly normal and decisive for most utilities. A few exceptions may occur—water and sewage, rapid transit, fire extinguishing, basic postal service, and crime control. These often go directly to public enterprise states, though often primarily because of content and public health consideration.

Points 2–8 in the text deal mainly with the temporary utilities. Much of this discussion appeared in "Entry as a Substitute for Regulation," *American Economic Review,* May 1973, pp. 98–105.

fer even more markedly. On the best predictions, it seems likely that the main Stage-2 utilities fifty years hence will be wired cities, parts of electricity and telephone supply, health insurance, and perhaps certain city utilities (transit, water).

Note that the whole scope of the utility sectors need not be constant. Indeed, it seems probable that the scope of utilities peaked in the 1920s and will continue to dwindle. Technology now appears to favor competitive forms in a wide range of possible "utilities," except perhaps for certain urban services. This could sharply alter the scope and nature of the utility problem within a few decades.

2. *Regulation usually starts in Stage 2, in harmony with the interests of the utility and its larger industrial customers.* The structure of mutual interests, the profit expectations, and the terms of exchange (the rate level and structure) therefore precede regulation, as in railroads, electricity, telephones, banks, and now the Postal Service. The contract is not under the regulators' control; they cannot change it. Regulation is able only to legiti-

Table 9.1 Stages of Utility Life-cycle: Approximate Intervals

	Stage 1	*Stage 2*	*Stage 3*	*Stage 4*
Manufactured gas	1800–1820	1820–1880	1880–1920	1920–1950
Natural gas	1900–1910	1910–1950	1950–	
Telegraph	1840–1850	1850–1916	1916–1930	1930–
Railways: All	1820–1835	1835–1910		
Passenger			1910–1935	1935–
Freight			1910–1960	1960–
Electricity	1870–1885	1885–1960	1960–	
Street railways	1870–1885	1885–1912	1912–1922	1922–
Telephone	1875–1880	1880–1947	1947–	
Airlines	1920–1925	1925–1965	1965–	
Television	1935–1947	1947–1965	1965–	
Cable Television	1950–1955	1955–		

mize, reinforce, and smooth these interest-group compromises. Webster's Third New International Dictionary's definition of *regulate* (2a) is "to reduce to order . . . [to] regularize." Regulation can alter the compromises ("1: to govern or direct according to rule") only marginally. (Often only Oxford English Dictionary definition 4 applies: "to make regulations.") Rate structure is never thoroughly assessed and changed.

If commissions were converted into Utility Advisory Boards—to define what utilities and major customers should do to protect their long-run interests, to legitimize their acts, and to avert reduction in their common stock prices—their behavior would be similar to what now happens. Regulation does use honorific terms and rituals. That has lulled academics, and it explains why their present disillusion with regulation runs deep. To doubt that 45 of 50 state commissions, and 7 of 10 federal ones, constrain matters of economic substance, one needs only to look closely and skeptically at their resources, behavior, and results.

Therefore, by contract as it were, regulation promotes and protects the utility, and its larger customers, on into Stages 3 and 4.

3. *Regulation has (barring the odd exception) inadequate funds and talent for its supposed economic tasks.* So those at its center have little motivation, or even understanding, to try to change the basic contract and the process.

4. *The contract excludes seller competition from the service area, in exchange for a review process. The efficacy of the review atrophies, from lack of funds, expertise, and powers. The exclusions spread and become absolute.* The contract is formally with utility owners, and it often becomes capitalized into equity values in Stage 3. Its key effects, however, are on managers. The exclusions protect management from evaluations, controls, or takeover. Few managements have ever been so privileged, and isolated. They (and their usually passive boards) occupy a strange position between shareholders and the commission. What, if anything, they are maximizing is unclear, as chapter 5 noted. Such a vacuum has attracted theorists, but it leaves incentives and responsibility—and the public interest—in limbo.

The managers often find it natural to maximize along both dimensions of profitability: (1) the rate of return (by influencing the commission as well as company behavior), and (2) risk-avoidance (to do this, they maximize their present and future market shares). Since profit rates are formally limited, the firm satisfices by devoting resources (or sacrificed profits) instead to market-share-maintaining activities of many kinds, including some noted by Averch and Johnson.[5] This differs from nonpecuniary maximizing and is probably larger in total resource loss. Therefore, formal profit limits induce hypercon-

---

[5] H. Averch and L. L. Johnson, "Behavior of the Firm Under Regulatory Constraint," *American Economic Review,* 1962, pp. 1052–69; Kahn, *Economics of Regulation;* Shepherd, "The Margin of Competition in Communication," in *Technological Change in Regulated Industries,* ed. W. M. Capron (Wash., D.C.: Brookings Institution, 1971).

trol of the market and hyperreaction against new entry. The franchise and regulatory processes themselves are among the instruments with which managers maximize the utility's value or minimize managerial uncertainty (in some cases, they do both). Since the utility's share prices capitalize the value of the franchise, any threat to their value, such as by unilateral new entry, is "confiscation." Therefore, new entry is intolerable to the *regulators* as well as the owners and managers.

So regulation is non-neutral toward entry; the bias arises from the contract, and it is accentuated by the profit constraints. This bias further increases the utility's bargaining power with the commission: the utility, being irreplaceable, must be propitiated. So regulation tends toward stable corner solutions on entry, preventing it entirely. That may be appropriate for Stage 2, but not for Stages 3 and 4.

5. *The contract de facto allots responsibility and service liability in large part, and increasingly, to the commission.* Penalties and rewards are not applied—either in general or specific directions—to utility performance. Instead of asserting or imposing the public interest, the commission ends up accepting a large degree of service responsibility. Under it, too, there are no practical, specific penalties on the utility for specific nonfulfillments (e.g., outages, crossed wires, late planes) or for general failures of management.[6] The contract lacks explicit performance standards, and it is devoid of mechanisms for enforcing any possible standards. The only penalties are political, which hurt the regulators as much as the utilities. The utility's and commission's shared objective therefore becomes simply to minimize political repercussions, to avoid redressing inequities, to gloss over. The strangeness of the manager's role is matched by that of the regulators'.

6. *So the contract hyperexcludes:*

    a. It excludes seller entry from primary markets and often even from secondary and tertiary ones.
    b. It excludes interarea competition for major customers.
    c. It excludes takeover or any lesser change in managerial and financial control, either by private interests or ultimately by the commission itself or other public groups.
    d. It excludes product-liability claims by legitimate plaintiffs.
    e. It excludes rivalrous innovation, of Schumpeterian or other types.
    f. It excludes regulatory choices that would cause significant reductions in utility share prices.

---

[6] This is plain from observation, research, and personal participation. Commissions simply cannot identify and induce the individual elements of optimal performance.

- g. It excludes thorough, neutral treatments of third-party effects of utility actions (e.g., on the environment).
- h. It excludes future revisions or termination of the contract itself.

Taken together, these exclusions are of large scope and permanence. Few of these exclusions, and their likely costs, are clearly recognized for what they are. And the contract breeds mutual vested interests against change, even among potential entrants.

In short, there is a *reversed evolution* of regulation, in the opposite direction from what utility evolution calls for. This is a rebuttable hypothesis: Regulation of utilities evolves contrary to the optimal trend, in light of the evolution of utility technology and demand.

7. *The regulatory contract, by removing constraints, induces inefficiencies of several sorts.* The new demonology of regulation has not fixed the relative importance of these costs, nor, probably, will it ever do so precisely. My appraisal is that the three leading costs are:

- a. Internal inefficiency. Railroads and, more recently, electricity and telephones are partial examples.[7]
- b. A greater degree of exclusivity in utility technology, which induces innovation below optimal levels and in nonoptimal directions. This may be largest in telephones and electricity.[8]
- c. Excess peak demand and capacity induced by non- and antimarginalist price structures.[9] It took several decades of analysis and pressure to get electricity firms to adopt promotional rates to explore demand elasticity and scale frontiers. The new scarcities of energy and capital are making it clear that marginal conditions now require reversing the price structures to fit true costs and to abate peak demand.

Averch-Johnson rate-base effects may be present in all three costs, but they alone are not the main problem. Also, as Kahn notes, rate-base effects may fit long-run optimizing, not obstruct it.[10]

---

[7] J. R. Meyer, M. J. Peck, J. Stenason, and C. Zwick, *The Economics of Competition in the Transportation Industries* (Cambridge, Mass.: Harvard University Press, 1959); Kahn, *Economics of Regulation;* A. Phillips, ed. *Competition and the Regulation of Industry* (Wash., D.C.: Brookings Institution, 1974).

[8] Capron, *Technological Change;* Kahn, *ibid.*

[9] Shepherd, "Marginal Cost-Pricing in American Utilities," *Southern Economic Journal,* July 1966, pp. 58–70.

[10] Kahn (*Economics of Regulation*) argues that the added margin of investment may explore new technology and scale economies so that the technological gains more than offset the added rate-base costs. The possibility can neither be proven nor disproven at this stage of ignorance.

We have clearly come lightyears since the 1930s, when Leo Sharfman could take the ICC largely at face value, with admiration.[11] Nor is regulation merely a Transylvanian drama, picaresque but trivial, as the Chicago muses tell us.[12] It applies and masks powerful economic influences. The mass of economically aware regulators (perhaps a small mass) must lead lives of quiet desperation, and even if economists were to replace lawyers in running the Dream Factory, most of the costs would still probably occur.[13] There would be too few alert, forceful economists, even perhaps for just the federal commissions. And, in any event, the contract would be unchanged.

The costs are piecemeal, difficult to detect, and *officially* are not to be permitted or admitted (ask any regulator how much inefficiency he/she permits). They often increase utility and commission security from breakdowns, and so they can be portrayed as giving "high-quality" service even if they are actually wasteful. They appear to be immune to any "incentive regulation" yet designed. There is also little inherent pressure from regulation toward equity, to protect poor, politically weak users from being overcharged relative to wealthy powerful ones.

These costs are likely to increase during Stage 3. The normal constraints on management are off, and the utility's incentives are to tighten the exclusions further.

8. *The exclusions tend to be stable and homeostatic.* Seller entry is difficult to force unilaterally upon a utility. Any such possible depressant on utility stock prices is said to be "confiscatory." Also, large firms are commonly reluctant to try to enter, probably because their other profit opportunities exceed those which regulation formally permits. Also, as in the classic Western Electric instance, both sides mutually fear new competition.[14] Small entrants are vulnerable and usually of trivial effect. "Better" regulation of rates—by hiring more brilliant commissioners or staffs, giving them

---

[11] I. L. Sharfman, *The Interstate Commerce Commission*, 4 vols. (The Commonwealth Fund, 1931–37); compare P. W. MacAvoy, *The Economic Effects of Regulation* (Cambridge, Mass.: MIT Press, 1965); G. Kolko, *Railroads and Regulation, 1877–1916* (Princeton: Princeton University Press, 1965); G. W. Hilton, "The Consistency of the Interstate Commerce Act," *Journal of Law and Economics,* 1966, pp. 87–114.

[12] G. J. Stigler and C. Friedland, "What Can Regulators Regulate? The Case of Electricity," in *Utility Regulation,* eds. W. G. Shepherd and T. G. Gies (New York: Random House, 1966).

[13] Donahue and others have urged replacing economists or other specialists with lawyers.

[14] See Shepherd, "The Margin of Competition in Telecommunications," in *Technological Change.*

bigger budgets, etc.—does not correct the basic structural problems or the inefficiencies.

The upshot is anti-Darwinian with a vengeance: regulation is ill-fitted from the start, evolves the wrong way to fit its proper economic function, and survives only too well. Abolition is usually too simple and abrupt an answer, except for Stage 4 cases. What is needed is regulation that lasts only as long as is appropriate, contains inducements for its own termination, and induces optimal choices by those in the regulated firm while it does last.

2   EFFECTS OF REGULATION

Now consider regulation as it operates upon its temporary "utility." The primary choices under regulation need a more detailed review, as a start toward defining the preferred treatment. I shall consider profit criteria, efficiency, investment and innovation choices, and marginal-cost pricing. In these four directions, utility managers have great latitude for choice, and so it is important to examine how to induce optimal choices.

A   RATE OF RETURN

The "fair" rate of return has been the main focus of regulatory effort.[15] There has been lengthy and often empty dispute over seemingly small differences in return, and very often the supposed ceiling on the rate of return has not actually been enforced. Still, small changes in the rate of return can cause large capital gains for shareholders, and so the issue will continue to be contested sharply.

If regulatory doctrine has progressed at all on the definition of a "fair" return, it has been toward a concept of "comparable" returns. That utility rates of return and risk criteria should be in line with risk-return conditions in the rest of the economy is prescribed, approximately, by second-best analysis.[16] This point cautions against a blind limiting of utility returns to minimal levels. And it may be, as many witnesses in rate hearings have

---

[15] Recall ch. 5; see also I. R. Barnes, *The Economics of Public Utility Regulation* (New York: F. S. Crofts, 1942); Kahn, *Economics of Regulation;* and Ben W. Lewis's contribution to *Utility Regulation*.

[16] See Kahn, *ibid.;* Bonbright, *Public Utility Rates;* C. F. Phillips, Jr., *The Economics of Regulation* (Homewood, Ill.: Irwin, 1969). Much of the effort to establish comparable risk as a criterion has come in recent decades from the Bell system.

maintained, that utilities bear substantial long-term risks, despite their apparently secure positions.

Yet for several reasons the criterion of comparable returns is not fully valid for setting profit ceilings. First, it is not practical. Acceptable definitions of "comparable" have not been forthcoming, even after concerted efforts. "Risk," in particular, has defied reliable definition and measurement. Cross-section and time-series variation in profit rates have been hypothesized as estimators of risk. But they are highly dubious and incomplete in concept. And in actual measurement they have not displayed the expected properties (recall chapter 4).

Therefore, second, the conceptual risk-return basis for a comparable-earnings standard has not yet been verified. Moreover, when risk is high, capital possibly should not be "attracted," but instead withdrawn. That has been true for several decades in the eastern railroads, for example. Therefore a low rate of return may be prescribed by high risks, rather than a high rate of return to "compensate" for the risk-bearing. In fact, the refusal to recognize that many utilities reach a phase when capital should be *depleted* is the blind spot that afflicts most of the simple criteria for fair rates of return.

Third, actual earnings of a firm should relate to relative efficiency, not to a guaranteed, if "comparable," return. While utilities are monopolies, their attainment of the target comparable return could happen even if they were inefficient, uninnovative, and possessed of a markedly irrational price structure. This proviso would hold even if the previous two problems were somehow solved. Therefore, the relation of comparable earnings to allocative efficiency is remote.

A fourth problem adds to the remoteness. The regulators themselves create much of the utilities' risk, so that the criterion is quite circular. The regulators do not find the degree of risk; they make it. If they are strict, the risk of a low profit rate is very high. If they are not, the risk diminishes.

In short, a comparable earnings criterion for regulation of fair returns is a will-o'-the-wisp. This is not to deny that the optimal rate of return may bear some relation to risk, and that it may be roughly in line with what commissions often set as a criterion in the belief that they are using a comparable earnings standard. But there should be no illusion that the standard has much scientific or practical substance.

There are no other criteria clearly superior on economic grounds, for the criterion depends on the social objective. Rather than trying to derive a universal criterion, one should incorporate the net after-tax rate of return into the whole strategy of social control. The optimal net rate of return can be said, in any event, to be somewhere between 15 and 5 percent on equity capital. The precise rate attained should depend *not* on regulatory choice but on company performance. One great fallacy of regulation is that by making the profit results look like competition, the other results of competition—efficiency, equity, innovation, etc.—could be guaranteed. Instead, the opposite effects have perhaps come about. An optimal strategy must have a more direct incentive mechanism.

B INCENTIVES FOR EFFICIENCY

Few managers have greater freedom from constraint and supervision than those in regulated utilities and in classical public firms in prosperous utility industries, such as electricity and telephones. Despite any subjective sense of personal career striving or of interindustry competition, the managers' scope for choice—and therefore for uncorrected inefficiency—is great, as chapter 5 noted. We shall now assess the several treatments to avert inefficiency that have been discussed or tried.

One possible treatment is "incentive regulation." Regulators could determine which utilities are the more efficient and then reward them.[17] The treatment must have a method for making objective estimates of "efficiency," and a method of applying rewards and penalties.

The most promising method of estimating efficiency has been applied to private electricity systems by William Iulo.[18] It shows both the strengths and the limits of the approach. The aim is to factor out exogenous and extraneous influences on enterprise activities; those factors remaining would represent true performance and not just insufficient specification or weak data. The distinctive trait of this work, its reliance on outside information, removes it one step from the actual processes in the utility enterprises. If the available data do not happen to include the true determinants (economic or other) or elements (what about fairness?) of performance, then performance will be neither measured nor explained.

Even if the principal variables are included and properly specified, the

[17] See Kahn, *ibid.* and H. M. Trebing, ed., *Performance Under Regulation* (East Lansing: Michigan State University Press, 1968).
[18] William Iulo, *Electric Utilities—Costs and Performance* (Pullman: Washington State University Press, 1961).

data at hand are likely to mask much of the real processes and differences. They will be averages, often grossing up disparate quanta, and even more often not closely fitting the economic elements sought. Iulo's study shows not only his skill in handling these problems, but also the stubborn difficulties with data that nonetheless remain.

It must also be noted that whatever success it may achieve with power supply, cross-section statistical analysis cannot easily be extended to other utilities, whose products are even more heterogeneous than is electric supply. The basic variables (such as output of telephone or transport services) are not only difficult to specify, but their determinants and interrelations are also likely to be more complex and shifting than in the case of power.

In addition, these econometric appraisals of performance are likely to confirm the preexisting informal folk-knowledge in management and regulatory circles. Most commissions already know fairly clearly, even without metrical affirmation, how efficient the firms in their jurisdiction are. In the profession of utility management generally, the appraisals are undoubtedly even sharper. Therefore econometric analysis is likely to systematize, double-check, and spruce up the folklore with scholarly coloration. But much of its results are perfectly (if privately) well known already. We shall all be especially interested in those unusual cases where the "objective data" clash with the folk-knowledge. Yet, given the difficulties caused by such statistical analyses feeding on outside data, the first presumption may usually be that the folklore is right.

This may account for the slight impact Iulo's first study, landmark though it is, has had upon regulatory activities. Where the data are right, their message is probably already known; where they challenge the folklore, they are presumed wrong and, explained away, laboriously and incorrectly, if not ignored altogether. Further work in this vein is therefore unlikely to evoke a greatly enlarged response, no matter how definitive the findings may be.

However, these studies do bring the inside opinion out into the open. Inefficiency becomes a published fact, not a private opinion. This gives commissions a new weapon to use in seeking improvements, if they have the resolve and wit to use it effectively. It also presents information that can help evaluate the commissions' performance. Accordingly one can applaud these research efforts, even though the approach inherently contains a number of severe limitations and is unlikely to succeed in other utility industries.

A second method is "if-then" regulation. This ties specific rewards to specific *tasks*. The tasks, defined by the commission, involve any feature of performance (e.g., completing a service network or reaching a target level of productivity). The commission is presumably able to judge the public interest in each such task; such judgments are indeed its primary task. Then a reward—such as a price or profit change desired by the firm—is made contingent upon completing the task.

This approach can have great power and exactitude. By contrast, conventional regulation scarcely provides any feedback to reward specific accomplishments. It is often devoid of any timely rewards. "If-then" regulation also permits the time lags to be set precisely; the reasonable time needed to do the task can be set so as to provide a fair interval for action. Moreover, the reward can be fitted carefully to the value of the task. It can be scaled, made into a rising sequence of rewards, or otherwise tailored to the objective.

Several small efforts at such "if-then" choices have been begun in recent years, but the method is virtually untried in the common run of commissions and utilities. It fills some of the most obvious voids in conventional regulation, by placing responsibilities upon firms in accord with opportunities. It also makes the regulators more responsible for their true tasks. Present regulatory conventions permit them to avoid such a responsible role.

A third incentive for efficiency is to order direct audits of managerial performance, to fill the void of control.[19] These outside audits would be a basis for specific changes in the firm's form, staffing, and activities. They would also give the regulators and directors a basis for differential rewards.

Managerial evaluation is a well-developed professional field, having a great variety of unbiased assessors to choose among.[20] The problem requires expert, sophisticated judgment. Efficiency includes not just allocational niceties, but also research and innovations, hard bargaining over supplies, and attention to consumer preferences. The lonely academic feeding published data into a computer cannot capture the whole of this or fully evaluate the cause, or appraise the enterprise's prospects for future performance.

[19] I urged this in *Performance Under Regulation;* O. E. Williamson took up the idea in "Administrative Controls and Regulatory Behavior," in *Essays on Public Utility Pricing and Regulation,* ed. H. M. Trebing (East Lansing: Michigan State University Press, 1971). And a few efforts to apply it have recently occurred.

[20] This is true even after discounting for all the many known limitations of management consulting for this purpose. One should not have illusions, though, about the depth of analysis.

The mere possibility of an audit may stimulate efforts to cut costs and to find new technologies. It would clarify the regulatory role too, by fixing responsibility for performance. These points hold equally for private, public, and mixed ownership. So far audits have only been tried once or twice, with no reinforcement. If the practice became routine, its effects could be thorough. If the regulatory process continues to create the incentive void, direct audits may be the only practical way to fill it.

A fourth incentive is to permit entry by relaxing regulatory bars, thus allowing entry by competitors. It is optimal to do this in Stage 3, and recently it—and its extreme form, "deregulation"—have been seen as the main route for regulatory reform. Actually, there are three forms of seller entry: by new firms against old utility sellers, by the old sellers against each other, and by revisions of the old sellers themselves. Recent commentary has favored the first, but the second and third are more promising in a wider range of utilities.

Reservations about the power of "new entry" have already been noted in chapters 2 and 4. For regulation, the main analytical lessons are, briefly, that entry is rarely distinct, in theory or in practice, from other structural changes (e.g., small-firm growth, oligopolists' strategies toward each other); the probability of entry is inverse to its scope—major entry is a rarity, and therefore normally a second-order decision variable; the impact of entry occurs via changes in the established firm's market share.

Recall also the recent econometric suggestions (in chapter 4): the market share of the firm, *not* barriers to its industry, appears to be the main structural determinant of profit rates; only when barriers are reduced to "low" levels are profit rates significantly reduced; barrier height is not at all related to the degree of stability of market shares. Finally, among all the postwar changes in U.S. industrial markets, major entry is rather a rarity and in almost every case it occurs slowly, with little surprise, and comes from large firms in related markets.

In many major industries—the hard-core market-power cases—it scarcely happens at all, although the established firms may have been enjoying high profit rates for decades.[21] Entry succeeds mainly when the prior firms are

---

[21] Recall chapters 4 and 7. The obvious cases are computers, automobiles, photographic film, detergents, razor blades, and canned soups. These and other aspects of entry are reviewed in Shepherd, "General Conditions of Entry," ch. 3 in *Regulation and Entry,* eds. M. W. Klass and W. G. Shepherd (East Lansing: Institute of Public Utilities, Michigan State University, 1975).

unusually slow-moving. Alert monopolists who can price-discriminate normally can head off significant entry (examples: IBM, United Shoe Machinery). Much of the observed postwar entry has in fact been arranged by the government (synthetic rubber, aluminum) or has been by public enterprises.

The upshot: for new-seller entry to take much effect, market share must go down soon—and far, toward 70 or 50 percent or even lower—and remain down. Technology must be readily available to entrants, and prior firms must be unable to use price discrimination to avert entry. Actually, most utilities can of course discriminate sharply, even under regulation, and many do. Recall again that regulated utilities are uniquely insulated. Entrants are vulnerable and resistance to entry is magnified: the seeming paranoia of utilities—to whom every entrant is the thin edge of a large wedge—is a natural result of this insulation.

If regulators merely permit seller entry, little will happen. Regulators will need to make entry, and to keep entry open for further new entrants. Short of total deregulation, entry will make the regulatory task more complex, not less. (Deregulation, in turn, makes the antitrust problem more complex.)

Such new entry is scarcely conceivable in utility markets under conventional regulation. If it is effective it lowers expected returns and share prices, and thereby actually threatens regulation. Experience is equally bearish. In telephones, prospective new entry is only peripheral and slow, despite the carriers' alarmist assertions.[22] In electricity, new sellers are less promising than existing ones (see below). A moderate policy favoring new seller entry may be the least rewarding possibility—the profit inducements for entry are modest, entry is technologically difficult, it unambiguously reduces carrier opportunities, and will therefore be resisted even to the point of congesting regulatory processes. It may be the least promising direction for entry policy. It conflicts with the regulatory contract, rather than revising it. It violates settled interests rather than redirecting them.

Another entry route may be created by an opening of competition among utilities in each others' "service areas." Bulk electricity supply markets have now become the best example of this.[23] For treatment, a range of regu-

---

[22] Kahn, *Economics of Regulation;* Shepherd "Margin of Competition in Communication."
[23] This is indicated in L. W. Weiss, "Antitrust in the Electric Power Industry," in *Competition and the Regulation of Industry;* see also the Otter Tail Power Case. For a contrary view see earlier writings of W. R. Hughes, including a paper in *Technological Change,* ed. Capron. But Hughes relies on unlimited scale economies, which are now realized to be limited after all. See

latory changes is possible, but they all boil down to letting utilities bid customers away from other utilities. This, too, simply restores normal economic behavior.

Where technology permits such a mingling of supply relationships—as it does in bulk electricity—the gains vould be large. Inefficiency would be under direct constraint, for the first time in generations. Service standards and cheapness would both be used to gain customers, as they should be; this would ease the probable present bias toward excessive service "quality." Utilities would be induced to develop and use the technology of large scale supply more fully.

The change could offer net gains to many utilities, since it widens their opportunities. It is a bilateral threat to managerial security and share values. Therefore it could dissolve, or at least reduce, today's balkanized status quo. Possibly it would be welcomed, not resisted, by most utilities.

In bulk electric power, the possibilities are quite good, according to Leonard W. Weiss, James R. Nelson, and others. Throughout the country, thousands of major customers—including both cities and private customers—are within range of alternative suppliers and presumably would seek bids. In Michigan, for example, about one-third of the largest commercial accounts at single locations are close enough to alternative suppliers to take bids, even if wheeling (the transmission of power for another firm) were not required. If wheeling were mandatory, the fraction would be much higher. Other industrial areas are similar.

Although full-blown interarea competition would only affect the larger customers, many smaller users could pool their demand and bargain as large units. This would naturally introduce complex game conditions into the present rigidity. Pooling and mergers would become strategic elements in the process, since many adjoining utilities would be both competing and cooperating. Some people might fear that intolerable discrimination, and possibly collusion, would result. I would prefer that we try it first. The utilities sector is neither more complex nor prone to natural monopoly than are many "competitive" markets in the industrial sector. The efficiency gains could be large, and there is already much discrimination and absolute noncompetition in the patchwork we have now.

---

the Federal Power Commission, *National Power Survey*, 1970 (U.S. Government Printing Office, 1970).

The basic revision in the regulatory contract is simple: contracts with an "outside" supplier would be unregulated. The rest of the utility's business would remain its "service area" and subject to regulation. Wheeling at reasonable charges—or as part of exchange agreements—would be required, within certain distances. Separate transmission lines would be built at will for outside supply, but—pending more detailed study and experience—possibly not using powers of eminent domain. Horizontal mergers that would adversely affect this competition (and most of them would) would require overriding evidence of scale economies. Indeed, many of the larger systems are probably already too large by this criterion, and further pooling and "coordination" may have negative results, because competition will be forestalled. In regions where mergers with large scale economies would do away with interarea bulk supply competition, or have already done so, the case for a public bulk power network on the lines of the British Central Electricity Board of 1926–48, would be strong.[24]

The result will be a more complicated and efficient industry. The mass of smaller contracts will still be regulated, but by a streamlined and focussed regulation process. Terms of service and the liability for all service will be explicit. Structure and contracts will be more flexible, in some cases the outcome of intricate strategy. In short, part of the industry will evolve properly through Stage 3 toward economic normality. A clear parallel is the New York Stock Exchange, where the decontrol of brokers' fees has led to highly effective competition.[25]

A third entry route is by revision and realignment among existing sellers. This has already been suggested as an important treatment for banking markets (chapter 6). It can also be effective for utilities. Regulated firms commonly provide a variety of services, with differing elasticities of demand and degrees of competition. These can be separated, for accountability. Present regulation permits finances to be overcombined and market structure to be kept more rigid than necessary, especially in Stage 3. This is now true of banking, air transport, communications, electric power, and combination electric and gas firms, among others.

Instead, structure should be changeable, and in some fields the separation

---

[24] See W. A. Robson, *Nationalized Land and Public Ownership* (London: Allen and Unwin, 1961); and W. G. Shepherd, *Economic Performance Under Public Ownership*.

[25] See H. M. Mann, "Antitrust and the New York Stock Exchange: The Issue—Minimum Brokerage Commissions," in *Competition and the Regulation of Industry*.

and realignment of activities should be routinely permitted. In banking, for example, key personnel responsible for key clients should be able to leave and form separate firms—as new "entrants" from within, as it were—using their special skills. This "entry by realignment" would be far more effective than entry by new banks could be. In communications, experts and managers to form new competitive entities could come from within the existing carriers—as many of IBM's small competitors have—were it not for tradition and regulations that require franchises. In the electric power industry, customer groups—including whole cities or other commercial users—could be formed anew to pool demand and take over distribution directly. Independent distribution would exist within the formerly monolithic service areas.

Such revisions would apply skilled inside talent acting in its own interests rather than vulnerable new outsiders. The key provision is, again, having explicit service liability standards, so that regulators need not evaluate the fitness of suppliers.

Finally, regulation could be revised to permit takeover of utilities. This is simply another kind of entry—entry to the managerial and supervisory function. But it may have the highest net social yield—and require the most care in regulatory treatment—of all the proposed reforms.

The regulatory contract has given *carte blanche* to managers and their boards. Were it not for regulation, takeovers and managerial changes would be more common. Utilities are, with one or two exceptions, perfectly amenable—in size, simplicity of technology, profit opportunities, etc.—to takeover or partial shifts of control. Only the regulatory laws exclude take-overs, supposedly to ensure stability and service at virtually any cost.

The proper solution is simply to write specific service criteria and liability standards into the contract, and then permit nearly any ownership and managerial change. Many service liabilities would be insurable. As for ownership changes, in electricity this would require revising the Public Utility Act of 1935 to permit all—or perhaps only certain categories of—nonutility firms to own utilities. The operations and accounts would of course be kept separate. The Act has served much of its original purpose, but now it shields management and protects inefficiency. So does the Bank Holding Company Act of 1970, which neatly protects large banks from takeover.

For such actual or potential entry to operate, a large share of each utility's—and its subsidiaries'—stock needs to be out in the market, so that independent ownership exists and can operate to check management performance. For telephone and electric utilities, this would require releasing at least 49 percent of the stock of major subsidiaries, both operating and supplying. Such a shift would assure accountability by keeping the books separate and subject to the markets' evaluation. Performance will no longer be buried in hierarchy.

Most such utility units are neither forbiddingly large nor complex. There are other large enterprises capable of perceiving, and of acting to correct, inefficiencies in utilities. These improvements require changed behavior, not necessarily drastic personnel shifts. The last decade of mergers has shown that takeovers commonly fail (1) when the aggressor firm is smaller and younger than its target, and can be discredited as being unreliable, and (2) when the target firm is protected by a public agency.

Therefore, regulators would need to take great care to be neutral to takeover, lest they unwittingly stop it cold. If strict neutrality is maintained, past experience suggests there would be active, diverse, and effective—and thoroughly normal—constraints on utility management, at long last. At present, the potential for unperceived and uncorrectable inefficiency is high, and takeover access—plus clear service liability—will reach it more directly than conventional regulation or new seller entry can.

C INVESTMENT AND INNOVATION CHOICES

Utilities can be viewed as choosing among a variety of technical alternatives, with a range of capital-intensity and riskiness. Regulation—or public ownership—may influence these choices strongly, perhaps away from the optimal patterns. These choices may also become part of the problem of optimizing the degree of competition in the utility, since technology supposedly defines the "proper" scope of utility monopoly at each point.

The possible overuse of capital is actually a fairly complex question which relates back to the regulatory franchise. Although its total impact may be limited, the topic has been intensely discussed, and so I shall explore it here at some length. I shall begin by restating the possible regulatory impact on investment, in terms of the neoclassical theory of investment choice by the firm.[26] I shall discuss criteria for evaluating "excessive" investment,

---

[26] Such as in Friedrich and Vera Lutz, *The Theory of Investment of the Firm* (Princeton: Princeton University Press, 1952); J. Hirshleifer, "On the Theory of Optimal Investment Decisions," *Journal of Political Economy*, August 1958, pp. 329–52; Myron J. Gordon, *The Investment, Financing, and Valuation of the Corporation* (Homewood, Ill.: Irwin, 1962). See

and consider several factors that may offset—or justify—the investment-expansion tendencies.

In this analysis it is assumed that the firm arrays its investment alternatives according to prospective returns on them, determines the cost of capital to it at each level of investment, and then invests up to the point at which the return on the marginal project is not less than the marginal cost of capital.[27]

Figure 9.1 represents the firm's investment choice under these conditions. The (declining) internal rates of return on successive additional investments are shown by *MRI;* the (rising) interest or interest-equivalent costs of additional funds are shown by *MCI.* For each of these marginal curves there is an average curve; *ARI* shows the average return at each level of investment, and *ACI* the average cost of investment funds from all sources.[28]

The firm will choose to invest up to I_U (*U* for unregulated), where marginal investment return and cost are 6 percent. At I_U, average investment return is 13.5 percent and average investment cost is 4.5 percent, leaving a net profit above minimum capital cost of 9 percent.

Now suppose that regulation is imposed on the firm, while all other conditions remain unchanged—implausible though this may seem. Reflecting the orthodox aim of preventing "exploitative" utility profits and providing services "at cost," the commission will attempt to force an equality between

---

also E. E. Bailey, *Economic Theory of Regulatory Constraint* (Lexington, Mass.: D. C. Heath, 1973).

Parts of this passage are drawn from my "Regulatory Constraints and Public Utility Investment," *Land Economics,* August 1966, pp. 349–354.

[27] For this simplified marginal-investment-productivity analysis, several assumptions (in addition to the usual ones for analysis of this sort) need explicit mention: (1) The schedules of investment returns and costs are continuous. (2) The firm maximizes its net profits, in neo-classical fashion. (3) The firm's predicted returns and capital costs at each level of investment are certain and precise; they are also orderly, with no odd patterns of losses and profits over time. (4) The return on a given project or level of investment is wholly independent of any project giving *lower* returns, although the lower-return projects may be dependent on higher-return projects. (5) The suppliers of external funds to the firm know the firm's financial prospects, at least partially; they supply funds not at a constant "cost of capital" but at a rising cost, corresponding to the increasing financial risk and declining prospective returns on additional investment. (6) The firm is in a steady-state or steady-growth situation. Therefore, effects on investment flows are the same as, and proportional to, effects on the entire capital stock of the firm. Alternatively, the horizontal axis could be the firm's investment or capital-stock growth *rate.*

[28] The vertical percentage-rate scale is purely illustrative. The shapes of the curves are arbitrary but do conform with common versions, and they do not predetermine the conclusions to be reached in what follows.

the average costs and average returns of utility investment. Assume that this does not affect cost-reduction behavior; that is, the investment-returns curves do not respond by shifting down. If so, the level of investment under regulatory constraint will be I_R (R for regulated), with capacity adequate to supply the load at the regulated output prices. Accordingly I_R minus I_U is the regulatory impact on utility investment. This impact varies inversely with the positive gap between the permitted rate of return and the cost of capital. The tighter the regulation, the greater the increase in investment—as long as

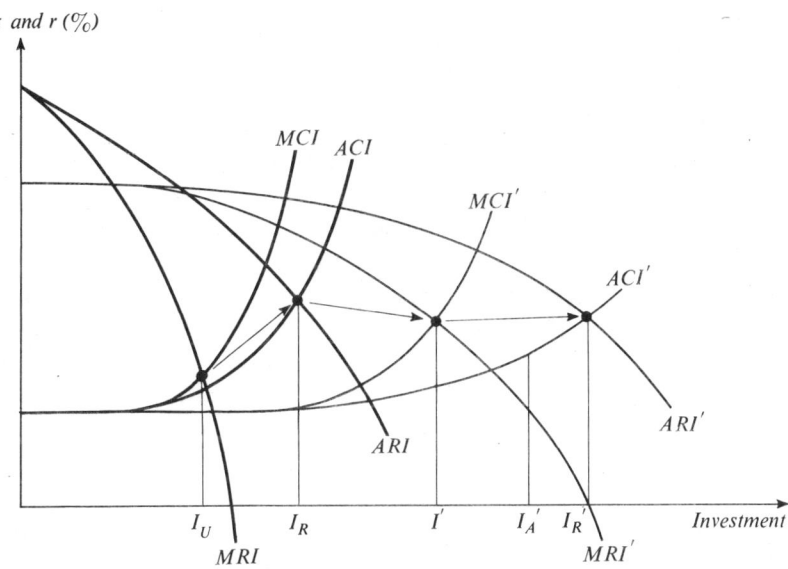

Figure 9.1 Regulation typically alters and extends the firm's profit opportunities and increases the level of investment. (Arrows show the shift.)

the permitted rate of return does not fall below the average cost of capital. At I_R, the marginal return on investment to the firm is far below the marginal cost of capital to it.

Now assume—as is likely—that the imposition of regulation *does* affect investment returns and costs for the utility. This impact will vary from case to case, and would be difficult to determine in each instance. Yet a common pattern might be the one shown in Figure 9.1. Regulation involves a mixture of protection and constraint. Enfranchisement of the firm as the sole supplier of a region or city may increase the utility's ability to charge profitable rates on additional services. This would raise the investment returns curves at the higher levels of investment. However, regulation may also reduce the utility's range of discretion in exploiting its basic consumers, thereby lowering the return curves at lower levels of investment. The resulting investment returns schedules, as modified by regulation, might be shown by MRI' and ARI'.

Since these changes are known at least partially by the utility's suppliers of external funds, the cost of capital curves will also shift—downward. Especially at higher levels of investment, which now promise higher returns than before, funds for investment will be provided at lower interest and dividend costs. The marginal and average cost-of-funds curves might become as shown by MCI' and ACI'.

The utility will now wish to invest to I', where $MRI' = MCI'$. The marginal return on capital (MRI') just equals the marginal cost of capital (MCI'). Yet if regulation succeeds in constraining average profit to the minimum average cost of capital, a much greater investment is called for, at I_R'. If there is slippage in the regulatory process, or if the regulators deliberately allow some excess profit, some intermediate result such as I'_A might occur.[29] In this example, the extra return above "bare bones" cost of capital would be 3.0 percent (10 − 7.0 percent).

One modification of the analysis may be added at this point. Assume that the permitted rate of return has been fixed at some level for the time being, and that the rate-of-return and cost-of-funds schedules, and the level of investment, adjust to this parameter. In Figure 9.2, RR is the now-fixed regulatory ceiling on the rate of return, while ARI', ACI', and the other schedules are as before. At every level of investment, RR is the maximum average (and marginal) realizable rate of return. The utility will now have particular incentives to add any further operations that can be included in the rate base, whether or not these operations are necessarily related to the utility's basic services. Innovation and diversification into entirely new lines may result, starting from the level of "utility" services (at I_R'). These new possibilities are represented by ARI^D (D for diversity). The assurance of the regulatory return on these new assets will further shift down the cost of funds curve, to

---

[29] Slippage could include accounting adjustments by the utility to increase the valuation of its assets and operating costs, dilution of the quality of utility services, or an inability of the regulators to reduce rates as fast as costs decline—the so-called regulatory lag.

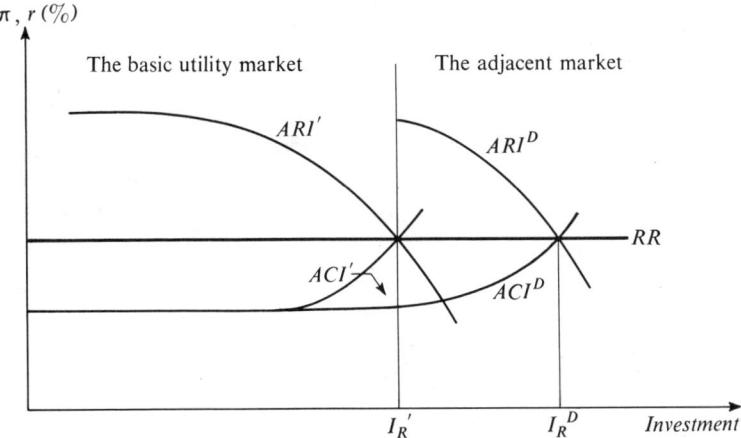

Figure 9.2 Regulation may induce capture of an adjacent market by the utility.

ACI^D in Figure 9.2.[30] Investment of I^D_R is made; the overall rate or return is "held down" to RR; the utility grows rapidly; and it provides a growing array of diversified, high-quality, progressive services. All parties—regulators, utilities, and customers—experience a sense of satisfaction and accomplishment. The regulators can show a record of "tough" regulation; utilities show profits, growth profits, growth, and progress; consumers have "cheap" but "high-quality" services, in increasing variety.

In several ways, the utilities' actual behavior may bear out these analytical possibilities of expanded investment. Perhaps best known is the relative encouragement of peak-load consumption under the standard promotional declining-rate schedules in electricity and gas. Along other lines, innovation in telephone, electric, and gas utilities has been heavily labor-saving and

---

[30] Though Averch and Johnson ("Behavior of the Firm") argue that the utility may branch into new lines that are entirely unprofitable in themselves, this will be most likely to happen if the utility is somehow constrained from adding equally unprofitable capacity in its basic services. Thus only a slow-growing and highly profitable and secure utility would be likely to branch into unprofitable lines. The cases discussed by Averch and Johnson do fit these requirements.

For further detail on patterns in telecommunications, see Shepherd, "The Margin of Competition in Communications," pp. 106–8 and 116–17, and Roger G. Noll, M. J. Peck, and J. McGowan, *Economic Aspects of Television Regulation* (Wash., D.C.: Brookings Institution, 1973).

capital-using. Much investment in suburban supply by these utilities may also provide a low or negative return.

But expanded investment—under regulatory constraints—does not necessarily constitute *excessive* investment.[31] Assume that Pareto optimality conditions hold in all other markets (including other utilities also). Then it might be supposed that, in Figure 9.1, I_R represents the efficient investment level, corresponding to what perfect competition "would have provided." However, this assumes a comparability—which may not exist—between the actual monopolistic utility (under regulatory constraint) and the competitive model. For one example, the range of utility discretion over joint-product pricing and combinations of outputs is incompatible with perfectly competitive conditions. Accordingly the regulatory constraint on utility profits can provide certain Pareto conditions, but even then the capital–labor ratios will be distorted. In a Pareto equilibrium environment, then, I_U in Figure 9.1 would be definitely inefficient; the efficient level is greater than I_U and may indeed be I_R, but is not necessarily so.

At I_R', by contrast, or at I_A', investment is more likely to be the efficient level. Profit-maximizing is able to induce the utility to go this far only because the public—through the regulatory system—protects the utility and absorbs some of its risks. As Figure 9.1 is (arbitrarily) drawn, I' might approximate an efficient investment outcome. The commission would accomplish this by deliberately doing little or no real regulating at all.

Whether regulation in fact causes the curves to shift as in Figure 9.1 is highly speculative and possibly a matter for research. The cost-plus-profit character of regulation may—by encouraging nonpecuniary maximizing—instead induce a downward shift in the investment-returns curves rather than a downward shift in the cost-of-capital curves. More generally this suggests that there might be a tradeoff between current-resources and investment-resources misallocation. There may be much of one or the other, or some of both; but probably not a lot of both. A recognition of non-Pareto (monopolistic or other) conditions elsewhere in the economy would, by contrast, strengthen the likelihood that regulation *does* induce excessive investment.

Several other points, on the contrary, would weaken the likelihood that

---

[31] Nor may there be an expansive effect at all, if regulation is loose and if the utility can arrange its accounting adjustments largely to serve its own purposes. Thus an expanded rate base might be attained without any actual increase in *real* investment. In such conditions, on the contrary, investment would be overly restricted rather than possibly overly expanded.

expansion would be excessive. Utility executives may simply balk at undertaking investments whose identifiable returns are low or negative. Management's general aversion to going to capital markets until it becomes absolutely necessary may further limit the expansion. Pressure from investor groups may be directed against investments which—owing to increasing risk relative to return—may lead to a dilution of the existing equity holdings.

To the degree that other factors determine investment decisions, the rate-of-return inducements for expansion may have only slight effect. This reasoning is not conclusive, because investment decisions may become conventionalized—in accelerator or physical-ratio patterns—at unduly high levels of investment, rather than at efficient or minimum levels. For example, a utility may always aim at a fixed ratio between peak load and capacity; but this ratio might involve a reserve capacity of 5 percent or 35 percent, either or neither of which may be the efficient amount.

The utility may also be in a capital-rationing situation, with a constraint that sharply limits its ability to expand investments. This would reflect relative noncircularity between regulatory policy and the cost of capital; that is, it would presuppose that the utility's suppliers of external funds do not fully know the risk-returns situation of the utility under regulation. Although this seems improbable, it need not be ruled out.

Also the extra capacity, the extra capital-intensity of utility processes, and the extra diversification by the utility may all have a very high value to users and to the economy altogether. Accordingly, a reduction of the probability of breakdown from 1.0 percent to 0.01 percent may be well worth the cost of a much larger investment in reserve capacity. Ample utility capacity may have other national-security benefits. The inducement for diversification may promote more rapid research and innovation.[32] Other social objectives may also be nicely met by this inducement mechanism, with or without explicit guidance from the regulators.

Finally, the possibilities of overinvestment, as judged by purely static criteria, may be largely swamped by the trends of speedy growth and technical change in the utilities. For example, a $2 billion excess in utility capital might conceivably be provable, using static marginal criteria. But if the capital stock is expanding by $4 billion yearly, the problem becomes largely

---

[32] A. E. Kahn has expanded on this point most usefully, if rather optimistically; see *Economics of Regulation*, 2:106–8.

one of the *timing* of investment rather than one of permanent overinvestment.

Despite these suggestions that the tendency toward overinvestment may be offset in several ways, the status of much utility investment must remain in doubt—permanently, or at least pending further research.[33]

The possibility of overinvestment opens important questions for research. Even without firm empirical support, it invites a rethinking of some of the traditional success indicators of utility—and regulatory—performance. Expansion, capital-intensive innovation, and diversification may usually be justifiable on a variety of economic grounds, but the possibility of excessive investment is distinct and pervasive.

D COMPARING PRIVATE AND PUBLIC CHOICES

The capital-intensity question is actually part of a broader set of *innovation* choices by the utility firm, in which it selects its technology for the future. The issues are subtle, and yet they ultimately may transcend the other static-efficiency issues. Does regulation discourage innovation? Are public enterprises likely to be less innovative than regulated private firms? There is practically no research on the topic.

Here I shall outline an analysis of the problem. The basic result is counter-intuitive—that private firms under conventional regulation are likely to assume less risk than conventional public enterprises do. The result is independent of managerial objectives in private and public firms. Much experience suggests that they are essentially the same. This is partly because the

[33] See Johnson's discussion in Shepherd and Gies, *Regulation in Further Perspective;* see also Bailey, *Regulatory Constraint.* Since profits under regulation fall within a narrow range—about 5 to 9 percent—a cross-section analysis of the differential impact of regulation under different commissions is likely to be fruitless. Comparisons with nonregulated firms, including publicly owned systems, might be a more promising first step, although many extraneous elements would have to be factored out. Various indicators of capital-use (including factor ratios, reserve capacity, and the rate of addition of new capacity for suburban services) would need to be included, but the criteria for appraising the effects of regulation are not clear at this point.

Further and wider studies of rates of return and cost of capital are needed, in view of the limited and disputed findings that have been made. In some cases, it might even be possible to estimate some of the investment-return and cost-of-capital magnitudes and elasticities. The extent of certain below-cost services and capacity might be indicated by cost analysis, such as the Federal Communication Commission required of the Bell System in the 1960s. Such below-cost services may be one manifestation of the expanded—though not necessarily inefficient—use of capital. Patterns of diversification of products may also show an association with regulatory constraints.

technology and constraints are similar and partly because managers are drawn from similar groups and are virtually indistinguishable. No special behavioral model is therefore necessary.

The key contrast is this: regulation of private utilities sets *ceilings* on profit rates, while the constraints on public enterprises usually act as *floors*.[34] Public enterprises commonly have difficulty in achieving these floors, because they are loaded with several sorts of special social burdens (recall chapter 5). Private utilities usually could make profit rates well above the ceiling levels. Therefore these parallel constraints may well have differing effects on the choices made by managers. Do they affect the bearing of risk, which innovation often entails? The question is important enough for us to venture into three dimensions, in some detail.

The average volume of profit (P) on planned expenditure on investment-innovation (E) is related to risk (σ):

$$P = f(E, \sigma)$$

At each point the firm has a profit "hill," as shown in Figure 9.3. E_0 is the level that will maintain the firm's growth rate. The preferred choice is set by the tangency of profit-risk preferences and the profit hill: it is point A for the unfranchised, preregulation firm in Figure 9.3. The tradeoff at this tangency (θ) will in equilibrium approach the tradeoff prevailing in the economy. Therefore, θ will tend to be part of the equimarginal Pareto conditions for efficient choice in this dimension.

Regulation shifts the hill, as shown in Figure 9.4, because it reduces the new utility's risk. Regulation also applies a profit constraint, shown by Plane I.[35] This truncates the hill, so that the private regulated firm now maximizes long-run profits at point B, which is somewhere between points a and b (depending on the new shape and position of the profit hill). This is shown in Figure 9.5, which is a vertical projection of the plane-hill slice onto the E-σ plane.

If, instead, public ownership occurs, the profit hill is moved more downward than to the left. This reflects the additional social burdens it bears.

---

[34] See Shepherd, *Economic Performance Under Public Ownership;* R. Pryke, *Public Enterprise in Practice* (New York: St. Martins, 1972). The profit-rate constraints are in the same range—6 to 12 percent return on assets.

[35] This method of analysis is parallel in some respects to that of E. E. Zajac, "A Geometric Treatment of Averch-Johnson's Behavior of the Firm Model," *American Economic Review,* 1970, pp. 117–25; and Bailey, *Regulatory Constraint.*

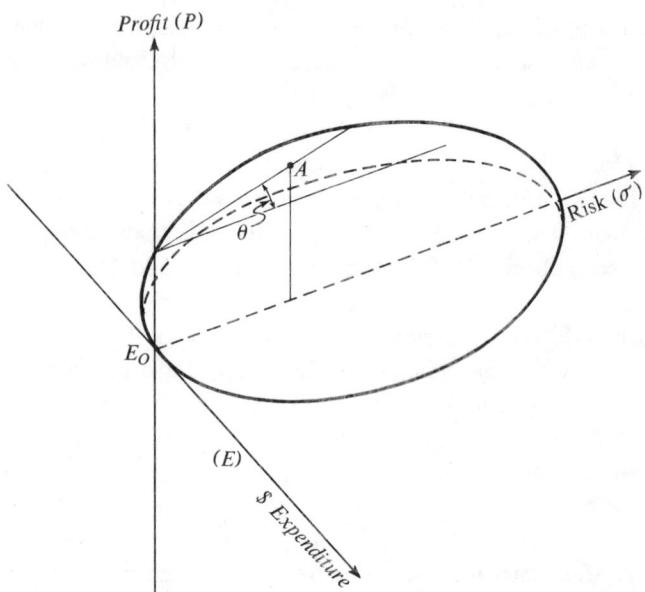

Figure 9.3 The optimum profit-risk choice by a firm.

Plane *I* is now a *floor*, not a ceiling, and the public firm maximizes its long-run profit and security at point *C*, which lies somewhere along line *cd*. This too is shown in Figure 9.5.

The implications are that (1) the average degree of risk-taking is less in the private regulated firm; (2) the marginal risk–profit tradeoff reached by the public firm is likely to be close to the economywide tradeoff (θ) for competitive firms, while the tradeoff for the private regulated firm is less determinate; (3) the level of investment is higher in the private regulated firm than it is in the public firm. Points 1 and 2 are counterintuitive; point 3 fits the Averch-Johnson hypothesis. The analysis is not conclusive—practical research is needed to estimate the actual conditions—but the odds seem to be that public firms will come closer to optimal investment-risk choices than will private regulated firms.

Taken altogether, conventional regulation is likely to include levels and directions of innovation that are nonoptimal. The nonoptimality is likely to be hardest to detect and correct precisely where it is the most severe. Public enterprises have parallel biases, but under conventional conditions these are likely to depart less from the optimum.

Policy Alternatives in Practice

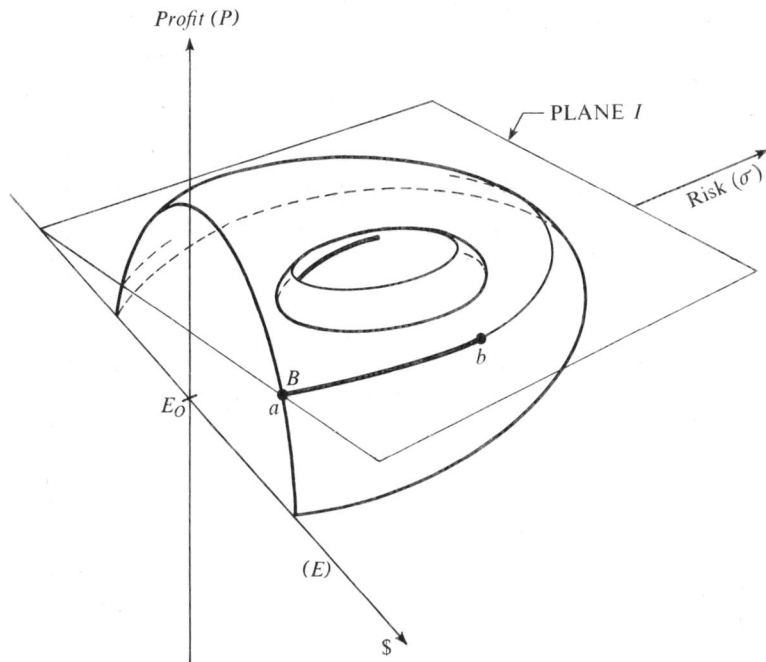

Figure 9.4 Comparison of the optimum profit-risk choice by a public firm and a regulated private firm.

These probabilities appear to fit the main lines of actual behavior in the U.S. and Britain. Electric and telephone managers in the U.S. have taken conservative approaches to innovation in a variety of directions.[36] Their British counterparts have been more ready to move boldly into new technologies.[37] The National Coal Board's investment program appears to have been aligned reasonably well with the prospective returns and risks from new technology,[38] and the possibility of a rate-base effect on capacity, on own-lease choices, and on moves into new markets appears higher in U.S. private utilities under regulation. These must be matters of judgment, but

[36] See Shepherd, "The Margin of Competition in Communications"; Weiss, "Evaluation of Antitrust in the Electric Power Industry"; W. R. Hughes, "Scale Frontiers in Electric Power," in *Technological Change,* ed. Capron.

[37] A summary of some features of this is in my "Public Expenditure" chapter in Caves, *Britain's Economic Prospects* (Wash., D.C.: Brookings Institution, 1968); Pryke, *Public Enterprise,* also covers it extensively.

[38] Shepherd, *Economic Performance Under Public Ownership;* Pryke, *ibid.*

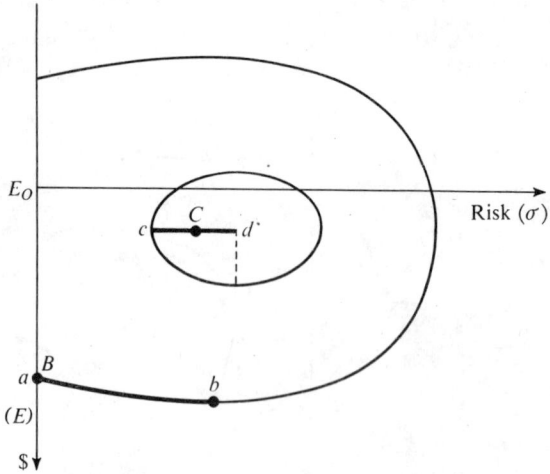

Figure 9.5 Vertical view of the comparative profit-risk choices in Figure 9.4.

the burden of proof now seems to rest upon those who would dispute this analysis.

E PRICE STRUCTURE AND CAPACITY

The utility—private or public—usually has much latitude in designing its prices. A greater variety of price structures will be consistent with global objectives (profit rate, efficiency, innovation). Various price structures may enhance the utility's financial security, increase its capacity or its political leverage, or deter new competition. Pricing is usually too complex for public policy to treat in detail. The costs and demand conditions are complicated and obscure, and are understood mainly by expert "feel" and study rather than precise research.

Most regulatory treatment has left price structure to the firm, offering only a broad encouragement to set prices promotionally, so as to stimulate residential use and total growth.[39] This has permitted or induced two non-optimal results: (1) excessive demand and capacity at peak periods, and (2) efforts to capture new, adjacent markets at cutthroat prices.[40] Only since the

[39] Kahn, *Economics of Regulation;* C. F. Phillips, Jr., *Economics of Regulation;* R. K. Davidson, *Price Discrimination in Selling Gas and Electricity* (Baltimore: Johns Hopkins Press, 1955); J. R. Nelson, *Marginal Cost Pricing in Practice* (Englewood Cliffs, N.J.: Prentice-Hall, 1964).

[40] See Davidson, *ibid.,* and Shepherd, "Marginal-Cost Pricing in American Utilities," *Southern Economics Journal,* July 1966, pp. 58–70.

1950s have these problems drawn serious commission resistance. Earlier—when capital was abundant and utilities were regarded as simple, isolated technologies—the cost of these deviations seemed insignificant. Now they are recognized to pose serious issues. Two sectors display them currently, for differing reasons.

In electricity and gas, an apparent "fuel crisis" since 1972 has combined with ecological problems to prescribe a reversal of the promotional rate structure. A reversal of this sort had long been in order, so as to align prices with true costs as much as possible. Marginal-cost pricing of this kind would accord with other performance objectives, including adequate profits for the entire firm.[41] Now an even sharper reversal may be needed, to reflect the true increasing costs of supply in most directions. This is accentuated by equity considerations, since inner-city users—who are generally of low income—regularly pay at effective prices up to double those of affluent suburban users. Yet the resulting shift toward rate reversal has been only slight, so far.

In telephones, marginal costs have been only partly reflected in costs, and so extra demand and capacity have been induced in a number of directions.[42] Since the quality and capacity of telephone service began to come under increasing stress in the 1960s, the firms' interest in fitting prices to true costs has grown. Their ability to do so is limited by the basic design of local equipment, which does not permit close metering of calls. That design in turn reflected the earlier promotional motives, under which metering of calls was irrelevant. Abroad, pricing has been more rational, with costs more closely allowed for.[43] In the U.S. telephone industry, regulation has been largely peripheral to the firms' own recent interests in a socially more rational price structure, but regulation could press it further.

In short, regulatory treatments need explicitly to encourage marginal-cost pricing. Though some services defy accurate cost determinations, many others can be treated fairly precisely.

---

[41] *Ibid.* The traditional view is that a deficit may result, because average costs are declining (in the "natural monopoly"). Yet an optimal growth path will normally keep capacity aligned with demands, so that peak and off-peak revenues can balance out to modest profits in toto; also, a stage-3 "utility" commonly does not have endlessly declining costs: it is a natural monopoly no more, except for portions of its business.

[42] *Ibid.*, and see also Kahn, *Economics of Regulation.*

[43] W. G. Shepherd, "Residence Expansion in the British Telephone System," *Journal of Industrial Economics,* July, 1966, pp. 263–74.

3 OPTIMAL TREATMENT

To many of us, regulation is like growing old: we would rather not do it, but consider the alternative. Regulation is a tenacious institution, which is broadly biased against entry and often follows a wrong-way evolution. Indeed, conventional entry from outside by new sellers may be nearly a dead end, since it goes so thoroughly against the regulatory grain. The other types of entry treat the problem more directly, and they can attract support from important private interests, including the utilities themselves. They offer ways to escape homeostatic border solutions.

At all stages of utility evolution, regulation thus revised may still be inferior to the alternatives, including various forms of public enterprise. Research and trials of new entry should be strictly experimental. If revisions of the treatment are not effective, we should find out soon, so better treatments can be applied.

Our strategy should be, above all, to *anticipate;* to study emergent conditions in traditional utilities and in "new" sectors (cable TV, hospitals, etc.), as well as to clarify the sequences of evolution of utilities and regulation. Our final objective is to design into the regulatory process incentive structures that will fit the sequence, be neutral toward entry, and give instant carrot-and-stick feedback from performance.

So, the conventional regulatory process offers certain clear nonoptimalities, some of them quite costly. The approach is probably salvageable, despite recent doubts. But changes are needed, both in what regulators do and in the basic utility franchise.

Four revisions are in order:

Evolution. Apply incentives for the firm to terminate its franchised monopoly status. The surtax on rates of return (chapters 6 and 7) provides such an incentive, and so it is essential to effective regulation. It would be written into the regulatory franchise, or simply applied as part of the standard taxation of enterprises. The utility would then qualify for lower tax rates as its market share decreased during Stages 3 and 4. Without this incentive, the utility would instead use the regulatory process in its strategy to avert competition. Only if the firm itself seeks the change will regulation evolve toward competition, rather than the reverse, as it now does. The surtax would also, in turn, dilute the need for constraining the rate of return formally.

Exposure to Evaluation and Takeover. All separable utility units would have a large share of voting stock held publicly and would report their accounts publicly in full. This would ensure full exposure of the utility's performance. It would also make takeover possible. Commissions would also order efficiency audits whenever they seemed appropriate, and these too would be published. Commissions would not impede takeovers, since service requirements and liabilities would be explicitly detailed in the regulatory contract. The public investment bank would be among those eligible to take minority or controlling holdings.

"If-then" Regulation. Commissions would define specific tasks which firms can reasonably be expected to perform. In some sectors there would be many such specific items to perform; in others, few or none. Specific rewards would be made contingent on doing the tasks. Firms would be given direct feedback for precise fulfillment of the objectives. Regulators would become more explicitly responsible for defining and inducing good performance.

Competition and Revisions of Structure. Interarea competition among utilities would be permitted. Commissions would also permit units within a utility's "service area" to split out and deal independently with that or other utilities. Utilities would thus evolve back toward more competitive structures by their own incentives rather than by coercion. All ventures by utilities into significant new markets would be by separate subsidiaries, with segregated accounts. The standard surtax would apply to these, too. Throughout, the reliance would not be on *new* entrants to attack established utilities, but on mutual competition or separation among strong established units.

Price Structure. All this would still leave certain parts of the price structure to be supervised. The main criterion in setting prices would be marginal costs, with particular attention to peak and off-peak rates. Commissions would focus their supervision and constraints on a relatively few such pricing dimensions. Often the socially rational price would also fit the firm's private interests. For the other cases, commissions would need to retain the power to require specific changes.

Altogether, these changes would sharply reduce the regulatory burden and clarify responsibility. Only in a few areas—mainly in price structure—would commissions need to derive expert findings and, perhaps, require their application. For the rest, "regulation" would be aligned with self-interest inside the current "utility" firms as well as in a range of other units capable of entry, takeover, secession from the utility network, or other natural actions. Present utilities would yield some privileges, but they would gain in other directions. New utilities would be on notice that their tenure is temporary, not insulated, and primed with incentives to revert to competitive status.

In all this, the degree of public ownership is indeterminate. In some cases it may be zero; in others, complete. The content criteria would be similar to those for firms in other sectors (recall chapters 6 and 7). The regulatory treatment would be largely the same regardless of the role of public ownership.

In short, regulation would need to "do better" over a much smaller set of problems, and there would be strong incentives working in its favor. These changes in the regulatory contract appear to be necessary. If they are made, regulation may turn out to be, at long last, sufficient.

CHAPTER TEN
The Supply of Weapons

WEAPONS SUPPLY has been a sensitive issue in virtually all societies. Weapons provide power, to exert against both external and internal forces. In earlier eras the State commonly produced its own weapons in public arsenals, partly to retain this power. During the last 30 years, with their high levels of peacetime weapons supply and large-scale sales of weapons among nations, there has been a movement toward contracting-out to private firms. This method is now common in western nations, especially the United States.[1]

The possible costs of the present methods—profiteering, inefficiency in production, and wasteful ordering—have long been known.[2] These problems are outlined in sections 1 and 2, and treatments for them are assessed

---

[1] See M. J. Peck and F. M. Scherer, *The Weapons Acquisition Process* (Cambridge, Mass.: Harvard University School of Business, 1962); J. K. Galbraith, *The New Industrial State,* Boston: Houghton Mifflin, 1967); H. O. Stekler, *The Structure and Performance of the Aerospace Industry* (Berkeley: University of California Press, 1965).

[2] Peck and Scherer, *ibid.;* Galbraith, *ibid.;* and for more intensive commentary on recent outcomes, one can consult the voluminous hearings and testimony for the U.S. Congress, Joint Economic Committee, Subcommittee on Economy in Government, since 1969. (Hereafter cited as Congressional Hearings.)

in section 3. A larger issue, whether the present methods add to the arms race, is considered separately in section 4.

1 THE "SECTOR"

The cardinal fact is a pedestrian one: weapons purchases are essentially made at the grass-roots levels of the procurement hierarchy, by middle-level officers, who are long and intimately familiar with their suppliers.[3] These people work out the contracting information, and are familiar with capabilities and costs. They also receive company suggestions for new weaponry and develop specific proposals. This information, when processed on up to higher levels, usually defines the choices actually made. Any treatments to alter weapons purchasing must somehow affect activities on this plane. Most of the officers have been trained as engineers, in the older, lower-grade specialties. The criteria they base their decisions on are therefore usually narrow, combining avoidance of risks with engineering standards. Cost is commonly regarded as a secondary (or tertiary) criterion. The apparent value of—or "need" for—a weapons system often arises from joint planning by these officers and the suppliers themselves.

Certain supplying companies are deeply—in some cases totally—engaged in weapons production.[4] Perhaps 10 to 20 major corporations are primarily weapons producers; many of them make the fairly complex innovative systems that constitute a large share of modern military purchases. Actually, this share is rather smaller than was commonly believed in the 1960s.[5] The great bulk of weapons are of routine character. Indeed, the crash-program Buck Rogers ambience of many programs in the 1960s magnified their seeming futurism. Handled more conservatively, they are mostly predictable and could be purchased on an efficient, competitive basis.[6]

---

[3] In addition to using the usual sources, I learned much about this process firsthand during 1967–68. I was one of two Antitrust Division members assigned as the "liaison" to the Defense Department, looking into competitive aspects of procurement. See also Galbraith, *ibid.*

[4] Some of these are indicated in W. G. Shepherd, *Market Power and Economic Welfare* (New York: Random House, 1970), ch. 5 and Appendix Tables 5 and 7; see also Peck and Scherer, *Weapons Acquisition Process,* and Congressional Hearings.

[5] Peck and Scherer (*ibid.*) wrote when the belief in complex systems was at a peak.

[6] Thus, two-thirds of military purchases occur with little or no competition at all (Shepherd, *Market Power and Economic Welfare,* Appendix Table 6). The fraction is so high partly because of the supposed urgency and complexity of the systems. A more measured treatment would make it possible to reduce that proportion sharply.

For weapons firms, the key economic fact is that their short-run *marginal* cost for new orders is quite low when their order backlog is small—when operations are expected to be below capacity. Yet the revenue from each order must eventually cover its average costs. Each supplier therefore tends to bid aggressively when short of orders but only nominally when the order backlog is long. A certain degree of this is routine in many other markets, but in weapons supply it interacts with the peculiar motives of the purchasers. The net effect is to reduce competition and cause a tendency to the "buying-in" of contracts. Firms knowingly bid below average costs—but at or above marginal costs—expecting to be able to push up the effective price at later stages. This is possible because the outputs are complex and undergo design and other changes during the long period between contracting and completion.

This simalacrum of "competition" creates illusions of low weapons costs, at the time when contracts are being prepared and let. It also prevents effective minimizing of costs. It encourages weapons "markets" to evolve a limited set of suppliers; each is heavily reliant on weapons orders, which are essentially rotated among them and which exceed the optimal total levels of weapons supply.

The focusing of R&D support—aside from actual purchases—is also very tight, with a high degree of interdependence between the military and a relatively few firms.[7] At the grass-roots level, there is no systematic attention to competitive effects in either the R&D support or the purchases.[8] Therefore, the purchasers tend to become "locked-in" with noncompetitive or sole-source suppliers in the majority of cases.[9] The dynamic marginal-cost choice logic is reinforced by the dynamics of R&D funds for several projects, and these mingle as overhead costs with the activities and costs for other ongoing production of weapons. This pooling of funds and costs further reduces the level of assignable costs to any one project—much of the resources are simply "on hand *anyway*"—and so identifiable marginal costs are reduced even further below true long-run average costs. Accordingly,

[7] See especially Galbraith, *New Industrial State;* Peck and Scherer, *Weapons Acquisition Process;* and Congressional Hearings.

[8] This emerges from various studies of the process; it was thoroughly confirmed by my direct experience.

[9] In 1965–66, some 38 percent of all defense purchases were "sole-source"; another 29 percent were purchased with no price competition. For details, see Shepherd, *Market Power and Economic Welfare,* Appendix Table 6.

The Supply of Weapons   261

the process of unrealistic and pseudocompetitive underbidding is accentuated even more.

A striking instance of this has been aircraft production.[10] With remarkable precision, successive models have been timed and allotted as if designed to keep the several private aircraft assembly lines in operation. This has amounted to *de facto* rotation despite appearances of competition and controls on costs. The unusually large cost overruns in these programs have been a natural outcome.

Beneath the narrow focus of primary contracts in a few firms and regions, there is a much broader substructure of weapons production. Subcontracting of components is widely spread across industries, company sizes, and regions of the country. Much of this private subcontracting can be provisionally assumed to be on an efficient basis, free of special distortions, yet this substructure does ensure that the motivation for high weapons spending is much wider than the narrow focus of prime contracts would suggest. Much the same has been true also of space flight and nuclear energy programs.

2 PROBABLE COSTS

Altogether, the weapons sector is managed in ways likely to generate appreciable net social costs. These can be identified with some clarity, but they cannot be estimated with precision.

Inefficiency in production is substantial, probably on the order of 20 percent of costs for the more complex systems.[11] This reflects both cost overruns and routine inefficiency. Further, weapons quantities and quality both tend to exceed the optimum. There is excess ordering of many items—in part because of the cost illusions fostered by underbidding—and supplies often embody service qualities—reliability, length of life, etc.—that exceed the levels of efficient design. These added costs are likely to be on the order of 10 percent of actual costs.

These forms of inefficiency probably account for approximately 30 per-

---

[10] See J. R. Kurth, "The Political Economy of Weapons Procurement: The Follow-on Imperative," *American Economic Review,* May 1972, pp. 304–11.

[11] This is a conservative summary of informal estimates by a number of analysts close to the problem. Some estimates are much larger. Cost overruns suggest truly heroic degrees of waste, but because they reflect a natural process linking the marginal-cost bid-in factor and rotation of orders, they overstate the actual level of direct waste.

cent of costs, on average. During the rapid expansions of programs in the 1960s they may have been higher in many large instances.[12] To this, one would add the capital donated to suppliers in a variety of industries, which has approached $25 billion.[13] How to determine the whole deadweight loss from these costs is not clear, since much of it did have hidden private yields.

Finally, there are equity effects from the profit flows. These too are hard to estimate, for the official profit figures are not complete or reliable. Moreover, capital gains during 1962–68 for shareholders of many weapons producers have been reversed by sharp drops in share prices more recently. Yet informed holders have presumably tended to liquidate their gains in good time, and so there has probably been a significant regressive effect from procurement policies that have permitted supernormal profits.

Among weapons suppliers, inefficiency and high profit rates may occur together. Indeed, that is precisely the effect of the various versions of cost-plus contracting. By contrast, market power in industry usually tends to cause either high profitability or inefficiency (recall chapters 2 and 4). This combination presents special problems of treatment for the weapons sector.

There are two primary causes of malfunctioning: the nature of grass-roots military decision-making, and overcommitment by some firms to weapons work. Reconstituting the lower-level decisions criteria might be both necessary and sufficient to achieve a reasonable cure. It is extremely unlikely ever to occur. By contrast, reducing weapons work to no more than, say, 30 percent of any supplier's total revenue would avert inefficiency in several ways: it would put the main body of the firm's activities under some degree of competitive discipline, as average costs would be under relatively strong constraints; marginal costs would not diverge nearly so sharply below average costs, because civilian production would absorb most of each firm's capacity; incentives for underbidding—with all its effects—would be less.

3 TREATMENT

Since the 1950s, experiments with new treatments have been directed mainly to the criteria used in contract decisions. We have seen that these decisions are formed basically at the grass-roots level. Incentive contracting, in various forms, has been seen as a way to induce greater efficiency, by al-

---

[12] See Congressional Hearings. [13] *Ibid*.

tering the basic cost-plus contracting situation.[14] Other suggestions have been to use past performance in deciding who shall get future contracts, to inject broader objectives—competition, efficiency—into procurement decisions, and, most recently, to convert weapons suppliers into public enterprises.[15] I shall consider three main directions for treatment, roughly in descending order of likely effectiveness.

A TAX ON WEAPONS INVOLVEMENT

The incentives for overcommitment to weapons contracts probably need to be reduced directly. A surtax parallel to the tax on market share (chapters 6–9) would be appropriate. The extra tax would be in line with the share (call it W) of the firm's total sales that weapons contracts represent. It could begin at a share of 30 percent, in order to induce reductions down to that level. Its precise design and graduation are of less importance than the mere presence of some such incentive.[16] The alternative would be to employ simply the general market-share surtax. If shares in weapons markets were easily measured, this might suffice; but weapons markets are notoriously difficult to define. By contrast, the W share can be measured precisely and reliably. In any case, the overcommitment is the primary target of treatment, and the profits are determined directly by the purchases. Therefore, weapons markets might be an appropriate exception to the general surtax on market share.

The terms of the contracts would naturally tend to adjust in response to the tax on W, thereby weakening its effect. Doubtlessly, contracting officers would find that reasonable, even necessary. But there would be limits, for low-W—and therefore more lightly taxed—firms would be favored in head-on bidding situations. It is instructive to compare this strong economic lever with the futility of "instructing" officers to allocate contracts to firms with low W. Such an abstract criterion would be nearly weightless against the tendency for firms to underbid and for officers to rotate contracts.

A tax on W would induce high-W firms to seek mergers with nonweapons

---

[14] For one analysis J. G. Cross, "Incentive Pricing and Utility Regulation," *Quarterly Journal of Economics,* 1970, pp. 236–53; and Peck and Scherer, *Weapons Acquisition Process.*

[15] Peck and Scherer, *Ibid.;* Galbraith, *Economics and the Public Purpose* (Boston, Houghton Mifflin, 1973).

[16] It would probably be scaled within a range of 0 to 3 percent of those weapons sales exceeding 30 percent of the firm's total sales; this would apply significant marginal incentives.

firms, so as to reduce W. Such conglomerate mergers could be a substantial side-effect; few weapons producers are large enough to be immune from takeover. But these takeovers need not pose a social problem, as long as the other treatments in this book are followed. The takeover effects could be beneficial for efficiency, and the accounts of divisions would remain separate and public. Although certain mergers might pose costs, the common run of them probably would not.

B OWNERSHIP REALIGNMENTS

In certain cases, the public provides capital and bears the risks of weapons supply. But it does not have ownership, nor the benefits (net revenues, capital gains, control) ownership provides. This is the worst of both worlds, and predictably it has coincided with some of the highest social costs. A natural remedy is to arrange public ownership, to align controls with costs.[17] Such a "nationalizing of the weapons industry" could improve on certain present cases, but its net yields are uncertain. It should be done selectively, in extreme moderation. The main objective should be to reduce the public subsidy.

As ever, the mere presence of public enterprise is not a treatment. The basic problems are the lowness of marginal cost and the overuse of public funds without compensating public benefits. The marginal-cost problem would continue. More likely it would intensify, for the pressure to keep public factories going would probably be greater than for private factories. That, at least, has been true of arsenals and Navy shipyards in the past. A large public weapons sector would tend to establish a floor under the level of weapons production.

The committal of public funds would also increase under any large-scale shift. And there would be no way to earn a high profit for the public, because the State is itself the customer. Therefore the main possible gains are only in efficiency and in averting excess arms levels; and these would not at all necessarily be achieved.

Yet certain selective shifts to public enterprise would be optimal. First, all public capital grants and loans to weapons suppliers might also entail a degree of direct control by the public investment bank. The forms would vary—stockholdings, directorships, etc.—but there would be tight financial

---

[17] Galbraith, *Economics and the Public Purpose,* has put the point persuasively.

supervision (including the authority to make management changes) of every firm relying heavily on public resources. The public bank would also be free to take holdings and control of weapons firms with high W, in order to realize the tax savings from taking actions to reduce W. This degree of public ownership would be only temporary (recall chapter 7), and selective.

The public bank would naturally avoid cases with extremely high risk. It would not be optimal to commit large amounts of public funds to risky military projects. The incentive instead would be for military planners to decompose risky projects into a sequence of stages, each of which is more predictable than the whole.[18] Otherwise, the extension of public enterprise would serve as a costly device to enable further military indulgence in improbable and wasteful schemes. It is precisely this sort of 1960s crash program for untried "systems" that should be minimized in the future. If private venture capital will not undertake a project, then the project is presumptively ill-defined or inefficient.

C INCENTIVE CONTRACTING

Much can be done to improve contract design in order to reward efficient performance,[19] but the practical gains will be the least precisely in those cases—e.g., complex systems still to be designed—where performance is chronically worst. The two most promising tactics are to adjust S (the degree of profit sharing) to optimize incentives for cost-minimizing, and performance contracting (in which good past performance gives a firm priority in getting future contracts).[20]

In principle, S can be optimized and then applied to strongly induce efficiency. In practice, it interacts with the other contract variables (profit rate,

---

[18] O. E. Williamson has developed the concept of "task decomposition" as a way to minimize the commitment of military purchases to large single contracts. It would introduce a sequence of learning steps, rather than prematurely lock onto one system and one supplier.

[19] The basic problem is in relating the company's profit reward to its cost performance. The basic reward situation is defined in terms of target and realized profit, thus:

Realized Profit = Target Profit + S(Target Cost − Realized Cost)

adapting from Scherer, "The Aerospace Industry," in *The Structure of American Industry*, ed. W. Adams (New York: Macmillan, 1962). The S ratio can be set between 0 and 1.0. At 0, it leaves the supplier indifferent to costs. At 1.0, it puts all the responsibility for costs on the supplier.

[20] On incentive contracting, see Cross, "Incentive Regulation." On performance contracting, see especially F. M. Scherer, *The Weapons Acquisition Process: Economic Incentives* (Boston: Harvard University Business School, 1963).

time deadlines, renewal prospects, etc.) and has little force where it is most needed. In fact, fixed-price contracts (in which S is 1.0 and has its maximum "incentive" effect) are workable mainly in the simpler, routine items. On those, such contracts are already common; but for complex systems, all parameters are uncertain. Raising S then causes firms to seek and get compensating adjustments in the other contract terms. And still later, when large losses nevertheless result, there ensues a political struggle in which the firm has a good chance of winning a price adjustment after all. Therefore, "incentive contracting" may offer new yields only for certain moderate-size contracts for intermediate weapons—those which are neither simple nor extremely complex—and the grass-roots contracting process will tend to erode even these yields, by permitting other compensatory adjustments. The prospects for incentive contracting (like those for incentive regulation; see chapter 9) are well below those entertained in the 1960s, when it was given fairly extensive trials. It is at most a supplement to other treatments.

"Performance contracting" also offers certain marginal new yields. To some extent it is already implicitly used. Firms with markedly poor past performance occasionally do suffer in later decisions, because the one strength of lower Pentagon officials is that they (usually) do know their suppliers' capabilities. However, a formal procedure of performance rating would be required in order to extend this treatment. This would appraise performance objectively, circulate the ratings to contracting officials, and then see to it that the ratings actually influence later decisions.

Unfortunately, there are severe practical difficulties in doing this. Performance is often not clearly ratable, especially in the middle range of cases where mitigating factors can always be turned up. The ratings will be difficult to enforce, for several reasons: later contracts for firm X will differ from what firm X supplied before; personnel come and go, both in the firms and the contracting offices, so that memories are short, forgiveness is long, and hope springs eternal; and in the most complex cases, the ratings would be just one among many considerations.

Altogether, a formalization of present judgments is not likely to improve performance to the extent that it justifies its costs except perhaps in special cases. Performance ratings are a valuable device—if only to apply an added discipline to suppliers' efficiency in the current contract—but would remain as a supplementary treatment.

Taken together, these three kinds of treatment may still be insufficient.

The surtax on W may need to be high to cause W to decline—so high as to be politically unacceptable. In any event, the lower-level contracting process may be largely untouched, so that rotation and reduced incentives for efficiency will continue despite the "correct" treatments.

4 PROLIFERATION

International weapons markets have grown to major scale in recent decades. The global selling of aircraft, munitions, and related equipment is a rapidly growing, extensive system of markets. It does impose competitive constraints on certain suppliers. Because the possession of weapons has external costs—in arms races, inducements to belligerence, and indiscriminate destruction when they are put to use—this industry probably constitutes a clear exception to the optimizing role of free international trade.

This intense competition occurs under certain special conditions: (1) low marginal costs of additional sales; (2) government assistance, in R&D funding, promoting sales, and applying related inducements (such as U.S. training of foreign officers, provision of technical support, etc.); (3) secondhand markets in which prices often bear little relation to costs, and in which corruption is frequent.

Even if the unsavory aspects were absent, this process of competition in proliferation would lead to outcomes that reduce the probability of world survival. Suppliers have strong incentives to increase foreign sales, even at "cutthroat" prices. Public policies accentuate these pressures, by further reducing sellers' costs and by applying pressures that stimulate demand. Each sale to a client nation raises its neighbors' demand for matching purchases; but even without the ratchet effect of such little arms races, proliferation and instability are increased.

The treatments in Section 3 will not remedy these conditions, though they may abate them in some degree, and a broad "nationalization" of weapons production would probably aggravate the proliferation problem, by making weapons production a more direct responsibility and interest of military officials.

Since competition is part of the problem, reducing it might seem appropriate. A global combination or cartel of major weapons suppliers would be the result, and indeed it would probably increase effective prices and reduce supply. Further, it might decrease efficiency and innovation in weapons— and thereby slow the arms race—but with such waste there would also be large excess profits and windfall capital gains. The international political power of these combinations would thus be increased. In short, the gains would be moderate and the costs extreme.

The optimal treatment would fit the problem: the external costs of proliferation. Proliferation intensifies world instability, and no mere prohibitions or unilateral decisions by any country will be effective. The direct treatment is to tax all international arms sales in proportion to these externalities. The revenues would go to the United Nations or possibly to other institutions that operate to avert warfare. This U.N. tax would, in theory, vary with the weapons type. Aircraft, missiles, and other offensive arms with great striking distances impose high external costs, and so they would be taxed heavily; more conventional items (jeeps, hand weapons) would have low tax rates; and strictly defensive or deterrent weapons would not be taxed.

Crude attempts at this goal are already made, by means of physical quotas and denials. Atomic weapons are simply not traded at all (they are instead "deployed"). Other sensitive items—attack aircraft, antipersonnal explosives—are rationed by seller countries to certain buyer countries. This system is crude, however, and it often collapses under the pressure of competitive weapons sales. This pressure is likely to intensify further.

Therefore the constraints need to be systematized on a worldwide basis, with incentives firmly attuned to the objectives. The proliferation of offensive arms would be made less profitable to those involved, and the flow of revenue to the U.N.—paradoxical though it may seem—will directly relate the levels of peacekeeping resources to the degree of need for them. The present disintegrating "system" of world arms control tends, by contrast, to align the large powers' interests with sheer proliferation.

Can world survival be treated by benefit-cost calculations in designing optimal treatments? Even though such an appraisal seems far-fetched and cannot in fact be done metrically, the direction of desired treatments is clear enough. Only a device like the proliferation tax would deal directly with the key condition. Even if it presently may appear to have slight chance of adoption, it is a promising treatment for reducing the probability of Doomsday.

CHAPTER ELEVEN
Industrial Policies in an Equalitarian Society

So FAR I have outlined methods for treating market power and its effects in an advanced industrial system. The discussion's scope has been reformist rather than radical, because a major change to a more equalitarian system is against the odds. In the first half of this chapter I discuss these odds, and show why it has been rational for us to direct our attention mainly to optimizing within the present framework. After this I shall turn to a discussion of an equal-shares system.

An "equal" distribution is conceivable and possible. It has indeed been approached in other important economies.[1] For the longer run and for a deeper understanding, we should inquire about treatments of market power that would be suitable for an equalitarian society, and also about those suitable for transferring wealth to achieve equality. These old and important questions provide an appropriate larger setting for the smaller lessons we

---

[1] China is presently an example. Despite the persistence of a degree of inequality, it is far less than previously existed. There have also been large changes in context and content. Certain East European countries also have reduced inequality sharply. I am not extolling their political systems, but rather suggesting that shifts toward equality can occur.

have drawn up to this point; would the State wither away? Or will controls spread? Can the choices be defined at all? What role might there be for competition? At the least, we can escape the tunnel vision that comes from thinking exclusively within the present system.

I shall first explore the conditions under which wealth might be transferred. Then I shall define the basic attributes of the alternative system—call it Equitania. Next, I shall discuss the role of public enterprise during and after the transfer, following which I shall consider the scope for competition. Finally, for added perspective, I shall turn to the set of treatments suited to the large structural changes sought by many "less-developed economies."

I do not here advocate an equalization, but merely analyze clinically what it might entail. What is required for a shift to be effective and lasting may be unacceptable on other grounds, or perhaps it may simply be impossible to achieve. Some of the conditions for a shift are indeed unattractive; the reader should not believe that, by recognizing them, I am advocating them. Indeed, some readers will regard this chapter as a case *against* an equalizing shift.

1 THE IMPROBABILITY OF A RAPID TRANSFER [2]

The yields from moderate treatments may be clearer if we first consider the conditions under which more thorough changes might occur.[3] The familiar model posits a markedly more equal distribution of personal wealth and power. In practice, such sharp shifts often engender violence and effective counteraction. Here we shall explore at some length the key elements of a "successful" shift, to see which conditions favor it and which constrain it. Industrial policies may turn out to be strategic both in the process and in a new system.

A number of propositions about the real world are basic to this analysis:

a. Wealth is presently unequally held.[4]

[2] Parts of sections 1–4 appeared in *Working Papers,* Summer 1973, pp. 62–71.

[3] Our context here is sharply limited; even a thorough equalizing of wealth need not alter content or the career syndrome. Compare R. Marris, "Is the Corporate Economy a Corporate State?" *American Economic Review,* May 1972, pp. 103–15.

[4] There can be no doubt about this, either for the United States or for other "Western" economies; see R. J. Lampmann, *The Share of Top Wealth-Holders in National Wealth, 1922–1956* (Princeton: Princeton University Press, 1962); E. C. Budd, "Postwar Changes in

b. Talent (legal, managerial, political, intellectual, etc.) can be and is hired to serve interests. The best (or at least the most energetic) talent normally will go to the highest bidders.
c. Therefore power (the ability to control social images and relationships) is related to wealth patterns, though not precisely.
d. Most participants in society behave rationally. That is, they maximize their own family's self-interest in line with their perceived opportunities, using their own and hired talent.
e. The democratic process has an uncanny ability to make marginal adjustments in social policy in the "right" directions, but it will tend to reflect, not alter, the underlying structure of wealth and power.
f. Therefore a well-functioning democracy, as an equilibrium system, will not bring about large changes. It will normally arrange just enough amelioration or seeming change to abate the pressures for basic change.
g. Information influences the process, by controlling peoples' images of their status and prospects and of the possibilities for changing the system. These images can depart from "reality."
h. Groups within the populace differ in their roles and skills. Thus there are owners, workers, military, and other groups, each with specific stakes, skills, and expectations.
i. Only sharp and unforeseen changes in peoples' images and conditions for action can precipitate a rapid transfer or other large changes. These changes must be more rapid than the present controllers can anticipate and prevent. They may come from new information, from new definitions of social roles, or from real events (e.g., wars, epidemics, earthquakes), which detach the social order from old formats.

These points have recurred again and again in human history. People at the upper levels endeavor to keep the rest ignorant about their true deprivation, by hiding facts, by persuading them of present and future blessings, by wars, by providing entertainment and other diversions, and by asserting the inviolability of the economic order and the political system. Modern societies, including our own, will reflect these natural tendencies.

Accordingly, a rapid transfer need not be expected through the normal

---

the Size Distribution of Income in the U.S." *American Economic Review*, May 1970, pp. 247–61; F. Lundberg, *The Rich and the Super Rich* (Seacaucus, N.J.: Lyle Stuart, 1968).

functioning of the democratic process. This process allows ample time for the wealthy to engage talent to protect their interests. The more one tries to rewrite laws without altering the basic information, images, and expectations held by the populace, the more one evokes counteraction and, in the end, seems to demonstrate that nothing can be done.

There are three classic means for making a rapid transfer possible. One is by force—coups, civil wars, invasions. However, violence is destabilizing and often more harmful in the end than no change at all. The second method of rapid change is the chance event (e.g., an epidemic) which upsets the old order. Such rare and unforeseeable occasions come by surprise and are as likely to yield reaction as progress. (Though world wars I and II may have led to significant improvements in social legislation.)

The third method is the creation of different images, expectations, and knowledge about status and roles. This requires new thinking and mass publicity. The managers of a coup attempt this, by announcing new—but usually only superficial—power relationships at the top. Our concern is with new images for the major gainers and losers of a rapid transfer. To effect these new images requires new thought and advance planning, so that the resulting new order emerges quickly as a stable, productive, and consistent whole. Those at the top will regard such preparation as subversive, so it must be prepared to seek the widest audience in the face of skillful and determined resistance.

It seems clear in principle that the third route is preferable. It is seemingly indirect and passive, but it does focus on the true objective—to show lucidly both the present defects and the alternative solutions, so that those who stand to gain will themselves act to bring changes about. The odds on achieving major changes are still long, and yet they may still be better than with the alternatives—violence and chance events. Also, this strategy prepares for the chance events, so that they cause progress, not regress.

The third route has not been tried to any great extent. Even an analysis of the economics of a rapid transfer has scarcely begun. Indeed, we barely understand the outlines of how (and how much) property is presently transferred from older to younger generations, under the present laws of private property and inheritance.[5] That routine transfer process itself is important,

---

[5] See F. L. Pryor, "Simulation of the Impact of Social and Economic Institutions on the Size Distribution of Income and Wealth," *American Economic Review,* 1973, pp. 50–72. This pioneering study explores one direction for analysis.

since an equalizing transfer would necessarily have to link with it as well as divert it. That process is also a massive shift in its own right, and much of it is imbued with conflicts among interests. Also, laws have certain limited but intricate effects on it.

To understand an equalitarian transfer, one must first identify the main groups of participants in it, their motives, and their alternative actions:

a. *Owners.* Those holding formal title to personal wealth and its income claims. These are mostly older people. Those with substantial holdings are included; those with small amounts belong primarily in other groups.

b. *Financial managers.* These are specialists in arranging paper and real investments. They operate in various banks, investment entities, insurance firms, and foundations. They are crucial in managing capital, both for personal and enterprise uses.

c. *Managers.* These are industrial and commercial executives in large and small enterprises. They are essential for keeping production and trade going.

d. *Military and police forces.* These control and manage the stock of weapons that underlie the power that may ultimately limit external and internal sources of change.

e. *Political professionals.* These accomplish the interest-group compromises that resolve civic conflicts, whether by democratic or other political processes. In seeking office, they serve the interests of the controlling groups, whoever they may be.

f. *Workers.* The rest, who work for wages or salaries.

Some persons may be placed in more than one group, but most may not. Dual roles may cause conflicting motivations, but these do not undermine the basic distinctions.

Members of these groups perform various accustomed roles under any social and economic system. The roles differ with the systems, but the skills and interests are basically constant. Thus enterprise management has much the same skill content in a large private corporation as in a large public corporation. And so—a crucial point—a successful rapid transfer requires that most people merely perform the same activities as before but in an altered environment. For many people this alteration is slight or irrelevant. The basic practical question is how to secure compliance and cooperation from the key actors.

The most efficient format for a transfer appears to have three stages. First, an administration sympathetic to transfer and capable of designing it gains office. It then prepares the content and strategy, using its access to information which—for reasons noted in chapter 1—is presently inaccessible.

Second, the transfer is announced without anticipation (as was the wage-price freeze of 1971). The new rules define both the new system as a whole and the terms by which each individual can determine his prospects in it. The change is not only thorough but is also *seen* to be thorough, universal, and certain of application.[6] Fair access to the means of communication would be essential in disseminating and justifying the changes and in countering misrepresentations.

Third, there is a period of adjustment and response, during which the transfer actually occurs. New entities to manage capital are staffed and begin operation. Specific distributions of wealth and related benefits are made among individuals, contingent of course upon compliance and participation. The other major changes in roles and rules are also made.

After the transfer would occur the long adjustment to the alternative society. New "permanent" social programs, made possible by a fair distribution, would be developed, and any necessary further constraints to prevent a reversion to excessive inequality would be worked out.

Now consider the transfer process. During it, members of each of the groups may choose to:

a. To cooperate or to refuse to do so.
b. To support or to resist it outside one's working role.
c. To use peaceful methods or to resort to violence.
d. Ultimately, to stay or to emigrate (with one's resources).

This last choice is often neglected but crucial to understanding the problem. Emigration (of people and their resources) is a key variable limiting social change within any political unit; any serious effort at rapid transfer must deal with it. All of the choices will depend on the returns that are believed to be available from the alternatives open at the time. A successful

---

[6] It is less effective, even suicidal, to propose a new order as a vehicle to *gain* office democratically and then implement the transfer. The proposal would have to be prepared secretly, with little access to facts. The authorities would strive to suppress it, condemn it as subversive, or divert attention to other issues (the examples of such episodes are legion). The announcement of the proposed transfer can be portrayed as a mere electoral stratagem to gain power, and so the result may be only factional strife.

transfer will retain at least most of the groups in their roles, so that society continues to function without great disruption.

The only group that would necessarily undergo a negative basic economic change by the transfer is the Owners, or, more precisely, only their heirs. These are, of course, a small fraction of the populace, on the order of roughly 5 percent, who would no longer be able to persuade members of the other five groups that a transfer would be against their interests.

Actually, many of the specific benefits of wealth could be provided to Owners and heirs while the wealth is being transferred; these include security, purchasing power, cultural activities, and certain honorific items (such as prominent positions and prizes, or public buildings, monuments, or local streets named after them). Therefore, with ingenuity, the Owners could be at least partly mollified.

Basically, though, each person's and each group's responses to a prospective rapid transfer will be highly influenced by the information it has about what it stands to gain or lose. This in turn depends on the actual array of opportunities available to the various members of society and the actual disparities in wealth and poverty among them, and the *information* about these actual patterns. Unless the data are circulated, the actual patterns are not known, and citizens cannot act on their true interests. For example, most citizens simply do not know the extremes of wealth in society, nor do they know accurately how little opportunity they and their children really have compared to their more furtunate fellow-citizens. This bias in information influences behavior in favor of a greater degree of acquiescence. Conversely, full information on these patterns could, by itself, raise the possibilities of a transfer. Secrecy about wealth and poverty is a large factor favoring the status quo, and information about the true conditions and opportunities will be a critical part of any effort to arrange a transfer—for it will affect the choices the participants make during the process. Although full information may not be sufficient to trigger a change, it may be necessary. In any event, it will be a prime element, both for those trying to cause the transfer and for the rest of those affected.

To a large extent, the effort to arrange a transfer is simply an effort to clarify honestly the individual opportunities throughout society. Conversely, the status quo is best preserved by secrecy and a denial of the true conditions of inequality and lack of opportunity. This information includes, of course, the true degree of efficacy of existing public policies. This is commonly exaggerated, as we have seen earlier in this book. In short, the process of information and education, passive and tedious as it may seem, is quite essential to an effective transfer.

Analyzing this new and complex subject, we discover that the main aspects of the transfer are an unforeseen shift in the levels of permitted wealth for owners (and heirs), the occupational orientation—and perhaps job security—of financial managers and political professionals, and the direction of control of enterprise managers (though not necessarily their job security).

The other groups need not face any essential change in their roles from the transfer. It is reasonable to assume that throughout the transfer process individuals act according to their best interest, which will normally have three elements:

> a. Money income and wealth, which give command over goods and services for one's self and descendants. They are denoted by I, for income (which also can be capitalized into wealth).
> b. Security. Personal survival is of course the minimal requirement, but there are also degrees of security from risks of ruin or harm. It is denoted by S.
> c. Honor goods of various kinds. These include job status, cultural advantages, and other sorts of honors. Such honors come in great variety: prizes, recognition, promotion, social status, having public buildings or places named after one. They are often ultimately a more powerful incentive than mere money. I label them H.

Each person's perceived level of welfare then depends on these levels:

$$W_i = f(I_i, \frac{I_i}{I_n}, S_i, H_k, \frac{H_i}{H_n}, \ldots) \tag{11.1}$$

where i refers to this person and n to the average of others. Note that a universal reduction in I and H would, in part, leave perceived welfare levels unchanged, because relative positions would remain. Equally, reductions in I for some groups could be compensated by rises in H_i and H_i/H_n (that is by honors and by honors relative to *other* people's honors).

For the mass of citizens, the expected rate of rise in I equals the average national rate of rise in income per capita. Fair-minded, realistic citizens will expect to share in the rate of aggregate economic gain as a matter of course. Deviations below the mean will strain their loyalties to their given roles, and reduce the likelihood that they will maintain productivity.

Let us consider productivity first in an open society, which permits emigration and immigration freely. The key question is whether the transfer will reduce productivity sharply. Productivity depends in turn on the skills supplied and the degree of effort put forth. Let us divide the populace roughly into those who will lose by a transfer (P_u, u for upper) and those who will gain (P_l, l for lower). Effort is represented by E_u and E_l. Also let F represent the flow of innovations, which may raise productivity over time. Then

$$\text{Productivity} = f(P_u, E_u, P_l, E_l, F, \ldots) \qquad (11.2)$$

That is, maintaining productivity requires the combined presence *and efforts* of the upper and lower "classes," and of those who innovate.

A rapid transfer is likely to affect these. P_u will fall if and as the "elite" emigrate. One critical constraint is whether wealth can also be taken out of the country by emigrés before or during the transfer. The central importance of such expatriation of wealth can hardly be overstated.[7] It must be a key concern in any effort at rapid transfer. E_u is not obviously reduced by the transfer. The income and substitution effects will be counterpoised, and the net effect cannot be predicted. The remaining upper-class members may work harder to maintain their status.

As for the rest, P_l and E_l are likely both to rise. P_l will be pushed up by immigration of people with little opportunity from other countries. These immigrants will predictably work harder, and thereby reinforce the probable rise in E_1. The influx is likely to provoke efforts to stop immigration, of course, since it would dilute the gains from the transfer. Worse, a free flow of emigration of P_u and their wealth will tend to strip the economy of its most highly skilled members. Therefore a rapid transfer is likely to be futile, even if it does occur, in an open economy. The privileged leave; the dispossessed enter and dilute the meager gains of the domestic poor.

Therefore, a transfer will usually require a degree of controls on entry and exit. The point is quite general: the prospects for rapid transfer in any and every individual economy are severely limited by the policies in force in other nations. If the others cater to the wealthy, the goal of rapid transfer will be correspondingly more difficult to attain in any single society. Conversely, a world order limiting the flight of the rich and their capital will

---

[7] It is obviously endemic in all small countries, in this era and others. "Leading" families maintain foreign accounts and are able to augment them quickly in crisis situations. As in classical Greece and imperial Rome, a large degree of shifting in residence and assets is quite normal. Only recently, and in the very largest countries, has this come to be disregarded.

raise the chances for transfer everywhere. This truth holds even though its implications maybe distasteful.

Accordingly, a key condition for rapid transfer is that outward movement of title to wealth be controlled. This is not always recognized in programs for internal redistribution, but it can be basic. Thus, if U.S. taxes or other treatments of wealth ever really began to touch the core of large wealth, there would be a quick outward flow, and the control of such a flight of capital could become critical. That such a flight has not occurred is a reflection that present policies do not deeply touch large-scale wealth. In short, rapid transfer (or any large transfer) is virtually impossible in an economy that permits free entry and exit of persons and wealth.

Invasions from outside must also be avoided. These—or other foreign pressures—are often invoked to protect the established groups. Their effects are highly unpredictable.

A key objective would be to substitute security and honor goods for the wealth of the upper classes, so that they remain in society and continue to supply their talents.

The six-part grouping of citizens suggests that only owners hold the wealth which is to be spread equally, and they may seem to be merely drones. Many owners are elderly and passive, but many are also financial managers, many of whom—along with some industrial managers—will believe that their interests lie with wealth. An exchange of their present or expected wealth may thus be necessary for transfer, for without the cooperation of financial and industrial managers, any transfer scheme is in difficulty (for technical as well as political reasons).

This identifies the focal point for a transfer effort. It must—however distasteful—put selective limits at the borders and come to terms with the elite, giving them honor goods and relatively favorable prospects in return for their participation. By and large, the same financial and industrial managers must continue to play their previous technical roles. To replace them outright is beyond the capability of even the most thorough revisions. But their cooperation may be achieved without sacrificing the whole effort, by astute substitutions of honors and security for wealth (or the prospect of wealth), and assurances that relative status will not be wholly eliminated.

Accordingly, leveling may be feasible, but only by leaving the former elite with at least a modicum of advantage over the rest. To narrow the differences is usually more effective than to churn the participants into new, unpredictable relative positions. This is suggested by equation (11.1), which reflects the tendency of many people to be motivated by their relative positions in society as well as by their absolute and relative levels of economic affluence.

So far I have outlined key limits on a rapid transfer, instead of presenting a theory of it. These limits will be the most sensitive elements in any general theory. Moreover, they have suggested the points at which a rapid transfer would apply stress to the familiar roles in society, and they have indicated directions for further analysis and policy-making.

In addition, it should be noted that a rapid change places great strains on the accustomed choices and loyalties of most "leaders" of the social and economic order. Many (perhaps most) of them will prefer pseudopolicies, which promise transfers but do not really bring them about. Therefore, many current leaders will advance deceptive policies, which substitute for real transfers and therefore make them more difficult to accomplish.

This strategy is reinforced by the ability—and the desire—of the wealthy to hire talented members of the other groups to serve their interests. The stakes are large, for many of this class have holdings in the range of many hundreds of millions of dollars, and are also accustomed to social leadership. The hiring of lawyers, economists, and other agents is perfectly rational in the circumstances. The indirect effect of this can be to condition and divert whole academic disciplines, especially the social sciences.[8] The ability to engage selected members of other groups to prevent transfer sets another limit on the possibilities of the transfer itself. To some extent this limit can be offset by efforts to clarify the true potential gains from the transfer, and by exhortations for "class solidarity," but these efforts operate against strong individual incentives to break ranks. The class defector has long, and justly, been a special focus of concern to his fellows.

We can define the conditions normally required for a successful transfer. They divide into *basic constraints* and *short-run conditions* that need to hold during the transfer.

    a. *Basic constraints*
        i. Productivity must remain approximately on its previous growth path, both on a microeconomic and macroeconomic basis. The system must

[8] Many perceptive observers now argue that this has indeed happened to the economics profession; for one example, see M. Bronfenbrenner, "Notes on Marxian Economics in the United States," *American Economic Review*, 1964, pp. 1019–26.

function in all its parts; investment and employment must be kept at least approximately on course, *and* efforts to invent and innovate must also be sustained.
   ii. Large-scale flight of capital must be prevented, if necessary by controls.
   iii. The wealthy must be unable or unwilling to engage other citizens in large numbers to work, either directly or indirectly, against the transfer.
   iv. Citizens with key skills must be induced not to emigrate. To some extent, therefore, the elite must be propitiated and retained in some form of elite status during and probably after the transfer.
   v. Large-scale immigration of poorer people must be avoided, at least for a period.
   vi. Interference by foreign powers must not occur, except in the form of broad support—at a distance—for the transfer.
b. *Conditions during the transfer*
   i. The transfer must occur quickly and without anticipation by those who will not profit by it.
   ii. It must define new choices and rewards for the former elite, so that at each stage in the process they rationally choose to remain in productive roles, rather than resist, and hire defenders or emigrate.
   iii. While it is similar to a coup—in which information and alternatives are managed by the new would-be rulers—the transfer must avoid a fluid situation in which extraneous forces can pre-empt power. It must rely not on controls and claims but on widespread recgonition of the new alternative society and its benefits.

The basic constraints alone are likely to be simultaneously unattainable, as sober reflection will suggest. The short-run conditions only add to the difficulties. They can perhaps be met by a complex, thorough system retaining some relative status and substituting honor goods for the withdrawn wealth. Yet it will be a vast task to design and put over such a system to the various groups, and the attractions of honor goods and maintained relative status may fall short of mollifying the wealthy. Perhaps the transfer effort will abort on the basic need to have a thorough program and a receptive citizenry. Preparations of both of these can be resisted on grounds of conspiracy, subversion, lack of patriotism, and scholarly quality, etc., and indeed they have been resisted and punished precisely on those grounds in the past.

A successful transfer may not be possible within a democratic process or indeed within any other political system. At each stage, hitches can develop and reaction may occur. Moreover, there is likely to be no middle ground.

Under certain vectors of favorable conditions, a major transfer just might be possible. But a partially completed one is almost a contradiction in terms, for it leaves intact part of the structure of wealth and this will generate strong countertransfer activities.

Many of my points may seem like platitudes, but their cumulative meaning for the possible roles of public enterprise is distinctive. Whether or not we wish it to occur, we are probably wise to look forward to a slight chance of a big transfer, and a near-certainty that transfer will only occur at a glacial pace, if at all. In this context, we can think about the roles and yields of industrial policies without illusion.

2 BASIC CONDITIONS

If Equitania were to come about, it would by definition have close to an equal distribution of wealth and income. The rudimentary benefits of wealth—a range of economic choice, security of income and health care, decent living conditions, education for children, legal counsel, and much else—would be available either by public program or at prices within reach of virtually all. The equity term in cost-benefit appraisals would be relevant only when a market was capable of generating enough private gains to restore sharp inequality. Taxation would presumably abate disequalizing tendencies, but—as now—more would be needed to constrain the extraordinary sources of new private wealth.

The occupational structure could be basically similar to the present one, although some reallocation of labor and output would occur, and a major redefinition of authority and job content would be appropriate. However, these are separable issues relating to the background conditions. The basic interest groups, as defined in section 1, could remain, but with ownership more widely spread. In fact, as we saw there, a premise of an efficient (or acceptable) transfer is that the basic economic roles would not be upset.

The transfer to near-equality would presumably be instituted by intercepting the inheritance process.[9] Under favorable conditions, a compressed range of wealth and income inequality could, in principle, be peacefully established, supplemented by a new treatment for honor goods of various sorts as a partial substitute for wealth. During transfer, policy treatment would

---

[9] Again, see Pryor, "Simulation," for perspective on this transfer.

need to foster this revision. After transfer, a major objective would be to prevent reversion to marked inequality.

Once again, the absence of equity would be a major factor in most policy decisions. This would be oddly parallel to present policy context, where equity has been routinely excluded. Yet there would be important differences.

The cardinal difference would be in the possible role of public enterprise. This ownership factor may not be directly related to choices about constraints; in section 1 we noted that it often is not. But in the transfer process and its aftermath, the replacement of private capital with public capital could be decisive. The one major "occupational" shift could be in the Owner group. Therefore the first question is the role of public enterprise during and after the transfer.

3 THE ROLE OF PUBLIC ENTERPRISE

A DURING THE TRANSFER

The basic objectives during the transfer are to disturb job roles as little as possible, while enabling new patterns of wealth, full provision of social services, an upgrading of job content for most people, and a shifting toward nonpecuniary, social, and honor-good motivations.

If public enterprise has previously existed the transfer may be eased, but less so than is commonly thought. Managers and employees of such enterprises might be more sympathetic to a transfer (or at least neutral to it) than their colleagues in private firms—and the larger the share of public capital, the less private capital there is to gain control over.

Yet, public enterprise is often a minor fraction of all capital in industry, trade, finance, and utilities, and so this possible effect is probably small. What is more, the transfer is aimed at private portfolio wealth, and such wealth can and does freely include public-enterprise (and government) securities. Therefore the pattern of industrial ownership may be largely irrelevant to the structure of private wealth and the chances for altering it. Indeed, if private owners must be bought out at prices favorable to them, the change could tend to consolidate private wealth rather than displace or alter it. Therefore, whether prior public enterprise assists or hinders a rapid transfer depends on its forms and financing, and the effect is likely to be small.

During the transfer process, public enterprise may be critical. First, support or acquiescence of public enterprises will often be essential, for they often manage such key activities as communications, power, transportation, and the banking system. Political strategy therefore requires asserting and assuring the public's control over such public entities, or at least their neutrality during the change.

Second, new public enterprises for financial management will need to be created and staffed in order to receive and manage much or most of the transferred wealth. This activity may only be needed until a more lasting dispersal of wealth is arranged, but it is essential. Such enterprises will perform three functions, similar to the public investment bank mentioned earlier. One is investment itself: managing the portfolios of the new beneficiaries who are unskilled in the Byzantine tactics of capital markets. This would be analogous to some mutual funds. A second function is to affect managerial behavior in a wide range of private firms, including greater efficiency and also behavior supporting the transfer. The third function is, as an investment bank, to fund new enterprises, public or quasiprivate, which will provide services now inadequate. Some of these services would be in the health and welfare areas, but others would relate to pollution, congestion, and other urban problems.

The capital thus managed would be a limited reserve, a specialized resource used to bring about real economic effects and to induce effort consistent with the transfer. This reserve of transferred wealth must be used efficiently and sparingly, by skilled managers. To do so requires the recruitment of the best capital-market talents (presumably from the younger ranks) and setting suitable criteria for their performance as managers of social and quasisocial capital. They will function much as their present-day counterparts in public investment banks, but on a larger scale. There could well be several or more such banks.

Third, the temptation to create and expand public firms to provide new consumption services and subsidies must be resisted. The key job is to maintain productivity, and this may strain the reserve of transferred wealth. To rush into a set of costly new services before the post-transfer productive base is secure is to imperil the whole process. Therefore, each new proposed public enterprise for services and subsidies must be strictly weighed for its net yield in efficiency and welfare.

In short, public enterprise would play a Spartan, seemingly commercial, and restricted role during the transfer. This may seem out of line with the conventional image of the alternative society, but the paradox is only temporary, and it is resolved by the transfer itself. Public enterprise is strictly a set of tools which, if used carefully, can assist the shift as well as form part of the new system.

B AFTER THE TRANSFER

We can assume that after the transfer capital would still need to be employed in large units in many sectors, and that not everyone would become a skilled portfolio investor. To that extent, much of the redistributed wealth would remain beneficially in large entities under some degree of direct public control and ownership. Probably some degree of public ownership and influence on many large firms would also be appropriate. Most financial and industrial managers might perform much the same functions as before, but in a modified setting.

The literature on the content of a radically improved society frequently mentions public enterprise as playing an important role. That reflects, perhaps, the socialist tenet during the last century that public ownership must replace private capitalism in a "true" socialism. But no scientific basis for this dogma has ever been established, and current radical literature—like Marx's own work—offers little or no substance on the role for public interprise.[10]

One must proceed without romantic notions about what public enterprise could do in a post-transfer economy. It is safe to assume that it will still be managed by people of ordinary talents, who will not hew strictly to rational economic and social optimizing criteria, nor to simple standards of efficient management. The strong points of such public enterprises will continue to be (1) improved content, (2) provision of services and goods that might otherwise be in short supply or not fairly distributed, (3) management of capital for those not professionally skilled at it (e.g., in insurance for old age, health and accidents, and in investing), and (4) policy uses to control or influence commercial behavior (e.g., by partial public enterprise). In a post-transfer society, public enterprise would, in varying forms, be important in these directions. Perhaps the greatest expansion would be in the management of capital and in influencing private firms (3 and 4 above), rather than

[10] See H. Sherman, *Radical Political Economy* (New York: Basic Books, 1972); R. C. Edwards, M. Reich, and T. E. Weisskopf, *The Capitalist System,* (Englewood Cliffs, N.J.: Prentice-Hall, 1972); and Karl Marx's "Critique of the Gotha Program."

in content and social programs (1 and 2 above). This is the reverse of the common expectation that the public provision of social welfare services will be more extensive in an alternative society. In fact, a transfer would increase everyone's ability to purchase the needed and preferred services, in the combinations suited to individual desires. Therefore, under an efficient treatment many of these might be provided by private firms under the general constraints common to other markets (recall chapters 6–9 and 11).

In short, public management of capital would be extended after a transfer, though perhaps not permanently, and conventional sorts of complete public ownership or public subsidies would not be widely used. Public enterprise in varying degrees and forms would probably have a much expanded role, in a variety of sectors beyond what are now regarded as its traditional domain of utilities and sick industries. But this role might differ only in marginal degree from an optimal scope and form of public enterprise might be close to the proportions in Western European economies now.

Changes in the role of public enterprise offer high yields in a pre-transfer society. They are also part of the groundwork for the transfer itself and for the subsequent changed society. In large part, to set optimal policies within the present framework is to prepare for an alternative system.

4 CONSTRAINTS AND COMPETITION

In Equitania, industrial policies would aim to avert inefficiency and any reemergence of marked inequality. The treatments outlined elsewhere in this book would suit this purpose, with only marginal adjustments. The graduated profit tax based on market share would supply a preventive inducement against a reemergence of major fortunes via new monopolizing. The full-information treatment would also still be efficient.

The most basic question perhaps is whether competition would still be appropriate. Earlier writers have been divided on the question, but economists usually have assumed that competition would largely prevail in any system of efficient allocation.[11] This reflects many economics' training and belief in

---

[11] The extreme form of this view is formalized in the Lange-Lerner analysis of Pareto outcomes under "competitive" socialism; see A. P. Lerner, *The Economics of Control* (New York: Macmillan, 1944); O. Lange and F. M. Taylor, *On the Economic Theory of Socialism* (Minneapolis: University of Minnesota Press, 1938); and J. Vanek, *A General Theory of Labor-Managed Market Economies* (Ithaca: Cornell University Press, 1970).

the competitive equilibrium system. It may also have roots in social psychology, for a significant share of the population may have strong competitive motivation, akin to Adam Smith's "propensity to truck, barter and exchange." For such persons, a strictly noncompetitive system may stifle effort and performance.

Yet two factors limit the reach of this point. First, personal competitive urges can be exerted within enterprises as well as among them. A large share of the population already strives for job positions or portfolio gain as individuals, not as proprietors. Second, even in a fully competitive system only a small minority of the population engages directly in the management of competitive enterprises. Thus, only about 11 percent of the work force are classified as "managers, officials, and proprietors," and only a tiny minority of these people actually are in controlling positions.

In short, the scope of competition in Equitania is surely not determinate on economic grounds. A wide scope for competition is not compelled. It can be regarded as a matter of social choice, to be applied, modified, or subordinated as part of the larger optimal set of treatments.

Similarly, the extent of public enterprise is not determinate above a minimal level, and the scale of graduated tax on market share will probably be at or below the optimal level for pre-transfer conditions. Altogether, industrial policies will need to be *less* severe in Equitania. This is not unexpected: current deviations, being greater, require relatively strict treatments. Equitania requires more preventive and fewer restorative treatments.

This conclusion conflicts with orthodox expectations that the State's role would be larger in a post-industrial, equalitarian society. On the contrary, if the equity problem were solved, the appropriate role of industrial policies would probably recede.

Let us suppose, nonetheless, that the accepted scope of competitive industrial behavior remains—by social choice—roughly unchanged. This supposition would apply also to the degree of competition impinging on various utilities. In such a setting, the post-transfer optimal treatments would be similar to the pre-transfer ones, which primarily reflects the melancholy fact that—in the pre-transfer setting—the yields from optimal treatment are primarily in efficiency and content; equity is largely beyond reach. Therefore, solving equity problems does not radically alter the optimal choice of treatments in efficiency and content.

The post-transfer relaxation in constraints on industrial policies would therefore be marginal at most. This is true both of conventional industrial sectors and of utilities: the scope of public enterprise and of competition would be matters of some choice. Only in the financial sector would strict—probably even stricter—treatments be indicated. Constraints on secrecy, security, returns, and financial ties would need to be at least as tight as the present optimal limits would be, for this sector is the primary one in which new fortunes and market power can be generated. An active and substantial public investment bank would be necessary, but not sufficient in itself. The graduated profit tax based on market share would remain important as a device for offsetting the effect of financial market power on industrial market power.

The motif therefore is one of continuity between the treatment for current markets and those in a genuinely equalitarian system. This conclusion might reflect conservatism and myopia on my part. But I believe it reflects instead the primary unity of preventive and restorative treatments, which chapters 6–9 made clear. Treatments that induce efficient choices and basic improvements are the most difficult to achieve. Attaining and preserving equity are, strange to say, simpler policy problems.

Note again that the shift does seem to require unusual and partly negative conditions, in order to be effective and lasting. The discussion here has not advocated these conditions, but it has suggested that they need to be understood.

5 DEVELOPMENT

So far, we have focused entirely on treatments for industrialized, "advanced" economies. But for still greater perspective and completeness, we can draw several basic lessons about industrial policies during the "development" phase through which an agrarian economy must pass to become industrialized.[12]

The main attributes of the end result are extensive product and financial markets, large and sophisticated enough to sustain reasonably competitive

[12] Among the better analyses of this development process are W. Elkins, *An Introduction to Development Economics* (Baltimore: Penguin, 1973); I. M. D. Little, T. Scitovsky, and M. Scott, *Industry and Trade in Some Developing Countries* (London: Oxford, 1970); and A. O. Hirschmann, *The Strategy of Economic Development* (New Haven: Yale University Press, 1958).

conditions. In most developing economies, competition will be abridged, for most undeveloped countries are small and will remain so; they will support loose oligopolies only in special cases. Instead, an imperfect process of gaps and responses will normally occur during the sequence of structural changes in the course of "development." [13]

Therefore, competition will never be close to perfect in these situations, but some degree of it may be quite critical in order to avoid inefficiency and inequity. The pre-development conditions commonly include a high degree of inequality (in every respect) and inefficiency. Usually, wealth is concentrated in a few families, the few industries are extremely highly concentrated, and capital markets are rudimentary. Structural change and entire new industries are required in the course of development; and of course the requisite upheaval in society and amenity are commonly severe.

Cost-benefit analysis cannot be fine-tuned in such conditions, and so the conclusions must be coarse-grained. They appear to prescribe an expanded role for public enterprise and competition during the transition. During development there will be extraordinary opportunities for monopolizing and disequalizing the distribution of wealth. This is plain from the past "industrial revolutions," and it still holds true. Also monopoly during the development phase is likely to persist during later periods, especially if the new enterprises are international firms, which are more likely to be able to retain their initial market positions.

In short, high market shares are virtually inevitable during the development phase, but this also retards the process and makes it less equitable. To this degree, public enterprise of certain sorts may be optimal. The efficient treatment is to establish public-firm competitors in major growth sectors, and then limit them to branching into other industries.[14] This will tend to equalize wealth holdings, and also to avert high inefficiency. It is an intermediate degree of public ownership, much less than the Soviet model and yet different from common patterns of actual development. The two prevailing models are Western development, with private enterprises—often monopolies—accentuating the preexisting wealth inequalities, and Soviet-bloc treatments, with reliance on controls and public enterprises. The middle course avoids obvious faults in both models, but it requires careful analysis

---

[13] See especially Hirschmann, *ibid.*

[14] W. C. Merrill and N. Schneider, "Government Firms in Oligopoly Industries," *Quarterly Journal of Economics*, 1966, pp. 400–12, offer an exploratory analysis of this approach.

and sufficient resources. In particular, public capital and management resources need both to be adequate and to be available to competitive public enterprises. Competition must be fostered from the outset.

In all, an optimal development path commonly requires a substantial degree of public enterprise, carefully designed and managed. This can recede as development occurs, so that the State can indeed wither away in the advanced stages of socialism. The choices of sectors and degrees of public enterprises are usually quite broad, and differences in national resources, temperament, reserves, and trade opportunities can often have a wide effect. Even if the scope of public enterprise is large during development, future patterns will not therefore be controlled. Advanced capitalism can usually bring a larger degree of private ownership, which only needs certain constraints (see chapters 6–9) in order to approach optimal conditions.

The extension of public enterprise in the development sequence requires careful sectoral choices, and it leaves a degree of selection about the forms and financing of public enterprises. It may usually be followed by an evolution toward private ownership, but it appears to be prescribed nonetheless by criteria for equity and efficiency.

A transfer to an equalitarian society is not likely, but the structure of optimal industrial policies would not be radically changed should the transfer occur. The scope of public enterprise would be somewhat larger during and after the transfer, and it would be markedly larger during the transition of agrarian economies to more advanced economic systems.

CHAPTER TWELVE
A Summary

INDUSTRIAL POLICIES—the method and design of treating market power—are evidently a wide and rich subject. The modern forms of market power and corporate reality do not simply pit antitrust against twentieth-century technology; that policy context has seemed barren, because in fact it is nearly so. The more correct context is, rather, rich and fruitful.

The conditions of markets do offer wide social choices, and the tools available are of many kinds and for many purposes. To see the choices and use the tools, we need to modify the technocratic view of industrial organization and revise many of our images of reality and of the choices open to us. This book has ventured a series of such revisions, testing them wherever possible with facts and logical criteria.

The main points and hypotheses can be summed up briefly. Policies arise in a setting of political economy, which shapes the treatments and influences their real effects. Very possibly, policies will reflect or accentuate the underlying structure of power rather than alter it. Information is critical in the design and evaluation of many policies, but usually the most critical data will be the least available. A complete availability of information would, in itself, abate many industrial problems and obviate many costly policy efforts.

We then restated certain concepts of industrial organization, adding context and content to the conventional range of industry concepts. And within the conventional set of structural concepts, we noted that market share is of central importance, both on logical and empirical grounds. In analyzing the context of enterprises, we found that financial structure is likely to foster a degree of market power in other markets. And content, though not yet rigorously defined, is an important part of market performance. The degree of content is likely to be neutral to production costs, or even to vary inversely with it.

From factual tests, we inferred that market structure is related to profitability more closely than has been thought. There is little evidence that high profit rates are explained by riskiness or superior efficiency; on the whole, the opposite is at least as likely. There is indeed a gradual tendency for high market shares to decline over time, and most "utilities" are "natural monopolies" only briefly; but among leading dominant firms in the U.S. industry, the rate of decay has dropped in recent decades, and it now appears to be low. The yields from antitrust restructuring in the past have been high. In short, there appear to be definite social yields from direct steps to abate market power in a core of major industries.

In designing optimal policies, one uses some form of cost-benefit evaluation. For industrial policies, there are several distinctive adjustments to be made in the benefit and cost estimates. These point up the critical role of burdens of proof and advantages of time. Also, an incentive structure to induce behavior will usually be preferable to enforced actions which go against the interests and expertise of the main actors in the process.

Among current conventional treatments, antitrust tends to protect dominant firms, and financial markets are made more monopolistic by such "regulation" as occurs. Utility regulation evolves perversely, tending to suppress possible competition and permit high degrees of inefficiency. Public enterprise is misapplied in several directions, and it usually evolves toward a regressive impact. Its potential for improving content is neglected. Still other policies (e.g., in public purchasing) also show deviant attributes.

We have therefore two sets of reasons for reevaluating and revising industrial policies: our perceptions of the nature of industry are now broader, different, and more distinct than they have been; and the present set of policies has definite nonoptimal features. The balance of the book proceeded through the main sectors where revised industrial policies would appear to offer high yields. Several types of tax incentives were explored, as therapy in place of surgery. A shift toward a full information policy, with virtually unlimited access to industrial information, was proposed. Treatments that are neutral to takeovers were explored, for finance, industry, and "utilities." An altered role for public enterprise was also outlined, including more experimentation with it in finance and industry, but less of the classical public corporation and public-agency monopoly in other sectors.

The mainstream sectors—industry, finance and trade, and "utilities"—would be under essentially a unified set of treatments relying heavily on information and specific incentives to induce optimal outcomes. Conventional treatments, and more radical ones, too, would play supplementary roles. Certain treatments would be quite drastic, but the whole set of treatments would involve less burden on public resources than at present, while yielding sharp gains in effiency, content, and equity. Weapons production, too, offers high yields to certain selective treatments which allow for the true sources of procurement inefficiency. In all of these, our thinking in cost-benefit concepts leads us to identify the problem and to design treatments that will induce behavior to shift toward optimal directions.

There may seem to be a paradox at the center of this thinking. Market power is defined and estimated as a structural problem, and yet the optimal treatments largely bypass the traditional structural remedies. Actually, each half of this approach is valid and essential. Certain structural conditions do indeed relate to certain losses of efficiency, content, and equity; market structure is a valid way to define and test out this problem. But the treatments must be sophisticated and realistic, applying incentives to modify behavior and structure, both for restoration and prevention. Classic restructuring, regulation, and public enterprise are defective and ineffectual in certain clear respects. That, perhaps, explains partly why they have been kept on so long, serving functions quite different from their official aims.

Once this is recognized, there remains a relatively wide scope for a procompetitive policy, if it is efficiently combined with other treatments. One could agree with Galbraith—and with current Chicago views—that restructuring has a limited role in future optimal treatment and still expect large net social yields from reducing market power by other means.

The pivotal point in the analysis is the central role of market share and its evolution over time. By recognizing this, one can at last reunify the analysis of competitive and utility sectors—of antitrust and regulatory policies. Without it, one is caught in a static world seemingly segmented between oligopoly and natural monopoly. Each of these categories is a detour from the main problem, and together they lead to policy confusion and costs. By creating artificial distinctions in a technocratic context, they have helped to create deep stresses and impasses in antitrust and regulation. And they have helped to detach discussion of public enterprise from its real hazards and from its real potential for altering content.

Broadening our perspective at the end, we explored the unlikely conditions under which a major equalizing of wealth might occur. They involved surprisingly similar industrial policies to those already outlined in the body of the book. The basic lessons for "reform," therefore, appear to remain valid for larger changes in the social context. Again there is unity in concepts and treatments.

One could not say that this book has applied cost-benefit analysis thoroughly or in detail. That may never be possible, and it scarcely is now. We are still in the stone age of information, for the really sensitive facts are indeed kept under quite thorough secrecy. That is why a full information policy might have such powerful optimizing effects. We cannot judge that well, while secrecy prevails. In any case, the reign of secrecy in which we now struggle cripples our understanding of reality and puts fundamental biases into policy treatments.

Still, cost-benefit concepts do help to identify some of the clear deviances in policies and to guide the design of rational treatments. A clairvoyant could develop optimal treatments with more precision than has been possible here, although the inherent character of the political economy might still turn aside all efforts to optimize.

In any case, such an ideal optimizing would be likely to fit within the lines drawn here, and those who would argue for different treatment must, I would maintain, put their case in the cost-benefit terms of chapter 3. Such a framework will not settle these issues; nothing ever will. Yet it will make for rational thinking and, perhaps, revisions of treatment so that, at least, they move toward the optimum rather than away from it.

APPENDICES

APPENDIX A
Methods and Data

THIS APPENDIX provides detail on the methods and data used in analyzing the elements of market structure. It also contains supporting material for other parts of chapter 4.

1 ANALYSIS OF ELEMENTS OF STRUCTURE

Estimation is based on information about the largest United States industrial corporations; data on their size and profitability have been available on a relatively standardized basis since 1960 in the *Fortune Directory,* and their aggregate importance in the United States economy is large. The years 1960–1969 provide a recent, relatively recession-free period, which is also long enough to show equilibrium patterns for many firms.

Coverage: The data primarily cover 216 firms among the largest 500 manufacturing corporations whose average market shares in the early 1960s could be estimated and which were not involved in a major internal or industry-wide disequilibrium. An additional 29 from the next largest 500 were also included for 1960–1969, making a total panel of 245 firms.

The panel includes a wide range of industries and of firms' positions within them.[1] Firms were excluded mainly for a high degree of internal

[1] A first analysis with 231 firms is reported in W. G. Shepherd, *Market Power and Economic Welfare* (New York: Random House, 1970). It fits the present results in all essentials.

diversification, a major merger during the period, high sales to the military (which would particularly affect post-1964 results), absence from the largest-500 group for more than one year of the 1960–1969 period, and major disequilibrium in the firm's primary industry or in its own condition.

The premise for the sample selection is that all firms and subsidiaries conform to the general structural patterns, so that those cases with identifiable market shares are representative of the universe. This assumption, if it is valid, mitigates sample bias which might arise from excluding diversified and other firms. The reduction of the panel from 500-plus to 245 means only that inferior or unobtainable market-share estimates have been omitted.

Profitability: Profit rates are measured by net income after tax as a percent of equity.[2] Though subject to accounting and measurement problems, this has become the conventional measure, as reported on a fairly standardized basis in the *Directory,* and it has been affirmed statistically (Hall and Weiss, 1967) as preferable to the rate of return on total net assets. It is not likely that the findings would be significantly altered by the use of an alternative estimator of profit rates.

One element of "risk"—year-to-year fluctuations in profit rates—was estimated by the standard error of the trend line fitted to each firms' profit rates for the 1960–1969 period.[3] This is labeled V and is used in exploring possible relations between risk, rate of return, and structure.

Market share is the estimated weighted average share of the firm in its markets in 1961. Individual shares are based on information in the *Fortune Plant and Product Directory* and a large variety of other official, company, industry, and financial sources. In the cases included in the panel, the firm's share in its primary markets could be estimated or approximated reasonably

---

[2] Equity is book value of equity plus retained earnings. The *Fortune* compilations are largely consistent, but the underlying data are known to contain accounting differences which introduce some variation.

[3] The high variance of profit rates of smaller firms may be regarded as a problem of heteroscedasticity which requires specific correction. Yet such differentials may represent true differences in the economic characteristics of the profit rates. If such profit variation causes disutility, then lesser stability of profits means an inferior quality and value of profits.

To adjust for such variation, one may introduce it as a separate variable, or adjust the profit rates downward. Both are tried in this study. For the profit adjustment, as a first approximation, the standard deviation around trend was subtracted from the mean profit rate. This is comparable to the risk adjustment made by Fisher and Hall. Pending an intra-industry analysis, a whole-panel treatment appears to rest securely on the assumption that investors choose among alternative risks and returns over the whole range of firms and industries.

well.[4] Alternative methods and sources of data now available do not appear capable of providing more reliable evidence about market shares—imperfect and provisional though these are. Pending further research to improve and extend them, the data appear reliable enough to warrant reporting the present exploratory findings.

In 80 cases, the firm's market share was known to have changed significantly between 1960–1963 and 1968. The estimated change was used in assigning the 1968 market share. In other cases, no change was assumed. Some changes may have been omitted, but the main instances of shift have probably been included.

Firms are assigned to individual industries or industry groups, at the 3- or 4-digit level, primarily following classifications by the S.E.C. This made possible the selection of specific subsets of firms, as noted earlier.

A weighted average of 4-firm *concentration* in the firm's markets was derived in parallel fashion, drawing on adjusted concentration ratios.[5] The ratios were used for direct analysis of concentration's possible role, for comparison with Hall and Weiss's findings, and for deriving measures of G.

Entry barriers in the firm's main markets are represented on a general basis for 177 firms by dummy variables for three categories (high, moderate,

---

[4] The residual, nonprimary activities of the firm were assumed to be at nonsignificant market shares. A weighted average of market shares for the firm as a whole was then estimated, with the weights based primarily on measures of sales and employment levels gathered from various firm and industry sources. A degree of estimating was necessary in some cases. This may introduce measurement error, but it does permit an approximation of true market conditions. Many genuine markets are regional and local, and are at varying degrees of 3- to 5-digit detail. A mechanical computing of shares from *Fortune Plant and Product Directory* data (even if they were quantitatively precise) would misrepresent many genuine market conditions more grossly than the procedure used here.

The methodological premise is that these estimates, though imperfect, do provisionally fill an empirical gap and should be rejected only in favor of better alternatives. Also, gross errors would be likely to cause clear inconsistencies in the regression results. In most cases included in the panel, the firm participated substantially in less than four markets and had more than one-half its sales in one primary market. Even so, the individual company market shares do contain a degree of weighted averaging among high and low market shares, so that some detail is suppressed. One effect of this is to reduce the number of very high market-share cases, with only one over 70 percent and five between 60 and 70 percent. This excludes the possibility of testing for curvilinearity in the ranges of share over 70 percent.

[5] The ratios are in my *Market Power and Economic Welfare* (New York: Random House, 1970), Appendix Table 8. These differed in some respects from the ratios prepared by Hall and Weiss in their sample, although the levels of estimated concentration were about the same and the individual ratios were highly correlated.

and low: *HB, MB,* and *LB*), using estimates by Bain and Mann. For the remaining firms, various other sources were used for making tentative estimates of barriers.

Firm size is measured by the natural logarithm of net total assets, following reasoning by Hall and Weiss that this represents the capital-cost aspect of entry barriers and that the effect varies with relative, not absolute, size.

Advertising intensity is measured conventionally by the ratio of advertising expenditure to sales revenue in *Advertising Age* and the Internal Revenue Service *Source Book of Income.*

Firm growth is measured as the percentage change in total revenues during the period under analysis. This accords with possible growth motivation

Table A.1 Large U.S. Industrial Firms, 1956–1969. Properties of Profit and Structural Variables

Variables		General Panel 245 Firms
Rate of Return (π)	Mean	11.78
	σ	5.16
Variation in Rate of Return (V)	Mean	2.59
	σ	.51
Market Share (M)	Mean	20.92
	σ	12.68
Concentration (C)	Mean	63.75
	σ	17.00
Rest of Group (G)	Mean	42.81
	σ	15.38
Size ($\log_e$ net assets) (S)	Mean	8.06
	σ	1.23
Advertising-Intensity (A)	Mean	2.56
	σ	5.19
Revenue Growth (E)	Mean	1.09
	σ	1.16
Change in Market Share (ΔM)	Mean	−.01
	σ	4.18

of the firm and its relation to total profitability, and it is consistent with the estimation of market shares and weights primarily in terms of sales. Since price changes during 1960–1969 were relatively moderate and parallel, revenue growth may reasonably approximate physical growth.

Table A.1 summarizes these variables. Some degree of heteroscedasticity in the residuals is present, primarily because the variance of profit rates is

Table A.2 Matrix of Simple Correlation Coefficients Among Variables

		π	V	M	C	G	S	A	E	ΔM
Rate of return	π	1.0	−.154	.681	.450	−.041	.106	.361	.374	.193
Variation in π	V		1.0	−.114	−.086	.001	−.188	−.099	−.011	.018
Market share	M			1.0	.510	−.209	.231	.194	.280	−.013
Concentration	C				1.0	.688	.484	.277	.197	.023
Group	G					1.0	.369	.160	−.002	.172
Size	S						1.0	−.080	−.085	−.104
Ad:sales ratio	A							1.0	.098	−.005
Growth	E								1.0	.604
Change in M	ΔM									1.0

inversely related to firm size and market position (as also in Hall and Weiss). Inspection of the residuals from unweighted regressions indicated that an appropriate correction is to weight observations by the square root of the logarithm of firm size, as measured by net total assets.[6]

Table A.3 Is Declining Concentration Associated with New Entry?
U.S. 4-Digit Industries, 1954–1970

	4-firm Concentration Ratio:		Major seller entry 1954–70?	Value of shipments 1970 ($ million)
	1954	1970		
Meat packing	39	23	Yes	2,630
Flour, etc.	40	30	No	2,410
Distilled liquor	64	47	No	1,757
Tobacco stemming	79	66	No	1,288
Plastics materials and resins	47	29	Yes	4,286
Organic fibers (non-cellulosic)	94 [a]	73	Yes	2,822
Blast furnaces and steel mills	55	47	No	9,328 [b]
Metal cans	80	72	Antitrust	3,912
Steam engines and turbines	93 [a]	77	Yes	1,791
Ball and roller bearings	60	54	Yes	1,314
Transformers	78	59	No	1,392
Industrial controls	56 [a]	47	No	1,170
Railroad and street cars	64	52	Yes	1,378

SOURCE: U.S. Census Bureau, *Value-of-Shipment Concentration Ratios, 1970*, Annual Survey of Manufactures, M70(AS)–9 (U.S. Government Printing Office, 1972), and various trade publications.

[a] 1963 (1954 not available).
[b] Value added (value of shipments is not available).

[6] The statistical significance of the observed patterns is debatable, for the panel is intended as a census of all large manufacturing firms with identifiable market shares in the United States economy during 1956–1969. To this extent one is simply measuring the patterns directly, not

The main body of econometric results are presented in chapter 4. For background, Table A.2 presents a correlation matrix.

2 ENTRY

Table A.3 presents the industries as described in chapter 4. The appraisal of "major entry" was necessarily subjective in part. It was based on a survey of trade and other materials about the industries.

3 RISK AND RETURN

Table A.4 gives details on the cross-industry comparison of profit rates and variation. Gaps in columns 9–1 are for industries not covered by Fisher and Hall.

---

estimating them, and significance tests are of doubtful relevance. Yet the panel can instead be regarded as a sample of all economic units, which include small firms, divisions of conglomerate firms, and all economic units in nonmanufacturing sectors, in other time periods, in other countries, and in international markets.

Table A.4 Alternative Measures of Rate of Return and Risk

Industry	Number of firms 1	Average Rate of Return, 1960–69		Average Risk Premium, 1960–69		Risk-Discounted Profit Rates, 1960–69				Fisher and Hall 1950–64		
						(Rate of return−σ)		$(\pi R - \frac{\sigma}{2})$				
		Unweighted 2	Weighted by sales 3	Unweighted 4	Weighted 5	Unweighted 6	Weighted 7	Weighted 8		Rate of return 9	Risk premium 10	$(RR-\sigma)$ 11
Toiletries	4	25.8	28.3	3.1	3.3	22.7	25.0	26.7				
Photographic	2	19.6	20.0	4.3	3.5	15.3	16.5	18.3				
Drugs	14	18.4	19.2	2.2	2.1	16.2	17.1	18.2		18.3	1.7	16.6
Soft drinks	3	15.1	18.0	2.8	2.8	12.3	15.2	16.6				
Office machinery	4	16.3	16.7	2.8	1.5	13.5	15.2	16.0		14.1	6.8	7.3
Automobiles	4	11.7	15.7	7.7	4.4	4.0	11.3	13.5		14.8	7.2	7.6
Tobacco	4	12.7	13.9	1.4	1.3	11.3	12.6	13.3				
Electrical machinery	10	15.2	14.2	2.5	2.3	12.7	11.9	13.1		12.0	3.4	8.6
Soaps	4	12.6	13.5	2.0	1.4	10.6	12.1	12.8				
Rubber	3	11.0	11.4	1.0	0.9	10.0	10.5	11.0		11.0	0.8	10.2
Grain milling	6	10.5	11.7	2.2	1.7	8.3	10.0	10.9				
Petroleum	17	10.4	11.1	2.1	1.2	8.3	9.9	10.5		11.5	1.2	10.3
Containers	5	10.8	10.2	2.2	2.0	8.6	8.2	9.2				
Glass	3	10.4	9.8	1.8	1.5	8.6	8.3	9.1				
Steel	16	7.9	7.7	2.8	1.8	5.1	5.9	6.8		8.3	1.2	7.1
Meat packing	5	8.7	6.1	3.2	1.9	5.5	4.2	5.2				

APPENDIX B
Changes in the Leading Dominant Firms, 1910-35 and 1948-73

THE OBJECTIVE is to estimate the degree of change in the market positions of the major dominant firms. This cannot be done precisely, for reasons set forth in the text. The data are scanty and, as chapters 2 and 4 note, there is room for debate about the main elements to be estimated. Still, first approximations can be derived, using a variety of sources.

The coverage is meant to include all firms among the largest 100 in 1910 and 1948 that held market shares above 50 percent. There are perhaps several omissions, owing to lack of information, but these need not bias the main findings from the research about the degree of change among such firms. If there is any bias, it is likely to understate the transience of the 1910 firms. Such bias would further strengthen the interpretation in the text, that the rate of erosion has declined.

The first task is to estimate the firm's market share, on the premise (see chapters 2 and 4) that it is the primary element of market position. That was done, using the sources listed later in this appendix. The result is a single figure representing the average market share among the firm's activities. In most cases, the firm has only one basic market, and the share can be estimated within an error margin of 3 or 4 percentage points. Alternative estimates—by other students, by the firms themselves, etc.—can and will differ in particulars. Yet the aim is only to indicate changes in positions, and to form a general estimate for the whole panel of firms. This larger finding is likely to be a matter of consensus even though the details may differ.

The estimated height of entry barriers is also added in for completeness (despite the reservations noted in chapters 2 and 4). These estimates are even more subject to error than the market shares, for they hinge on a disparate set of entry-barriers factors; patents in some cases, selling expenses in others, and still others of several kinds. For recent decades, Bain's and Mann's estimates can be used directly; and in many cases they are a helpful guide even for the 1910 period.

These two elements are then combined to estimate the "degree of monopoly" for the firm, using the coefficients derived in chapter 4. The premise is that these coefficients can be extended backward in time from the 1960–69 period. That seems a reasonable presumption, since contrary evidence from earlier periods does not exist. Further study may test this assumption.

Tables B.1 and B.2 present the outcome of this approach. Since the methods are evidently debatable, the estimates are to be used with care. Those cases where an important policy step influenced structure are indicated in Tables 4.8 and 4.9. This too is a matter for interpretation, about which chapter 5 and 7 and appendix C say more. Yet, again, the larger picture can be shown with some confidence, even though the details are individually debatable.

The main sources for the estimates in Tables B.1 and B.2 are as follows. Trade sources of the period included a variety of technical journals and reports. The financial and business press provides a large but scattered volume of data, of varying quality, about individual firms and industry shifts over time. There were also many more scholarly studies to draw on, plus a number of official reports and data sources.

The following are among the principal sources, useful both for their data and for references to other information.

> Adams, W., ed. *The Structure of American Industry,* 4th ed. New York: Macmillan, 1971.
> Chandler, A. D., Jr., and S. Salsbury. *Pierre S. duPont and the Making of the Modern Corporation.* New York: Harper, 1971.
> Dougherty, C. R., M. G. de Chazeau and S. S. Stratton. *Economics of the Iron and Steel Industry,* 2 vols. New York: McGraw-Hill, 1937.

Dewing, A. S. "A Statistical Test of the Success of Consolidations." *Quarterly Journal of Economics,* 1921, pp. 84–101.

Eichner, A. *The Emergence of Oligopoly: Sugar Refining as a Case Study.* Baltimore: Johns Hopkins Press, 1969.

Foreman, C. J. "Theories and Tests of Monopoly Control." *American Economic Review,* 1919, pp. 482–501.

Fortune Magazine, *Directory of the 500 Largest U.S. Industrial Corporations.* New York: Time Inc., yearly from 1955.

Fortune Magazine, *Plant and Product Directory of the Largest 1,000 U.S. Industrial Corporations,* Time Inc., 1965–66.

Hidy, R. W., and M. E. *Pioneering in Big Business, 1882–1911.* New York: Harper, 1965.

Kaplan, A. D. H. *Big Enterprise in a Competitive System,* rev. ed. Wash., D.C.: Brookings Institution, 1965.

Livermore, S. "The Success of Industrial Mergers." *Quarterly Journal of Economics,* November 1935, pp. 68–96.

McKie, J. W. *Tin Cans and Tin Plates.* Cambridge, Mass.: Harvard University Press, 1959.

Moody, J. *The Truth About the Trusts.* Original edition 1904, reprinted by Greenwood Press, 1968.

Ripley, W. Z. *Trusts, Pools and Corporations,* rev. ed. Lexington, Mass.: Ginn, 1916.

Seager, H. R. and C. A. Gulick. *Trust and Corporation Problems.* New York: Harper, 1929.

Shepherd, W. G. *Market Power and Economic Welfare.* New York: Random House, 1970.

Shepherd, W. G. "The Elements of Market Structure." *Review of Economics and Statistics,* 1972, pp. 25–38.

Stocking, G. W. *The Oil Industry and the Competitive System.* Boston: Houghton Mifflin, 1925.

Stocking, G. W. and W. F. Mueller. "The Cellophane Case and the New Competition." *American Economic Review,* 1955, pp. 29–63.

Tennant, R. B. *The American Cigarette Industry.* New Haven: Yale University Press, 1950.

U.S. Bureau of Corporations: various studies during 1960 to 1916 on International Harvester Co., 1913; the Beef Industry, 1905; the Petroleum Industry, 3 vols., 1907–09; the Steel Industry, 3 vols., 1911–13; and the Tobacco Industry, 3 vols., 1909–15.

U.S. Federal Trade Commission. *Report on the Motor Vehicle Industry.* U.S. Government Printing Office, 1939.

U.S. Senate Subcommittee on Antitrust and Monopoly. *Report on Administered Prices: Drugs.* U.S. Government Printing Office, 1962.

U.S. Senate Subcommittee on Monopoly. *Hearings on Competitive Problems in the Drug Industry,* Parts 1–14. U.S. Government Printing Office, 1967–70.

Ward's *Automotive Yearbook*. Detroit, annual.

Whitney, S. N. *Antitrust Policies: American Experience in Twenty Industries,* 2 vols. New York: Twentieth Century Fund, 1958.

A large number of antitrust cases have also yielded important court records which illumine, with varying clarity, the conditions of industry. These include:

United States v. Aluminum Co. of America, 148 F. 2d 416 (2d Cir. 1945).

United States v. Pullman Co., 50 F. Supp. 123 (E.D.Pa. 1943), aff'd per curiam 330 U.S. 806 (1947).

United States v. United Shoe Machinery Corp., 110 F. Supp. 295 (D. Mass. 1953), aff'd per curiam 347 U.S. 521 (1954).

Standard Oil Co. of New Jersey v. United States, 221 U.S. 1 (1911).

United States v. American Tobacco Co., 221 U.S. 106 (1911).

United States v. E. I. du Pont de Nemours & Co., 188 Fed. 127 (C.C.D. Del. 1911).

United States v. International Harvester Co., 214 Fed. 987 (D. Minn. 1914), petition for additional relief denied 10 F. 2d 827 (D. Minn. 1926), aff'd 274 U.S. 693 (1927).

United States v. Corn Products Refining Co., 234 Fed. 964 (S.D. N.Y. 1916), appeal dismissed 249 U.S. 621 (1919), decree modified Oct. 18, 1921.

United States v. Eastman Kodak Co., 226 Fed. 62 (W.D.N.Y. 1915), decree entered 1 D & J 477 (1916).

Hartford-Empire Co. v. United States, 323 U.S. 386 (1945).

United States v. United Shoe Machinery Corp., 110 F. Supp. 295, 347 (D. Mass. 1953) aff'd per curiam 347 U.S. 521 (1954).

Also, U.S. v. Eastman Kodak Co., 1954 Trade Case. 67,920 (at 70,009) W.D.N.Y. 1954; U.S. v. Swift & Co., summarized 189 F. Supp. 885, 890–91 (N.D. Ill., 1960); U.S. v. Bethlehem Steel Corp. *et al.,* 168 F. Supp. 576 (1958); and U.S. v. E. I. du Pont de Nemours & Co., 353 U.S. 586 (1957).

Table B.1 Instances of "Dominant" Firms in Major U.S. Industrial Markets, 1910-35

Company	Estimates for 1910			Estimates for 1935			Change, 1910 to 1935, in degree of market power
	Market share (%)	Entry barriers	Imputed degree of market power [a] (%)	Market share (%)	Entry barriers	Imputed degree of market power [a]	
U.S. Steel	60	Medium	22.0	40	Medium	17.0	−5.0
Standard Oil	80	Medium	27.0	35	Medium	15.3	−11.7
American Tobacco	80	Medium	27.0	25	Medium	13.3	−13.7
International Harvester	70	High	25.5	33	Medium	15.0	−10.5
Central Leather	60	Low	21.0	—	—	6.0	−15.0
Pullman	85	High	29.3	80	Medium	27.0	−2.3
American Sugar Refining	60	Low	21.0	35	Low	14.7	−6.3
Singer Manufacturing	75	Medium	25.7	55	Low	9.7	−6.0
General Electric	60	High	23.0	55	High	21.8	−1.2
Corn Products	60	Low	21.0	45	Low	17.3	−3.7
American Can	60	Medium	22.0	51	Medium	19.7	−2.3
Westinghouse Electric	50	High	20.5	45	High	19.3	−1.2
E. I. duPont de Nemours	90	Medium	29.5	30	Low	13.5	−16.0
International Paper	50	Low	18.5	20	Low	11.0	−7.5
National Biscuit	50	Low	18.5	20	Low	11.0	−7.5
Western Electric	100	High	33.0	100	High	33.0	0
United Fruit	80	Medium	27.0	80	Medium	27.0	0
United Shoe Machinery	95	High	31.7	90	High	30.5	−1.2
Eastman Kodak	90	Medium	29.5	90	Medium	29.5	0
Aluminum Company of America	99	High	32.9	90	Medium	29.5	−3.4

SOURCES: See the accompanying list of references.

[a] This is the degree of predicted profitability for a firm with the given values for market share and barriers. The coefficients are $\pi = 6.0 + .25M$, plus 1 point for medium barriers, 2 points for high barriers.

Table B.2 Instances of Dominant Firms in Major U.S. Industrial Markets, 1948–73

Company	Estimates for 1948			Estimates for 1973			Change, 1910 to 1935, in degree of market power
	Market share (%)	Entry barriers	Imputed degree of market power [a] (%)	Market share (%)	Entry barriers	Imputed degree of market power [a]	
General Motors	60	Medium	22.0	55	High	21.8	−.2
General Electric	50	High	20.5	50	High	20.5	0
Western Electric	100	High	33.0	98	High	32.6	−.4
Alcoa	80	High	28.0	40	Medium	17.0	−11.0
Eastman Kodak	80	Medium	27.0	80	Medium	27.0	0
Procter and Gamble	50	Medium	19.5	50	Medium	19.5	0
United Fruit	80	Medium	27.0	60	Medium	22.0	−5.0
American Can	52	Medium	20.0	35	Low	14.8	−5.2
IBM	90	Medium	29.5	70	High	23.5	−6.0
Coca-Cola	60	Medium	22.0	50	Medium	19.5	−2.5
Campbell Soup	85	Medium	28.2	85	Medium	28.2	0
Caterpillar Tractor	50	Medium	19.5	50	Medium	19.5	0
Kellogg	50	Medium	19.5	45	Medium	18.3	−1.2
Gillette	70	Medium	24.5	70	Medium	24.5	0
Babcock & Wilcox	60	Medium	22.0	50	Medium	19.5	−2.5
Hershey	75	Medium	25.8	50	Low	23.5	−2.3
duPont (cellophane)	90	High	30.5	60	Medium	22.0	−8.5
United Shoe Machinery	85	High	29.2	50	Low	18.5	−10.7

SOURCE: See the accompanying list of references.

[a] See footnote a, Table 1.

Table B.3 U.S. Industries with Substantial Market Power

Name [a]	Value of shipments 1970 [b] ($ million)	Minimum Estimate of [c]		Basic industry structure was formed [d]	Possible public-agency or public-firm constraint
		Imports as a % of all domestic sales, 1970 (%)	Foreign-firm branches' sales as a % of all domestic sales, 1969 (%)		
Telephone equipment	2,247	0	0	pre-1900	Indirect regulation
Computers	2,816	0	0	1950–55	
Motor vehicles	13,780	11	0	pre-1930	
Heavy electrical equipment	5,757	0	0	pre-1910	Numerous public entities comprise 25% of purchasing sector
Iron and steel	9,328	19	0	1960–65 [d]	
Petroleum products	22,738	0	2	pre-1940	
Pharmaceutical products	6,028	5	3	pre-1950	Some public agencies are buyers
Soaps and detergents	2,989	0	5	pre-1950	
Electric lamps	892	0	0	pre-1930	
Photocopying equipment	2,000	0	0	1960–62	
Photographic supplies	4,372	10	0	1950–55	
Industrial chemicals	12,801	5	3	pre-1930	
Flat glass	670	0	0	pre-1935	
Copper	4,600	0	0	pre-1935	

SOURCES: Various official and trade sources were searched. A number of Antitrust Division sources were also used, consistent with disclosure rules. See Shepherd, *Market Power and Economic Welfare* (New York: Random House, 1970) and the U.S. Bureau of the Census, *Value of Shipments Concentration Ratios, 1970*, Annual Survey of Manufacturers, M70(AS)-9, U.S. Government Printing Office, 1972).

a Refers in most cases to the specific industry; in some cases refers to a group of related industries, most of which have substantial market power.
b Shipments data refer as accurately as possible to specific industries. Some are estimates. Data are intended solely to indicate approximate size for illustrative purposes.
c See note 3, Table B.4.
d This is based on the rise of imports since 1960, which could be regarded more as a change of degree than of structure.

Table B.4 U.K. Industries with Substantial Market Power

Name	Total sales 1970 [a] (£ million)	Minimum Estimate of [b]		Basic industry structure was formed	Possible public-agency or public-firm constraint
		Estimated imports as a % of all domestic sales, 1970 (%)	Foreign-firm branches' sales as a % of all domestic sales, 1970 (%)		
Iron and steel	1,840	10	0	1968	British Steel Corp.; Public ownership of 70% of capacity
Flat glass	125	0	0	1945–51	
Tobacco products	309	0	35	pre-1930	
Metal containers	85	0	0	pre-1950	
Sugar	198	0	0	pre-1950	Sugar Board "regulates" it
Cement	84	0	0	1948–56	
Compressed gases	41	0	0	pre-1950	
Film	30	0	70	1966–68	
Man-made fibres	172	10	5	1956–62	
Electrical machinery	440	20	10	1968	Central Electricity Generating Board
Communications apparatus	154	20	20	1968	Post Office
Soaps and detergents	77	2	45	1945–54	
Pharmaceutical products	41	20	60	pre-1960	National Health Service
Electric lamps	23	0	20	pre-1950	
Petroleum products	506	40	35	1960–65	British Petroleum is partly publicly owned
Motor vehicles	2,081	10	50	1968	
Computers	32	20	37	1968	

SOURCES: A variety of private and official sources was canvassed. They include John H. Dunning (with W. Jensen), *American Investment in British Industry*, Political and Economic Planning Broadsheet 304, January 1969; Richard Evely and I. M. D. Little, *Concentration in British Industry* (Cambridge: Cambridge University Press, 1960); U.K. Board of Trade, *Overseas Trade Accounts of the United Kingdom*, H.M.S.O., December edition, annual; U.K. Board of Trade, *Report on the Census of Production*, 1963, Vol. 131, H.M.S.O., 1969; U.K. Committee of Inquiry into the Aircraft Industry, 1964–1965 (Plowden Committee), *Report*, Cmnd. 2853, H.M.S.O., 1965; U.K. Committee of Inquiry into the Relationship of the Pharmaceutical Industry with the National Health Service, 1965–1967 (Sainsbury Committee), *Report*, Cmnd. 3410, H.M.S.O., 1967.

Also various reports by the U.K. Monopolies Commission; Reports on *The Supply of Cigarettes and Tobacco and of Cigarette and Tobacco Machinery*, H. of C. 218, 1961; *The Supply of Household Detergents*, H. of C. 105, 1966; *The Supply of Flat Glass*, H. of C. 83, 1968; *The Supply of Man-made Cellulosic Fibres*, H. of C. 130, 1968; *The Supply and Export of Pneumatic Tires*, H. of C. 133, 1955; *The Supply of Chemical Fertilizers*, H. of C. 267, 1959.

[a] Sales data refer as accurately as possible to the specific market. Data are intended primarily to indicate size for illustrative purposes.
[b] Estimates are for conditions in 1970 wherever possible; in several cases data are drawn from earlier years. Estimates are minimum; in several cases the true value may be substantially higher.

APPENDIX C
Estimates of Yields from Certain Antitrust Actions

THE OBJECTIVE is to measure the economic return to major actions taken under Section 2 of the Sherman Act. There is virtually a clear methodological field, since the two previous studies looked only for hints of the changes in company position, and they found few of them at that. The economic yield depends on the resources used in getting the change, the extent of the change, and the effects of the change. For all three of these elements one can only prepare rough estimates of the probable magnitudes.

The basic method used here is simply to try to make reasonable assumptions about the probable values for each of the first two elements. The estimates of effects are based on the model presented in chapter 4 and appendix A. The result is a set of final estimates for these cases, based on explicit assumptions from which the reader can make selections. The sources of information about the individual instances are the same as those discussed and listed in appendix B.

There must be a rough-hewn quality to the whole procedure, for most of the data are soft and the proper assumptions for time-discounting, allowing for price-level changes, and defining public and private costs are open to debate. The aim here is to put the orders of magnitude into a fair perspective, using reasonable—though rebuttable—assumptions.

We begin by discussing the three elements of the estimation.

1 POLICY COSTS

The absolute levels of the costs of studying and litigating these cases are not definitely known, but their trend has clearly been strongly upward. Most costs are incurred as a part of "normal" functioning of the agencies and courts. Therefore, their true opportunity costs for any one task are not clear. In some conditions, the cost is zero, for the resources may have had no good alternative use. At the other extreme, the true cost may be a multiple of the direct cost, when courts are congested, agencies are overstrained, etc. Here we shall use very rough amounts, based on the time involved, staff estimates, and other resources required for cases of this sort. It will turn out that the results are not very sensitive to these estimated magnitudes.

Rough estimates were also made of the adjustment costs incurred by the firms. These reflected a reading of the actual changes and a comparison with the adjustments the firm would have been making anyway, in response to natural forces.

2 EFFECTS OF TREATMENT ON STRUCTURE

First, three time points were estimated: the date the treatment began (either a court decision or the acceptance of a degree of informal constraints on company choice), the date the treatment reached its "fullest" effect on the firm's market position, and the date this effect would probably have occurred by natural processes, even if no treatment had been tried. The effect is then defined as the difference between the actual change and the change that would have occurred "naturally." This is shown in Figure C.1 as the shaded area A.

The estimates are partly conjectural, but they are made conservatively, in accordance with a wide range of observers. They are of course subject to reestimation in further research. The main conclusions are not highly sensitive to the estimates of dates.

For simplicity, only the market shares and barrier conditions of the firms are included in defining structure and the degree of market power. This will understate the total possible effect, for the increase in degree of competition would have some degree of additional effect on behavior and performance throughout the market. Moreover, reductions in the other, lesser elements will be ignored. Therefore the estimates contain those downward biases.

A large number of actions were begun but aborted; U.S. Steel, International Harvester, American Can, Western Electric (in 1913 and 1956), IBM, and Cellophane are leading examples. These incomplete efforts did exert some effect by deterring the target firms from some actions (mergers and pricing) that would otherwise have been taken. For most of these and many others, large net yields would almost certainly have resulted from complete action, and so the stoppage of treatment was economically irrational. Estimates are made for some of these cases, for comparison. By contrast, the du Pont gunpowder treatment is omitted because it was entirely reversed by the effects of World War I.

3 THE POLICY YIELDS

The effects on performance are simplified down to efficiency, the rate of innovation, and equity. This leaves aside such items as external effects (which are difficult to ascertain) and content (which may be important but is conjectural at this stage). Therefore the method contains this additional degree of understating the probable net benefits.

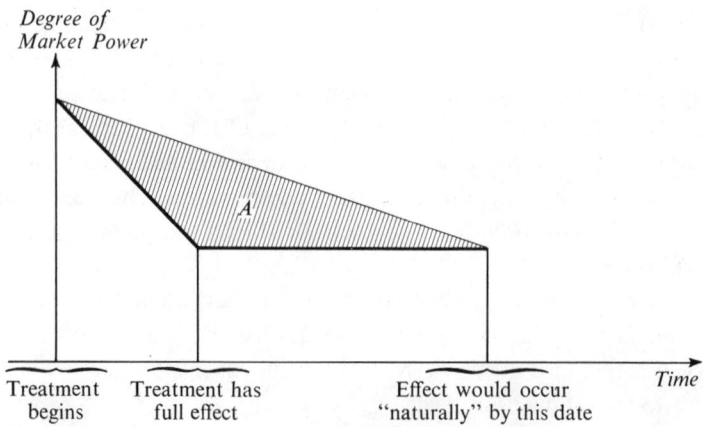

Figure C.1 Schematic illustration of the method for estimating the effects of antitrust restructuring.

Appendices 316

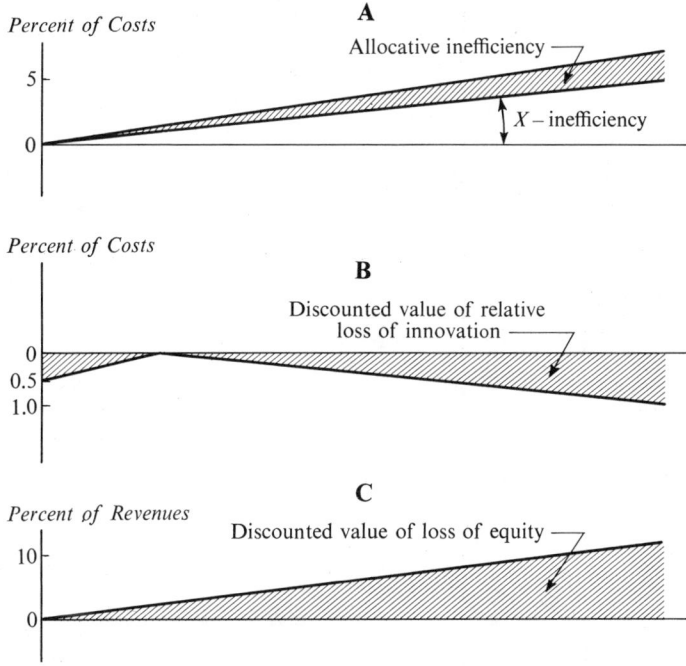

Figure C.2 Assumed effects of market power on performance, reflecting recent research consensus.

The yields are estimated using the simple consensus assumptions about the effects of market power noted in chapter 4. They are diagrammed in Figure C.2. X-inefficiency is assumed to increase linearly from 0 at a market share of 0 percent to 5 percent of revenues at pure monopoly. It is accompanied by an additional sliver of allocative inefficiency, up to 2 percent of revenues. The rate of innovation is assumed to peak at a market share of 20 percent. Equity shifts are assumed to rise linearly, as shown by the standard share-profits function in chapter 4. Since the innovation effect is less firmly a matter of consensus, the values for it are discounted by one-half, to reflect the uncertainty, and the equity effect may not be strictly regressive, so it too is discounted by half.

The whole streams of benefits and costs are not discounted for time. This reflects the fact that we are appraising them retrospectively, over the interval during which they occurred. The discounting would be highly sensitive to the rate of discount used. Moreover, in some cases, the benefits are still ac-

Table C.1 Estimates Used in Calculating Possible Yields of Policy Treatments, Major U.S. Cases [a]

	Dates of Treatment			Market Shares			Change in entry barriers?	Change in Monopoly Effect (as a % of Revenues)		
Company	Initial Year 1	Full effect Year 2	Terminal Year 3	Year 1	Years 2 and 3			Total	Years 1 to 2	Years 2 to 3
Standard Oil	1911	1935	1950	80	35		—	−9.1	−5.5	−3.5
American Tobacco	1911	1920	1935	80	30		—	−10.1	−3.8	−6.3
International Harvester	1915	1935	1950	70	33		High to Medium	−11.2	−6.4	−4.8
Corn Products Refining	1918	1935	1950	60	45		—	−3.1	−1.6	−1.5
United States Steel	1913	1928	1945	15	17		—	−4.2	−2.0	−2.2
Alcoa	1946	1955	1973	80	40		High to Medium	−8.4	−2.8	−5.6
American Can	1950	1960	1965	52	35		Medium to Low	−3.9	−2.6	−1.3
United Shoe Machinery	1953	1973	1983	85	50		High to Low	−9.4	−6.3	−3.1

[a] Omissions include du Pont gunpowder (effectively nullified by the effects of World War I); American Sugar and the Meatpackers decree of 1920 (effects, if any, are obscure); Pullman and Paramount (not industrial); and American Tobacco, 1946 (no remedy).

Table C.2 Calculations of Estimated Policy Yields, Major U.S. Cases
($ millions)

Company	Average Revenues		Aggregated Estimated Yields from Improved Performance			Total, (adjusted for price changes) [a]
	Years 1 and 2	Years 3 and 4	Years 1 and 2	Years 2 and 3	Total	
Standard Oil	(793) [b]	(2105)	1055	1103	2158	3021
American Tobacco	(178)	(173)	61	162	223	312
International Harvester	(199)	(302)	128 [c]	109 [c]	237	331
Corn Products Refining	(125)	(146)	17 [c]	16 [c]	33	46
United States Steel	1086	1557	163 [c]	291 [c]	454	636
Alcoa	572	(1023)	72 [d]	516 [d]	588	470
American Can	(700)	(850)	182 [e]	25 [e]	107	96
United Shoe Machinery	(80)	(70)	101	23	124	93

[a] Based on the wholesale price index of the U.S. Bureau of Labor Statistics, base period 1947–49.
[b] Parentheses indicate estimates.
[c] Discounted by half to reflect uncertainty about the effect.
[d] Discounted by half because the effect occurred via the disposal of war plants, not directly via court action.
[e] Discounted by half because remedy under the consent decree was a partial one.

Table C.3 Estimate of Costs and Benefits, Major Treatments Under Section 2

Company	Public agency costs [a]	Private adjustment costs [a]	Sum of costs [a,b]	Sum of benefits (from Table C.2) [a]	Ratio of benefits to costs
Standard Oil	20	25	45	3,021	67.1
American Tobacco	10	5	15	312	20.8
International Harvester	15	0	15	331	22.1
Corn Products Refining	5	1	6	46	7.7
United States Steel	25	2	27	636	23.6
Alcoa	25	0	25	470	18.8
American Can	15	3	13	96	7.4
United Shoe Machinery	20	5	20	93	4.7

[a] $ millions.
[b] Adjusted to 1947–49 values using the U.S. Bureau of Labor Statistics wholesale price index.

cruing, even though they were far ahead at the initial point of departure. We are not testing the rationality of the decision at the time, so much as the total accumulated effect of the action.

Actually, this method is probably quite free of bias. The simplest device for giving effect to a discount would be to assume that the agency resources (costs) were invested and grew at some compound rate. But for symmetry, one would also have to treat the sequence of benefits as if they too were reinvested and grew at a compound rate. This would, if anything, have biased the measured net benefits sharply upward. Therefore, it is reasonably neutral, and conservative, to cumulate the yields without discounting, for a first approximation.

The amounts are adjusted approximately to reflect general price changes, in order to show the values in constant dollars. The base period is 1947–49.

Index

Adams, Walter, 13n, 103n, 139n, 266n, 305n
Advertising: 48, 93–98, 300–301; policy treatment of, 210–11
Alhadeff, David A., 171n, 175n, 177n
Allen, George C., 42
Allocative efficiency, 3–5
Aluminum Corp. of America, 114, 115, 187, 188, 193, 220, 307, 318–19
American Can Co., 114, 115, 186–88, 316, 318–19
American Sugar Co., 114, 186, 318n
American Telephone & Telegraph Co., 186, 187, 191n, 209n
American Tobacco Co., 114, 116, 186–89, 201n, 307
Antitrust, 12–17, 63–69, 127–28, 141–48, 183–224
Antitrust Division: 13, 15–16, 68, 141–48, 185–90, 218, 260n; internal processes of, 145–47
Areeda, Phillip, 14n, 185n, 201n, 220n
Arrow, Kenneth J., 8n, 74n
Atomic Energy Commission, 141n
Automobile industry, 192–93
Averch, Harvey A., 153n, 154n, 229n, 231n, 247n, 252

Backman, Jules, 181n
Bailey, Elizabeth E., 224n, 250n, 251n
Bailey, Martin J., 30n
Bain, Joe S., 4n, 11n, 12n, 23n, 29n, 40, 44n, 45–46, 48n, 63n, 96n, 119

Balassa, Bela, 207n
Banking relationships, 171–82
Barlow, Robin, 30n
Barnes, Irston R., 14n, 16n, 148n, 150n, 233n
Barriers to entry, 29, 39–50, 96–103, 129–30, 230–33, 238–43, 299–301, 305, 308–9, 318
Baumol, William J., 5n, 33n, 38n, 40, 41n, 45n, 153n, 160n
Beckenstein, Alan, 119n, 124n
Becker, Gary S., 34n
Berle, Adolf A., 33n
Bernstein, Marver H., 148n, 154n
Berry, Charles H., 101
Blair, John M., 11n
Bonbright, James C., 14n, 148n, 152n, 226n
Boulding, Elise, 32n, 133n
Bowen, William, 160n
Brazer, Harvey E., 30n
Breit, William, 201n
British industrial structure, 116–18
Bronfenbrenner, Martin, 280n
Brozen, Yale, 129n
Budd, Edward C., 90n, 271n
Burden of proof, 73–74, 79–80
Bureau of Corporations, 147, 190, 306
Butters, J. K., 165n

Campbell, James S., 144n, 203n
Campbell Soup Co., 115, 117, 192
Capron, William M., 154n, 229n, 231n, 239n
Career, 34–35

Caves, Richard E., 63n, 106, 107, 140n, 154n, 159n, 194n, 253n
Celler-Kefauver Act, 119
Chamberlin, Edward H., 11n, 39, 45
Chandler, Alfred D., Jr., 305
Clark, John Bates, 27n, 42, 45
Clark, John M., 11n
Clark, Ramsey, 192n
Coleman, J. S., 32n
Collins, Norman R., 94n
Comanor, William S., 34n, 40n, 43n, 49n, 91n, 97n, 131n, 147n, 154n, 192n, 210
Comparable returns, 233–35
Concentration, 39–50
Conglomerate mergers, 203–4
Conrad, G. R., 106
Content (of the firm), 1–7, 18, 31–38, 49–50, 133–34, 205, 285; treatment of, 213
Context (of the firm), 1, 18, 24–31, 88–91
Cootner, Paul, 106
Corden, William M., 165n, 207n
Corn Products Refining Co., 114, 186, 188, 307, 318–19
Cost-benefit analysis: 2, 4–7, 62–86; biases in, 70–86; by private firms, 76–77, 82–83; by public agencies, 69–86
Cost of capital, 26–29, 151, 243–55
Cramton, Roger C., 151n, 153n
Cross, John G., 264n, 266n

Dahl, Robert A., 8n, 57n, 67n
Dalton, J. A., 75n
Davidson, R. K., 254n
Davis, K. C., 8n
de Chazeau, Melvin G., 305
Defense, Department of, 15, 259–69
Democratic process, 8–10
Demsetz, Harold, 129n
De-regulation, 238–43
Development, policy during, 288–90
Dewey, Donald J., 4n, 27n, 29n, 41n, 43n, 45n, 47n, 151n
Dewing, Arthur S., 306
Dirlam, Joel B., 41n
Discrimination in employment, 133
Distribution, 90–91, 270–90; see also Equity
Donahue, Charles, Jr., 69n, 232n
Dougherty, C. R., 305

Douglas, G. W., 109n
Downs, Anthony, 8n, 57n, 67n
Dunning, John H., 313
du Pont, E. I. de Nemours & Co., 114, 115, 116, 185n, 189, 307, 316, 318n

Eads, George, 140n, 147n
Eastman Kodak Co., 114, 115, 117, 192n, 307
Economies of scale, 41–44, 119–20, 180, 185, 217–18, 239–41
Edwards, Corwin D., 48n, 204
Edwards, Franklin R., 39n, 109n
Edwards, R. C., 285n
Efficiency, 57–61 (see also X-efficiency)
Eichner, Alfred, 306
Electricity industry: 239–41, 242–43, 255; competition in, 239, 242
Elements of market structure, 5, 11, 38–50, 61, 92–105
Elkins, W., 288n
Elzinga, Kenneth G., 147n, 201n
Entry, 28–30, 45–49, 92–105, 230–33, 238–43, 301–2
Equalitarian society: policy in, 270–90; role of competition, 286–88; role of public enterprise, 283–88; shift to, 273–85
Equity, 4, 29–30, 57, 60–61, 130–32, 270–90
Evely, Richard, 313
Evolution of market structure, 50–57, 113–29, 196–206, 225–33
Exemption, 139–41

Federal Communications Commission, 16, 225n, 250n
Federal Deposit Insurance Corp., 172n, 176n, 179n
Federal Power Commission, 16, 225n
Federal Trade Commission, 15–16, 79n, 141–48, 193n, 201, 209n
Fellner, William J., 44n, 45
Financial markets: 5–6, 23–31, 89–90, 140, 169–82; effects of, 170–74; policies toward, 169–82; structure of, 171–72
Fisher, I. N., 39n, 106–12, 302
Fleming, M., 69n, 160n
Foreman, C. J., 306
Foster, Christopher, D., 157n
Franchise, 229–33

Index   322

Franklin, Stephen D., 29n
Friedland, Claire, 153n, 232n
Friedman, Milton, 75n
Friend, Irwin, 171n
Fusfeld, Daniel R., 209n

Galbraith, John Kenneth, 3n, 166n, 212n, 259n, 260n, 261n, 264n, 265n
Gale, Bradley T., 94n
Gaskins, Darius W., 42
General Electric Co., 114, 115, 117, 192
General Motors Corp., 115, 117, 185n, 187, 193n, 217, 221
Gies, Thomas G., 149n, 150n, 151n, 153n, 154n, 226n, 232n, 250n
Gillette Corp., 192n
Goldschmid, H. J., 129n
Goode, Richard, 30n
Gordon, Myron J., 243n
Gray, Horace M., 139n, 150n
Green, Mark J., 141n, 187n, 192n, 193n
Grinnell Corp., 220n
Gulick, C. A., 306
Guttentag, Jack M., 89n, 140n, 171n

Hall, George R., 39n, 106–12, 302
Hall, Marshall, 29n, 40n, 48n, 301
Hamilton, M., 166n
Hamilton, Walton, 145n, 184n
Harberger, Arnold, 30n, 58n
Hart, Senator Philip A., 97n
Hay, George A., 147n
Heggestad, A. A., 39n, 109n
Hellman, Richard, 155n, 161n
Herman, E. S., 89n, 140n, 171n
Hession, Charles H., 103n
Hester, Donald D., 75n, 107n
Hidy, M. E., 190n, 306
Hidy, R. W., 190n, 306
Hilton, George W., 232n
Hirschmann, Albert O., 288n, 289n
Hirshleifer, J., 243n
Holland, Daniel, 106
Holland, Stuart, 155n, 161n, 177n, 194n
Horvitz, Paul M., 25n, 171n
Hughes, William R., 239n, 253n
Hurdle, Gloria J., 107n

If-then regulation, 237, 257
Incentive contracting, problems of, 267–68
Incentives, 83–84, 196–206, 216–24, 235–43, 259–69
Incipiency, 216–22
Industrial Reorganization Act, 97n
Information, problems of, 9, 17, 67–68, 78–79, 87–88, 145–48, 183–84, 291–94
Insider problem, 174–82
Internal growth, policy toward, 220–21
International Business Machines Corp., 75, 115–17, 144n, 146, 187–89, 191, 195n, 198, 209n, 217, 316
International Harvester Co., 114, 116, 186, 188, 307, 316, 318–19
Interstate Commerce Commission, 16
Iulo, William, 235–36

Jensen, Michael C., 108n
Johnson, Leland L., 153n, 154n, 229n, 231n, 247n, 250n, 252

Kahn, Alfred E., 13n, 14n, 148n, 149n, 150n, 152n, 153n, 154n, 165n, 226n, 229n, 231, 233n, 235n, 249n, 254n
Kahn, R. L., 32n, 133n
Kaplan, A. D. H., 41n, 42, 114n, 115n, 306
Katz, D., 32n, 133n
Kaufer, Erich, 119n, 124n
Kaysen, Carl, 12n, 44n, 96n, 97n, 139n, 192, 193, 201n
Kendrick, John W., 58n
Klass, Michael W., 238n
Klevorick, Alan K., 153n
Knight, Frank H., 3n, 39n, 75n, 106n, 108
Kolko, Gabriel, 232n
Kurth, James R., 161n, 262n

Lampmann, Robert J., 29n, 90n, 271n
Lange, O., 286n
Lanzillotti, Robert F., 41n, 166n
Lawyers, role of, 69
Leibenstein, Harvey, 33n, 43n, 104n
Lerner, Abba P., 30n, 286n
Letwin, William, 184n, 190n
Levin, Sharon G., 34n, 133n
Levin, Stanford, 75n
Lewis, Ben W., 151n, 233n

Index   323

Life-cycles of industries: 51–53, 217, 226–33; of utilities, 226–33
Likert, Rensis, 32n, 134n
Limit pricing, 40, 46
Lindblom, Charles E., 8n
Lintner, John, 165n
Little, Ian M. D., 288n, 313n
Livermore, Shaw, 306
LTV Corp., 203–4
Lundberg, Ferdinand, 29n, 90n, 272n
Lutz, F. and V., 243n

MacAvoy, Paul W., 154n, 232n
McGee, John, 11n, 129n
McGowan, John, 247n
Machlup, Fritz, 3n, 153n
McKie, James W., 306
McLaren, Richard A., 203n
Mancke, Richard B., 52n, 97n
Mann, H. Michael, 48n, 129n, 147n, 241n
Manne, Henry G., 90n
Mansfield, Edwin, 74n, 104n, 103n
March, James G., 33n
Marginal cost, in weapons supply, 261–69
Marginal-cost pricing, 151–52, 231, 254–55, 257
Market power, 2–4, 23–61, 92–134, 148, 185–90; effects, 129–34; rate of decline, 113–29, 148, 185–90, 304–9
Market share: 5, 25–30, 39–50, 92–129, 196–206, 216–24, 238–39, 298–301, 304–5, 308–9, 317–18; tax on, 196–206
Market structure: elements, 38–50, 92–105; evolution, 50–57
Markham, Jesse, 66n, 148n
Markowitz, H., 75n, 107n
Marris, Robin, 33n, 38n, 271n
Marshall, Alfred, 3n, 11n, 39n
Marx, Karl, 3n, 285
Mason, Edward S., 5n, 11n
Means, Gardiner C., 33n
Meatpackers consent decree, 186, 188n, 318n
Mergers, 102n, 118–19, 143–48, 171, 202–6, 216–24, 316
Merrill, William C., 161n, 289n
Meyer, John R., 231n
Minimum efficient scale, 35–36
Mishan, Ezra J., 70n

Monopolies Commission (U.K.), 206n, 211n
Moody, John, 306
Morgan, James N., 30n
Morgenstern, O., 40n
Motivation, 31–39, 53–57, 69–83, 145–59, 213, 226–33, 235–53, 260–62, 264–69, 271–83, 287; and content, 31–38; in private firms, 38–39, 53–57, 82–83, 213, 226–33, 235–53, 260–62, 264–69; in public agencies, 69–82, 145–59, 226–33
Mueller, Willard F., 11n, 115n, 306
Murphy, Richard D., 119n, 124n
Musgrave, Richard A., 90n

National Coal Board (U.K.), 162, 253
National Health Service (U.K.), 211n
Nationalization, see Public Enterprise
Natural monopoly, 51, 63, 225–33
Neale, Arthur D., 4n, 185n, 201n
Neale Report, 201n
Nelson, James R., 240, 254n
Neumann, J. von, 40n
Noll, Roger G., 247n
Nordhaus, William D., 208n

Okner, Benjamin A., 30n
Otter Tail Power Co., 239n

Paramount Pictures Corp., 187, 318n
Pashigian, B. P., 47n
Patents, 120, 208–9, 217–19
Pechman, Joseph A., 30n, 90n, 165n
Peck, Merton J., 16n, 161n, 219n, 231n, 247n, 259n, 260n, 261n, 264n
Pengilley, Warren, 194n
Performance, 3–7, 23–50, 57–61
Phillips, Almarin, 118n, 140n, 171n, 175n, 180n, 231n
Phillips, Charles F., Jr., 15n, 233n, 254n
Pigou, Arthur Cecil, 153n
Plotkin, I. H., 106
Polanyi, Karl, 3n
Policy choices, biases in, 193–94
Policy effects, estimates, 314–20
Posner, Richard A., 69n, 143n, 154n
Precedent, 75–76
Prest, Alan R., 62n
Preston, Lee E., 94n

Index 324

Preventive policies, 143–44, 216–24
Price discrimination, 41, 151–54
Price fixing, 143–45
Price structure, 151–52, 157, 231, 254–58
Price-wage controls, 166, 212–13
Prices and Incomes Board (U.K.), 194, 212
Procedural bias, 80
Procter & Gamble, 115, 117
Profitability, 38–50, 151–53, 157–62, 222–23, 229, 233–35
Pryke, Richard, 159n, 160n, 251n, 253n
Pryor, Frederic L., 90n, 132n, 273n, 282n
Public enterprise, 12–17, 63–69, 155–63, 251–55, 265–66, 283–90; in weapons supply, 265–66; investment and innovation choices, 251–55; objectives, 157–63
Public investment bank, 177, 180–81, 204–6, 210
Public purchases, 13–17, 211–12, 259–69
Pullman Co., 114, 187, 307

Random processes, 51–52, 104, 120–25
Rate base, 151–53, 212, 243–50
Rate of return, 151–53, 157–59, 233–35, 243–55; *see also* Profitability
Rawls, John, 30n
Raw materials, 209–10
Redistribution, 270–90; *see also* Equity
Regulation, 12–17, 63–69, 128, 144, 148–54, 212, 225–58; basic contract, 226–33; effects of, 233–55; investment and innovation choices, 243–55; processes, 151–54
Reich, M., 285n
Restorative policies, 144, 183–215, 256–58; conditions for success, 189–90; new treatments, 196–206; past actions, 184–91; prospective yields, 191–96; speed, 186–89
Ripley, William Z., 306
Risk and return, 106–13, 234, 302–3
Roberts, B., 166n
Robinson, Joan, 39, 153n
Robson, William A., 155n, 157n, 160n, 241n
Rowley, Charles K., 194n
Rozen, M. E., 25n, 89n
Ruggles, Nancy, 154n

Savage, Leonard J., 75n
Scherer, F. M., 4n, 11n, 13n, 16n, 23n, 27n, 38n, 51n, 63–64n, 74n, 104n, 119n, 124n, 129n, 130n, 155n, 161n, 163n, 208n, 219n, 259n, 260n, 261n, 264n, 266n
Schneider, Norman, 161n, 289n
Schumpeter, Joseph A., 2n, 3n, 11n, 74
Scitovsky, Tibor, 288n
Scott, M., 288n
Seager, H. R., 306
Securities and Exchange Commission, 140, 141n
Share-profit relationship, 41–44, 92–105, 197–200
Share-time relationship, 54–57, 120–29, 217
Sharfman, I. Leo, 16, 232
Sheahan, John B., 166n, 194n
Shepherd, William G., 4n, 14n, 15n, 23n, 26n, 34n, 48n, 78n, 89n, 92n, 97n, 164n, 107n, 116n, 119n, 129n, 130n, 131n, 133n, 144n, 147n, 149n, 150n, 151n, 153n, 154n, 155n, 157n, 159n, 161n, 184n, 191n, 192n, 194n, 203n, 226n, 227n, 229n, 231n, 232n, 238n, 241n, 244n, 247n, 250n, 251n, 253n, 254n, 255n, 260n, 261n, 297n, 299n, 306, 311n
Sherman Antitrust Act, 15, 68, 141–48, 183–90, 220
Sherman, Howard, 285n
Sherman, Roger, 46n
Shubik, Martin, 40n
Shull, Bernard, 171n
Simon, Herbert, 33n
Simons, Henry C., 3n, 30n
Smiley, Robert H., 91n, 131n
Smith, Adam, 2n, 165n, 206, 287
Smith, James D., 29n
Standard Oil Co. (N.J.), 114, 116, 186–90, 193, 307, 318–19
Steiner, Peter O., 62n, 70n, 203n
Stekler, H. O., 259n
Stenason, J., 231n
Stigler, George J., 3n, 11n, 26n, 40, 45n, 68n, 120, 150n, 153n, 163n, 232n
Stocking, George W., 115n, 306
Stratton, S. S., 305
Subsidies, 13–17, 160, 164–65
Swidler, Joseph C., 154n

Takeover, 180, 202–6, 257, 264–65
Tariffs, 206–8

Index 325

Tax: on market share, 221–24; on weapons involvement, 264–65; policies, 164–66, 179–81
Taylor, Fred M., 286n
Technical progress, 130
Telephone industry, 239, 242–43, 255
Telser, Lester, 49n
Tennant, Richard B., 306
Tennessee Valley Authority, 162
Thorelli, Hans, 184n
Tight oligopoly, treatment of, 201–6
Till, Irene, 145n, 184n
Time bias, 79–80
Tobin, James, 75n, 107n
Trade barriers, 206–8
Trebing, Harry M., 235n, 237n
Troxel, Emery, 150n
Turner, Donald F., 12n, 44n, 96n, 97n, 139n, 144n, 192–93, 201n, 203n
Turvey, Ralph, 62n, 70n, 157n, 160n
Tybout, Richard A., 163n, 219n

United Fruit Co., 114, 115, 187
United Shoe Machinery Co., 114, 115, 185n, 186–88, 220, 307, 318–19
U.S. Steel Corp., 114, 116, 186–88, 217, 316, 318–19
Utility franchise, 150–51
Utility sectors, 225–58

Vaccara, Beatrice N., 207n
Vanek, Jaroslav, 32n, 286n

Wealth, 3–7, 270–90; *see also* Equity
Weapons purchases, 3, 161, 163, 211, 259–69; incentive contracting, 263–64, 266–68; probable costs, 262–63; proliferation, 268–69; treatment, 263–69
Weiss, Leonard W., 4n, 29n, 40n, 48n, 49n, 63n, 75n, 92n, 94n, 97n, 147n, 154n, 239n, 240, 253n, 301
Weisskopf, Thomas E., 285n
Werboff, Lawrence L., 25n, 89n
Western Electric Corp., 114, 115, 116, 187–88, 193, 220, 316
Weston, J. Fred, 11n, 129n
Whitney, Simon N., 4n, 116n, 187n, 188n, 307
Wilcox, Clair, 15n
Willett, Thomas D., 46n
Williams, Alan, 62n
Williamson, Oliver E., 5n, 33n, 147n, 221n, 237n, 266n
Wilson, Thomas, 40n, 49n, 97n, 210
Wood, A., 33n
Worcester, Dean A., Jr., 43–44, 120

X-efficiency, 33, 58–59, 99, 104, 129–31, 173–75, 179–80, 202–3, 208, 212, 231, 234, 240, 262–63, 317
Xerox Corp., 115–18, 118, 187, 191n, 209n, 217, 220

Yamey, Basil, 106, 107

Zajac, E. E., 251n
Zwick, Charles, 231n